Public Education and Social Reform

A History of the Illinois Education Association

THOMAS J. SUHRBUR

Library of Congress Cataloging-in-Publication Data

Names: Suhrbur, Thomas J., 1946– author.
Title: Public education and social reform : a history of the Illinois
    Education Association / Thomas J. Suhrbur.
Description: Urbana : University of Illinois Press, 2025. | Includes
    bibliographical references and index.
Identifiers: LCCN 2024040466 (print) | LCCN 2024040467 (ebook) |
    ISBN 9780252046360 (cloth) | ISBN 9780252088438 (paperback)
    | ISBN 9780252047657 (ebook)
Subjects: LCSH: Illinois Education Association—History. |
    Education—Illinois—History. | Education—Social aspects—
    Illinois—History. | Public schools—Illinois—History. | Teachers'
    unions—Illinois—History. | Teachers—Political activity—
    Illinois—History.
Classification: LCC L13.I35 S86 2025 (print) | LCC L13.I35 (ebook) |
    DDC 370.9773—dc23/eng/20241204
LC record available at https://lccn.loc.gov/2024040466
LC ebook record available at https://lccn.loc.gov/2024040467

Public Education and Social Reform

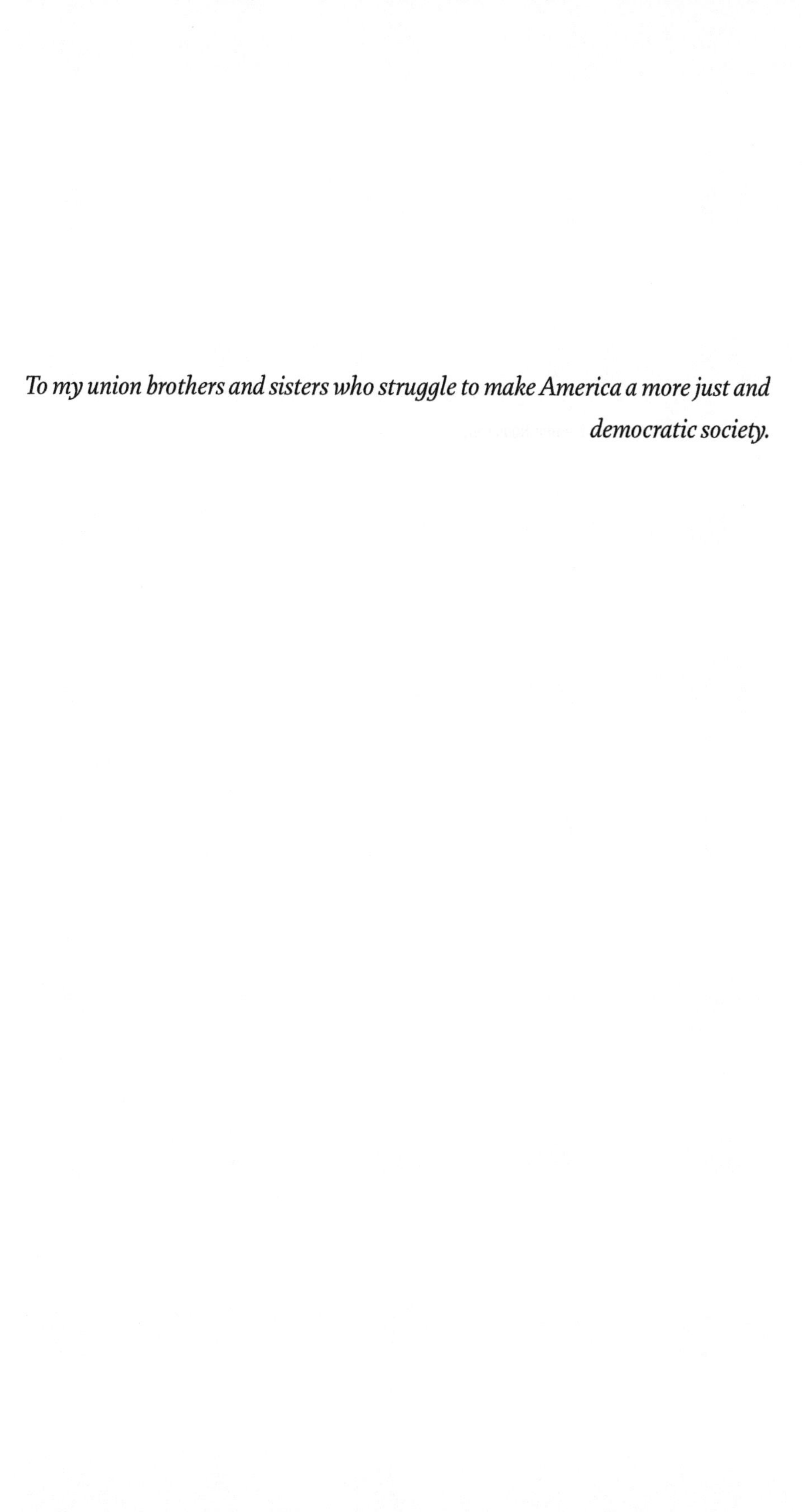

To my union brothers and sisters who struggle to make America a more just and democratic society.

One of the best ways of enslaving a people is to keep them from education...

—Eleanor Roosevelt

Contents

Photographs follow page 165

Prologue

The motivation for writing this book is deeply rooted in my own personal experiences. I grew up in a large working-class family in the 1950s. My father was a union pipe fitter, while my mother worked full time at home raising seven children. I was the first in my family to attend college, earning a BA in history at the University of Illinois Chicago. I taught at a Chicago middle school as a full-time substitute from 1968 to 1973. During that time, I participated in three strikes by the Chicago Teachers Union (CTU). After earning an MA, I taught high school social studies for twelve years in a suburban district that had a local union affiliated with the Illinois Education Association (IEA).

My first experience with IEA, other than attendance at local union meetings, occurred when I was elected as an alternate delegate to the 1980 IEA Representative Assembly (RA), the highest governing body in IEA. It was held at the Marriott Hotel on Michigan Avenue in Chicago. I was naturally upset that the state organization was having its meeting at a hotel that had recently defeated a union-organizing effort. Why would a union meet there?

As an alternate delegate, I sat in the back of the room. I could not submit motions on the floor, participate in debates, or vote. My only job was to observe the proceedings and replace my local's delegate if an emergency arose. Between the working sessions of the RA, delegates and alternates would break up into their respective regional groupings to discuss the proposed annual budget, dues, by-law amendments, and resolutions. Since the RA delegates also elected the IEA president and other statewide officers, candidates would make the rounds to solicit support from the delegates at these briefings.

At the first delegate briefings, IEA secretary-treasurer Jim Nagle attended on behalf of Reginald "Reg" Weaver, a candidate for IEA president. Nagle was sporting a button for Solidarność (Solidarity), the independent trade union that helped end Communist Party rule in Poland. Noticing the button on Nagle's lapel, I asked him: "If you believe in what that button means, why is IEA at the Marriott?"

Jim indicated that he was not happy to meet there either but explained that IEA had no choice. Its bylaws required an annual RA, and Marriot was the only hotel available. IEA had booked the hotel well in advance and could not make any other arrangements. Jim assured me that the IEA RA would be held at a union hotel the next year. In fact, there was a resolution to require IEA to use only union hotels in the future. Jim put me in touch with the delegate who had submitted the motion.

When the motion came up the next day, it failed without much discussion. I was dismayed. I asked Jim why. He stated that the motion was too restrictive. If IEA was unable to book a union hotel, how could it hold its annual RA as required under the bylaws? Hearing his explanation, I wrote a sharply worded resolution condemning Marriott for its anti-union practices and stating that IEA would meet only in a union hotel as long as one was available.

I asked the delegate from my local to introduce the resolution. He refused, saying that the issue was already defeated and that it might offend the leadership. My region chairperson concurred and refused to submit the proposal. So I asked Jim Nagle. He readily agreed and introduced me to a delegate from another region, who put the resolution on the floor. It passed unanimously. I was amazed. Even though I was a first-time, alternate delegate, the IEA secretary-treasurer not only shared my concerns but also helped me get a resolution passed. We eventually became good friends.

Over the next two days, I listened to the lively debate among the delegates and came to realize that IEA was an open and democratic union. Delegates introduced numerous bylaw proposals and resolutions that were debated and acted on by simple majority. In contrast, a proposed budget and dues increase, by far the most contentious issue facing the RA, would require a two-thirds majority. Since salaries in the Chicago metropolitan area are generally much higher than in the rest of the state, the proposed dues increase generated vigorous debate among the delegates. Downstate members generally supported lower dues increases, and so the amount supported by the leadership and the majority of delegates did not pass. Compromise resulted in a lower-figure dues increase.

On the last day of the RA, the delegates elected Reg Weaver for state president. Reg, who is African American, was a dynamic speaker and an inspirational leader. This experience impressed me to the point that I decided to become active in the state organization. Here was a union that was democratic and not top-down. I was hooked. The next year, I was elected president of my local union. Following the 1983 passage of the state's collective bargaining law, IEA hired me as a temporary part-time organizer of support staff unions.

In 1985, as I was about to finish a certificate of advanced studies in labor history at Northern Illinois University, IEA hired me as a full-time organizer. At the time, IEA was engaged in a bitter struggle with the Illinois Federation of Teachers (IFT) over union representation in public schools. In order to be an effective organizer, I decided to learn as much as possible about the history of the two unions. I read all the books written about IEA, IFT, and their affiliated national unions. I also began to collect literature used in organizing campaigns, monthly union newsletters, flyers, membership reports, and other documents published by the two unions. In 1988, I wrote a forty-page (unpublished) history of IEA and urged IEA leaders to professionally preserve its historical records. In response, IEA hired an archivist to organize documents dating back to the 1853 founding of the association. IEA also established a special committee that I co-chaired to encourage local associations to preserve and write their own histories. In my twenty-six years on IEA staff, I often did presentations on IEA history at training conferences. I continued to collect literature left behind by retired staff, with the intent to write a history of IEA and public education when I retired.

Throughout its history, Illinois has played a leading role in the establishment of public schools in the United States; it also has been a key state in the organizing of unions. It is my hope that this book on Illinois public education and the labor movement will shed light on the contributions of these two institutions to our nation's democratic traditions.

Acknowledgments

First and foremost, I want to thank my wife, Barbara, for her patience and assistance in preparing this book for publication. Drawing on her experience as a school secretary, an Illinois Education Association (IEA) associate staff employee, and a National Education Association (NEA) member benefits specialist, Barbara provided many valuable suggestions that improved the manuscript.

I appreciate the encouragement that I received from IEA and the Illinois Labor History Society (ILHS) in the writing of this book. IEA has supported my research and has promoted interest in the book among members and staff. I especially thank IEA archivist Lisa Schnell. Her knowledge of the association's history provided me with numerous leads in my research. Lisa assisted me in acquiring IEA documents and contact information of retired leaders and staff whom I interviewed for the book. I thank University of Illinois Press editors Alison Syring and Leigh Ann Cowan for their guidance in helping me prepare my manuscript for publication.

My research for this book, especially regarding IEA's history prior to the 1960s, relied heavily on sources from the HathiTrust Digital Library, IEA archives, the Chicago Public Library, the Illinois State Board of Education (ISBE), and documents that I received over my twenty-six years as an IEA organizer. I also collected files of retiring staff that would have been otherwise discarded. There are two published histories of IEA and public education. In 1912, John Williston Cook wrote *Educational History of Illinois: Growth and Progress in Educational Affairs of the State, from the Earliest Day to the Present*. In 1961, George Propeck and Irving Pearson wrote *The History of the Illinois Education Association*. Cook's book was very helpful, but the latter, while it had some useful information, was limited in its scope, failing even to mention the Chicago Teachers Union (CTU), the Illinois Federation of Teachers (IFT), or collective bargaining. Mary J. Herrick's *The Chicago Schools: A Social and Political History* (1971) assisted me here, providing a detailed study of IEA's involvement in Chicago and its interaction with the labor movement, CTU, and IFT. Finally, I read numerous studies that dealt with state and national education policy, NEA, and the American Federation of Teachers (AFT), as well as related historical publications.

I owe a debt of gratitude to the more than thirty-five IEA leaders and staff whom I interviewed for this book. Reg Weaver, Ken Bruce, and Larry Lawlyes were especially helpful in my writing about the 1983 passage of Illinois's collective bargaining law, as was IEA general counsel Mitch Roth, who explained the legal strategy behind the implementation of the bargaining law. Besides Reg Weaver, I thank IEA presidents Bob Haisman, Cinda Klickna, Kathi Griffin, and Al Llorens for their help. Patti Brown-Barnes and Reg Weaver answered my questions about minority involvement following IEA's transformation into a union. Clay Marquardt provided insights into its successful membership organizing following the passage of the bargaining law. I thank the following individuals for their recollections about IEA strikes: Earl Rudolph and Vern Thistlewaite (Decatur), Mary Ann Beil (Sandwich), Bob Jensen and Gerry Gordon (Elgin), Kathy Wessel (Wheaton), Pat Bihn (Rock Island), and Steven Fischer (Lake Park). Dave Sneddon, Mike Cook, Jim Clark, Dave Vitoff, Dave Rathke, Marcus Albrecht, John McCluskey, and Ellen Nore contributed to my understanding of organizing campaigns and strikes among downstate K–12 districts and Southern Illinois University employees. Steve Vaughan provided information about higher education organizing at Illinois State University and the University of Illinois Urbana-Champaign. Jim Nagle, Larry Lawlyes, Bruce Lund, and Chuck DesEnfants contributed to my understanding of the chaos IEA faced due to the staff lockout and IEA Staff Organization (IEASO) strike. When I had questions about the relationship between IEA and its staff union after the strike, I contacted Lynn Adler. In addition to Adler, I interviewed Bob Ray, Audrey Soglin, Jo Anderson, Will Lovett, and Mary Jane Morris for information about IEA since my 2011 retirement. A special thanks goes to Anderson, who recruited me as a local association activist and later mentored me as an IEA organizer.

I appreciate the help that I received from Joseph Pasteris (DeKalb IFT) and Robert Breving (retired IFT staff). University of Illinois professor Robert Bruno's suggestions significantly improved my manuscript.

Finally, I received valuable suggestions about writing a proposal to publish the book from my good friend Richard Schneirov, professor emeritus at Indiana State University, as well as Northern Illinois University professor Rose Feurer.

Abbreviations

AAUP—American Association of University Professors, 1915

AFL—American Federation of Labor, 1886–1955

AFL-CIO—American Federation of Labor and Congress of Industrial Organizations,1955

AFT—American Federation of Teachers, 1916

AFSCME—American Federation of State, County and Municipal Employees, 1932

ATA—Affiliated Teachers Association, 1940–49

CAPE—Coalition of American Public Employees, 1973–80

CEC—Consortium for Educational Change, 1987

CFL—Chicago Federation of Labor, 1896

CPS—Chicago Public Schools

CSBO—Civil Service Bargaining Organization, 1976

CTF—Chicago Teachers Federation, 1897–1967

CTU—Chicago Teachers Union, 1937

DEA—Decatur Education Association, 1927

DFT—Decatur Federation of Teachers, 1946–89

DUTU—District U-46 Transportation Union, 1974

EBR—exclusive bargaining representative

ESP—education support professional (support staff employee)

ETA—Elgin Teachers Association

FOCB—Faculty Organization for Collective Bargaining, 1969

IACT—Illinois Association of Classroom Teachers, 1949–72

IAF—Industrial Areas Foundation, 1940

IAHE—Illinois Association of Higher Education, 1960s–70s

IASA—Illinois Association of School Administrators, 1946
IASB—Illinois Association of School Boards, 1933
IBB—interest-based bargaining
IEA—Illinois Education Association, 1936
IEASA—IEA Secretaries Association, 1971–88
IEASO—IEA Staff Organization, 1971
IELRA—Illinois Educational Labor Relations Act, 1984
IELRB—Illinois Educational Labor Relations Board, 1984
IFT—Illinois Federation of Teachers, 1937
ILHS—Illinois Labor History Society, 1969
IPA—Illinois Principals Association, 1971
IPACE—Illinois Political Action Committee for Education, 1971
IPI—Illinois Policy Institute, 2007
IRTA—Illinois Retired Teachers Association, circa 1960s
ISBE—Illinois State Board of Education, 1970
ISNU—Illinois State Normal University, 1857
ISTA—Illinois State Teachers' Association, 1855–1936, forerunner of IEA
MBC—Metro Bargaining Council, 1975
MIP—majority interest petition
NEA—National Education Association, 1870
NLRA—National Labor Relations Act, 1935
NLRB—National Labor Relations Board, 1935
NSO—National Staff Organization (NEA staff union), 1968
NSUBC—North Suburban Unified Bargaining Council, 1974
NTA—National Teachers Association, 1857–1870, forerunner of NEA
NTTFA—Non-Tenure Track Faculty Association, 2004
P-Fac—Part-Time Faculty at Columbia College, 1997
PN—professional negotiation
PSA—Professional Staff Association, 1985
PSOC—Professional Staff Organizing Committee, 1985
RA—representative assembly
RIEA—Rock Island Education Association
RIFT—Rock Island Federation of Teachers
SEIU—Service Employees International Union, 1921
SFL—Illinois State Federation of Labor, 1884
SIU—Southern Illinois University
SIUC—Southern Illinois University Carbondale
SIUE—Southern Illinois University Edwardsville
SXU—Saint Xavier University
UIUC—University of Illinois Urbana-Champaign, 1867
ULP—unfair labor practice
UTC—United Teachers of Chicago, 1972–73

Public Education and Social Reform

Introduction

The Illinois Education Association (IEA), an affiliate of the 2.3-million-member National Education Association (NEA), is the largest labor union in the state, representing more than 135,000 education employees. Founded in 1853, IEA played a central role in the education reform movement that swept through the free states on the eve of the Civil War. In 1857, it and nine other state associations organized the National Teachers Association (NTA, forerunner to NEA). IEA has been the most influential voice in the creation and subsequent development of the Illinois public school system over the past 170 years.

IEA was first organized in 1853 as the Illinois State Teachers' Institute. Two years later, it was renamed the Illinois State Teachers' Association (ISTA). Finally, it was renamed the Illinois Education Association in 1936. From 1853 into the 1960s, IEA (like NEA) was an all-inclusive professional organization that encompassed K–12 teachers, school administrators, state and county education officials, college professors, retirees, and others working in education. Although the overwhelming majority of its members were teachers, K–12 administrators and other education officials held sway over the association's leadership until after World War II, when a rising tide of teacher militancy resulted in the radical transformation of the association into an education union in 1971. Despite its transformation into a union, IEA (like NEA) has remained an independent organization, unaffiliated but closely aligned with mainstream organized labor.

Public education has always been a top priority of the Illinois government. It is critical to the state's economic development and directly affects virtually every business and resident in the state. In 2020, 1.9 million children attended Illinois PreK–12 public schools. In addition, more than 700,000 students were enrolled in the state's forty-eight community colleges and nine public universities. Except for Chicago, all of the 852 PreK–12 districts have locally elected school boards (Chicago began transitioning to an elected school board in 2024). Illinois public PreK–12 and higher education institutions employ over 250,000 faculty and staff. In 2020, the state spent over $41 billion on education, accounting for 26 percent of the state's budget (the largest share of the state expenditures), with 82 percent of this total spending derived from local property taxes. Given this massive commitment of public resources and community involvement, it is not surprising that public education has generated a great deal of political controversy.

Since the early nineteenth century, public education has involved many of the most contentious social and economic issues facing Illinois politics. This book examines the impact of race, gender, and religion in shaping education policy. It also describes the struggle over financing the public school system. Finally, the book describes how IEA's transition into a democratic labor union greatly expanded membership involvement in the association.

Race and Racism

Beginning with the earliest efforts to establish a public school system in Illinois, racism played a major role in formulating public policy. Prior to the Civil War, the Illinois General Assembly passed legislation that allowed school districts to exclude Black children from public schools. ISTA actively supported free schooling for all children regardless of race or social circumstance. A public school system, it held, would provide all Americans with the opportunity for social advancement. Following ratification of the 1870 Illinois State Constitution, which guaranteed public education for "all children," school districts in fifteen southern Illinois counties as well as some districts as far north as Springfield and Quincy maintained segregated facilities into the 1950s. There is very little evidence that ISTA/IEA took measures to confront segregation in Illinois schools until the 1940s. Throughout the post–World War II era, IEA was an outspoken advocate of civil rights, integration, and social justice, but its elected leadership and staff remained almost exclusively white. After the teachers seized control in 1971, IEA adopted policies that ensured minority participation at all levels of IEA governance. By 1990, eleven members (20 percent) of the board of directors were of an ethnic minority. Hiring minorities for professional staff positions proceeded slowly, but today minorities constitute over 20 percent of the IEA professional staff.

Gender

Public education was one of the first professions opened to women. Male-dominated administrations and school boards often viewed women as an accommodating and pliable workforce, further advancing the notion that young, unmarried women were best suited to teach young children. For tax-conscious conservatives, the fact that female teachers were paid considerably less than men was a bonus. But women were far from a compliant workforce, and the reliance on young, mostly unmarried women as teachers unwittingly fueled a growing political consciousness among women. Margaret Haley and Catherine Goggin helped organize the Chicago Teachers Federation (CTF), the first teachers union in Chicago. By 1900, an increasing number of women were being hired as elementary school principals. In 1909, Ella Flagg Young became Chicago's first female superintendent. Women teachers, especially in Chicago and other urban centers, were active in the suffrage movement and other progressive causes. While women held leadership positions in IEA, male administrators dominated association leadership into the 1970s. After teachers seized control of IEA in 1971, women organized a caucus to increase female involvement in leadership positions. Today, women hold 70 percent of the elected IEA board of directors and 53 percent of the professional staff positions. Four of the last seven presidents have been women.

Religion and Privatization

While there was agreement that schools should include public "morality" in the curriculum, ISTA leaders resisted efforts to include religious instruction in public schools; they wanted a nonsectarian school system that welcomed all children regardless of their religious backgrounds. Professors from Millikin, Knox, Wheaton, and other Protestant colleges regularly attended ISTA annual meetings to promote Bible readings, school prayer, temperance, and "Christian values" in the public schools into the early 1900s. The controversy within ISTA over Bible readings and other religious practices continued in many school districts, especially in conservative Protestant communities, well into the twentieth century. As public schools became more secular due to court decisions and the increasing religious, cultural, and ethnic diversity of students, conservative evangelical support for public education waned; many evangelical congregations responded by establishing their own schools and supporting homeschooling and religious-based charter schools. By the 1980s, evangelical religious groups joined forces with anti-tax organizations in support of policies designed to divert public dollars to private schools through indirect subsidies such as tuition tax credits and vouchers. Efforts to divert public funds to privatize public education have been an ever-present issue in state politics. The association has never wavered from its opposition to public funding of religious and other private schools.

Taxation and Equalization Funding

The public school system requires a huge commitment of resources. Conservatives have long sought to limit taxation and spending on public education. The Free School Act of 1825 provided public funding to maintain a public school system but was undermined in 1828 by legislation that made the tax voluntary. The Free Public School Act of 1855 provided a two-mill property tax that funded the establishment of public schools across the state. In 1873, the General Assembly replaced the two-mill tax with a $1 million grant, which remained unchanged until 1907. Consequently, Illinois schools became increasingly reliant on local property taxes, creating widespread funding inequity between the property-rich urban districts and downstate rural communities. In 1920, ISTA dropped its support for reinstating the two-mill tax in favor of a graduated state income tax. In 1927, the association successfully lobbied for an equalization formula in state aid that guaranteed a district, no matter how poor, a minimum level of funding for education. In subsequent years, changes in the equalization formula have eased some of the inequities resulting from the reliance on property tax funding. In 1932, Illinois passed a graduated income tax, but the Illinois Supreme Court declared it unconstitutional several months later. The association has continued to support a graduated state income tax. A graduated income tax amendment failed in 2020.

Besides tax policy, conservative businessmen and anti-tax interests supported other policies to limit spending on public education. Introduced in 1915, the Cooley Bill was a plan to establish a two-year, part-time vocational education program that would serve chiefly working-class children entering the workforce after elementary school. A comprehensive curriculum of learning at four-year high schools would serve middle-class students seeking careers in business or college education. ISTA, the Illinois State Federation of Labor (SFL), CTF, and other teacher unions defeated attempts to limit access to public education and supported a universal four-year high school education for all children.

Conservatives have long backed programs to shift education funding to less expensive private schools so as to lower taxation. After teachers organized unions, their salaries and benefits steadily improved. Anti-tax conservative support for privatization became even more pronounced. Since federal courts have ruled against direct aid (parochial aid) for religious schools, conservatives have pushed for indirect aid for private and religious schools through such programs as tuition tax credits, vouchers, and for-profit charter schools.

IEA and the Labor Movement

Labor unions have long been at the forefront of support for public education. Since the early 1900s, ISTA/IEA has worked closely with organized labor on a wide range of legislative matters, such as funding, compulsory education, tenure, free textbooks, and vocational training. Robert C. Moore, the association's first executive secretary (1915–38), regularly addressed the annual SFL conventions, just as SFL secretary Victor Olander did at the annual ISTA meetings. Not only was the association the leading voice for public education in the legislature, but its Chicago division was the largest educational organization in the city. After 1940, the Chicago Teachers Union (CTU), an affiliate of the American Federation of Teachers (AFT), became the dominant teacher organization in the city, largely due to its aggressive advocacy for teacher welfare (e.g., improved pay, benefits, and employment rights).

After World War II, the labor movement's success in improving the lives of working people inspired a generation of young militant teachers, especially in heavily unionized suburban and downstate school districts, to organize local unions with the Illinois Federation of Teachers (IFT). IFT participated in forty strikes in the 1960s and bargained some of the earliest union contracts in the state. It challenged IEA for teacher representation in school districts across Illinois.

In 1971, teachers took control of IEA from school administrators and reorganized the association into a militant, independent labor union. The restructuring of IEA left unsettled the question of how its central office management, governance, and hired staff would function in the new organization. A power struggle developed within IEA, leading to a month-long IEA lockout in 1977 of the IEA Staff Organization (IEASO), the professional staff union. In 1980, IEASO initiated a strike against IEA that lasted over two months. The turmoil of these events resulted in huge membership losses to IFT. Under the effective leadership of president Reginald "Reg" Weaver (1981–87), IEA resolved its internal strife and made a dramatic turnaround after the staff strike.

No longer in control, many school boards and superintendents vigorously opposed collective bargaining. Even though teacher strikes were illegal, IEA locals participated in more than 250 strikes from 1971 to 1983. "Recognition strikes" were often sparked by the refusal of districts to agree to bargain with the local associations. Without any legal protection for participants, strikers often faced reprisals. Some strikes ended with court injunctions, jailing of union leaders, and firing of striking teachers. Once the state enacted the Illinois Educational Labor Relations Act (IELRA), a comprehensive collective bargaining law that went into effect in 1984 and legalized strikes, the number of education strikes steadily declined. While conflicts still occurred, the IELRA pressured school boards and administrators to deal with education unions on a more equal footing and paved the way for a surge in union organizing. Today, almost all PreK–12 teachers and community college faculty, as well as a significant number of support staff personnel, university professors, graduate students, and other education employees have organized unions. Together, IEA and IFT represent more than 240,000 public school employees.

IEA currently represents almost a thousand local unions scattered across the state. Bargaining in so many local units requires grassroots involvement. Unlike unions that bargain regional or national contracts, these IEA unions bargain directly with local school boards. Each IEA local elects a governing board consisting of officers, building representatives, and regional council delegates. In addition, locals have a bargaining committee, and some also appoint committees for grievances, research, social planning, and other purposes. Local members elect delegates to the annual IEA and NEA representative assemblies (RAs). Despite the IEA's size and complexity, decision-making is primarily at the local association level. Its greatest strength is its internal democracy, which generates a great deal of involvement and ownership in the association.

After more than thirty years of bitter fighting over teacher representation, IEA and IFT entered a "no raid" agreement in the mid-1990s, as the political climate shifted to the right. The two unions have since worked together to oppose attacks by free market and religious conservatives. In 1998, a national merger of NEA and AFT failed, as only 42 percent of the 10,000 NEA delegates voted for the merger. IEA was among the key organizations opposing the merger at the NEA RA. Organizational differences, and not political perspectives, were the main reasons behind this opposition. IEA and IFT generally worked together on legislation in Springfield, but IEA had local associations in all Illinois counties, whereas more than half of IFT locals were concentrated in five counties—Cook, Lake, Will, St. Clair, and Peoria. IFT had no locals at all in fifty of the 102 Illinois counties. IEA feared that any requirement to join the American Federation of Labor and Congress of Industrial Organizations (AFL-CIO) would result in membership losses in conservative, heavily Republican, and rural areas of the state. In addition, there were major differences in how the state officers and governing board members were elected, how dues were collected, how field staff were hired, and what services were provided by the state organizations, including legal, research, and political organizing.

The IELRA has had a positive impact on school improvement initiatives. The law provides that all decisions regarding terms and conditions of employment are mandatory subjects of bargaining. School districts are required to deal with employee concerns in good faith. Districts can no longer unilaterally impose decisions on union employees. In effect, the law makes IEA local unions partners in the development of school policies. In the 1980s, IEA created the Consortium for

Educational Change (CEC) to work with school districts and parents to improve public education.

The education reformers who organized IEA in the 1850s believed that all children regardless of race, gender, religion, or social class should receive a "common" learning experience. Public education would teach democratic values, moral behavior, and civic responsibility. Public schools would be essential in creating a sense of national identity amid the diversity of American society. It is not surprising that many of the most contentious political issues throughout Illinois history have been directly related to public education, given the huge commitment of revenue and human capital involved in sustaining a free public school system. From the beginning, IEA has been at the center of the debate over public education. The democratic ideals that inspired the creation of the Illinois public school system in the 1850s have continued to guide IEA policies involving race, religion, women's rights, economic justice, and labor unionism throughout its history. Today, a well-organized coalition of free market profiteers, religious fundamentalists, and tax-conscious conservatives seek to undermine public education and education unionism. A vibrant labor movement is critical to the survival of public education and our democratic republic.

Democratic Ideals and the Creation of the Illinois Public School System, 1825–1900

It was built of round logs, the spaces between them chinked and then daubed with mud. . . . There was no danger of burning the floor, as there was none. The seats were made of stools or benches, constructed by splitting a log, hewing off the splinters from the flat side and then putting four pegs into it from the round side for legs. The door was made of clapboards. On either side a piece of one log was cut out, and over the aperture was pasted greased paper which answered for a window. Wooden pins were driven into the log running lengthwise immediately beneath the window, upon which was laid a board, and this constituted the writing desks.

—Unnamed speaker, description of an early rural schoolhouse

The public education system in Illinois was created during the political crisis leading up to the Civil War. Southern slavery as well as ethnic and religious tensions generated by Irish immigration to the North threatened the social fabric of American society. Reformers, primarily in the free states, viewed universal public education as essential to the survival of the republic. Self-government required an educated citizenry. They believed that public education would foster a sense of nationhood, morality, and democratic ideals amid the increasing diversity of American society and provide all citizens with an opportunity for economic advancement. As Horace Mann, an abolitionist and public education champion, succinctly pointed out: "Education is the great equalizer of the condition of men—the balance-wheel of the social machinery."[1] He explained further, "If we do not prepare children to become good citizens—if we do not enrich their minds with knowledge, imbue their hearts with the love of truth and duty, and a reverence for all things sacred and holy, then our republic must go down to destruction."[2] By the 1850s, there was a developing consensus in the North that there should be free public education and that teachers should receive professional training.

Slavery and the Public Education Movement

The movement in Illinois to create a state-sponsored public school system was directly linked to the increasing anti-slavery efforts throughout the North in the 1850s. Abolitionism provided the moral, ideological, and political underpinnings of the education reform movement. Illinois common (public) school advocates were united in their condemnation of slavery as a threat to democratic institutions. Slavery raised fundamental moral and political issues about the future of the American republic. Slavery concentrated economic and political power in a European-style planter aristocracy that not only oppressed the enslaved but also limited opportunities for most free white people. Free public education, on the other hand, was the road to social and economic progress. New York governor William H. Seward called universal education "the leveler we must use to prevent wealth and power from building up aristocratic institutions, and dividing society into unequal classes."[3] As the opposition to slavery in the North gained momentum in the 1850s, so too did the public education movement.

Prior to the Civil War, education in the slave states was largely reserved for the few. Of the 1,516,000 free white families in the South in 1860, 385,000 (25.4 percent) were enslavers. About 10,000 of these families made up the planter aristocracy, enslaving fifty or more people.[4] At the time, planters were among the richest people in the United States, and they dominated the political and civic life of the South. Public education was stymied as a result. Wealthy planters hired tutors or sent their sons (and sometimes their daughters) to private academies in the United States and England. They did not need or want a public school system. Since they possessed such a large share of the wealth, the tax burden to support a public system would fall largely on them. They saw very little benefit in taxing themselves to pay for the education of lower-class white children. Consequently, taxes were kept low.[5]

In 1860, enslaved people constituted about a third of the twelve million people living in the South. As early as 1740, southern states had begun enacting laws prohibiting the education of enslaved people. Planters viewed literacy as a threat to their control of the enslaved workforce. Education could encourage enslaved individuals to challenge the enslaver's authority or even inspire rebellion. Following Nat Turner's rebellion in 1831, all southern states had enacted harsh anti-literacy laws that prohibited the education of enslaved (and free) African Americans, punishable by fines and whippings.[6]

As the brutality and degradation of slavery became increasingly apparent to those in the free states, northern opinion galvanized around the belief that slavery threatened the very existence of democratic institutions. Public education reformers viewed southern society as a backward feudal system that oppressed the enslaved population, impeded economic development, and impoverished most southern white people for the benefit of the few.

The majority of southern white people were not enslavers. Most had limited access to education. Southern education was primarily a family responsibility and not a social obligation. A tax-supported public school system did not exist in the Antebellum South, except in a few larger cities and among some yeoman farming communities in the Piedmont. Most white southerners relied on homeschooling or parochial schools if they wanted their children to be educated.[8]

Poverty among white people was widespread throughout the South. The southern plantation system maintained an agrarian economy that suppressed internal development and impoverished those white farmers who were not enslavers. Small farms could not compete with the large-scale production of plantations. Planters owned the best lands. Since the economy was based on the export of cotton and other cash crops in exchange for manufactured goods from New England and Great Britain, the market for local industry was limited. Railroads were mostly used to move crops to ports for export. Southern cities were small compared to those in the North. In 1860, the largest city in the South, New Orleans, had 168,675 people, compared to 813,669 in New York. Of the twenty largest US cities, it was the only one in the Confederacy.[9] Slavery retarded economic development. In his travels through Virginia, William Seward noted: "An exhausted soil, old and decaying towns, wretchedly-neglected roads, and, in every respect, an absence of enterprise and improvement, distinguished the region through which we have come, in contrast to that in which we live. Such has been the effect of slavery."[10]

Not surprisingly, Confederate Army officers were chiefly planter aristocrats, while the majority of soldiers in the Confederate Army were poor landless white people and yeoman farmers with little access to schooling. Many Confederate Army enlistees signed their names with an X. The *Illinois Teacher*, the official publication of the Illinois State Teachers' Association (ISTA), reported after the Civil War that "with the exception of Ireland, there is not a country in Europe where the peasantry are so illiterate as the native whites of our southern states."[11]

BENAIAH G. ROOTS: EDUCATOR AND ABOLITIONIST

"Father Roots," as he was known within the Illinois State Teachers' Association (ISTA), moved to southern Illinois in 1837. Like many of the New England educators who settled in Illinois prior to the Civil War, Roots came with a commitment to public education and opposition to slavery. He opened a school from his cabin home in 1839 and later operated the Sparta Seminary near Tamaroa. In 1851, he surveyed a route for the Illinois Central Railroad that passed by his Tamaroa home, where he sheltered freedom seekers on the Underground Railroad. His abolitionist sentiments were not popular with some of his neighbors. He was forced into hiding for a few days due to threats of tar and feathering. After the Civil War, some freedom seekers returned and built homes on his farm. He was a founding member of ISTA and served as its president in 1858.[7]

The Beginning of Public Education in Illinois

Prior to the 1850s, the establishment of common schools was left up entirely to local communities. Illinois had no centralized education standards to guide communities in their efforts to establish public schools. Most schools prior to the passage of the Free Public School Act of 1855 were public tuition-based, private, or parochial. In the 1849–50 *Biennial Report of the Superintendent of Common Schools*, secretary of state David Gregg reported, based on incomplete reports submitted by county officials, an estimated 161,751 students attending 4,410 public schools. Of the buildings described in the reports he received, 1,370 were log cabins, 925 were frame construction, and only 176 were brick or stone construction. Except for Chicago, Peoria, and a few other large cities, almost all these schools were ungraded, one-room buildings. They were crudely constructed, lacking adequate heating, sufficient lighting, and proper ventilation, and furnishings were typically of the poorest quality. Gregg wrote: "It is evident, that, as a general thing, but little attention is paid to the character of school houses. Any old and shattered tenement is, in many communities, deemed good enough as a place of education."[12] In discussing the poor conditions of many Illinois schoolhouses, Chicago superintendent William H. Wells wrote that a school "should be elegant and convenient; fit for human beings to occupy, not a mere herding place nor a prison."[13] Funding was a major problem. Many communities did not have tax-supported schools, and tuition-based schools were out of reach for poor families. Teachers typically had very little, if any, pedagogical training; some were barely literate themselves. In 1842, education reformer John S. Wright stated: "We believe that four-fifths of the teachers of common schools in Illinois would not pass an examination in the rudiments of English education."[14]

In many cases, the Bible was the only book used in rural schoolhouses. The moral character of the teacher was often more important than educational qualifications in hiring decisions. Gregg reported: "There is, undoubtedly, a great want of good teachers in our schools. Majority of those employed are, perhaps, more suited to the position of pupils than instructors. Their qualifications are represented to be generally of inferior grade." Textbooks and other supplies were not widely available. The "school year" was only four or five months. In addition, male teachers were typically paid twice that of female teachers. Student attendance was often sporadic; many school-age children did not even enroll.[15]

Neither the 1818 Illinois Constitution nor its 1848 successor made any mention of public education. However, based on the US Land Ordinance of 1785, the Illinois territorial government in 1818 provided for the sale of section 16 (a plot of land) in each township to finance public school. This was an important first step in the creation of a public school system, but taxation would be necessary to provide ongoing financing for a statewide education system. Following the defeat of a convention to legalize slavery, Illinois passed the Free School Act of 1825, which provided for state-funded schools "open and free to every class of white citizens," implicitly excluding African Americans and other minorities. The law also included a provision that gave local communities taxing power to fund public schools.[16]

Many conservative property owners and businessmen believed that they should not be required to pay taxes to educate the children of another family, especially those poor who were deemed lazy and good for nothing (and who seemed to have the largest families). In addition, the earliest Illinois settlers came from slave states, mainly Kentucky and Tennessee. They settled mostly in southern and central Illinois. These migrants had no public education tradition, and many opposed taxation to support public schools. In 1828, opponents of the education tax amended the 1825 law so that "no person shall hereafter be taxed for the support of any free school in the state unless by his own free will and consent, . . . obtained in writing." A few communities, such as Joliet, Galena, Alton, Jacksonville, and Springfield, used public revenue to support some limited education opportunities, but this amendment, in effect, stalled the development of a statewide school system until the 1850s.[17]

Despite this setback, support for public education slowly gained momentum. Abraham Lincoln was an early advocate of public education. In 1832, Lincoln indicated his support for public education, saying that education is "the most important subject that we as a people can be engaged in."[18] Starting in 1833, with an educational convention held in Vandalia, the state capital, while the legislature was in session, there were regular efforts to promote public education. As the Sangamon County representative, Lincoln attended the second educational convention in Vandalia, the following year. These conventions lobbied unsuccessfully for legislation to support free public schools. Following the Vandalia conventions, education organizations continued to spring up, but none were able to sustain themselves very long. In 1836, the Illinois Teachers' Association was organized; it published a short-lived journal, the *Common School Advocate*.[19] Bills that provided for a state-funded free education were introduced in 1835 and again in 1836 but did not pass. As a member of the General Assembly, Lincoln introduced a resolution in 1840 that called on the Committee on Education to propose legislation establishing qualifications for "persons offering themselves as school teachers." In 1841, the Illinois Education Society was organized; in response to this effort, Illinois passed the Common School Act of 1841. Although Lincoln's proposal was included in the 1841 act, the law itself did little to improve the situation because it failed to include any state revenue or provision for local taxation to finance education.[20] Besides the Vandalia conventions of 1833–34, education conventions were held in 1841, 1844, 1846, and 1849. All these efforts met with little success, but the stage was set for real progress.[21]

The education movement in New England provided the impetus for public schooling in Illinois. By 1845, Massachusetts, New York, and Rhode Island had organized education associations that had successfully lobbied for the creation of tax-supported state school systems. Other states soon followed. As migrants from New England moved into Illinois in the 1830s, they provided the leadership for the education reform movement. John S. Wright, a New England transplant, was a key leader of the reform movement of this period. In 1839, Wright, only twenty-four years old at the time, headed a delegation to Springfield that sought a not-for-profit charter for the Union Agricultural Society. The society was incorporated by the state and began publishing a periodical, the *Union Agriculturist and Western Prairie Farmer* (later renamed the *Prairie Farmer*), with Wright as editor, in 1841. Its original purpose was to promote "western agriculture, mechanics, and education." The biggest problem in creating a free public school system was the shortage of qualified teachers. In its very first issue, the *Union Agriculturist* called for the establishment of a normal school to train teachers using the Illinois College and Seminary Fund, which had been endowed in 1825 by Congress. Wright was deeply concerned about the poor state of public education in Illinois. He believed that democracy was threatened if quality education was only available to those who could afford private schools.[22] Wright pointed out that private schools are "generally more expensive, and being supported independent of aid from the state, children of poor parents will be unable to attend. . . . Such schools create erroneous distinctions between children." In public schools, all children, regardless of social standing, would be provided with a common education. "Children should be made to feel that true excellence consists in moral and intellectual work, and the distinctions of property should be kept out of view as far as possible."[23]

In 1842, the Mechanics' Institute of Chicago affiliated with the Union Agricultural Society based on the premise that workers in the towns and farmers in the field shared a common interest regarding public education. One of its leaders, John Gage, ran a regular column in the *Prairie Farmer*. By the late 1840s, this publication had a statewide circulation of six thousand. Ironically, Wright lived in Chicago and had never worked on a farm.[24]

The *Prairie Farmer* laid the groundwork for reforms enacted in the 1850s. Wright called for teacher certification, local property taxation, a full-time state superintendent of schools, and a postsecondary normal school for teacher training. He also urged the abandonment of ungraded, one-room buildings and the construction of multiple grade-level schools. In the 1880s, Illinois State University professor William L. Pillsbury paid this tribute to Wright: "He made the *Prairie Farmer* a most excellent school journal, all the more effective because it reached the patrons of the schools more than the teachers. From the start of 1841 until the publication of the *Illinois Teacher* was begun in 1855, this newspaper occupied the field of school journalism in Illinois. The school history of this period must be largely written from its pages."[25]

As a result of the growing pressure to improve education and make it more accessible to the public, the secretary of state was designated as the ex officio superintendent of common schools in 1845. His duties included recommending appropriate maps, books, and other materials for use in public schools, publishing periodic newsletters to advise teachers on best practices based on the counsel of experienced educators, and submitting biennial reports to the governor on the progress of public instruction throughout the state. This did little to improve the situation. Being occupied with his regular duties, the secretary of state had little time to devote to his new role as chief education officer.[26]

The Illinois State Teachers' Association

A chance meeting in Bloomington of James Hawley (a book printer representative from Dixon in northwestern Illinois), Henry Lee (principal of Garden City Institute of Chicago), and Daniel Wilkins (president of the Central Illinois Female Institute) resulted in a call for an education summit in fall 1853. Among the thirty-one delegates at the summit were the Illinois secretary of state, school superintendents, seven professors from Illinois Wesleyan, Knox, and Shurtleff Colleges, pastors from various Protestant churches, a medical doctor, and private school principals. The delegates adopted a constitution, establishing the Illinois State Teachers' Institute. Responding to the inadequate teacher preparation in the state, the constitution declared the organization "not only essential to raise the standard of teaching, but conducive to the promotion of the greatest diffusion of knowledge throughout our state."[27]

To achieve this goal, the Illinois State Teachers' Institute was committed to "promot[ing] the formation of county institutes." Since the 1840s, teacher institutes had been held sporadically throughout the state, usually at the county level, to provide badly needed teacher training. They were at the time the primary venue open to teachers to upgrade their skills in the "art of teaching." At these meetings, professors would address attendees about education theory and practice. In the spirit of collegiality, teachers would share their classroom experiences, "listening and practicing upon the best methods of instruction." The newly organized state institute not only advocated a statewide system of teacher institutes but also called on the legislature to use the Illinois College and Seminary Fund to establish a state normal college devoted to teacher education.[28]

The following goals were adopted at the state institute's founding convention:

1. Create a permanent Illinois teachers' institute
2. Appoint a committee of three to achieve this objective
3. Revise the state's school law
4. Create a full-time, salaried state superintendent of public instruction

5. Establish a state normal school to train teachers in best practices
6. Publish a journal devoted to the cause of public education
7. Secure funds for printing minutes of the institute's meetings[29]

William H. Powell was elected the first president of the state institute. The organization had an immediate impact on education policy. In February 1854, the General Assembly created a full-time superintendent of public instruction. The following December, the Illinois State Teachers' Institute was renamed ISTA. Ninian Edwards, who was both the son of a former governor and Lincoln's close friend, was appointed interim state superintendent until the 1856 election. He published reports that highlighted the poorly administered conditions of schools, especially in rural Illinois. Edwards believed that it was the duty of the state to provide free high-quality education for all children: "The only way to bring in the children of the poor is to bring them in on the same footing and on terms of equality with those of the rich. . . . Let the poorest child feel that he has as much right to be there as has the child of the millionaire, and that the only distinction known is that of merit, and then you will reach the poor, while no injury will be done to the rich."[30] In 1856, Powell became the first elected superintendent of public instruction.[31]

Comprehensive legislation soon followed. The Free Public School Act of 1855, which was proposed by Edwards, provided universal free public education for all children (although the act passed by the legislature included the words "white children," contra Edwards's initial proposal) and established a two-mill state property tax that initially accounted for 61.5 percent of the total state spending on education. It also authorized local school districts to levy local property taxes. As a result of the law, school construction rapidly increased in 1857–58; three thousand schools were built.[32] As local property taxes increased, the state share of the education spending declined. By 1873, the two-mill tax accounted for only 13.4 percent of total education spending. In that year, the state substituted the tax with a $1 million state aid grant—about the same amount that the two-mill tax would have generated. State aid remained frozen at that amount until 1907. Consequently, Illinois schools became increasingly reliant on local property taxes, creating widespread funding inequity between the property-rich urban districts and poorer rural communities.

Religious and Private Institutions

From the beginning, ISTA had opposed any appropriation of public funds for religious or private institutions. At the 1869 annual meeting, ISTA adopted the following resolution:

Let it also be provided that no part of the capital or proceeds of the school-fund, or of any school-tax levied by authority of the legislature, shall ever be appropriated or used, directly or indirectly, for the exclusive benefit of any sect or party in church or state, under any circumstance or pretext whatever. . . .

Once admit that, any sect or class may have and control its share of the school-fund, and, of inexorable necessity, the same right must sooner or latter [*sic*] be conceded to every sect or class, and the whole fabric of public education, *as an organic state system*, is in ruins at once. There is no middle ground—no stopping place. It is the whole system, intact and inviolable, or no system at all.[33]

The growing public education system created a demand for teachers. There was general agreement over the necessity of state support for a normal school to train teachers for the growing public school system, but the question of how to achieve that goal generated controversy. A bill introduced by a state senator to use the College and Seminary Fund to endow private colleges to train teachers met stiff resistance. There were at least fourteen private colleges or academies in Illinois; most had religious affiliations. The curriculum of these schools emphasized theology, Latin, Greek, and the classics. Illinois farmers saw little use for classical education; they wanted a curriculum of science, horticulture, botany, agriculture, and similar fields of study. Education reformers viewed private schools as elitist and those with religious affiliation as sectarian and inappropriate for training teachers. They wanted a school system that would diminish class, ethnic, and religious distinctions. It would unify the nation behind democratic values. The legislation to fund teacher education through the private, mostly religiously affiliated, colleges failed.[34]

Despite this setback, educators from Illinois Wesleyan, Knox, and other Protestant colleges continued to be active in the association into the early 1900s. Bible reading in public schools was a common practice in nineteenth-century America, especially in rural, Protestant communities. The Bible was the book most readily available in most homes. It often served as a reading and spelling text in the earliest nineteenth-century public schools. Many Protestant clergymen strongly supported public education on the premise that it would provide youth with a "moral education" based on "Christian" values. For them, biblical readings were an essential feature of public schools. In contrast, many ISTA leaders, especially those from Chicago and other large urban areas, supported a strictly nonsectarian school system. They feared that Bible readings could be sectarian and divisive.

The issue of Bible reading stirred a vigorous debate within ISTA. At the association's annual meeting, Daniel Wilkins, president of the Central Illinois Female Institute, proposed the following resolution: "that we, as teachers, consider the use of sacred scripture in all our schools, and the application of the moral principles and motives deduced alone from this sacred volume, indispensable to our success in securing the great object for which we labor."[35] Wilkins's resolution was referred to a committee on the use of the Bible in schools, charged with reporting on the matter at the next annual meeting. In 1860, the committee rejected Wilkins's resolution. Former ISTA president Benaiah Roots reported back:

> That they believe that the plan of government of these United States recognizes the principle that *the majority have a right to govern in things temporal* ONLY, and the religion of every citizen of the United States is a matter *exclusively* between him and his God. So far as his fellow citizens are concerned, he has a right to believe in no God, one God, or any other number of Gods. No man can rightfully be *compelled* to assist in the propagation of *any religion whatever.* . . . If the believers in the Protestant-Christian faith, where they are a majority, have a right to order the Bible to be read in schools, other districts, in which the majority are of a different opinion, have a right to order the reading in school of the Roman Breviary, The Book of Mormon, or the Age of Reason . . . Your committee believe it to be inexpedient to drive any of the children of the State from the public schools by an attempt to compel the children to receive religious instruction there.[36]

In effect, Bible reading had the potential to open a Pandora's box, given the religious and cultural diversity of American society. The committee proposed the following resolution as a compromise: "That every teacher should carefully consider the propriety of reading the Bible in his school, availing himself of the advice of the wise and the good who are acquainted with the peculiar circumstances of the community in which he is to teach, and do that which he believes to be right."[37]

The compromise continued to spark considerable debate over the merits of Bible reading in public schools. Although not opposed to Bible reading, Chicago superintendent William H. Wells urged caution. He warned that England had failed to establish free public schools due to the divisiveness caused by those who insisted on having religious training in the curriculum. No one should be compelled to participate. Conservative Protestants, especially those downstate, disagreed. Springfield superintendent L. M. Cutcheon argued: "Because a few Catholics raise a clamor, shall we yield and banish the Bible from our schools?" Finally, a compromise was reached, with the association recommending "reading of the Bible, without notes or comments, in all of our schools."[38] ISTA was unwilling to support a ban on the use of the Bible in public schools, but it rejected the notion that the Bible be used as a religious book. Dr. Samuel Willard, editor of the *Illinois Teacher*, commented:

> The State knows no God, no religion, no holy days, no sacred things. . . . But there is a ground on which the educational function of the state may recognize the Bible as worthy a place in our schools, and even may require the use of selected portions of

it as a text-book. . . . It is a classic book in the highest sense of the term: its language is more familiar to the people than that of any other book, and its history, poetry, and ethics, are proper subjects of study and thorough knowledge.[39]

In Chicago, both Irish Catholics and German Lutherans objected to the reading of the King James Bible in public schools. This issue played a major role in the establishment of elementary schools in Catholic and Lutheran immigrant communities. Free-thinking German and Czech immigrants fleeing Europe after the failure of the 1848 revolutions also opposed such religious teachings. In 1874, after years of controversy, the Chicago Board of Education removed Bible reading from the curriculum and other school functions. Faculty from various Protestant colleges continued to attend ISTA annual meetings to promote Bible reading, temperance, and moral education in the public schools. They supported the public system as a means to instill "Christian" values and citizenship in the young.[40] Bible reading and other religious practices continued in many school districts throughout the state well into the twentieth century.

While ISTA wanted a nonsectarian normal college to train teachers for the elementary school system, the highest priority for some educators was an agricultural and industrial university. In 1851, professor Jonathan B. Turner of Jacksonville organized the Illinois Industrial League, which was "composed of members of the industrial classes of the state, actively engaged in agricultural and mechanical pursuits." The Industrial League met five times from 1851 to 1855 for the purpose of having the state use its College and Seminary Fund to establish a four-year state university devoted to the study of agriculture and manufacturing. It proposed that a two-year normal school for teacher education be part of the university. This proposal had a good deal of support. But so great was the need for teacher recruitment and training that most educators believed that a normal school should be the highest priority. In 1857, the General Assembly enacted legislation that created the Illinois State Normal University (ISNU) near Bloomington to train public school teachers. It was designated as a "university" to win the support of the Industrial League (the designation being an indication that the new school could be expanded into a four-year university). Abraham Lincoln was hired by the State Board of Education to handle the legal work for the new school. Professor Turner served on a national committee that petitioned Congress to provide land grants for states to establish agricultural and industrial universities. In 1862, the Morrill Land Grant College Act passed by Congress enabled the establishment of a four-year agricultural and industrial school. The University of Illinois opened in 1867.[41]

In 1855, the association began publishing a journal, the *Illinois Teacher*. It lost a large sum of money due to the low number of subscriptions in its first year of publication, but after Charles E. Hovey took over as editor in 1856, the journal

CHARLES E. HOVEY

In 1854, Charles E. Hovey and his wife, Henrietta, moved from Massachusetts for teaching jobs at private schools in Peoria. Only twenty-seven years old at the time, Charles quickly became a key leader of the education movement. In Peoria, he successfully organized leading citizens to enact legislation to establish free public schools in the city; he also lobbied legislators in Springfield to fund a statewide system. In 1855, Hovey was elected president of ISTA and began serving as editor of its journal, the *Illinois Teacher*. He served on the normal school location committee and became principal of ISNU, the state's first teachers college. Hovey supervised the construction and the opening of ISNU. When the Civil War broke out, he organized and trained his male students as the "Normal Rifles" and commanded the Thirty-Third Regiment Illinois Infantry, achieving the rank of brigadier general.[42]

amassed 2,070 subscribers within two years. It had subscribers in twenty-three states, as far away as Massachusetts and California. Besides publishing the proceedings of ISTA's annual meetings and related news, the *Illinois Teacher* promoted the cause of free, universal education for all children. It published progressive articles on such topics as pay equity for female teachers and free college education. In an article entitled "Every Adult and Every Child Must Be Able to Read and Write," the journal called for compulsory education for all children and evening classes for adult education. It also covered reports from other state associations, teacher institute schedules, book reviews, best teaching practices, new discoveries in science, school statistics, and a host of other education-related topics. In 1858, the *Illinois Teacher* was turned over to a private printer, due to financial difficulties following Hovey's departure when he became principal at ISNU.[43] The *Illinois Teacher* continued to be published as an independent education journal until 1873. It maintained the format established by Hovey, reporting extensively on ISTA and education news from Illinois and the nation.

In 1855, ISTA hired a full-time "state agent" to promote the organization's agenda. This staff position was eliminated after just one year. ISTA would not hire any staff again until its reorganization in 1913. In just four years, ISTA had accomplished all of the goals adopted at its 1853 meeting. In 1903, ISTA president William L. Steele described those years as a "period of organization, of construction, when the foundations of our educational system were laid. All that has come since has been a natural growth from the creations then made."[44]

ISTA was a leader in the education reform movement that swept through the free states in the years leading up to the Civil War. In 1857, it was one of twelve associations from various states and the District of Columbia that attended the founding convention of the National Teachers Association (NTA, later renamed the National Education Association, NEA).[45]

Public Education for All Children Regardless of Race

After more than two hundred years of slavery and the ideology that justified its existence, racist attitudes about African Americans were not only engrained in the minds of most southern white people but were widely accepted among many white people in the free states. Even though there were relatively few Black people living in Illinois, race played a major role in Illinois politics in the decades leading up to the Civil War.[46] Despite the fact that Illinois entered the United States in 1818 as a free state, there was a movement in the southern counties among migrants from Tennessee and Kentucky to legalize slavery. In 1824, the proslavery Convention Party ended in defeat, but racism remained a powerful political force. The first public school law, in 1825, stated that schools should be "open and free to every class of white citizens." As early as 1829, Illinois enacted Black Codes that sharply restricted the rights of free Black people. Many Illinoisans viewed abolitionism as a threat to national peace and racial purity. Racism was especially virulent in southern Illinois. In 1837, abolitionist editor Elijah Lovejoy was murdered and his press was destroyed by a mob in Alton. By 1853, laws prohibited any African American from another state from remaining in Illinois for more than ten consecutive days. After that, the "colored" person was subject to arrest. Nevertheless, a number of individuals stood in defiance of the law, often with the protection of sympathetic white people.[47]

ISTA's efforts to use the Free Public School Act of 1855 to end the exclusion of Black children failed. As a concession to racist sentiment, the General Assembly allowed school boards to continue excluding Black children. School boards actually benefited financially from this racist exclusion: school boards kept the per capita state funding that they received from the state; Black families were reimbursed only for the amount they paid in local education property tax. On this matter, John W. Cook, who would serve as ISTA president in 1880 and later as president of Northern Illinois Normal University, pointed out that the 1855 act provided that

> in townships where there were persons of color, the board of education should allow such persons to withdraw from the school fund the amount which they had contributed. They were counted in the enumeration by which the amount of the state fund was distributed, and the township, therefore, profited by their presence as much as would have been the case if they had been as white as the snows of winter. If they had been allowed to use their share of the State fund as well as what they had personally contributed, they might have been able to do something in the education of the young of their race. It is another instance of the inhumanity of man.[48]

Prior to the Civil War, there was also a strong undercurrent of nativist bigotry and prejudice against Irish Catholic immigrants promoted by the xenophobic

Know-Nothing movement, formally organized as the Native American Party. This right-wing populism tried to rally Protestant public opinion against the perceived threat of Irish Catholics overwhelming America. In the late 1840s, Know-Nothingism remained neutral on the question of slavery. Know-Nothings gained support in all sections of the nation. The movement was viewed by some as an alternative to abolitionism. In the North, abolitionists and many hard-core Free Soilers rejected nativism.[49] ISTA, like Lincoln, wholly denounced Know-Nothingism. Lincoln wrote: "I am not a Know-Nothing; that is certain. How could I be? How can any one who abhors the oppression of negroes be in favor of degrading classes of white people? Our progress in degeneracy appears to me to be pretty rapid. As a nation we began by declaring, 'All men are created equal.' We now practically read it, 'All men are created equal, except negroes.' When the Know-Nothings get control, it will read, 'All men are created equal except negroes, foreigners and Catholics.'"[50]

ISTA stood in sharp opposition to racial and religious bigotry. It supported free universal education for all children, regardless of race or religion. It held the planter aristocracy responsible for the Civil War and for the stalled development of public education in the South. At the 1861 ISTA annual meeting, the following resolution was adopted: "Slavery, debasement of politics, disloyalty, indifference to the public welfare in a thousand forms—these are the true roots of the war and the cause of our evils."[51] Though the Civil War would end slavery, racism remained firmly embedded in the minds of many white Americans. After the war, Reconstruction established political rights for freedmen but not economic independence. For education reformers, the road to economic and perhaps social equity was through public education. ISTA and other NEA affiliates urged the creation of public school in the South for all children, regardless of race.

In 1862, the association passed a resolution stating that the "direful civil war against republican government and human rights was kindled . . . by a want of general information among the common people in the Southern states consequent upon the discouragement of public instruction."[52] In effect, had there been an educated citizenry in the South, slavery would not have been tolerated and the Civil War would have been avoided. After ISTA president Newton Bateman announced Lincoln's Emancipation Proclamation at the annual ISTA meeting on January 1, 1863, the *Illinois Teacher* reported: "Immediately there arose a tremendous cheering and clapping of hands; which having somewhat subsided, the whole assembly sang the Star-Spangled Banner with great spirit."[53] Richard Edwards, president of ISNU from 1862 to 1876, stated in 1862, "Secession and education are incompatible. I have seen the influence of slavery upon young whites, making them intractable." Two years later, Edwards was elected ISTA president.[54]

As the Union Army occupied southern territory, the *Illinois Teacher* printed numerous articles about the establishment of public schools in the South. The journal published a lengthy report debunking the racist myth that "the colored race have not the capacity to receive an education." The report cited detailed examples of the determination of freedmen for education, and the hostility they faced in pursuit of that goal.[55]

At the end of the Civil War, association leaders celebrated the newly won freedom of African Americans. In a speech at ISNU, Enoch Gastman stated: "The downtrodden, although their skins be black, have received their long-denied rights: for the first time in the history of our government can it be said, practically as well as theoretically, that all men are entitled to life, liberty and the pursuit of happiness." At its annual meeting in 1866, ISTA passed a resolution offering to assist in the establishment of public schools in the South.[56]

In 1865, Illinois became the first state to ratify the Thirteenth Amendment, which ended slavery. So powerful were the forces of social justice that the infamous Black Codes enacted by Illinois before the war were repealed. Governor Richard Oglesby pardoned Black people who had violated the maximum ten-day stay imposed by these laws. At the 1865 NTA convention, NTA president J. P. Wilkerson condemned slavery and demanded that former Confederate states not be readmitted into the Union unless they provided free public education for all students, regardless of race.[57]

The 1818 and 1848 Illinois Constitutions made no mention of education, but statutes governing schools included numerous instances of the term *white*, clearly indicating that the intent was to exclude African Americans from constitutional protections. This was consistent with the state's harsh Black Codes. As a result, in many school districts, African Americans were excluded from attending public schools. At ISTA's 1868 annual meeting, a resolution proposed by Newton Bateman, superintendent of public instruction, was adopted, calling for "the word 'white' [to] be stricken" from the law.[58] The 1870 Illinois Constitution did indeed do so, including the following words: "The general assembly shall provide a thorough and efficient system of free schools, whereby all children of this State may receive a good common school education."[59]

ISTA strongly supported free public education for all children. It stated in 1871 that "the right of colored children to share equally with others in the benefit of our free schools is clearly and undeniably granted in the first section of the eighth article of the Constitution, and that the right does now exist in virtue of the Constitution itself." ISTA interpreted the 1870 Constitution as negating all local laws that prohibited Black children from attending public schools. It called for all school districts to make immediate arrangements to provide equal education opportunities for all children. Despite ISTA's opposition, however, segregated schools were created in many southern Illinois counties.[60]

ISNU president Richard Edwards, an abolitionist and former ISTA president, was also a strong proponent of education for students regardless of race. When he admitted a Black female student to the Model School (elementary) in May 1867, the *Chicago Republican* reported:

> The other morning a little girl of color was found sitting in her right mind in the Model School waiting to have her idea taught. . . . The world didn't hear of the circumstance or it would immediately have come to an end; but the one and a half Democrats of the place had a regular conniption. . . . However Topsy stuck to her seat. The teachers taught her; the president treated her as he thought the Savior would have treated her if she had come to Him to be taught. All is now quiet at Normal.[61]

In February 1868, the conservative *Chicago Times* spewed out a racist rant about the situation, saying: "Here is an institution supported at great expense by the taxpayers of Illinois, and run in the interest of n——r-radicals and radical n——rs. Our hope is that if ever white people have a voice in controlling the affairs of Illinois again, they will blot out of existence this, and all similar institutions, that are carried on for the benefit of the radical party and the n——rs, at the expense of people. There are no benefits, save only as miscegenation and money-squandering establishments."[62]

Edwards's position on education was well known. He organized a teacher institute in 1867 at which those participating adopted a resolution "that all children of lawful age, without regard to race or color, should be freely admitted on terms of entire equality to the public schools of the state."[63] In 1871, a number of African Americans enrolled at ISNU. The board, at Edwards's urging, issued the following statement in response: "In our opinion, neither the Board nor the faculty has any right to recognize distinctions of race or color in determining who shall or shall not be admitted to several departments of the University, the equal rights of all youth of the state to participate in the benefits of our system of public education."[64]

Despite the 1870 Constitution, there was an effort in Springfield to continue to deny African Americans the right to attend public schools. The *Illinois Schoolmaster* reported that "Springfield has a sensation. The school board has stricken the word 'white' out of the regulations, and thrown open the doors of the public schools to applicants of every variety of color from mauve to jet black. The [Illinois State] *Register* is reported as greatly troubled thereat [*sic*], and there are rumors that the haut monde will withdraw its children."[65] The Springfield district complied with the law. In order to clarify the situation, the legislature passed a law the following year "to protect colored children in their right to attend public schools." This act provided for a fine of up to one hundred dollars per offense for any school official who violated the law. It also included a fine of up to twenty-five dollars for any person who threatened, menaced, or intimidated any Black student to prevent them from attending school.[66]

Even though Illinois public schools were made open to all students regardless of race, many county and local officials created segregated schools for Black children in the wake of the US Supreme Court's 1896 "separate but equal" decision in *Plessy v. Ferguson*. In Alton, Scott Bibb sued the city in 1897 after being told that his children could no longer attend a racially mixed school in their neighborhood; instead, they had been transferred to a new segregated facility across town. The African American community in Alton was incensed. The case dragged on for eleven years, but the Illinois Supreme Court eventually settled in Bibb's favor. Nevertheless, Alton refused to enforce the court order, and the school district remained segregated until 1958. Schools in fifteen southern Illinois counties as well as some districts as far north as Springfield and Quincy were also segregated.[67]

The Labor Movement and Public Education

Trade unions and labor organizations always supported universal public education. The political agenda of the Knights of Labor and the American Federation of Labor (AFL) included school funding, equal pay for female teachers, child labor laws, and compulsory school attendance laws. Child labor was a scourge; it retarded the physical and social development of working-class children. Children working in factories and mines suffered from a higher rate of accidents and disease than did adult workers. Child labor denied them educational opportunities and limited their hopes for a better future. It also suppressed wages by flooding the labor market with low-wage employees—which then buttressed the practice of child labor. ISTA and labor unions consistently supported mandatory attendance laws, a longer school year, and a four-year high school education for all children.

For union activists, education was a step toward achieving economic and political power. It meant a better future for their children. Only an educated working class could protect its interests in light of the growing power of the capitalist class. In 1883, Robert Layton, grand secretary of the Knights of Labor, testified before the US Senate Committee on Education and Labor that "if education were successful, . . . social reform would follow as a matter of course."[68] In 1881, the founding convention of the Federation of Organized Trades and Labor Unions (renamed AFL in 1886) adopted a platform that called for "the passage of legislative enactments as will enforce, by compulsion, the education of children" and that would forbid "the employment of children under the age of fourteen years in any capacity under penalty of fine and imprisonment."[69] The Illinois State Labor Association, a precursor to the Illinois State Federation of Labor (SFL), added the demand that students "shall be furnished with all books and other articles necessary to their education . . . at the expense of the State."[70] In 1936, the SFL reported that it "has given unwavering support to the maintenance and extension of the public school system in all divisions from kindergarten to the university" and that "the public school is the most important single item of American government."[71]

Unlike affiliates in conservative states, especially in the South and the West, ISTA was among NEA's most progressive state associations. It worked closely on education legislation with organized labor throughout its history. Illinois had a powerful labor movement and a democratic tradition dating back to the Civil War era. It was a natural ally of public education advocates. In *The History of the Illinois Education Association* (1961), George Propeck and IEA executive director Irving F. Pearson wrote: "Organized labor was another force which affected the development of public education. The pressure groups of organized labor added the weight of their influence and pressed office seekers for their stand on free public schools. They believed that only an educated citizenry could nourish and promote the interests of a democratic state."[72]

Feminization of Education

Teaching was the first profession open to women. Early education reformers such as Catharine Beecher and Horace Mann believed that women were better at nurturing and shaping the lives of young children. According to Beecher: "To enlighten the understanding and to gain the affections is a teacher's business," and "since the mind is to be guided chiefly by means of the affections, is not woman best fitted to accomplish these important objectives?" Male-dominated administrations and school boards often viewed women as an accommodating and pliable workforce, further advancing the notion that young, unmarried women were best suited to teach. For tax-conscious conservatives, the fact that female teachers were paid considerably less than men was a bonus.[73]

Abolitionism had a major impact on the women's rights movement. It was only natural for female abolitionists to draw parallels between the subjugation of enslaved people and that of women. The obvious question raised was: if enslaved people were denied an education and voting rights, how could opponents of slavery accept the same for women? Women's rights advocates such as Susan B. Anthony and Elizabeth Cady Stanton were outspoken in their opposition to slavery and their support for public education. This thinking resonated among the women entering teaching.

Female teachers rejected a second-class status in education from the start. In 1857, ISTA passed a resolution favoring equal pay for men and women. The *Illinois*

Teacher published an article written by an angry teacher. Titled "Inequality," the article argued:

> Our education has required as much hard toil as man's; our instructions have been of as pure a nature as his, so far as we have been permitted to pursue them; our board and clothing in this age of delirious fashion fully equals his, and why, we would ask of the superintendents and committee-men of schools in this State of Illinois, why are we not permitted to draw the *same amount of money* for performing the *same amount of labor* as he? Why should we, standing upon the same floor, presiding over as great, if not a greater number of pupils, hearing one third more recitations per day, and those often more complicated, receive from one hundred and fifty to two hundred dollars less per annum than he? Is it right that man, merely because he is a man, should be thus partially treated?[74]

Teaching not only gave economic independence to women but also increased their engagement in the civil life of their communities. It encouraged a greater degree of personal freedom than most women typically experienced at the time. Catherine Goggin, Chicago Teachers Federation (CTF) union leader, stated that a woman teacher "learns to govern, not to be governed . . . she cannot be molded to suit any man. Her individuality becomes too strongly developed."[75] Many women teachers became activists in the suffrage movement. It made no sense to them that male politicians governed school districts yet female teachers could not participate in the election process that put them in power.[76]

Teaching increasingly became a woman's profession as the public school movement advanced. With the demand for teachers rapidly increasing following the Civil War, thousands of women entered the profession. In 1858, 43 percent of Illinois teachers were women; by 1900, women accounted for 74 percent of the teaching workforce. Most women taught at the elementary level. The fact that teaching in the elementary grades required only a high school education or, at the most, a two-year certificate from a normal school, rather than a more costly four-year degree, meant that the profession was open to many working-class and lower middle-class women.[77] Rather than being a compliant workforce, the young, mostly unmarried women teachers fueled a growing political consciousness and activism.

Women had secured full membership in ISTA, including the right to vote on all business, in 1873, but the association's leadership remained predominantly male. Women began taking on more leadership roles as their active involvement increased. In 1874, a Miss M. E. Hughes served as secretary, and there were also three female vice presidents.[78] After that, women regularly held the position of secretary and served on the executive committee. In 1900, all seven officers were men, but three of the five members of the board of directors were women.[79] Caroline

Grote served as association secretary from 1902 to 1912. In 1906, ISTA endorsed "suffrage for women on equal terms with men."[80]

Achievements

By 1900, Illinois had made great strides in improving public education. The association supported the consolidation of one-room schoolhouses into larger, graded buildings. These larger schools, which housed dedicated first- through eighth-grade classrooms, consolidated the resources of small districts and greatly improved educational opportunities. Graded schools slowly replaced one-room schoolhouses. In 1860, only 292 (3.7 percent) of the 7,929 schools in Illinois were graded. In 1880, 62.1 percent of students still attended ungraded, mostly one- or two-room schoolhouses. By 1900, 63.9 percent of all students attended schools with graded classrooms, although the actual number of ungraded schools had not decreased significantly. One-room schools continued to serve communities in rural areas of the state well into the twentieth century. Most of these ungraded schoolhouses were frame structures, but there were still twenty-two log buildings remaining at the end of the nineteenth century. Brick and stone buildings were, for the most part, large, graded elementary or high schools (see table 1). The improvement in school facilities corresponded with a steady increase in the length of the school year, from 6.75 months in 1857 to 7.6 months by 1900.[81]

The association also supported access to universal high school education. Except for a few large urban areas, the early publicly funded schools were K–8 districts. The first Illinois high school supported by public funds was established in Jacksonville in 1851. Peoria established a high school in 1856 under the leadership of Charles Hovey. In the fall of that same year, Chicago opened its first high school.[82] But high schools were impractical and too expensive to build in the sparsely populated, rural communities. In 1867, Illinois enacted "the township system of schools . . . in the place of our present cumbrous district system." The association suggested that "the organization of a high school in every township would be an easy task." In 1868, Princeton organized the first township high school under the new law.[83] Many high schools, especially in poorer, rural areas, had only two-year or three-year programs.[84] By 1900, Illinois had 321 high schools, but only 38,758 (4 percent) of the 958,911 enrolled students attended high school.

Following the enactment of the Free Public School Act of 1855, the state raised the standards for teaching and administrative certification. Teacher training rapidly improved. In 1858, 52 teacher institutes were reported; that number had increased to 225 by 1880.[85] Prior to the 1890s, counties held four- to six-week summer institutes that served as the main source of training. Teachers were required to attend these institutes in order to pass their certification exams. But, as attendance

Table 1. The Development of Illinois K–12 Public Schools

	1860	1870	1880	1890	1900
Number of students	472,247	652,715	704,041	778,319	958,911
Ungraded	437,220	376,160	346,037		
Graded	266,821	440,159	612,385		
School buildings	7,847	10,783	11,883	12,252	12,809
Log	1,447	1,089	495	114	22
Frame	5,561	8,498	9,910	10,470	10,796
Brick/stone	839	1,196	1,478	1,668	1,991
Type of school					
High school	3	108	110	208	321
Ungraded	7,634	10,262	10,933	10,715	
Graded	292	641	921	1,761	
Teachers	14,708	20,285	22,255	23,164	26,313
Male	8,223	8,826	8,834	7,522	6,950
Female	6,485	11,459	13,421	15,642	19,363
Average monthly pay					
Male	$28.82	$48.35	$41.92	$54.63	$60.30
Female	$18.80	$36.66	$31.80	$44.41	$52.40

Sources: Biennial Report of the Superintendent of Public Instruction of the State of Illinois, for years 1859–60, 1878–80, 1888–90, 1898–1900.

at normal schools increased, county institutes were eventually replaced by institute days conducted by local school districts throughout the school year. The main sources of training became the state normal schools. By 1900, Illinois had six teacher colleges. Besides ISNU, Cook County Normal School (later Chicago State University) was established in 1867, followed by Southern Illinois Normal University two years later. In 1899, Illinois added normal schools in DeKalb, Charleston, and Macomb. As of 1905, 4,112 of the 27,860 teachers in the state still had not finished high school, but, increasingly, younger elementary teachers had attended one to two years of normal schooling, and many, especially those teaching at high schools, had four-year degrees.[86]

Organizational Developments

ISTA had a very simple structure. Officers and committees were elected at the annual meeting by those in attendance. From 1880 to 1909, all of ISTA's annual meetings were held in Springfield, specifically over three days in late December. The timing of the annual meetings as well as the expense of traveling to Springfield made it difficult for many low-paid teachers to attend. Though ISTA had members in virtually every county of the state, the majority of attendees came from Springfield and school districts in central Illinois. Attendees from outside the Springfield area were mostly K–12 and higher education administrators. Annual dues were one dollar. Any member attending the annual meeting was eligible to participate fully, including voting on the election of officers, bylaws, resolutions, and other matters. To accommodate concerns of constituents, "sections" met on the second day of the meeting to discuss papers submitted by prominent members, and raise issues regarding educational policies for the association to consider. Reports of the sectional meetings were published in ISTA's annual *Journal of Proceedings*. Primary, grammar, and high school sections were the first to meet, convening in 1868. The number of sections gradually increased to include county superintendents, colleges, high schools, principals, village principals, music, parent-teachers, and other interest groups.[87]

Following the Panic of 1873, the US economy experienced the worst business downturn of the nineteenth century. The "Long Depression" had a devastating effect on ISTA. Having achieved so much in its first twenty years, ISTA barely survived the depression. ISTA reported 216 members and a scant $131.85 in its treasury in 1874; five years later it had only 85 members. Membership increased slowly thereafter. In 1901, the association reported 1,128 members.[88] The independent education press likewise collapsed during the depression. In 1873, the *Illinois Teacher* merged with the *Chicago Schoolmaster*, becoming the *Illinois Schoolmaster*. This consolidated journal ceased publication three years later.[89]

ISTA's political credibility was further undermined by the fact that thousands of teachers joined regional associations that were not affiliated with ISTA. These regional bodies convened around teacher colleges and universities, primarily during teacher institutes. The Southern Illinois Teachers' Association was organized in 1881, followed by regional associations in northern Illinois (1882) and eastern Illinois (1898). By 1900, there were seven independent regional associations organized throughout the state. Most members of these regional associations did not join ISTA. Though not viewed as rivals, these regional associations called into question the credibility of ISTA as representative of Illinois teachers.[90]

Conclusion

ISTA laid the groundwork for the state's public school system. The association successfully organized educators, reformers, and public opinion behind passage of the Free Public School Act of 1855. ISTA secured legislation that provided a state property tax to fund education; established a full-time superintendent of public instruction, who issued biennial reports that included recommendations on policies to improve education; and was instrumental in the creation of ISNU. By 1900, Illinois had six normal colleges to train teachers and an industrial university (the University of Illinois). Many other reforms advocated by ISTA were enacted to varying degrees, including graded schools, teacher institutes, kindergarten, compulsory attendance laws, school libraries, teacher certification standards, and high school education.

While much progress was achieved, many problems persisted. Despite ISTA's early support for pay equity, male teachers continued to receive higher pay than their female counterparts. While the 1870 Illinois Constitution and subsequent legislation protected the rights of Black children to attend school, racial segregation subsequently became widespread throughout the state. As a testament to ISTA's declining influence, the $1 million state subsidy that replaced the two-mill property tax in 1873 remained frozen for thirty-four years, resulting in an ever-increasing reliance on local property taxes and exasperating funding disparities among school districts across the state.[91] ISTA barely survived the depression that followed the Panic of 1873. In 1876, the monthly education press that had chronicled public school events since 1855 ceased publication. By the early 1900s, ISTA's influence over education policy had eroded. Membership had remained relatively stagnant since 1895, even though the number of teachers statewide had steadily increased to almost 28,000. In 1905, ISTA reported just 1,116 members. According to Chicago principal R. W. Hatfield, "more than one-half of the membership of this body comes from within a radius of sixty miles from Springfield and of that membership, two-thirds of it comes from the two counties of Sangamon and Christian. It is almost a local association." In failing to organize teachers across the state, ISTA missed the opportunity to build a powerful political coalition; however, events in Chicago would have a profound impact on the future of ISTA and Illinois teachers.[92]

CHAPTER 2

Chicago Teachers Federation
The First Public Education Union

When you teachers stayed in your school rooms, we men took care of you,
but when you go out of your school rooms as you have done, and attack
these great, powerful corporations, you must expect that they will hit back.

—Illinois state representative David Shanahan (R-Chicago)

The political influence of the Illinois State Teachers' Association (ISTA) in Springfield politics declined following the Panic of 1873. The association barely survived the ensuing depression, which lasted until 1879. Legislative priorities such as school consolidation and funding languished in Springfield. Writing in 1926, state superintendent of public instruction Francis Blair recalled a speech by Chicago principal Walter R. Hatfield at the 1915 ISTA annual meeting: "He said that in the beginning the State Teachers Association had sought to further the educational interests of this commonwealth, and for twenty-five years carried on the work well. But for the next twenty-five years, the association existed in a sort of academic atmosphere."[1]

While ISTA was floundering, teachers under the leadership of Margaret Haley and Catherine Goggin organized a largely female, elementary union—the Chicago Teachers Federation (CTF)—in 1897. Within its first six months, over half of all Chicago elementary teachers joined CTF. It was the first education union in the nation.[2] CTF challenged the idea that female teachers in elementary schools would be a compliant workforce. Chicago Public Schools (CPS) teaching staff accounted for over 22 percent of all Illinois teachers, and CTF's successes inspired a major reorganization for ISTA, making it a statewide organization.[3]

CTF Organizing

The issues that fueled the drive to organize CTF involved teacher pay and pensions. CPS had a seven-step salary schedule. The salary steps had not been increased since 1877, despite the rising cost of living. As a result, many teachers on the seventh step had not received a pay increase in twenty years. Besides salary, the pension fund was another major concern of CTF.[4] In 1895, under governor John Peter Altgeld, the state enacted a pension for Chicago teachers, which included a tenure provision that teachers could not be dismissed mid–school year without a hearing on the charges. From the start, revenue problems plagued the pension law. The pension plan was underfunded and near bankruptcy by 1898, just three years after it was created.[5]

To address the pay issue, CTF circulated a petition signed by 3,567 elementary teachers, demanding a ten-step salary schedule. Shortly after agreeing to the ten-step schedule, CPS reneged on the promised improvements, claiming a shortage of funds. In response, CTF launched an investigation into the Chicago Board of Education's finances and the property taxes paid by the city's largest corporations. The investigation exposed fraudulent tax assessments that cost the school system millions of dollars in revenue, and CTF filed in court a writ of mandamus to recoup lost revenue. After CTF won an Illinois Supreme Court decision in 1901 that ordered Chicago public utilities to be assessed at their actual value, ISTA praised CTF at its annual meeting: "What women can do in public service, has been admirably illustrated by Miss Margaret A. Haley and Miss Catherine Goggin of Chicago. . . . Although capital and the best legal talent the country afforded were united against them, they won."[6] The corporations appealed the decision in federal court, which greatly reduced the judgment of the state court. Nevertheless, CTF eventually recouped tax revenue and won back pay for over 2,300 teachers.[7] CTF also fought CPS superintendent Edwin Cooley's merit pay system, which was based on secretive principal evaluation. In the system's first three years in use, only 61 of the 2,600 eligible teachers received a merit increase. The merit pay system was not dropped until Ella Flagg Young replaced Cooley as superintendent in 1909.[8] Another key victory for CTF was defeating efforts to repeal the teacher pension and, subsequently, winning legislation in 1911 that put the pension on a solid footing. Once the pension was secured, CTF defeated efforts by the corrupt alderman William Rothmann to take control of the fund from the elected pension governing board.[9]

CTF's success in dealing with Chicago's corporate and political establishment was a direct result of its organizing the majority of CPS teachers. Having thousands of dues-paying members enabled CTF to pay Goggin and Haley full-time salaries equivalent to their teacher pay. While Goggin worked tirelessly behind the scenes, Haley served as the federation's chief spokesperson. They published a weekly bulletin that kept members informed of union activities and helped CTF organizing efforts across the city. Dues dollars also paid for CTF's lawsuits against the corporate tax cheats and the Chicago Board of Education.[10]

CTF built powerful alliances within the community. In 1902, it affiliated with the powerful Chicago Federation of Labor (CFL). CFL played an instrumental role in the passage of teacher pension and other legislation supported by CTF. Through their involvement in the women's suffrage movement, Haley and Goggin developed close political ties with Ella Flagg Young, Jane Addams, Florence Kelley, and other progressive reformers.[11] As a testimony to CTF's power and influence, Chicago Board of Education member Jacob Loeb complained in 1915 that CTF was a "curse to the school system," and that CPS was in the "grip of Margaret Haley."[12]

National Education Association

CTF never affiliated with the National Education Association (NEA), but Haley worked to build a national movement among women teachers within the association. She battled the all-male "old guard" leadership of NEA—education professors, city and state administrators, and college presidents—challenging them to be more responsive to the concerns of women teachers. While there were progressive leaders in union strongholds like Chicago and New York, many NEA members were from conservative rural communities across the nation. As a result, NEA tended to be politically more conservative than state associations like those in Illinois, with its large cities and powerful unions.[13]

Haley hoped to translate the CTF success into a national movement within NEA. At the 1898 NEA convention, CTF organized the National Federation of Teachers to pressure the association to address salary, pension, and tenure concerns of its members. This organization continued to agitate within NEA on behalf of teachers in the early 1900s. In 1901, Haley became the first female delegate to address the NEA annual meeting.[14] After hearing a speech by Dr. William Torrey Harris, US commissioner of education, Haley cited the CTF tax fight, explaining how Illinois railroads and public utilities had cheated Chicago schools of badly needed revenue. She suggested that other states might also be facing similar tax cheating. Dr. Harris responded with a personal assault: "Pay no attention to what that teacher down there has said. I take it that she is a grade school teacher, just out of the classroom at the end of the school year, worn out, tired out, and hysterical. . . . Chicago is no criterion for other parts of the country. It is morbid, cyclonic, and hysterical. You can never tell what is going to happen in Chicago."[15] Haley shot back with biting sarcasm, forcing Harris to apologize:

> I plead guilty to one charge made against me by Dr. Harris. I am a grade school teacher, but I'm not just out of the classroom. I have been out for two years working on this tax question as it affects the railroads and public utility corporations. I know what I am talking about. I have the facts. . . . If it be morbid to go into court and get an opinion, which I have little doubt will be sustained by the higher courts, ordering the taxing officers to assess property of five public utility corporations, amounting to two hundred million dollars, that for years have escaped taxation;

and if it be hysterical to go before people to tell them these facts, then we in Chicago plead guilty to your charge of being morbid and hysterical.[16]

This incident exposed the low regard of the conservative NEA leadership for women teaching in elementary schools. So began a fight to force NEA to be more responsive to the needs of its member teachers. In 1903, Haley led a successful floor fight against the old guard leadership. Under NEA bylaws, a committee composed of delegates from each of the state affiliates nominated a slate of officers. In effect, this nominating committee elected the officers for the next year. Harvard University president Nicholas M. Butler submitted a motion that would give the NEA president the power to appoint the nominating committee. Haley argued against this power grab by the leadership: "If the president appoints the nominating committee and the nominating committee appoints the president, this amendment establishes a self-perpetuating machine." Much to the chagrin of the old guard, this effort to consolidate power in the presidency was defeated, resulting in a barrage of lampoons in the press, which poked fun at NEA leadership "being taking to the woodshed by Haley."[17]

At the 1904 NEA convention, Haley delivered a speech entitled "Why Teachers Should Organize." In her speech, she defended the ideal of a professional teacher union, an ideal that even today resonates with NEA and the American Federation of Teachers (AFT): "The character of the teachers' organizations is twofold. Organizations on professional lines existed before the necessity became apparent for those for the improvement of conditions. . . . The closer the union between these two kinds of organization, the fuller and more effective is the activity possible to each."[18]

Throughout this period, Haley hoped that NEA would be the vehicle to create a national union. While the National Federation of Teachers ceased to exist in 1905, Haley did have an impact. Responding to pressure from its members, NEA established a committee on teacher salaries. Haley continued to agitate for issues at subsequent NEA conventions. The National League of Teachers' Associations was organized in 1912, and, one year later, NEA established a department of classroom teachers to research and make recommendations regarding salary, pension, and tenure. As a result of CTF's efforts, the professional and economic concerns of classroom teachers became increasingly more important within NEA.[19]

The CTF successes gained national attention. As the public face of the union, Haley was invited by reform groups in other cities to speak about education taxation, unionism, and women's rights. Haley traveled extensively coast to coast, urging teachers to organize unions. As a result of her efforts, women teachers became increasingly active, especially in urban schools. From 1902 to 1910, at least thirty-one teacher associations organized in cities across the nation.[20]

THE FIRST TEACHER STRIKE

The Saline County Teachers' Association conducted the first teacher strike in US history. As was the case throughout southern Illinois, teacher pay was pitifully low in Saline County, compared to the rest of the state. The success of a newly organized coal miners' union in Harrisburg in the early 1900s inspired the association to take action. Prior to the 1904 county institute, a teacher committee developed a plan to raise teacher salaries, with the help of Lewis York, the progressive county superintendent of schools. The association publicly announced a minimum salary scale based on an analysis of the fiscal condition of each district in the county. At the August county institute, teachers signed a pledge to return to work only if their districts paid according to the association's scale. Since the county superintendent in those days controlled the teacher certification process, York was able to limit the number of certificates so that school boards could not replace the current staff if teachers refused to work. Some districts ended up delaying the start of school. The plan worked. The Saline County Teachers' Association had control over teacher salaries for years to come, even after Superintendent York left office.[21]

CPS Superintendent Ella Flagg Young and CTF

In 1909, CPS hired Ella Flagg Young as superintendent, largely due to her strong support among CTF teachers. She became the first female school superintendent of a major urban system. The Chicago Board of Education believed that Young would be most effective in dealing with CPS's largely female teaching staff. That December, Young was elected as the first female president of ISTA. Her election as president inspired a complete reorganization of ISTA that made it one of the most influential organizations in Illinois politics.[22]

Young earned her PhD at the University of Chicago under professor John Dewey. She was the first woman to serve as director of the University of Chicago Lab School (1899–1905), principal of Chicago Normal School (1905–9), CPS superintendent (1909–13), ISTA president (1910), and NEA president (1911). Dewey said: "More times than I could well say I didn't see the meaning or the force of some favorite conception of my own till Mrs. Young had given it back to me." He was also quoted as saying that "I would come to her with these abstract ideas of mine and she would tell me what they meant."[23] Besides Dewey, Young was closely allied to Margaret Haley, Catherine Goggin, Jane Addams, and other progressive reformers. She was an outspoken feminist and supporter of women's suffrage. Haley stated that "her intellect was a machine gun," but that it was Young's "moral courage rather than her mental capacity that made her a leader of women."[24]

Young believed in a student-centered approach to education. Public schools were the training grounds for citizenship and equal opportunity. All children, regardless of social class, should attend a common school and have access to a curriculum that provided a broad range of learning opportunities for them. Instruction should also take into consideration the individual talents and interests of pupils. Teachers should be included at every level of school decision-making. The superintendent should be a person "of power," not simply someone "in power." Young established teacher councils (which she had proposed in her 1901 doctoral dissertation, "Isolation in the School") as a way to increase teachers' involvement in education improvement. In each school, a building council would regularly meet without administrators to discuss concerns; each school, in turn, sent representatives to an area council, and each area council elected one representative to a central council that met every five weeks with the superintendent. Recommendations of the teacher councils were not binding, but they did affect decisions at the building level and by central administration.[25] Haley said that the teacher councils "seemed to be [on the surface] merely a co-operative measure to promote understanding and good will. In reality, [they were] the declaration of independence in the war for academic freedom."[26] Teacher councils provided teachers with an opportunity to participate in the management of the schools—a step in the direction of collective bargaining and academic democracy.

A Turning Point

ISTA's annual meeting in December 1909 marked a turning point in its history. Not only was Ella Flagg Young elected as the first female president for 1910, but it also initiated a discussion about membership that ultimately led to the sweeping reorganization of ISTA.[27]

Membership had remained relatively static since 1895, even though the number of teachers statewide had steadily increased. Most ISTA members from outside the Springfield area were K–12 administrators, education professors, county school superintendents, and college presidents. A proposal to hold the 1910 annual meeting in Chicago rather than in Springfield so as to honor Young raised strong opposition from downstate members, reflecting the long-term tension between Chicago and downstate teachers. A Chicago principal, Grace Reed, responded: "I don't think it is the notion of anybody to move this Association to Chicago. I think we need a shaking up of the Association. The fact that Illinois has only 1,200 members is a scandal. . . . We ought to have at least three or four thousand active members. I think there is nothing like a little variety and change to awaken interest in this Association."[28] Reed concluded by saying that a Chicago meeting "would be a magnificent tribute to the new president," and she guaranteed that 1,000 teachers would attend.[29]

ISTA did indeed meet in Chicago the following year—and an unprecedented 5,555 teachers paid dues and attended.[30] CTF packed the meeting. Obviously, if

Table 2. ISTA Membership prior to 1912 Reorganization

Year	K–12 teachers	Members
1900	26,998	1,138
1905	27,860	1,116
1910	29,281	5,555
1911	29,860	974

Sources: Biennial Report of the Superintendent of Public Instruction of the State of Illinois, for years 1908–10, 16; 1910–12, 620; Journal of Proceedings of the Illinois State Teachers' Association, 1900 meeting, 89–95; 1905 meeting, 78; 1910 meeting, 95; 1911 meeting, 64.

Chicago and the other six regional associations merged with ISTA, membership would increase significantly. CTF's successes on taxation, salaries, and pensions demonstrated the potential power of a mass teacher organization. Moreover, the turnout at the 1910 annual meeting reinforced the idea that the association could be a political powerhouse if it organized teachers statewide—but also that to do so it would have to address teacher welfare issues. This realization was reinforced by the fact that ISTA's membership numbers dropped to under 1,000 in 1911 (see table 2).

Young's close ties to CTF and the labor movement were evident at the 1910 annual meeting, which she presided over. In the past, annual meetings had focused almost entirely on school organizational issues, such as funding, certification, libraries, kindergartens, textbooks, vocational education, district consolidations, "moral education," and township high schools. The 1910 meeting, in contrast, adopted a number of wide-ranging and progressive resolutions. Besides reiterating support for the restoration of the two-mill tax, it strengthened ISTA's stand against public funding of "private or sectarian" education. ISTA called for a law that ensured suitable and effective sanitation, purified drinking water, and proper ventilation and lighting in classrooms. In rural areas of the state that were lacking high schools, particularly in southern Illinois, it called for "free school extending to and through the twelfth grade for every child." It demanded a state minimum teacher salary. Finally, responding to CTF's successes in improving teacher pensions and the fact that in 1909 Peoria teachers had invited the president of the CPS pension board to address a meeting, ISTA committed itself to supporting "a state system of pensions for public school teachers."[31]

Three years later, ISTA clarified its position so as to avoid political and monetary entanglement with the existing Chicago plan: "we favor a Teachers' Pension Law which shall be State wide in its application and which shall not in any way impair the existing agreement in force in the State." In 1915, the legislature created a separate pension system for teachers funded partly by the state. Like Chicago, Peoria had previously established its own teacher pension fund. In the 1930s, the

Peoria pension was merged into the state system. The Chicago pension fund still remains separate from the state system.[32]

ISTA's Reorganization

ISTA's 1911 meeting began with a long and bitter debate over spending one hundred dollars for an Illinois state flag and ended with the decision that such an expenditure was unnecessary, given the meager funds in the treasury. State superintendent of public instruction F. G. Blair complained of "wasting an hour's time here talking about the expenditure of $100." How could ISTA be taken seriously in the state legislature if this minor expenditure raised budgetary concerns? Obviously, having a membership of fewer than one thousand when there were twenty-nine thousand K–12 teachers in the state was not just a budget problem; it was also a political embarrassment for an organization claiming to represent public schools. John W. Cook, president of Northern Illinois State Normal School, joined in stating, "I have just found that in a little state with only six or seven thousand teachers they have two thousand people in attendance and 4,516 enrolled." Cook even raised concerns about the continued survival of the state organization.[33]

The huge turnout in Chicago in 1910, largely a result of the power of CTF and the popularity of Young, inspired a plan to reorganize the association. At the 1911 meeting in Springfield, Chicago principal Walter Hatfield proposed a merger of the seven regional associations with ISTA. Hatfield stated: "With eight independent bodies going out alone we never get anywhere doing that sort of thing. We have gone down to defeat before many a legislator because they have thrown it at us and said 'you teachers don't know what you want.' Let us go with a solid front and say we are all after this thing and we are 30,000 strong." The 1911 convention unanimously endorsed a reorganization plan.[34]

A committee representing ISTA and the seven regional associations was given the task of drafting a merger plan for consideration at the next annual meeting. The plan called for a consolidation of the eight associations under a single banner, and was unanimously adopted at the 1912 annual meeting in Peoria.[35] The seven regional associations became divisions of ISTA. The dues dollars generated by the merger enabled ISTA to begin publishing a monthly newsletter, the *Illinois Teacher*, in 1913. The *Illinois Teacher* reported that the association "cannot hope to become as effective as it should unless it enrolls a larger percentage of the teaching force of the state."[36] Following the merger agreement, ISTA membership increased from 1,117 to 26,541 in just ten years (see table 3).

Under the merger agreement, the divisions were regional governing bodies of ISTA. Each division elected officers and three representatives; these latter served on the three state governing committees (appropriations, legislation, and resolutions).

Table 3. ISTA Membership and Staff after 1912 Reorganization

Year	No. K–12 teachers	No. ISTA members (%)*	No. staff
1912	30,366	1,177 (3.9)	0
1914	31,805	9,803 (30.8)	1
1922	39,590	26,541 (67.0)	1
1937	48,714	36,473 (74.9)	5

Source: Propeck and Pearson, *The History of the Illinois Education Association*, 90.

* The figures in parentheses represent the percentage of K–12 teachers who belonged to ISTA.

The three standing committees met regularly, developed policies, and assisted the state organization in carrying out its programs. In addition, ISTA created, as needed, ad hoc committees to make recommendations on specific issues such as teacher training, school sanitation, rural education, tenure, school district consolidation, and state funding. As with the governing committees, these ad hoc committees also included representation from each division. The three governing committees also met in a joint nominating session to slate the president and other officers for the next annual meeting to consider. The annual meeting normally elected the slated candidates.[37] Since each division had an equal voice in the nominating process, executive committee members typically included representation from districts across the state, thereby reducing regional rivalries (which was critical, given that the Chicago division accounted for over 25 percent of ISTA membership). Mattoon superintendent Gilbert Randle stated: "the new organization is not in the interest of any ring, nor is it an agency for the advancement of the interests of any particular community. It stands for the best interests of all of our schools, and the more humble the teacher the more willing he should be to lend his aid to this cause."[38] As membership expanded, the number of divisions increased, as did teacher involvement. In 1961, the association (now called the Illinois Education Association, IEA) had 61,181 members in twenty-one divisions. The IEA president was a county superintendent of schools. Five of the six state directors were school administrators, and the remaining director was a counselor. However, eleven of the twenty-one division chairpersons were teachers.[39]

The rapid increase in membership would not have occurred without an agenda that addressed the economic and professional concerns of classroom teachers. The issue of low salaries, especially for elementary teachers, attracted support particularly in the poor, rural districts throughout the state. In a presentation on the minimum wage for teachers, Robert C. Moore, who was later hired as ISTA's full-time executive secretary, stated that preparing teachers for the classroom: "requires time and money, and very few young people care to take the vows of poverty and consecrate their lives and devote their energies to teaching merely for the sake of teaching. . . . There are still many employers scattered over the state who rejoice when they can get a girl to try to feed the minds, build the characters, and cultivate the immortal souls of their children for lower wages than they pay to an ignorant hired man to feed their pigs."[40]

Already committed to women's suffrage, a minimum teacher salary, and a statewide pension, the association added to its legislative platform tenure, multiyear contracts, vocational education, consolidation of small school districts into larger units, free transportation for consolidated schools, increased state aid including the two-mill tax, health and safety regulations, compulsory education increased to sixteen years old, consideration of questions related to moral and religious education, use of school space for community events, a ban on the sale of cigarettes in Illinois, promotion of world peace, and the nonpartisan election of county superintendents of education.[41]

Besides merging the seven regional divisions with ISTA, the constitution adopted in 1912 made several other important changes. A full-time executive secretary position was created to manage the growing state association. In 1913, George Conn was hired, but he resigned the following year. A temporary part-timer, Lotus D. Coffman, was hired until a suitable replacement for Conn could be found. In 1915, Robert C. Moore was hired. Moore, a former Macoupin County superintendent of schools and Democratic Party candidate for state superintendent of public instruction, served as the executive secretary until 1938. His duties included being chief spokesperson, lobbyist, editor of the *Illinois Teacher*, and membership coordinator.[42]

In 1916, the constitution and bylaws were further amended to accommodate the rapid increase in membership. A representative assembly (RA) replaced the annual membership meeting. Under this system, each division selected delegates on the basis of one delegate per one hundred members or major fraction thereof. The RA met annually to elect officers, approve committee reports and resolutions, adopt a budget, amend the constitution and bylaws, and act on any other association policies. As was the case in the past, any member in good standing could still participate in the floor debate, but now only delegates could vote on matters before the assembly.[43]

The RA had a major effect on the association. In the past, any member in good standing could participate fully in the annual meetings. As a result, districts in the Springfield area, where the annual meetings were normally held, had an inordinate influence on ISTA business. The delegate system ensured fair representation across the state based on the membership in each division. At first, the delegate system resulted in administrators, not teachers, dominating the RA. In 1917, only 14 of the 167 elected delegates were teachers. The rest of the delegates included county superintendents, principals, and district superintendents. But, over time, as the membership increased, so did the number of teacher delegates. Chicago teachers were especially active in ISTA. In 1922, the Chicago division had 7,365 members, accounting for 28 percent of association membership. Of its 78 RA delegates, it sent 45 elementary and 14 high school teachers to the RA. The remaining 19 delegates were mostly principals and CPS administrators. The president of the Chicago division was a school principal, but the other four members of the executive committee were teachers. The delegate system greatly enhanced the influence of the Chicago division in the association. Being the largest and most powerful division, Chicago had a major impact on educational policy across the state.[44]

The annual RA became the voice of democracy in the organization, and even today it is the ultimate authority for all association policies. Once a year, hundreds of delegates from across the state would meet. The RA not only increased membership involvement, but also improved democratic decision-making within the state organization. Keeping with the spirit of collegiality, issues were thoroughly debated in an open, democratic manner. The fact that any association member had the right to participate in debate (if not to vote) led to a high level of teacher activism that would become even more pronounced over time. At the division level, teachers had the most representation. In 1937, the *Illinois Teacher* reported that at the annual meeting, "classroom teachers usually constitute a majority of the Chicago Division," but it pointed out that "some delegations have been made up almost altogether of principals and superintendents." That year, the association adopted a resolution proposed by a Chicago teacher calling on every division to include classroom teachers in their delegations. Teachers began accounting for a growing portion of the RA delegates. It was this body that would transform IEA into a teachers union focused on collective bargaining in the 1970s.[45]

At first, the work of the ISTA executive secretary was mostly clerical in nature, including keeping records of membership, publishing the *Illinois Teacher*, and handling other business. But, as its membership continued to increase, ISTA added programs and hired a research director, newsletter editor, and secretarial staff. The executive secretary became the chief administrator of the staff, official spokesperson, and legislative representative in Springfield. With ISTA's focus of attention mostly on the state legislature rather than on matters at the local level, the day-to-day operations of ISTA were left to the executive secretary in Springfield.[46]

The ISTA president and other statewide officers were elected for one-year terms. Only once in over one hundred years was a person elected for two consecutive terms: William H. Powell (1854–55), the first association president. In reality, presidential power was usually limited. The president received neither compensation nor release time. The president and the board of directors, consisting of the division presidents, met monthly to oversee association activities in accordance with the directives passed by the annual RA.[47]

ISTA became a powerful lobbying force for education in the state legislature. It was very successful at mobilizing political pressure on state leaders through its members and the public. To supplement these efforts, the association developed a prodigious research capacity. It worked closely with the Illinois State Board of Education (ISBE) and the National School Board Association in developing information on Illinois public schools. In 1924, ISTA hired Lester Grimm as full-time director of research to coordinate these activities. Through its research department, ISTA/IEA published data related to such issues as state aid equalization, attendance, school consolidation, teacher salaries and benefits, and local property taxation. Such information was invaluable in promoting its political agenda.[48]

Public Funding and Religious Education

ISTA had always taken a strong stand against public funding for "private or sectarian" purposes. In the 1850s, the association had insisted on a state-sponsored, secular normal school rather than relying on private, mostly religious colleges to train teachers for the growing public school system. In 1909, after a bill was introduced in Congress to provide funding for George Washington University in Washington, DC, ISTA passed a resolution stating that this bill violated the long-standing principle that there should be "no division of public educational funds among private institutions."[49] The association has never wavered from its opposition to public funding of private schools. But this incident did not end efforts, especially by Protestant college section members, to promote religious teaching in public schools.

In the early 1900s, faculty from Protestant institutions including Wheaton, Knox, Millikin, and Monmouth Colleges were active in ISTA through its college section. They supported public education as a means of instilling in children "Christian values" and morality. They promoted Bible reading, school prayer, and religious hymns in public schools. They also joined with the Woman's Christian Temperance Union in an effort to include "temperance physiology" in textbooks and curriculum.[50] In 1910, the college section, which was led by Charles Blanchard, president of Wheaton College, asked ISTA to consider the issue of Bible reading in public schools. That year, in response to Catholic parents seeking a writ of mandamus to order the Winchester School District in southern Illinois to discontinue its requirement that Bible reading, religious hymns, and school prayer being regularly included in classrooms, the Illinois Supreme Court issued an injunction against the practice. ISTA president Ella Flagg Young referred the issue to a three-member committee that included Blanchard. It was to report back the following year.[51] The special committee on the Supreme Court decision reported that "at least one-half of the schools of the state" prohibit such practices and that, in districts where such religious practices were permitted, "one-fourth of the teachers refrained in whole or in part from such exercises."[52] The committee also stated that should religious practices be permitted, they would be a continuing source of discord, much to the detriment of public schools. The majority on the committee recommended that the court decision should stand:

> The public school cannot be used for proselytizing or converting its pupils to any particular faith or creed. But it can and should teach a system of ethics and moral conduct based upon general and fundamental laws. . . . The court opinion really strengthens the cause of public education by reaffirming in language clearer and stronger than ever uttered before, the constitutional prohibition against the appropriation of any public funds for the aid or use of private, religious or sectarian institutions, a doctrine stoutly and constantly proclaimed by this Association.[53]

Blanchard, however, submitted a minority report with a motion to establish a committee to seek a reversal of the court decision. A heated floor debate ensued. Chicago principal Grace Reed argued: "We teachers are not paid for that. . . . It should not be required of us with our other numerous accomplishments. Let the children attend twice a month at their Sunday school and churches and there receive their religious instruction."[54]

Blanchard's substitute motion passed in a roll call vote, 207–84. A committee on Bible reading in public schools was created and hired legal counsel to investigate the matter. In 1911, the committee reported that the Supreme Court decision on Bible reading was not conclusive and "that there is no legal obstacle to bible reading in our public schools." Bible reading and other religious practices in public schools had stirred controversy within the association from its earliest days, and such practices still continued, especially in conservative, rural areas of the state. The adoption of Blanchard's report reflected the strength of religious sentiment within the association. The report justified Bible readings on the grounds that the United States was founded on "Christian" principles and that the King James Bible was widely viewed even by many Catholics as not being sectarian. This religious sentiment was, in part, a reflection of the fact that the ISTA meetings were held in Springfield, in heavily Protestant central Illinois.[55]

The issue of school-sponsored religious practice lost much of its support after 1917. Under the delegate system, power shifted to the divisions representing mainly K–12 school districts. The Chicago division was, by far, the largest division, representing over a fifth of the state membership. Chicago, with its diverse religious and ethnic population, opposed efforts to include religious practices in its schools. The Chicago Board of Education had ended Bible reading and other religious practices in schools in 1874. The college section, which included Blanchard and other members from religiously affiliated institutions, lost much of its influence. Though the annual meetings continued to be held in Springfield, attendees from the largely conservative counties of central Illinois would no longer have an inordinate influence over the association. The delegate system ensured statewide representation; ISTA became a truly statewide public school organization.

In 1919, the RA adopted a resolution that opposed "any appropriation or pay from any public fund whatever, anything in the aid of any church or sectarian purpose, or to help support or sustain any school, academy, seminary, college, university, or other literary or science institutions, controlled by any church or sectarian denomination whatever; nor shall any grant or donation of land, money or any personal property ever be made by the state to any such public corporation, to any church or for any sectarian purposes."[56] Regardless, Bible readings, school prayer, and religious hymns continued in many Illinois school districts unabated for years to come. In 1963, the US Supreme Court ruled in *Abington School District v. Schempp* that school-sponsored Bible reading for religious instruction in public schools was unconstitutional. Given the diversity of the US population, school-sponsored religious practices have been, for the most part, eliminated in public schools.[57]

NEA Reorganization

The success of ISTA following the 1912 reorganization gained the attention of other state associations as well as NEA. In the first five years of reorganization, ISTA membership increased from 1,177 to 16,171. Other states soon emulated the ISTA organizational model. At the time, there was no requirement for local association members to join NEA. In 1917, NEA had just 8,466 members, while ISTA had almost twice as many.[58] ISTA played a major role in the subsequent NEA transformation. In 1918, a conference of state associations met to develop a plan to reorganize NEA. An ISTA committee on reorganization headed by W. B. Owen pushed the Illinois model. However, Margaret Haley and CTF opposed the reorganization plan. Haley wanted to maintain the old system, under which any members who attended the annual NEA meeting had voting rights rather than having elected delegates vote on issues. Haley feared that the conservative old guard, whom she had battled in the early 1900s, would constitute the majority of the delegates and reduce the influence of progressive teacher activists in the large cities where the annual NEA meetings were held.

Having already broken its ties with AFT, CTF withdrew from NEA in 1918. At the time, Haley expressed frustration with NEA being controlled by administrators. According to Haley, "It required years of struggle to get the NEA to give any consideration whatever to the living and working conditions of the classroom teachers and to recognize salaries, pensions and tenure as legitimate subjects for discussion. It actually took a revolution in 1903 to secure the appointment of a committee on salary, tenure and pensions. For the first 50 years of the NEA, no classroom teacher was ever elected to any office."[59] Sensitive to this criticism, ISTA increased the size of the committee on reorganization to ten members, adding Robert C. Moore and female elementary teachers.[60] The reorganization plan was defeated at the 1919 NEA meeting in Milwaukee, Wisconsin, but passed the next year in Salt Lake City, Utah, not without controversy. In the debate over the issue, NEA leadership refused to recognize Haley from the convention floor, causing bitter feelings within the Illinois delegation. The *Illinois Teacher* reported: "The ISTA voted to affiliate with the NEA. There was no determined opposition to affiliation, but there was severe criticism of the methods used to bring about the re-organization of the NEA. Margaret Haley, Edgar C. Pruitt, Wm. B. Owen and others condemn the autocratic, czaristic, steam-roller methods used at Salt Lake City last July."[61]

Haley and many CTF members joined the ISTA Chicago division. Belonging to NEA was not a prerequisite for ISTA membership, but local education organizations, state associations, and divisions had the option to affiliate with NEA, paying a five-dollar fee and obtaining one delegate for the NEA RA. Every affiliate organization was also assigned one additional delegate per one hundred individual NEA memberships (with delegates to be chosen in the manner "provided by the separate divisions"). So for example a thousand-member division that affiliated with NEA would receive three delegates in total if only two hundred of its members also joined NEA. ISTA's Chicago division was, by far, the largest division in the state. It was the unifying force for the various teacher organizations in the city, and it served as the vehicle for CTF, the Chicago Principals' Association, AFT locals, and other education organizations to remain active in NEA. Haley continued to attend NEA meetings. As late as 1930, Haley served as a Chicago division delegate to the NEA RA. In 1928, Chicago teacher R. Ross Smith, vice president of the NEA department of classroom teachers, praised Haley, saying, "I'll name just one classroom teacher leader who by her ideal of democracy, by her vision, by her ability to think and act upon her thinking, has done more than any other to bring about the present state of your national body—Miss Margaret Haley."[62]

Following the reorganization, NEA membership increased very rapidly. In 1927, NEA reported 141,212 members; by 1957, it had 703,829. As was the case in Illinois, the NEA RA greatly increased participation, while the membership growth forced the organization to focus its attention on teacher concerns. Speaking in 1929 about NEA, R. Ross Smith stated: "it is true that the classroom teacher has only recently begun to have influence in it; for many years he merely paid his dues; and it is true that he had to fight for the recognition he has got and fight for years. But this recognition now is coming just about as rapidly as he develops leaders in his own particular organizations who can lead with credit in the larger group."[63]

School administrators continued to hold an inordinate amount of influence over NEA policy until the 1960s, but teachers became increasingly more involved and assertive.

Conclusion

The reorganization made ISTA a statewide, mass teacher organization and a powerful force in education politics. By 1922, 67 percent of Illinois teachers were ISTA members in sixteen divisions. Membership increases enabled the association to hire Robert C. Moore as a full-time executive secretary and publish *Illinois Teacher*, a monthly newsletter. The reorganization brought unity to the diverse education community across Illinois. The association billed itself as "the only big all-inclusive teacher organization in the state." It was a broad coalition of public education interests that included the County Superintendents Association, various school administrator organizations, the Parent Teachers Association, and teachers unions. It generated research, mobilized public support, and lobbied in Springfield on behalf of its members for educational funding and programs. Though not a union, it worked closely on education legislation with CTF, CFL, and the Illinois State Federation of Labor (SFL). While these labor organizations were never affiliated with ISTA, they shared a common interest in promoting the public school system. Most CTF members also joined ISTA's Chicago division, which, in concert with CFL, served as its conduit for the concerns of city teachers' unions in the state legislature. These relationships remained intact until the 1950s, when the Illinois Federation of Teachers (IFT) began to mount a challenge to IEA leadership in the state.

CHAPTER 3

ISTA and Labor Union Allies

Advancing the Cause of Public Education

That education is one of the chief means of fitting the child for worthy membership in modern society cannot be denied. In brief, to have a democracy at all we must guarantee to our children a reasonable equality of educational opportunity. . . . The daughter of the window-washer woman and the son of the wealthy banker stand equal beneath the banner of the district common school. . . . Equal educational opportunities for the children of the state whether they are in poor or in wealthy communities.

—Illinois Teacher

As a result of its 1912 reorganization, the Illinois State Teachers' Association (ISTA) had reestablished itself as the voice of public education. ISTA vigorously fought to increase state funding of public schools and to expand access to K–12 education for all children. It maintained strong political ties with the Chicago Teachers Federation (CTF) and organized labor. ISTA executive secretary Robert C. Moore praised the Illinois State Federation of Labor (SFL) for "promoting good school legislation."[1] He worked closely with Victor Olander, SFL secretary, on legislation for a wide range of education issues, such as compulsory education, tenure, free textbooks, vocational training, and state funding. The association often had its legislative program adopted without amendments at the SFL convention.[2]

Moore also served on the Joint Labor Legislative Board of Illinois. This joint committee included the Chicago Federation of Labor (CFL), Women's Trade Union League, United Mine Workers, and other unions. SFL president John Walker chaired the joint committee. It lobbied not only for education but for a broad range of labor legislation, such as workers' compensation, women's eight-hour day, and mine safety. The joint committee also defeated efforts to require military training in high schools and to use convict labor in manufacturing, among other conservative proposals. In 1915, Moore wrote: "Organized labor has been very helpful to us by strongly advocating some of our measures and helping defeat others. President John Walker of the State Federation of Labor, Secretary Victor Olander and Miss Margaret Haley have spoken several times before the committees on education and they are very forceful, logical, and convincing speakers. . . . If we succeed in getting some good school legislation this year, a part of the credit should be given to organized labor."[3] The close ties between the association and the labor unions were particularly evident in the fight over the 1915 Cooley Bill.

The Cooley Bill: Vocational Education

By the late 1890s, there was a growing movement nationally to include vocational education or what some termed "industrial arts" in public schools. Though public schools were successful in teaching reading, writing, and arithmetic in kindergarten through sixth grade, most educators recognized the need to include industrial arts in the school curriculum. In 1913, 46.2 percent of Illinois students dropped out prior to sixth grade, and 84.4 percent did not attend high school.[4] In light of this alarmingly high dropout rate, educators believed that classes designed to teach manual skills would keep students in school longer, with the hope of qualifying for higher-paying jobs when they joined the workforce. Businessmen and manufacturers wanted practical skills taught in order to fill jobs that increasingly required higher skills. They pointed out that Europe, especially Germany, had already established schools teaching industrial arts. By the 1890s, Chicago had introduced some basic manual training classes, including sewing, cooking, drawing, science labs, woodworking, and skilled trades. The demand for a comprehensive program of vocational education continued to gain momentum over the ensuing years.[5]

Though there was a general agreement over the need for vocational education, a bitter debate ensued over how the program should be organized. In 1911, Edwin Cooley, former Chicago Public Schools (CPS) superintendent, was hired by the Commercial Club to travel throughout Europe to study vocational education. He was especially impressed by the German school system. Two years later, his report became the basis of a vocational education bill introduced in Springfield. The Commercial Club, Civic Federation, Association of Commerce, and Illinois Manufacturers' Association rallied behind the Cooley Bill. The bill provided that starting in the seventh grade, students would be placed in either a vocational education track or an academic program. An appointed school board headed by business executives would govern the vocational training track. This dual-track education system envisioned by the Cooley Bill, in effect, would give corporate interests direct control over a large portion of the public school system. Not only was the bill intended to supply businesses with a trained workforce, but many believed that it would teach the children of blue-collar families a work ethic and an aversion to labor radicalism.[6]

ISTA condemned the Cooley Bill as "un-American and un-democratic," stating that it "attacks the very roots of our public education system."[7] ISTA supported expanding vocational education within the existing school system but opposed the Cooley Bill. It adopted this resolution: "We favor the establishment of vocational courses as part of the present school system and under the present school boards and . . . we strongly oppose the establishment of separate schools under separate boards of education."[8] ISTA held that all students should have access to the same educational opportunities, regardless of social class. It supported a single-track common school system, whereby students would have equal access to academic and vocational educational classes. The association also opposed the use of intelligence testing for placement in high school programs. High schools should include classes designed to meet all the needs and interests of the student population. ISTA president Walter R. Hatfield explained the association's position:

> The friends of the unit or present system of schools believe that separate system of schools would tend to stratify society, would not give the boy or girl a fair chance to find himself or herself thru working for a time in several lines of industry, would increase enormously the cost of education by duplication of teaching, equipment and buildings, would draw away from the present public school the children, the interest of the parents and consequently their financial support. It would tend to make friction and rivalry between two classes of schools in the division of public school funds and in segregating the children.[9]

CTF and its union allies, too, vehemently opposed the Cooley Bill. They believed that it would deny working-class students the full benefits of public education. It would segregate working-class students and train them to serve the needs of the business class. John Walker of the SFL stated that a dual-track education system would serve as "a training place for cheap labor, beasts of burden, at the expense of the development of children as broad-minded, bighearted, intelligent, fine types of citizenship."[10]

A coalition of labor unions, progressive reformers, and ISTA successfully lobbied against the Cooley Bill. ISTA executive secretary Moore wrote: "Is it possible that we must classify children at this tender age and extremely early stage of educational development with regards to vocations and thus preclude a freedom of choice at a more mature age? This would certainly be a long step backwards from where we have always stood heretofore."[11]

The Illinois General Assembly killed the Cooley Bill when it was introduced in 1913, in 1915, and for a final time in 1917, ending efforts to create a dual system in Chicago. After the United States entered World War I, Moore was quick to condemn Cooley's dual system of education as "made in Germany," saying, "Now we are told that the reason the German people do not rise in revolt against their wicked, oppressive and autocratic ruling class is that their educational system and methods for the last 25 years have been devoted to the purposes of developing industrial efficiency, of sterilizing the germs of democracy, and of making the people subservient to the Kaiser and the Junkers."[12]

A few communities established dual systems despite the defeat of the Cooley Bill, but for most districts, the vocational education programs would be included within the existing public school system. In 1917, Congress passed the Smith-Hughes National Vocational Education Act, providing for federal grants-in-aid for vocational training programs. To qualify for federal dollars, states were required to provide revenue matching the federal grants and develop programs consistent with the provisions in the act.[13] In 1919, Illinois created a State Board for Vocational Training, with the superintendent of public instruction serving as the board's executive officer. The board was charged with overseeing the implementation of the act and associated teacher training, and approving programs designed by school districts. Within this legal framework, school districts had a large degree of discretion in developing programs to accommodate the needs of their local communities.[14]

By 1938, 403 vocational education programs had been established by school districts throughout Illinois. These programs offered classes in home economics, construction, woodworking, automotive mechanics, machine shop work, agriculture, and numerous other industrial-related occupations. They included full-time and part-time high school programs as well as evening school. High school students, young adults working part time, and older adults "fully established in a vocation" could choose to take classes. CPS established the Washburne Apprentice and Continuation School for out-of-school students seeking entrance into the building trades and other occupations. Other four-year CPS vocational schools were established across the city. Targeted federal and state funding encouraged vocational education throughout the state. Some communities established separately managed vocational education centers based on the dual system model, but the governing boards of these cooperatives were administrators of the participating districts. Executive secretary Moore stated that the association motto was "one system and one administration, and equal opportunities for all children to obtain twelve years of free school education in general culture, in the vocations, and in good citizenship."[15]

The Loeb Rule

At the same time that CTF was fighting powerful business interests over the Cooley Bill, it was facing a more serious challenge from the Chicago Board of Education, which sought to remove superintendent Ella Flagg Young and break the power of the federation that supported her. Mayor William "Big Bill" Thompson appointed anti-union board members and called CTF leaders "character assassins" and "lady sluggers."[16] William Rothmann (who had been defeated by CTF a few years earlier when he tried to control the teacher pension) and Jacob Loeb (a holdover from the previous mayoral administration and brother of the vice president of Sears, Roebuck and Company) launched a campaign to destroy the teachers union. The business community, angry about the defeat of the Cooley Bill and Young's close ties to organized labor, backed Loeb's efforts. In September 1915, Loeb passed a resolution through the Board of Education rules committee that prohibited Chicago teachers from holding membership in any organization that was affiliated with a trade union or that hired a business agent.[17] According to the so-called Loeb Rule: "Membership by teachers in labor unions or in organizations of teachers affiliated with a trade union or a federation or association of trade unions, as well as teachers' organizations which have officers, business agents, or any other representatives who are not members of the teaching force, is inimical to proper discipline, prejudicial to the efficiency of the teaching force, and detrimental to the welfare of the public school system. Therefore, such membership, affiliation, or representation is hereby prohibited."[18] The Illinois Manufacturers' Association sent a letter to the board in support of the Loeb Rule. ISTA was quick to respond: "This fight is certainly of interest to all members of the ISTA because it involves the principle of their rights to organize, to make an organized effort to promote legislation, and to cooperate with other organizations."[19]

Loeb made it perfectly clear in a public statement that his target was CTF and not the other teacher organizations. The board refined the Loeb Rule to single out CTF on the grounds that it was "hostile to discipline, prejudicial to efficiency of the teaching force and detrimental to the welfare of the schools."[20] ISTA quickly came to the defense of the federation, reporting:

> before teachers criticize the Board of Education, they should remember that the Chicago teachers have been guilty of unpardonable activity in raising the tax assessments of several tax-dodging corporations many millions of dollars; that they have fought for the conservation of the school lands for the benefit of the schools against land and rent grabbers; that they have assisted the State Association in preventing the enactment of a law providing for a dual system of schools, which was a favorite measure of the business and factory interests of Chicago; that in all these measures they have cooperated with the labor unions; and they have claimed the right to continue this cooperation in order to promote the common interests and the interests of the public schools in the future.[21]

The federation obtained a court injunction that blocked any teacher firings based on the Loeb Rule. The Illinois Supreme Court upheld the injunction, citing the First Amendment right to freedom of association. Carl Sandburg wrote: "Margaret

Haley wins again! . . . For fifteen years this one little woman has flung her clenched fists into the faces of contractors, school land lease holders, tax dodgers and their politicians, fixers, go-betweens and stool pigeons."[22]

Amid the fight over the Loeb Rule, CTF suffered two losses. In December 1915, Ella Flagg Young resigned as superintendent. Her stand against the Cooley Bill, support for the teacher pensions, and close ties to progressive reformers and unions had angered conservative business interests. With the election of Big Bill Thompson in 1915, Young knew that her CPS contract would not be renewed. She remained one of the most influential education leaders of her time until her death in the 1918 influenza pandemic.[23] Haley praised her, saying, "[Young] gave all her worldly possessions to two institutions, the Mary Thompson Hospital for Women and Children and the Chicago Public Library. To the people of Chicago, she left an infinitely greater gift, an ideal of democracy in education which has heartened the fighters for freedom through long and sometimes dreary years since she went away."[24] One month after Young's resignation, Catherine Goggin, the highly respected CTF leader, died in a traffic accident. Her death was a serious blow to CTF. ISTA paid this tribute to Goggin: "She was a pioneer in the movement that resulted in increased wages and a pension for teachers; and, in fact, she took an active interest in every movement in the last twenty years to advance the cause of education."[25]

In defiance of the Loeb Rule, Haley responded by calling for the formation of a national teachers union. On April 15, 1916, representatives from three Chicago teachers unions—CTF, the Men's Teachers Union, and the Federation of Women High School Teachers—met with a teacher group from Gary, Indiana, to organize the American Federation of Teachers (AFT). Teacher unions from New York and four other cities sent letters asking to be chartered with this new organization. In May, AFT was granted a charter from the American Federation of Labor (AFL). Haley's CTF, the largest of the unions, was designated as Local 1. Charles Stillman, a high school teacher

MARY HERRICK

Mary Herrick, a teacher at Chicago's DuSable High School, had a storied career as a leader in the teachers union movement. She served as president of the Federation of Women High School Teachers in the 1920s and became a progressive leader in the Chicago Teachers Union (CTU). Unlike Margaret Haley, who was, at best, ambivalent about racial discrimination against African Americans, Herrick championed the cause of equal rights and racial justice. Herrick served as an AFT vice president and as a member of the CTU board. She held various positions in labor, academic, and civic organizations. She was a prolific researcher and writer. She contributed articles to *School and Society*, the *Nation*, and the *American Teacher* magazines. She authored a detailed history of the Chicago public school system: *The Chicago Schools: A Social and Political History* (1971).[27]

from the Chicago Men's Teachers Union, was elected president of the new national union.[26]

In May 1916, despite the court injunction against the Loeb Rule, the board fired sixty-eight teachers on the grounds that it was a management right to hire and fire employees "at will." It argued that the tenure provision enacted as part of the pension bill during the Altgeld administration did not apply to summer staff changes; in theory, the board could replace the entire teaching staff prior to the start of the next school year. The intent of this mass firing was clear. Of the sixty-eight fired teachers, forty-seven were current or former CTF officials. While almost all of the remaining twenty-one non-union teachers were rated as inefficient, none of the union teachers had received negative ratings.[28] These firings created a public outcry against the board. CTF challenged the firing in court. In April 1917, the Illinois Supreme Court ruled that "the Board has the absolute right to decline to employ or to re-employ any applicant for any reason whatever or for no reason at all."[29] Ella Flagg Young had supported tenure so that teachers would feel free to participate in teacher councils without fear of retaliation. She called the court's decision the "Dred Scott Decision of Education" since it, in effect, made teachers subject to the political whim of the school system.[30]

Loeb's campaign against the union had its intended effects. CTF membership declined by half from 1915 to 1916. In order to stave off disaster, CTF withdrew from AFT, CFL, SFL, and the Women's Trade Union League in May 1917. It never rejoined. Soon after, all the fired CTF members were rehired.[31] Years later, the Chicago Teachers Union (CTU) would be chartered as AFT Local 1, the designation held by CTF prior to its withdrawal from AFT.

CPS Teacher Tenure

The Loeb firings provoked widespread opposition. In Springfield, SFL and ISTA raised their voices in protest. The Chicago City Club, the Municipal Ownership League, the Illinois Congress of Parents and Teachers, and several city women's clubs organized the Public Education Association (PEA), calling for legislation to reform CPS operations. Ralph Otis, a Chicago Board of Education member who had supported the Loeb Rule but opposed the mass firings, led an effort along with several other board members to address the concerns raised by PEA. After a series of public hearings by the city's committee on schools, fire, police, and civil service, PEA prepared three reform bills for the legislature to consider. Of the three, the Otis Bill passed. It limited the power of the mayor and city council to interfere in board decisions. It also defined the powers and limits of the board: only the superintendent could recommend the appointment or dismissal of teachers; the board only had final approval on such recommendations. After a three-year probationary period, CPS teachers were covered by tenure and could only be dismissed for "cause." The law provided that a teacher facing dismissal had the right to a hearing "together with counsel" before the board, which then made the final decision on the firing. The Otis Bill was signed into law in April 1917.[32]

The Otis Bill "localized" tenure in that it only applied to Chicago teachers.[33] ISTA had proposed a statewide tenure law as early as 1900. The association argued that a tenure law would improve public education: "Schools will never receive the best instruction it is possible to give as long as teachers are hampered in their tenure of position by political pulls, and factional quarrels—therefore a law should be enacted granting to tried teachers greater security of position and compensation proportionate to their experience and ability."[34] A statewide tenure law modeled after the Otis Bill was passed in 1941. As in the case of teacher pensions, events in Chicago preceded statewide change.

World War I and Its Aftermath

In response to the outbreak of World War I, ISTA urged an immediate end to the conflict. In 1914, the association passed a resolution favoring a committee to promote "the ways and means by which public education will contribute with increasing effectiveness to the foundation of permanent world peace." Many educators believed that future wars could be avoided if only children were taught to understand and respect the racial, ethnic, and cultural differences of other nations. On the eve of the US declaration of war, the association passed a resolution opposing a bill that had been introduced in Springfield mandating "compulsory military training in public and private schools."[35] Once the nation entered the war in April 1917, ISTA wholeheartedly supported President Woodrow Wilson's war aims to make the "world safe for democracy." Nevertheless, the association, along with its labor union allies, opposed mandatory military training in schools; instead, it advocated physical education as a requirement for all public school students.[36]

ISTA viewed the war as an opportunity to promote democratic values. Once the war was concluded, public education would be key to a lasting peace. The *Illinois Teacher* published numerous articles about the role of education in democracy. It heralded the British Labour Party's adoption of an education reform program that called for free, universal public education until eighteen years of age "without any form of military training." All students should have equal access to school facilities and education programs, without social class distinction. The Labour Party program mirrored the democratic ideals being advanced by the association and seemed to prove that the war was advancing democracy.[37]

ROBERT C. MOORE

Robert C. Moore was the first full-time executive secretary of ISTA (1915–38). Growing up in southern Illinois outside Carlinville, a coal mining area of the state and a hotbed of unionism, he started his career as a teacher in a one-room schoolhouse. He later served as the Macoupin County superintendent of schools and was named the Democratic candidate for state superintendent of public instruction (although he lost this election). Moore was acutely aware of the inherent educational inequality, especially in rural school districts, caused by the state's reliance on local property taxes. During his time at ISTA, association membership increased from 9,803 to 44,457, and Moore was politically aligned with SFL. Upon his death in 1950, the *Chicago Union Teacher* wrote: "The Chicago Teachers Union honors and reveres Mr. Moore for his outstanding contribution to the welfare of the public schools in Illinois." The union also noted that his son Paul Moore was a teacher at Chicago Vocational School and a CTU trustee.[38]

Financing the huge expense of the war effort was a major concern. ISTA criticized war profiteers as "voracious 'patriots' . . . making enormous fortunes" from the conflict. It supported a "heavy tax on war profits." Otherwise, it argued, government borrowing in the form of war bonds would constrain education funding. Robert C. Moore wrote: "These enormous loans must be paid sometime and paid with interest; and it is likely that for the next fifty years such payments will be made the excuse for beating down wages of all workers, especially of teachers because their wages, the bonds and interest must all be paid by some form of public taxation."[39] He was right. An excessive war profit tax was not enacted, and taxation accounted for only 22 percent of the financing of the war. Borrowing was the main source of revenue. The Consumer Price Index nearly doubled from 1916 to 1920; salaries lagged far behind. School budgets could not keep up with rising prices and the growing student enrollment. The postwar period was marked by a teacher shortage, public debt, and high inflation. President Warren G. Harding and a conservative Republican Congress swept into power with an anti-tax fervor. When prices fell during the postwar depression, some newspapers suggested cutting teacher salaries to ease the funding crisis. ISTA responded: "Very little is said about reducing the salaries of presidents of railroads and other corporations or of the officers, chief executives, and other high positions in Big Business."[40]

The economy improved for teachers in the 1920s. After a 19.2 percent decline in the cost of living during the 1921 depression, the economy recovered and prices stabilized over the next six years. Teacher wages continued to rise over this time, from a average salary of $1,287 in 1921 to $1,589 in 1927.[41] Despite this improvement, teacher pay remained comparatively low. In 1928, the average annual salary for Illinois elementary teachers (including administrators) was $1,460, compared to $1,465 for blue-collar wage earners. High school teachers (including administrators) were better paid, averaging $2,050, but still received lower salaries than most semiskilled and skilled workers. A survey of seventy-five trade unions (839,955 workers) in sixty-seven cities indicated an average pay range of $2,008 for forty weeks to $2,497 for forty-eight weeks.[42]

Not all teachers benefited from the economic recovery in the 1920s. The war in Europe raised food prices in America and encouraged investment in farmland and equipment. After the war, the farm economy suffered from overproduction, low prices, and debt. The rural economy never fully recovered from the 1921 depression, driving many small farmers out of business. The heavy reliance on local property taxes to fund public schools meant inferior education programs and lower teacher salaries in many rural counties. In 1930, the ten counties that paid the highest median teacher salaries raised an average of $2,447 per teacher, whereas the ten counties with the lowest teacher salaries raised an average of only $821 per teacher.[43]

Taxation and Funding

Restoring the two-mill state property tax was critical to ISTA's political agenda. In 1873, Illinois had replaced the two-mill property tax with a $1 million state aid grant, which remained unchanged until 1907. Consequently, an increasing portion of public school funding relied on local property taxes. In 1907, the state increased education funding by an additional $1 million. However, had the two-mill tax remained intact, it would have generated $4.6 million annually by 1913, instead of the $2 million state aid allotment. Increasing state aid as a larger portion of public school funding has been a major focus of the association ever since, in large part to mitigate the funding inequity between property-rich urban districts and downstate rural communities. ISTA argued on behalf of low-paid teachers downstate, "where mining is the chief industry, and also where agriculture has lost its vigor because of an impoverisht [*sic*] soil." Revenue generated by the two-mill tax would remove the "economic barriers that tend to make a fair minimum-wage impossible at the present time."[44]

Reforms such as a minimum teacher salary, free textbooks, equalization of funding, and compulsory education until the age of sixteen were not achievable unless the state increased its share of the cost of public education. ISTA and its allies launched an ambitious campaign to increase the common school fund. ISTA had long lobbied unsuccessfully for the reinstatement of the two-mill tax. Going into 1919, the state allocated $4 million for public schools; the two-mill tax would have raised $8 million. Out of frustration, ISTA dropped its call for the two-mill tax in favor of a $10 million state grant. The state responded with $6 million for 1919—still less than what the two-mill tax would have generated. The next year, the association supported the adoption of a graduated income tax, which is to this day a fixture of the association's tax reform agenda (Illinois now has a flat income tax).[45]

In December 1920, ISTA, SFL, the School Board Association, and other allies called for $20 million in funding. In June, the Chicago division of ISTA organized a public rally in Springfield to lobby for education funding. The rally coincided with a "mass meeting" of the anti-tax Illinois Manufacturers' Association. CTF funded the rally; Margaret Haley and others made the arrangements. About three hundred Chicago division members attended the rally. Association members from other cities as well as representatives of the Congress of Parents and Teachers, School Board Association, women's clubs, and civic organizations also participated. About two hundred teachers quietly attended the manufacturers' meeting in the afternoon, before meeting with the governor and legislators. According to Robert Moore, the rally achieved its goals: "It brought a large number of teachers and other friends of education in direct contact with the legislative machinery of the state," and "it counteracted the effects of the demonstration planned by the Manufacturers' Association and its associates."[46]

In 1921, ISTA issued a report entitled "The Crisis in Public Education in Illinois," in which it described the funding problems facing public education. Though the cost of living had nearly doubled since 1916, education funding had increased only 33 percent. School districts were facing mounting debts. Inflation had undermined K–12 teacher salaries, which had risen only 9 percent across those five years. Schools also faced deteriorating conditions. There were 160,000 students that were being taught in unsuitable classrooms and school basements. The reliance on property taxes rather than state aid to fund education exacerbated the situation. Huge funding disparities existed among school districts. The ISTA report concluded that "the only way to prevent this situation from becoming worse is to increase the state school fund from $6,000,000 to $20,000,000 immediately."[47] Seven years later, in 1928, ISTA reported that the disparities continued: "In the poorest district in Illinois the assessed valuation of property is less than $9,000 and there are two or three others each less than $10,000. In marked contrast, in the wealthiest district in Lake County which happens to be also the wealthiest in the State, the assessed valuation is $2,420,000 or from 230 to 270 times that in the districts in Saline and Pope counties." As a result, wealthy Winnetka (Cook County) spent $140 annually per child, compared to only $18 in rural Brookport (Massac County).[48] In some parts of the state, children did not have access to high schools; other communities only provided two-year or three-year high school programs. Students in poorer districts were less likely to graduate high school and attend college than those in adequately funded school districts. The General Assembly increased state aid by only $2 million. From 1915 to 1925, the total education spending increased from $40 million to $122 million, but only $4 million of this increase was due to state aid. Between the years of 1921 and 1928, aid to education remained unchanged at $8 million, despite the fact that state revenue had increased by 73 percent. By 1929, local property taxes accounted for 94 percent of K–12 funding. The state contribution to the cost of public education was less than half of the amount that the two-mill tax would have generated if it had still been in effect.[49]

Illinois state government had always been reluctant to be the main funding source for public schools, preferring instead to allow local government to set property tax rates for public education. High schools, moreover, did not receive any state aid and had to rely totally on local property taxes to fund their programs. Local property assessments encouraged bribery of township and county officials in exchange for lower assessments. Such corruption has a long history in Illinois. In an article entitled "Corporations Escape Taxation," Robert Moore stated: "If all property were listed and fully assessed, the tax rate could be reduced by almost two-thirds and still yield the same revenue as at present."[50]

School Consolidation

"The Crisis in Public Education in Illinois" was ISTA's opening salvo in the 1920s to address the "inferior" educational opportunities in rural Illinois. The reliance on local property tax educational funding created "gross inequalities." The association reported in 1928 that Illinois had 10,148 one-room schoolhouses. Most of these schools taught the three R's and little else. They provided an education more suited for nineteenth-century rural America. ISTA pointed out that only 12 percent of the teachers in the schoolhouses had two or more years of postsecondary education; 37 percent had a single year of training beyond high school; and the remaining 51 percent had a high school education or less. In 1932, the association reported that 83 percent of teachers in cities with more than 10,000 people had two or more years of college training, as compared to 23 percent of those who taught in rural, one-room schools. Moreover, the rural schoolhouses were typically frame structures, whose physical conditions varied greatly. The poorest schools were shabby, inadequate structures. About 2,300 held classes for only seven months of the year, even though the state curriculum guides were based on an eight-month school year. Most teachers in these schools not only were paid less, but also had less teaching experience than those in urban, property-rich school districts. Student health screenings and enrichment programs were generally unavailable.[51] The *Illinois Teacher* noted that: "The typical rural school has standards much lower than the consolidated and urban schools, according to studies in Illinois and several other states."[52]

To improve education in rural counties, ISTA called for the consolidation of the poorly funded rural one-room schoolhouses into larger township high schools and unified K–12 (unit) districts that would be economically more "efficient" and provide students with a broader range of classes to meet their individual needs. The *Illinois Teacher* argued that "one community common school district for the purpose of support and administration is all that any one community needs."[53] ISTA also supported raising certification standards, increasing funding for normal colleges, and expanding teacher education programs so as to improve the supply of properly trained teachers available for rural schools. Additionally, since students would have to travel longer distances to school, ISTA lobbied for transportation funding for rural communities served by consolidated school districts and township high schools.[54] Despite ISTA's push for consolidation, however, very little was accomplished until after World War II. In 1944, there were still 9,700 one-room schoolhouses operating in the state.

Sometimes the geographic location of commercial property created an advantage for small districts over larger neighboring districts. Such was the case near Litchfield, where a local rural school district was home to a large manufacturer of heating radiators. ISTA reported that most of the factory workers lived in the city and sent their children to school there: Litchfield "must pay for educating the children of these workmen but receives no taxes from the factory. Country school district No. 99 receives the taxes from the factory, but has very few pupils. One result is that Litchfield district, No. 83, must levy a school tax of $2.75 on the $100, while district No. 99 levies only 24 cents on the $100."[55] Today two of the wealthiest school districts in Illinois are Rosemont near O'Hare Airport and Salt Creek in Oakbrook. Both have large concentrations of commercial property and very low property taxes.

Equalization Formula

Given the dire funding inequities, ISTA demanded that the state live up to its constitutional obligation to provide "a thorough and efficient system of free schools whereby all children of the state may receive a good common school education." The association believed that state aid should be based on an equalization formula that ensured poor districts enough revenue to provide their students with a satisfactory level of education:

> The state must assume its due and rightful responsibility in support of the common schools if the children in numerous districts of Illinois are to be given a square deal. It follows, too, that in the apportionment of the state school fund, the principal equalization must be the one that is emphasized; and that any feature of apportionment that tends to counteract equalization must be cast aside as unfair, and as being in conflict with the spirit of our State Constitution, and destructive of the fundamental essence of democracy itself.[56]

ISTA proposed several ways to remedy this inequity. It lobbied to change the School Fund Apportionment Law of 1923, which rewarded schools based on their ability to hire highly trained teachers and maintain lower class sizes, thereby providing additional funds to already-wealthy school districts. A new law in 1927 created an equalization formula that somewhat addressed ISTA's concerns. The law provided that districts would receive a flat dollar amount for all elementary students, and that if a district levied the required minimum tax rate but could not raise enough revenue to meet a foundational level of funding per student as established under the act, the state would provide the difference. This equalization formula guaranteed that all districts, no matter how poor, would have a minimum amount to educate their children. However, not all districts levied the dollar, and so not all were eligible for the supplemental state aid.[57] In 1929, a one-room district in Hamilton County levied only 87 cents, paying its teacher $315 that year. The 1927 law did not significantly address the extremes in student expenditures.[58] In 1928, Margaret Haley and Robert C. Moore were chosen to represent ISTA at the Illinois Tax Conference to address tax reform. The association proposed state aid increases in annual increments over a few years, until the state reached a 25 percent share of school spending "for an approximate equality of educational opportunity for the children of Illinois upon a reasonably high level." In 1929, the state increased its funding to $10 million—still far short of the goal to properly fund rural school districts.[59]

Friction between elementary teachers and those in the upper grades over salary also needed to be addressed. Junior high and high school teachers, especially men, received higher pay based on the fact that their employment required more academic training than needed for elementary schools; many elementary teachers believed that years of teaching experience should be rewarded. ISTA responded by encouraging districts to adopt a single salary schedule that rewarded teachers based on educational achievement as well as years of teaching experience. The single salary schedule ensured "equal pay for male and female teachers rendering equal service," regardless of the grade level taught. It was a major step in addressing the concerns of teachers at all levels of public education and overcoming division within the profession.[60]

Junior High Schools

The idea of creating junior high schools for seventh- and eighth-grade students gained wide acceptance among many in the education community in the early 1900s. In 1913, the National Education Association (NEA) endorsed the idea of junior highs. Many high school teachers and administrators complained that elementary students were not properly prepared for the academic rigors of secondary education. They argued that students in seventh and eighth grade were physically and emotionally different from those in the lower grades. Junior high schools would prepare them for high school. They also believed that an educational program designed for adolescent students could stymie the high dropout rate after sixth grade. Business leaders and the *Chicago Tribune* supported the junior high plan because it would include vocational education classes, making it possibly a less expensive alternative to high school education for many working-class kids. Chicago labor unions, in particular CTF, opposed the plan. They viewed it as an attempt to limit the formal education of working-class students at the age of fourteen. CTF also perceived the junior high plan as an organizational threat in that it created a distinct employment division within K–8 teaching staff.[61] Given the continuing efforts of business groups to limit access to secondary education, the unions had some reason to be concerned. In his address at the 1926 ISTA representative assembly (RA), SFL president Victor Olander characterized the junior high plan as an effort to create a "social caste system." He argued that these junior high schools were intended to serve as a "terminal degree" in lieu of high school for working-class children. ISTA disagreed with him on this point and strongly supported the plan.[62]

Despite CTF opposition, CPS introduced a junior high plan in 1924. The junior high movement did not detract from access to high school education. CTF's opposition to the junior high plan was organizationally costly. Junior high teachers did not gravitate to CTF. Instead, the Elementary Teachers Union was organized in 1927; it attracted mostly young junior high teachers.[63] Since junior high teachers required more specialized training in subjects such as math, science, social studies, and practical arts than did K–6 teachers, they, like high school teachers, favored higher salaries based on level of education.

High School Education

Although there was a consensus in all quarters supporting free K–8 education, conservative newspapers and business groups opposed universal high school education. In the 1870s, the *Chicago Times* editorialized against free high school education as a luxury that wasted taxpayers' money.[64] Enoch A. Gastman, a former ISTA president, recalled: "Many persons argued that it was nothing short of robbery to use the people's money for the education of children beyond what are known as the common branches; that high schools were for the benefit of the rich alone since the children of the poor could not afford to attend."[65] Nevertheless, public high schools increased in number across the state, from 108 in 1880 to 321 in 1900. In the early 1900s, critics of universal high school education argued that having all students attend high school was too costly and unnecessary: separate vocational education centers were deemed best for children of blue-collar families, while high schools would serve as academic institutions designed to prepare students for college or business careers. There was even an effort to create high school fraternities and sororities at this time. In 1919, ISTA successfully lobbied for a law that prohibited fraternities and sororities on high school campuses. It considered the law an important step in preventing high schools from becoming exclusionary, elitist institutions rather than a democratic meeting ground for all students, regardless of social class.[66]

In the early 1920s, the *Illinois Teacher* reported that Dr. Henry S. Pritchett, president of the Carnegie Foundation for the Advancement of Teaching, had published an essay criticizing universal access to high school education. According to Pritchett, due to the rapidly increasing high school enrollment, the cost of public education "has reached its enormous expense" and "the schools are overrun by a flood of pupils, many of whom would never have been admitted under reasonable conditions."[67] Following this publication, "reactionary governors and legislators" cited this report to criticize universal access to high school education. An educational finance inquiry commission appointed by the American Council on Education and funded by the Carnegie Foundation and three other foundations criticized the rising cost of education. A report entitled "The Financing of Public Schools in the State of Illinois," following up on Pritchett's study, argued that "the issue is perfectly clear: there is no way to reduce the cost . . . except by lopping off the school enterprises above and beyond elementary school wholly or in part." The report claimed that high school education "is two or more years longer than it need be."[68]

An article in the *New Republic* pointed out a major reason for the wealthy's opposition to high school education for working-class children: "It is well known that the greater part of the taxes—direct taxes that is to say—are paid by the better-to-do members of the community, the responsible pillars of society, who have but few children anyway, and many of them have private schools for the children where they pay tuition besides taxes. The larger part of the parents who send their children to public schools pay next to no taxes—direct taxes."[69]

The *Chicago Tribune*, of course, agreed with the Carnegie Foundation study. It opposed enrichment programs such as music, art, sports, and home economics. According to Mary Herrick: "For fifty years, the *Tribune* had consistently fought new services in the schools, calling them 'fads and frills,' and several times had stated that any education beyond elementary school level should not be given at the public expense."[70] Some right-wing critics blamed public education for real and perceived social ills. Bulletins published by the Association for Retrenchment in Public Expenditures included these statements:

The Only Tax Reform—Spend Less

> The evils and abuses of the public school system have become so numerous and so gross they can no longer be concealed.... Public education today is at the lowest level it has ever reached in America and juvenile crime is at its highest level.

> No Daniel is needed to interpret the handwriting on the walls of certain of our great city high schools. The automobile, the hip flask, the girl, the sexual anarchy spell out not only social degeneracy but mental and moral imbecility.[71]

Despite the staunch conservative opposition, high school attendance steadily increased after World War I. ISTA, labor unions, and progressive reformers argued that high schools would provide all students entering adulthood with equal access to a broad range of educational opportunities that would help shape their lives.[72] The Illinois superintendent of public instruction reported that in 1900 the state's 321 high schools had only 38,758 students. Over the next twenty-five years, high school attendance increased by 502 percent, to 233,682. By the mid-1920s, high schools accounted for 20 percent of all public school funding, despite the fact that high schools would not receive any state aid until 1938. High school attendance continued to increase during the Great Depression; by 1938, 358,768 attended high schools, an 826 percent increase since 1900. Not all high schools were four-year institutions. By the early 1930s, Illinois had 726 four-year high schools in addition to almost 200 three-year and 100 two-year schools. The two-year and three-year programs were primarily located in rural communities with low assessed evaluations. Many students in rural areas still did not have access to high schools at all. In 1917, the legislature enacted a law that provided local property tax funding for students living in a community without a district or township high school to pay tuition to attend high school in a nearby township.[73] Eventually, after World War II, a four-year high school education became the accepted norm—free and universal.

CTF's Declining Influence

Throughout the 1920s, CTF was the largest and most powerful education union in Chicago. Its influence started to decline, however, as junior high and high school attendance increased. CTF remained largely a female elementary school union; high school teachers, male and female, were not included. In 1900, 5,410 (94 percent) of CPS K–12 classroom teachers taught in elementary schools, and almost all were women. There were only 306 high school teachers, most of whom were men. The fact that male high school teachers received higher salaries caused resentment among CTF members. Conversely, high school teachers felt that they deserved higher salaries as compensation for their higher certification requirements (K–8 teachers were not required to have a four-year degree until 1940). The number of Chicago high school teachers rose dramatically after 1900: to 1,342 in 1920 and to 4,866 in 1940, by which point they accounted for 36 percent of CPS staff (see table 4). In 1912, male high school teachers organized the Men's Teachers Union. Two years later, the rift over pay equity led to the organizing of the Federation of Women High School Teachers. In 1927, junior high teachers organized the Elementary Teachers Union, and Chicago truant officers, playground teachers, and education clerks followed soon after. While all these unions were AFT affiliates, CTF remained an independent organization—one that represented a diminishing portion of CPS teaching staff.[74]

Margaret Haley maintained a loyal following among teachers, especially among those older elementary teachers who remembered her courageous fights on their behalf and for women's rights. She served as a delegate to the ISTA RA into the early 1930s. She retired in 1935, but her influence had steadily declined in the years preceding her retirement. Haley died penniless in January 1939. She was seventy-seven years old. Her estate was worth only twenty-five dollars. Haley was in her time one of the most influential feminist and education leaders in the nation. She was a fierce defender of public education, social justice, and unionism; she helped organize the first education union. Despite the power and wealth of large corporations and the era's political corruption, Haley, with Catherine Goggin, successfully fought for pay increases, pension reform, teacher rights, and improved educational standards.[75]

Haley's influence was far reaching. Her successes inspired not only other teacher groups in Chicago but also teachers across Illinois and the nation; she had a major impact on the development of NEA, AFT, and the Illinois Education Association (IEA). Sadly, at the time of her death, she was almost forgotten. That summer, there was no mention of her death at either the AFT or the NEA annual meetings. CTF

Table 4. Chicago K–12 Public School Teachers and Students

Year	Teachers		Students	
	No. K–8	No. high school (%)*	No. K–8	No. high school
1890	2,591	120 (4)	131,341	2,625
1900	5,104	306 (6)	215,660	10,201
1910	5,800	640 (10)	257,620	17,781
1920	7,398	1,342 (15)	291,678	36,433
1930	10,171	3,208 (24)	326,000	103,851
1940	8,613	4,866 (36)	318,443	144,671

Source: Herrick, *The Chicago Schools*, 403–6.

* The figures in parentheses represent the percentage of total K–12 teachers who taught high school.

lingered on for another twenty-nine years. It disbanded in the 1960s after CTU won exclusive bargaining rights for CPS teachers.[76] Haley's words from her autobiography, *Battleground*, best sum up her forty years of activism: Chicago was "the proving ground of American democracy" between "two great opposing forces of American life: the defenders and the exploiters of true popular governments. The war of privilege against people has been waged in and around the public schools of Chicago."[77]

Conclusion

Following its restructuring, ISTA built a powerful organization. Executive secretary Robert C. Moore maintained a close relationship with SFL. Moore worked with Margaret Haley's CTF and the other Chicago unions on legislation that affected CPS. By the 1920s a majority of Chicago teachers were members of the ISTA Chicago division. Through its alliance with organized labor and progressive reformers, ISTA achieved some important legislative victories that have had a lasting effect on Illinois public education. First and foremost was the defeat of Cooley's proposed dual school system, which ran counter to ISTA's support for a common school education for all students. In the 1920s, ISTA defeated efforts by the Carnegie Foundation, the *Chicago Tribune*, and anti-tax conservatives to limit high school attendance to middle-class students. Raising state revenue and taxation was a much more difficult problem to tackle. The reliance on local property taxes to fund education resulted in huge disparities among Illinois school districts. While ISTA failed to get a two-mill tax reinstated, it did get the state to increase funding from $2 million to $10 million by 1929 (still far short of its $20 million goal). In 1927, it did get an equalization formula passed to provide additional state funds for property tax–poor districts. The equalization formula provided the poorest districts some relief. Due to ISTA's coalitional advocacy, laws raising teacher certification standards, improving curriculum, implementing mandatory student attendance, and more were enacted prior to the 1929 stock market crash. The Great Depression would have a devastating effect on public education.

CHAPTER 4

The Great Depression

Business men sometimes refer sarcastically to teachers as having little business sense. They frequently remind us and our school boards that we ought to adopt "business methods" in financing and administering our schools. But when we view the mess that business men and financiers have got us and the whole country into, we are not sure their advice is worth much attention. . . .

Hereafter, when big business men tell us to put business methods into our schools, suppose we say: "Oh, go on! Your business methods nearly wrecked us in 1932. You had better put some education into your business."

—Robert C. Moore, ISTA executive secretary

Following the stock market crash in October 1929, school districts across the state faced rapidly deteriorating fiscal conditions that threatened to undo much of the progress of the past thirty years. Skyrocketing unemployment, bankruptcies, foreclosures, and declining property values undermined school board budgets. In Chicago, the situation was especially dire. On the eve of the Great Depression, Chicago Public Schools (CPS) and the county's schools were already facing a fiscal crisis. A disastrous reassessment of the 1927 quadrennial property assessment in Cook County resulted in protracted litigation and delayed revenue collection until 1930.[1]

Under the direction of Robert C. Moore, the Illinois State Teachers' Association (ISTA) pursued a progressive reform agenda that mobilized members to take direct action against the devastating impact of the Great Depression on public education. ISTA lobbied for a graduated state income tax, property assessment reform, a minimum teacher salary, school consolidation, and other reforms. In Chicago, the ISTA division was the largest education organization. It served as a meeting ground for the Chicago Teachers Federation (CTF), American Federation of Teachers (AFT) unions, the Principals' Club, and other education organizations, and it was a conduit for Chicago interests. Most members of these other organizations readily joined the Chicago division. In 1935, 80 percent of Chicago teachers were members of the ISTA Chicago division.[2] For thirty years, CTF had been the most powerful teacher organization in the city, but by the late 1920s, a number of CPS employees had organized additional unions. During the Great Depression, draconian cuts in CPS programs resulted in a merger of four AFT unions; they formed the Chicago Teachers Union (CTU), AFT Local 1, in 1937, under the leadership of John Fewkes. While the Chicago division remained the largest education organization until 1940, CTU quickly established itself as the leader in the city. In the 1940s, CTU became the dominant education organization in Chicago.

A Crisis in Funding

Based on evidence of blatant irregularities in the 1927 property assessment, CTF and other reformers supported a reassessment of Cook County property. This action opened the door to a protracted political fight that ended in fiscal disaster not only for Chicago but also for the rest of Cook County and, to a lesser degree, the entire state school system. As early as December 1929, Robert C. Moore called the revenue system in Cook County "a broken-down failure." Districts outside the city faced revenue shortfalls as the legal fight over the reassessment dragged on and tax collection remained in limbo. ISTA noted that many school districts "are in dire need of funds."[3] This delay also meant much less revenue for the state, since Cook County was the state's wealthiest county. Moore called the Illinois tax system "a fossilized, retarding barnacle of the ship of state."[4] Cook County did not begin to collect 1928 taxes until 1930, after all litigation on the issue was resolved.[5] In February 1931, the *Chicago Tribune* reported that Cook County had still not collected about $37 million of its 1928 real estate taxes. Of that uncollected amount, over $1 million was earmarked for state aid for school districts across Illinois. Even worse, contrary to the expectations of its supporters, the reassessment actually lowered rather than increased revenue—and Cook County was behind on collecting 1929 taxes. The governor warned that the state was in "grave danger that it will not be able to meet its financial obligations." For these two years, Cook County owed $17 million to the state. As a result, the state was short about $1.5 million to the University of Illinois fund and about $5.5 million to the K–8 common school fund, even before the full effects of the Great Depression took hold.[6]

While the urban industrial economy flourished during the Roaring Twenties, Illinois farmers faced financial hardship due to lower prices for their products as the European farming industry recovered from World War I. Many marginal farmers, especially in southern Illinois, were driven out of business. The Great Depression devastated urban America. Factories closed. High unemployment caused many homeowners to fall behind on mortgage payments and property taxes. Tax delinquencies increased from 11 percent in 1928 to 25 percent by 1933. The depression wrought havoc on property values. By 1932, the total assessed evaluation of property had fallen by 29 percent. Being heavily dependent on local property tax, school district revenue declined precipitously. Adding to the crisis, revenue for the common school fund that was derived from state property tax declined. Consequently, the state fell into arrears for its share of school funding, falling behind by a total of more than $7.8 million between 1931 and 1934. By 1936, the state was over $16.7 million in arrears to the public schools.[7] Bank failures wiped out invested school funds; facing severe cash shortage, many solvent banks tied up district investments to avert bankruptcy. Lending came to a virtual standstill. Unsurprisingly, school expenditures across the state were drastically curtailed: the total expenditure for the 1933–34 school year represented a 32 percent decline (a $50 million decrease) from four years earlier.[8]

Many school districts cut teacher salaries by as much as 25 percent within a year of the stock market crash. By January 1931, the *Illinois Teacher* reported that "even the richest districts are in distress. . . . There are school districts now entirely without funds, in debt to the legal limit, and with assessed valuation decreasing."[9] Districts were burdened with debt; some defaulted, unable to make payments on their bonded debts. Districts delayed paying teachers. Many teachers worked for months without being paid. In lieu of salary, some teachers received teacher orders (i.e., promissory notes), which they ended up selling to speculators at discounted prices because banks either refused to accept them or would only redeem them at much less than their face value. Districts cut programs and increased class size. Threatened layoffs further depressed salaries. By September 1931, about 25 percent of the state's teachers had not yet been paid their full salaries from the previous year.[10] Layoffs, pay cuts, and missed payroll meant that many teachers lost their life savings and insurance policies. Some teachers joined the breadlines and soup kitchens.

The crisis spurred efforts to cut spending. In 1931, ISTA defeated proposed legislation to end state support for the teacher pension fund and to cut the school year to seven months to "reduce taxes." Robert C. Moore reported that, at least, "no reactionary or dangerous bills passed."[11] Many districts slashed weeks or even months off the school year. By 1934, the average high school term had been reduced from 192 to 175 days. That same year, ISTA reported: "Almost every school is offering boys and girls fewer opportunities than they had two years ago. Drastic cuts in salaries and operating expenses of from 30 to 50 per cent are still in effect. Certain districts in the State are even now paying teachers in orders which may never be cashed due to the fact that the orders represent obligations in excess of the 5 per cent constitutional limitation upon debts of the district."[12]

The Illinois Teacher reported that ninety school districts were closed or would be closed before the end of the 1935–36 school year due to running out of money. It cited Western Springs District 101 in Cook County to illustrate the problem. By 1936, the district was experiencing a high rate of tax delinquency and a 42 percent decrease in its assessed valuation. It reduced its teaching staff by 40 percent. Kindergarten was eliminated, and the curriculum offerings were pared down. Teacher salaries were cut by 40 percent.[13]

Chicago Retrenchment

No major US city school system suffered as much devastation during the Great Depression as did CPS. The tax reassessment debacle forced CPS to assume a huge debt. By 1929, it owed $101.5 million to banks, along with $49 million to other creditors, largely due to the reassessment. Banks tightened credit and refused to buy tax anticipation warrants issued by the Board of Education. To make matters worse, graft and patronage had reached epic proportions under the mayor, William "Big Bill" Thompson. Douglass Sutherland, director of the Civic Federation, stated in 1930 that "corruption and inefficiency on a vast scale have plunged our second largest city so deep into bankruptcy that it is on the verge of closing its schools and losing police and fire protection."[14]

Already on the verge of bankruptcy prior to the stock market crash of 1929, Chicago schools hit rock bottom in the Depression. In June 1932, the CPS budget was cut by 14 percent. The school year was shortened two weeks; teacher salaries were reduced by 11.5 percent. Sick leave was stopped. No new teachers were hired. Class size increased to the point that some rooms did not have enough seating for students. Building construction and repair were slashed. The budget for truant officers, clerks, Crane Junior College, and Chicago Normal were sharply reduced, but patronage remained untouched, as Mary Herrick pointed out: "No one suggested reducing the maintenance patronage jobs."[15]

In July 1932, a committee on public expenditures—representing bankers and large corporations and chaired by Fred Sargent, president of the Chicago and North Western Railway—demanded additional cuts in the CPS budget. Sargent declared: "What is important now is retrenchment, and then more retrenchment."[16] The Sargent committee insisted that the Board of Education cut $15 million in addition to the $17 million (14 percent) already slashed from the budget. Sargent issued an ultimatum, saying that "banks have shown that they will positively not lend money for any municipal function which does not have our active support." As a result, CPS cut two weeks off the school year. Sargent justified his committee's action, saying that it was necessary for "men of sufficient stature to take charge for the people of the people's affairs." The committee continued to push for more cuts the following year.[17]

Secretary Moore dubbed the Sargent committee "a small, self-appointed oligarchy, of which one member seems to be rapidly assuming the role of despotic dictator," and "a super-government of bankers and other big business dictators." The Sargent committee used its influence to steer CPS policy. Moore wrote: "the committee is made up of men of wealth, power and influence, who like to do business and make fortunes in Chicago, but who reside outside of that city and dislike to pay taxes to educate its children. Some of these men send their own children to private schools of high per capita cost, but are taking steps to make the public schools cheap and inefficient for other children."[18] The Sargent committee continued to demand limits on government expenditures. In 1934, it called for a $20 million cap on state aid to education and sought to lower a proposed property tax levy in Chicago. In a scathing condemnation of the Sargent committee, Moore called it "Fascism in Illinois," saying, "In Illinois we have a small, self-appointed, extralegal, irresponsible group of big businessmen, with one man as their chief spokesman, who are asserting a power of dictation in governmental affairs."[19]

Although school employees were paid in cash until April 1931, payments due to them between September 1930 and March 1931 were distributed several months late. In June and July, teachers were offered paper scrip stamped "Not Sufficient Funds" rather than cash. From March 1930 to September 1934, teachers received eight late payments; on seven other occasions, they were paid in scrip or tax warrants. The scrip and tax warrants were difficult to redeem, and teachers often sold them to speculators at less than 70 percent of face value.[20]

Things would get much worse. In Chicago, wealthy property owners organized a "tax strike," refusing to pay their property taxes and demanding instead that the state cut expenses. Commenting on the situation, Robert C. Moore wrote: "The ideal of liberty is sometimes distorted into the ideal 'personal liberty,' or license, or the right of the individual to do as he pleases regardless of the effects of his acts upon society."[21] In July 1932, the Association of Real Estate Taxpayers organized a second tax strike. It only ended when courts declared the strike illegal; the names of the participants were publicized, and the teacher organizations led a boycott that targeted businesses involved. That August, Middle West Utilities collapsed, leaving $1.6 billion in now-worthless securities and wiping out the savings of six hundred thousand people. Its president, Samuel Insull, fled the country. In December, the US Chamber of Commerce produced a circular entitled "Possible Fields of School Retrenchment" that suggested school budget cuts to its state affiliates. Its suggestions included postponing capital outlays on school buildings, increasing class size and teacher hours, shortening the school day by one hour, cutting days from the school year, simplifying the curricula, suspending automatic teacher salary increases, discontinuing kindergarten and evening classes, reducing elementary school from eight to seven years and high school from four to three years, charging high school tuition, and requiring that one-third of the cost of higher education be paid by students.[22]

MOLLIE WEST

In the early 1930s, Mollie West was a student at Marshall High School. When CPS cut the music program in response to the financial crisis, Mollie and a group of music students staged a walkout in protest. She was arrested and spent a night in jail. Her parents were mortified. So began her activism! As a teenager, she attended a demonstration in support of the Republic Steel strikers. Ten people died in what is known as the Memorial Day Massacre of 1937. Mollie was knocked to the ground, and a company guard put a gun to her head and threatened to kill her if she moved. This episode began her long career of union activism and progressive feminism. As an adult, she entered the printing trade, became an activist in Chicago Typographical Union No. 16, and served as a delegate to CLF and the Illinois AFL-CIO. She was a founding member of the Chicago Coalition of Labor Union Women. She also served as administrative secretary and full-time volunteer at the office of the Illinois Labor History Society for over twenty years. Mollie died in 2015.[24]

These suggested cuts likely served as a model for the draconian downsizing approved by the Chicago Board of Education the following year.

Chicago Teachers Union

By the early 1930s, there were six unions in the city affiliated with AFT: elementary teachers, playground teachers, men teachers, women teachers, truant officers, and education secretaries. These locals formed a Joint Board of Teacher Unions and published a magazine, *Chicago Union Teacher*. Chicago always had a reputation as being a "union town." The Chicago Federation of Labor (CFL) was a powerful and respected force in Chicago politics. Through its radio station, WCFL, and its newspaper, *Federation News*, the teacher unions could readily communicate their concerns across the city. More importantly, the union movement's tradition of mass protest was ideally suited to pressure officials to respond to concerns. Affiliation with CFL was a crucial factor contributing to teacher membership in the AFT locals.[23]

In March 1933, a voluntary emergency committee led by John Fewkes, president of the AFT-affiliated Men's Teachers Union, organized a series of mass demonstrations to protest payless days and the unwillingness of the major banks to redeem board-issued scrip. The voluntary committee also organized neighborhood meetings with parents in every ward and set up a communication structure in every school. It published a list of businesses that were tax delinquent. It sent delegations to Springfield and Washington to lobby for funding to pay Chicago teachers. Fewkes led several hundred teachers in a protest march on the mayor's office. They vowed to return every week until teachers received their pay. On April 5, Fewkes led fifteen thousand students on a march to the mayor's office. Ten days later, he led a parade of twenty thousand teachers, parents, and students. On April 24, five thousand teachers set off on a march toward to the mayor's office, but, at a prescribed moment, the group split into five sections and marched into the largest banks in the city. Once inside the banks, the teachers chanted "pay us, pay us." They overturned desks, emptied wastebaskets, spilled inkwells, and severely frayed the nerves of bank officials. Two days later, a smaller group of teachers marched again, occupying Chicago Title and Trust Company with similar results. The committee published a list of tax-delinquent hotels, stores, and other businesses. The National Education Association (NEA) even threatened to move its 1934 annual meeting (planned in conjunction with the 1933 Century of Progress exposition) from Chicago to another city. These incidents in Chicago resulted in the teachers receiving some of their back pay in cash.[25]

After the assassination of Mayor Anton Cermak in early 1933, Edward Kelly was appointed his successor. Kelly was a protégé of *Chicago Tribune* owner Robert C. McCormick. The archconservative McCormick was no friend of public education. His newspaper had constantly criticized the expense incurred by what it termed the "fads and frills" of public schools and demanded cuts in school programs such as music, art, and sports. Mayor Kelly appointed a pliable school board to do his bidding soon after taking office.[26]

Ahead of the board's scheduled public meeting of July 12, 1933, ten school board members met privately to discuss the budget. Without consulting the school superintendent (let alone civic organizations, the Chicago division, or any labor unions), the board announced draconian budget cuts—laying off 1,400 teachers (10 percent of the staff) and shuttering dozens of programs—at the public meeting. The audience was stunned. Helen Hefferan, the only independent voice on the board, was not informed ahead of the meeting of the planned cuts. Enrichment programs that were eliminated included art, music, bands, athletic teams, physical education, manual arts, home economics, special education, swimming, printing classes, Crane Junior College, and adult education. Kindergarten and physical education were also sharply reduced, and a number of elementary principals and central office administrative staff were laid off.[27]

Faced with a desperate situation, teachers, parents, and civic groups organized a Save Our Schools (SOS) committee that very night. On July 21, the SOS committee, Chicago teacher organizations, and Congress of Parents and Teachers held a mass rally at the Chicago Stadium before an overflowing crowd of 30,000. Within two weeks of the July 12 meeting, 350,000 signatures had been gathered on a petition calling on the board to rescind the budget cuts. The board met again on July 26 but ignored all efforts to modify its decision. These massive cuts threw the school system into chaos. Teachers, students, and parents seethed with anger. Class size increased so much that some rooms did not have enough seating for the students. Teacher workloads became unbearable. As a result of a 10 percent salary cut coupled with a twenty-day decrease in the school year, teachers suffered a

23.5 percent cut in pay. Rumors circulated about mental breakdowns, suicide, and malnutrition among teachers.[28]

These dramatic events illustrated the need for a strong, disciplined teacher organization. Fewkes gained national notoriety, and the Chicago unions won a reputation as a tough leader. Despite the militant protest of the voluntary committee, Fewkes was basically a cautious, bread-and-butter unionist. He was more prone to compromise and settle on incremental gains rather than to seek radical change. Membership in the AFT local unions rapidly increased. Fewkes called for the merger of all teacher organizations under one local union banner. In 1937, four AFT locals—the Men's Teachers Union, the Federation of Women High School Teachers, the Playground Teachers Union, and the Elementary Teachers Union—surrendered their charters and reorganized as the Chicago Teachers Union, taking the Local 1 charter that had originally belonged to Margaret Haley's CTF. CTU was an immediate success. Within six months, two-thirds (8,200) of Chicago's teachers and many of its principals had joined the newly organized AFT affiliate.[29] Fewkes was elected the first president of CTU and would serve in that capacity for much of the next twenty-eight years.

ISTA Calls for Action

One early ISTA response to the Depression was to reform the complex, multilayered property assessment bureaucracy that enabled political interference. The rate at which property was assessed varied widely across the state, adding to funding inequities. ISTA called for "equalized" property assessments that would require a fixed assessment rate for property taxes throughout the state. Even though the Illinois Constitution called for properties to be assessed at their "fair market value" (i.e., 100 percent), the average rate of assessment statewide was 36 percent; in addition, the property of some large corporations was assessed well below the state average, if at all. The Chicago representatives in the General Assembly opposed property tax reform since it threatened their political power. Officials often sought to curry political favor by assessing property at low rates. Money graft (payoffs to local officials for lower assessments) was widespread but reached scandalous proportions in Chicago. In an *Illinois Teacher* editorial, Robert C. Moore claimed, "only half or less of the legally taxable property in Illinois is assessed; and this half is assessed at only about 40 per cent of its value."[30]

ISTA continued to press for school consolidation to ease the inequality facing small rural school districts. ISTA proposed the mandatory closing of all districts that had ten or fewer students for two or more consecutive years. It also supported a voluntary process for consolidation with larger districts as determined by the voters, similar to the current Illinois legislation. Students would be transported at state expense to neighboring districts. Consolidation would create larger taxing districts and eliminate wasteful duplication of administration and school boards. Consolidated schools could also offer curriculum programs that small, under-funded rural districts could not provide. Money saved by consolidating school districts could help pay for higher teacher salaries. ISTA noted that teachers in consolidated school districts were "better trained and better paid" than those in nearby one-room schools.[31] The consolidation of small rural schools with larger school districts met resistance in the legislature and among entrenched local school officials. Legislators were concerned that consolidation would increase state expenses for student transportation, construction of new central school buildings, and highway improvement. Many farmers worried that they would lose control over the small districts that served their children and end up paying higher property taxes on their land and farm equipment. A *Prairie Farmer* editorial referred to Moore as a "school dictator," criticizing school consolidation as a costly burden on farmers "to pay for educating city children" and "to take away from country people of Illinois local control over their schools."[32]

ISTA also pressed for a state minimum teacher salary of $800. The state superintendent of public instruction reported that the number of K–12 teachers earning less than $800 annually increased from 5,839 in 1931 to 11,892 in 1933. About 25 percent of the state's 47,922 teachers made less than $800 in 1933. This number includes 343 teachers making less than $400 annually, more than double the number in 1931.[33] Wayne County had the lowest average annual teacher salary at $444.95, followed by downstate Pulaski, Jasper, Hamilton, and Lawrence Counties. Cook County had the highest average at $2,003.92. The state average was $1,305.31. But, even in Cook County, seventy-four teachers made less than $800.[34] A minimum teacher salary would pressure small, poorly funded rural districts into consolidating. In addition, it would provide teachers with a "living wage" and discourage districts from saving money by hiring less-educated, inexperienced staff.[35]

Given the funding inequality inherent in a system that relied almost entirely on local property taxes, ISTA argued that only a large increase in state aid could significantly improve education in rural communities. ISTA's position was that the common school fund (state aid) should be used to create a reasonably high level of educational opportunity for all children, whether they lived in poor or wealthy communities. It campaigned for an increase in the common school fund to pay 25 percent of the cost of public education so as to improve educational standards in poor communities, provide access to secondary education for students living in communities not being served by high schools, raise teacher salaries, and fully fund the teacher pension fund. Since the state only provided funding for elementary school districts, the association also lobbied for state funding for secondary education. Achieving these reforms would require a new stream of revenue.[36]

State Income Tax

Following World War I, ISTA had supported a graduated income tax to reduce the reliance on property taxes to fund education. The collapse of property value in the Depression accentuated the need for an income tax. As the funding crisis deepened, the association, labor unions, and progressive allies organized for the passage of a graduated income tax that would provide the state with the necessary revenue to finance public education.

By 1931, Cook County and a number of downstate counties were facing default and bankruptcy. In response, Governor Louis Emmerson convened a tax conference that included industrial leaders, bankers, newspaper owners, civic organizations, Chicago mayor Cermak, and Victor Olander of the State Federation of Labor (SFL) to study the current problems of the Illinois tax system and to recommend reforms. The conference met thirty-three times. In October, it called on the General Assembly to replace the state property tax with a graduated income tax and to reform the corrupt property assessment system in Cook County. Speaking before the legislature on behalf of the tax conference, Melvin Traylor, president of the First National Bank, called for the graduated income tax plan, as opposed to the sales tax plan that was also being discussed. The *Chicago Tribune*, Illinois Manufacturers' Association, Cook County Real Estate Board, and other conservative business interests opposed the graduated income tax.[37]

Teacher organizations across the state organized in support of the graduated income tax. They obtained 937,339 signatures on petitions in support of the tax. In January 1932, they delivered truckloads of petitions to the General Assembly. The Chicago division and the city teachers unions rented the Chicago Stadium for a mass rally urging the legislature to enact the income tax; it was attended by an overflowing crowd of 27,000. The income tax bill easily passed the Senate but stalled in the House due to stiff opposition from conservative business interests. Faced with the mounting public outcry, the General Assembly finally passed the tax bill, only to have it declared unconstitutional by the Illinois Supreme Court in April. The court ruled that a graduated income tax violated the tax "uniformity" provision of the 1870 Constitution, dashing hopes of new revenue for the next school year.[38]

In September, following the court's ruling, legislators started planning for a general sales tax bill as an alternative. Four months later, in January 1933, a flat-rate income tax was also proposed: 2 percent on individual income and 3 percent on corporations.[39] ISTA and its allies, meanwhile, supported efforts to amend the Constitution to enable the passage of a graduated income tax. Robert C. Moore wrote that teachers "believe a tax on net income of corporations much fairer than a sales tax." He explained that the sales tax was regressive taxation. It "levies tribute on the bread and shoes a poor unemployed man buys for his children with the last dollar of his savings."[40]

To generate support for the graduated income tax and fight cutbacks being demanded by conservative business groups, ISTA announced, in February 1933, a "Save the Schools" campaign "to mobilize teachers and all other friends of education . . . to counteract all reactionary movements and forces" seeking to undermine public schools. The campaign had a straightforward message. Schools were no longer simply teaching basic literacy (i.e., the three R's); they had changed with the times. Public education prepared children for life in the modern world. Communities needed to understand the value of public education. The association organized a community outreach program to rally the public behind the schools in order to secure the necessary state funding to keep education programs operating. ISTA created a special Save the Schools fund to support the campaign.[41]

The state organization used its research capacity to publish pamphlets, newsletters, and posters highlighting the fiscal crises facing school districts across the state. A speakers bureau was established to address meetings of labor unions, parent-teacher organizations, farmer institutes, and other civic organizations. Local associations were asked to promote parent visitation days, exhibit student projects in school buildings and storefronts, participate in Fourth of July and Labor Day parades, and write letters to the editor of local newspapers. Teachers and parents were also encouraged to attend school board meetings to monitor and to oppose, if necessary, any effort to undermine the education programs. Individual teachers were urged to carry the message to the churches, women's clubs, and other civic organizations in which they were members. Public demonstrations were organized. Starting in February 1934, hundreds of teachers, school employees, administrators, students, and parents from across the state attended a series of rallies in Springfield to demand action by the legislature. On March 21, the Chicago division sent five hundred supporters to Springfield. They paraded to the Capitol, carrying banners and led by a color guard of teachers from the local American Legion hall.[42]

The flat-rate income tax met stiff opposition from the business community. Anti-tax conservatives backed by the *Chicago Tribune* called for "retrenchment," demanding an end to "fads and frills" such as kindergarten, home economics, art, music, sports, and band. The *Illinois Teacher* declared that some "super-patriots" had even dubbed the income tax as communism and were promoting legislation requiring teachers to take loyalty oaths. Such red-baiting by anti-tax conservatives was a convenient tactic used to attack public education. The income tax bills were tabled. A 2 percent retailers' occupation tax (i.e., sales tax), effective July 1, 1933, was enacted. Moore noted: "still most of the corporation officers and directors boosted the sales tax and strongly and effectively oppose the corporate income tax. This is only another example of the 'dictatorship of plutocracy.'"[43]

The fifty-cent state property tax was repealed to provide some tax relief once the sales tax was enacted. ISTA reluctantly supported the sales tax, even though it was structured to offset the state property taxes but did not increase the level of state funding for education. Local property taxes would continue to pay over 90 percent of the K–8 and all the high school expenditures. In fiscal year 1933–34, the sales tax generated over $36 million. All the receipts from the tax in the first six months went to unemployment relief for food, clothing, and shelter, but after February 1, 1934, the sales tax became the chief source of state revenue. Shortly thereafter, the sales tax was increased to 3 percent, and it generated $74.5 million in 1936. School districts received 17.5 percent of this revenue, which paid just over 9 percent of the total expenditures on education. ISTA continued to agitate for a graduated income tax as a means to increase the state's share of education funding.[44] Eventually, in 1969, a flat-rate income tax was enacted. Illinois still does not have a graduated income tax. A constitutional amendment for a graduated state income tax was soundly defeated in the November 2020 election.

The fight over taxation and protests by teachers over the hardships created by the Great Depression provoked many conservatives to question the patriotism of teachers and to criticize what was being taught in public schools. In June 1930, the *Illinois Teacher* reported that the annual meeting of the Daughters of the American Revolution had adopted a resolution expressing alarm at the "disloyalty in the schools and demanding that teachers be required to take an oath of allegiance." That September, the state convention of the American Legion called on Illinois to require all teachers to take an oath agreeing "to teach nothing derogatory to the flag" as a requirement of employment.[45] Attacks on public education continued throughout the 1930s. In 1934, House Bill 175 was introduced in Springfield; it would compel teachers to swear an oath of allegiance. Any violation of the oath would result in fines of up to $500 and possible imprisonment. Robert C. Moore sharply condemned the proposed legislation, charging that what these "super patriots . . . really want is a body of cowardly and cowed teachers . . . to force their own interpretation" of loyalty to the Constitution on teachers and the public. He further argued that such laws would "develop a class of unthinking automatons, afraid to teach anything." Those objecting to the loyalty oath would typically be labeled communist. Moore stated: "Teachers are silenced by propaganda that teachers are turning 'red' when they differ even slightly from the controlling minority on social and economic issues."[46] House Bill 175 failed in the legislature, but Moore warned that ISTA must protect members "from being bulldozed by ignorant school boards who themselves are often acting under pressure from 'local' patriots."[47] In 1937, Elmer Schnackenberg, Republican leader in the General Assembly, called for a purge of "un-American" teachers in Illinois schools, asserting that they were "poisoning the impressionable minds" of their students.[48] These efforts of the "super patriots" failed during the Great Depression, but loyalty oaths and other forms of suppression gained support during the Cold War years.

The state government eventually took several modest steps to provide school districts with fiscal relief. In July 1933, the legislature authorized a $40 million bond sale to help pay teacher salaries. In 1934, the state diverted $6.7 million (33 percent) of the gasoline tax fund to schools. An emergency relief bond issue committee (a broad coalition of education, civic, and business organizations) supported the addition of two referenda to the November ballot: a $30 million bond sale and a constitutional convention to reform property tax assessment. The bond sale proposal easily won voter approval, but the ballot measure for a constitutional convention failed. The federal government helped ease the situation somewhat in 1934. The Reconstruction Finance Corporation issued a $75 million loan, with school district property serving as collateral. Chicago received a $22.3 million loan that was used to pay teacher salaries. ISTA encouraged other Illinois districts to follow suit.[49]

In 1934, ISTA pressured NEA to take action in the crisis facing public schools. The Progressive Education Association on Social and Economic Problems and several other newly organized teacher groups criticized NEA and AFT for failing to take militant action in defense of "public education, children's rights, and teacher welfare."[50] Robert C. Moore rejected calls for a new organization to address the problems facing public education, but he warned: "If we can quickly develop a more militant spirit and make more aggressive and effective efforts in support of really progressive programs of objectives, we shall make such organizations as those discussed above unnecessary. But, if we do not play our full part in these trying times, we cannot blame the teachers for forming other and more aggressive organizations."[51]

In July 1934, the NEA representative assembly (RA) adopted a motion introduced by ISTA to hold peaceful "mass direct action" of support by teachers, students, and parents across the nation. ISTA was given the responsibility of producing a "Mass Meeting Packet" for the demonstrations. NEA produced packets of posters, leaflets, stickers, and other materials to generate support among teachers, rural schools, colleges, churches, newspapers, and others. Rallies were held during American Education Week, on Thursday, November 8.[52]

Organizational Changes

Since the primary focus of the association was to secure legislation to advance the interests of public education, ISTA changed its name to the Illinois Education Association (IEA) in 1936. Though "teachers' association" accurately described the fact that classroom teachers accounted for the overwhelming number of ISTA members, the new name was intended to reflect the broad purpose and membership of the organization. The association included school superintendents and principals as well as state and county education officials. Of the 47,677 Illinois "teachers" reported by the superintendent of public instruction in 1936, 287 of these were full-time superintendents. Another 1,130 were principals and superintendents teaching less than half time. The remaining 46,260 reported were mostly classroom teachers, some with part-time administrative duties. Except for the larger urban districts, the distinction between teacher and school administrator was often blurred. These roles became more clearly defined (and grew more at odds with each other) after World War II, with the consolidation of small rural districts. The name change also reflected IEA's sense of mission. Since its founding in the 1850s, the association had sought to project itself as an all-inclusive organization for a host of public education groups. The term "teacher" seemed too narrow to reflect its membership and purpose. Accordingly, IEA changed the name of its newsletter to *Illinois Education* in 1940.[53]

The organization's name change was, in part, a response to political perceptions. ISTA's drive for increased taxation riled conservative opponents. A speaker at a Kiwanis club was quoted as saying that ISTA "is merely a labor union camouflaging their activities under a smoke screen of better education for the children, when in reality they are interested solely in promoting better wages and working conditions for teachers and in monopolizing control of the state school system."[54]

As an all-inclusive organization, IEA sought to maintain "professional solidarity" by providing a voice for all groups involved in public education. Starting with the Association of County Superintendents of Schools in 1873, various employee groups and school subject areas had organized loosely affiliated sections within the association. These sections included school administrators, parent-teacher organizations, music, normal school, child study, and others. The sections met in conjunction with the annual ISTA/IEA RA to influence its political agenda. Following the 1912 reorganization, the relationship between sections and state association became more formalized and limited to school employment groups. The "sections" became affiliated organizations; they were recognized by IEA as the official representatives of their particular constituency. These affiliates included various administrative groups such as county superintendents, city superintendents, elementary principals, and high school principals.[55] Though classroom teachers constituted 90 percent of IEA's membership, they did not have an affiliate until the 1940s.

Affiliate status provided a format to influence IEA policy. Affiliates would meet several times a year to discuss their concerns and take positions on education policies that they presented to the IEA. Many members of these affiliated organizations, especially school administrators, also joined ISTA and were elected as division officers and delegates to the IEA and NEA RAs. In addition, affiliated officials would regularly write articles for IEA's newsletter and address the RA.

Besides changing its name, IEA raised and restructured its dues. Previously, the dues had been an annual fee of two dollars, unchanged since 1924. Received dues were split evenly between the divisions and the state organization. Though membership had increased by 52 percent over fourteen years, the dollar that IEA received per member could not sufficiently fund IEA staff and programs. Travel and meeting expenses, too, increased with the growing organization. IEA had hired a newsletter editor, a research director, and a publicity director, as well as associate staff to assist them. A building maintenance worker was hired to take care of the new Springfield headquarters. In 1938, IEA reported a 40 percent budget deficit that eroded much of its cash reserves. In response, the RA passed a graduated dues structure, which the divisions ratified in the spring. The dues increase took into account the wide range of salaries received by teachers, administrators, and education officials across the state. Why should a superintendent in a wealthy urban district pay the same dues as a low-paid teacher in poor rural district? Annual dues for members earning under $1,500 remained unchanged at $2; those earning between $1,500 and $2,499 paid $3; and anyone earning over $2,500 paid $4. The divisions continued to receive a dollar share of the dues for each member.[56]

Restoring Cuts and Improvements

By 1937, the state had realized a huge increase in revenue, largely as a result of an improving economy and the recently enacted sales tax. Revenue had increased by 84 percent since 1930. By the 1936–37 fiscal year, tax receipts had jumped by nearly $71 million (45 percent), but the common school fund remained unchanged at $13 million. The total expenditure for public education including the state colleges and universities amounted to 6.8 percent of the state budget.[57]

Even as the economy began to recover, many districts were slow to rescind pay cuts. Though small rural districts faced the worst salary reductions, ISTA reported that eighty-eight districts in cities with populations above 1,500 still faced pay cuts of over 20 percent in the 1936–37 school year. The list even included wealthier districts such as Chicago (23.5 percent), Waukegan (20–25 percent), Rockford (28 percent), and Brookfield (40 percent). As late as 1937, 604,000 students, 44 percent of the state enrollment, had a shorter school term than in the late 1920s. By 1939, the state average teacher salary had finally recovered to the pre-Depression level.[58]

In Chicago, fiscal conditions slowly improved. Increased state aid and a federal loan allowed CPS to restore some budget items. In August 1934, teachers received seven and a half months in back pay; 900 of the 1,400 laid-off teachers were rehired. Overcrowded classrooms and split shifts were ended, except for thirty-five South Side elementary schools, mostly in African American neighborhoods. In 1935, the remaining 500 teachers were rehired. In 1938, all local government employees *except teachers* had their pay restored to pre-Depression levels (16,000 city employees even received a pay increase above those levels). The Kelly-Nash machine (i.e., Mayor Kelly and local political boss Patrick Nash) took care of patronage workers such as sanitary district workers, school janitors, and other city employees, but did not feel the urgency to lessen the burden on the unionized teaching staff, whose 23.5 percent pay cut (steeper than for any other group) would not be fully restored until 1944. In 1940, CPS finally restored the forty-week school year, making Chicago the last of the fifteen largest American cities to do so.[59] CTU leader Mary Herrick wrote: "Only in Chicago was one-tenth of the teaching force dismissed without warning. Only in Chicago were teachers paid in scrip and warrants, or delayed three-fourths of a school year for pay of any kind. Even in Chicago, the police and firemen had been paid in cash—on time and with less reduction in pay. . . . There was no question that the damage done to the educational structure of Chicago in 1933 was greater than that of any other large city in the United States."[60]

The state teacher retirement fund had suffered funding shortages throughout the Depression. In 1932, the association established a pension committee to study the problem and make recommendations to ensure the survival of the retirement fund. In 1935, the committee reported that the fund had a $9.7 million liability to currently retired teachers but only $1.2 million in cash on hand to pay them. Its total accrued liability was $60.9 million.[61] The committee hired an actuary with expertise in drafting teacher pension legislation. A pension reform plan was introduced in 1937 and enacted into law two years later. IEA reported that the legislation shored up the pension system.[62] The new law raised the contributions paid by teachers and the state. Benefits were improved. It consolidated the Peoria system with the state pension. All new teachers hired after July 1, 1939, would be required to participate. Those teachers who had opted out of the pension system, as permitted under the 1915 act, could sign a waiver to remain out of the system. If they joined the system, they would be allowed to purchase service credit over a five-year period for those years that they did not participate.[63] The law put the pension system on a solid footing for many years to come.

Until the late 1930s, high schools were funded entirely by local property taxes. In 1938, there were 101 rural communities that did not have a local high school. To resolve this situation, the state legislature had provided that elementary districts not served by a high school could levy a property tax to pay student tuition and transportation costs for attendance at the nearest high school in the area. During the Depression, many of these districts without high schools defaulted on their tuition payments, creating a significant financial burden for the high schools and unit districts receiving their students. In 1937, the state approved a $1 million emergency relief fund for high schools.[64] The following year, the legislature enacted a permanent equalization formula for high schools. Under the formula, the state paid five dollars for each student and guaranteed an additional seventy-five dollars per student, provided that the district maintain a required local property tax rate (levy) for its high school. If the district levy failed to raise the seventy-five dollars per pupil, the state would make up the rest. The law established a minimum high school funding amount of eighty dollars (i.e., five plus seventy-five) per pupil.[65] State funding for high schools would play an important part in the efforts to consolidate schools into unit districts after the war.

Robert C. Moore Retires

After twenty-three years at ISTA/IEA, Robert C. Moore retired in 1938. During his career as executive secretary, IEA became a powerful force in Illinois politics. In 1915, less than one-third of the state's teachers belonged to the association; by the time he retired, IEA had 44,475 members—about 90 percent of the state's K–12 teachers. At first, Moore worked out of his home, but in 1924 the association raised dues to two dollars, rented rooms in the Springfield Mineworkers Building, and hired Lester Grimm as full-time research director. By 1938, the association had eight full-time staff. To accommodate the growth of staff and programs, divisions pledged money to build a headquarters. Work on the new headquarters was completed in 1931, and the association moved into its current location, the William Bishop Owen Memorial Building at 100 East Edwards Street, a short distance from the State Capitol. The building has undergone several additions over the years, but it is still the IEA state headquarters.[66]

Under Moore's progressive political guidance, IEA fought for compulsory education and child labor laws, a graduated income tax, school consolidation, an equalization formula, and transportation funding. He also sought to improve the teaching profession, calling for higher certification standards, improved teacher salaries, pension reform, and a tenure law. He sharply criticized the money graft of the property assessment system, fended off tax cut proposals in the General Assembly, and fought efforts by business conservatives to limit educational opportunities for working-class students. Some of IEA's goals were achieved during his tenure; others (such as school consolidation, a significant increase in state funding, a tenure law, and a teacher minimum wage) would be realized after Moore's retirement; and some, like the graduated income tax, have yet to be enacted.

As IEA's chief spokesperson, Moore reflected the democratic vision on which public education was founded in the mid-nineteenth century. He believed that public education was essential for a democratic society. Once students learned the basics of reading and writing in elementary school, universal high school education offered them the opportunity to cultivate their individual interests and talents rather than simply enter the workforce at age fourteen. Public education was the key to social progress. *Social Frontier*, the official publication of the John Dewey Society for the Study of Education and Culture, inducted Moore upon his retirement into its Teachers Honor Roll, with the following citation: "Robert C. Moore, former Executive Secretary of the Illinois Education Association—for his labors in awakening the economic intelligence of the group he served and in convincing legislators that democracy cannot survive ignorance."[67]

Moore maintained close ties to organized labor throughout his career. He admired Margaret Haley for her efforts on behalf of elementary teachers. She, in turn, praised his "economic intelligence" and commitment to social justice in a retirement tribute to him recalling the very first time they met, at the 1910 ISTA annual meeting.[68] Moore also often addressed annual meetings of SFL and included reports of union support for public education. CTU leader Mary Herrick wrote of him:

> The understanding and cooperation between Moore and Victor Olander, secretary of the State Federation of Labor, was a bond lasting until Moore's retirement in 1938. Robert C. Moore was a regular attendant at the annual conventions of the State Federation of Labor with badge and button. The union teachers from Chicago, represented in the education committees of the labor convention, presented the State Association legislative program and frequently got it adopted completely without change. Olander and Moore worked together in the legislature for compulsory education laws, free text books, increased state funds, pension legislation, [and] tenure. . . . They also fought together against the Cooley legislation for a dual vocational system. Olander was a speaker at the annual state teachers' convention in 1925 and at other times.[69]

Moore also respected the rights of teachers to affiliate with the labor movement. He wrote:

> Teachers in rich districts and the principals and superintendents in higher paid positions . . . should not condemn or criticize teachers who form unions and look to organize labor for help. It is significant the delegates from many local teacher unions in Illinois recently held a meeting and organized a State Federation of Teachers, which is affiliated with the American Federation of Teachers, which in turn is affiliated with the American Federation of Labor. Some of the subjects discussed were the social significance of the teacher union movement, the report of the President's Advisory Committee on Education, state pensions for teachers, a state tenure law, and Illinois taxation.[70]

Moore concluded that if IEA did not " have the sense" to lead the fight for fair wages, pensions, and tenure "for the many poorly paid and insecure classroom teachers in Illinois . . . then some other organization must."[71]

The close ties between the association and the labor movement lent credibility to unionism among Chicago teachers. According to Mary Herrick: "These long years of cooperation between teachers and labor on the state and local level, and the absence of conflict on labor affiliation with the Chicago Division of the State Teachers Association, helped to create a climate in Chicago which had conditioned Chicago teachers not to consider labor affiliation as unusual or dangerous."[72]

Conclusion

Before he retired, Robert C. Moore pointed out the need for teacher involvement at the school district level. Moore urged teachers to organize local associations. Since school boards made most decisions about taxation, budgets, and teacher welfare, local associations were critical to the success of IEA and the improvement of public education. In the late 1930s, IEA had locals in only a dozen large urban districts. It began a campaign to organize local associations across the state. IEA's Chicago division had long been the largest education organization in the city, but after 1939 CTU became the dominant organization. CTU's militant protests against the Chicago Board of Education's cuts in curriculum, staff, pay, and length of school year, as well as other welfare issues, rallied teachers to the union. The successes of CTU and the private sector unions during the Great Depression inspired teachers to organize unions in large urban districts across the state. CTU assisted these local unions in organizing the Illinois Federation of Teachers (IFT) in 1937. While public attention was focused on winning World War II, public education became one of the most important issues of postwar politics and social reform.

CHAPTER 5

Democratic Reform and Increasing Teacher Militancy

Our entire system of education today needs to be analyzed and, in some respects, modified because of rapid technological developments and on account of the problems growing out of the present war and coming post-war era of reconstruction.

—Lester Grimm, IEA research director

Robert C. Moore's 1938 retirement came at an important juncture in the history of the International Education Association (IEA). The Great Depression was finally coming to an end. State revenues had significantly increased since the late 1930s. Franklin D. Roosevelt's New Deal had created a friendly environment for labor organizing and progressive reform. As the economy pulled out of the Depression, the political climate was improving for many of IEA's legislative priorities, such as teacher pension funding, state aid for high schools, expansion of curricular programs, and a statewide tenure law. The Chicago Teachers Union (CTU) had demonstrated through its successes the importance of having teachers directly involved in the association. In the late 1930s, IEA launched a campaign to increase membership involvement in its divisions and to organize local associations in school districts across the state. Many larger IEA locals were teacher-only associations, but other locals often included administrators as members. The newly chartered Illinois Federation of Teachers (IFT), on the other hand, was a teacher organization. After World War II, the state made significant investments in school consolidation that eliminated thousands of small rural schoolhouses and improved the quality of public education. IEA continued to work closely with the State Federation of Labor (SFL) and IFT on tenure and other legislative issues into the early 1950s. Throughout the postwar era, IEA and the public education community supported civil rights, school desegregation, equity for women teachers, and other progressive ideals of John Dewey. Not surprisingly, much like after World War I and during the Great Depression, public education became a target of right-wing politicians. They called for so-called "communists" to be banned from teaching, and for loyalty oaths, merit pay, and curriculum censorship to be instituted.

Democratization

Even though IEA membership continued to increase throughout the Depression, the need for more rank-and-file teacher involvement became painfully apparent. By 1938, about 90 percent of all K–12 teachers in the state were IEA members. Despite this impressive growth, IEA had failed to achieve many of its key legislative goals, including pension reform, tenure, minimum teacher salary, and school consolidation. Paying a few dollars in annual dues was not enough. Only a high level of member involvement could rally public support behind the IEA legislative agenda and pressure elected officials to act on its demands. The public relations department reported as much to the representative assembly (RA): "We need more active participation of our members in the affairs of the Association."[1] Democratization was a campaign to increase rank-and-file teacher involvement in IEA.

IEA divisions were not conducive to membership involvement. The eighteen divisions covered large geographic areas, making it difficult to effectively engage members in the association. Outside the Chicago metropolitan area, divisions covered five or more counties. The southern division alone included fourteen counties. The long distances required to attend division meetings made membership participation difficult. In addition, divisions often held their annual meetings in the spring, at the end of county teacher institutes. Tired teachers, eager to get home, would often leave at the end of the institutes and not stay for the division meetings. Since those attending the annual meetings selected officers and determined policy matters, low attendance meant that leadership primarily consisted of "old standbys," mostly male administrators who had the time, resources, and professional ambition to attend.

The division governance structure almost ensured a top-down continuity in leadership that discouraged teacher involvement. Prior to the annual meeting, the executive committee of the divisions appointed a nominating committee to recruit a slate of candidates to run for office. This slate-making process normally guaranteed that the executive committee controlled the outcome of who would be elected. The newly elected officers, in turn, assigned committees, and appointed delegates to the annual IEA and National Education Association (NEA) RAs. This system left most members entirely out of the decision-making process. No wonder many teachers felt that "they had nothing to say about things." Some delegations

Table 5. Leadership of IEA Divisions Excluding Chicago, 1940

	Division officers	Executive committee	Standing committees[*]
Administrators/ professors	51	49	42
K–12 teachers	18	14	9
Total officials	69	63	51
Total women	12	11	4

Sources: Illinois Teacher 28, no. 3 (November 1939): 76, 91–92; 28, no. 4 (December 1939): 124; 28, no. 5 (January 1940): 153; 28, no. 6 (February 1940): 176; 28, no. 7 (March 1940): 215; 28, no. 8 (April 1940): 258, 267, 269–70; 28, no. 9 (May 1940): 286–92.

[*] There were three standing committees: resolutions, legislation, and appropriations. Every division had one representative on each of the three state standing committees.

to the annual RA did not even include any teachers, prompting the adoption of the following resolution at the 1936 RA: "We further urge every division that classroom teachers shall be represented in their delegations to the annual meeting of the association."[2] Similarly underrepresented at the RAs were women. Despite the fact that 75.8 percent of IEA members were women, they made up only 16 percent of delegates at the 1940 RA.[3] In the seventeen divisions outside Chicago, there were only 41 classroom teachers and 27 women among the 183 division officials in 1940 (see table 5).

In a 1938 article titled "Who Runs the Show?," Galva superintendent C. A. Weber sharply criticized divisions as "benevolent autocracies." He called on divisions to institute democratic reforms that would "engender active, interested participation of a far greater number of teachers than at present."[4] This was one of many articles published by the *Illinois Teacher* in the late 1930s calling for more "democratic functioning of the divisions." The Lake Shore division was the first to adopt a delegate assembly system that would be more responsive to members. Under this system, delegates were elected by school district members to represent their concerns at the annual division meeting. Attendance at these division meetings was an important step toward engaging members at the school district level.[5] Other divisions followed suit in adopting delegate assemblies. Rather than relying on "old standbys" to run the show, locally elected delegates established division policies and elected officers. School districts were allotted delegates based on their membership numbers. In the central division, delegates were allotted based on a formula of one delegate for every twenty-five members or fraction thereof; small districts were combined to ensure that they had an aggregate number of members to elect a delegate. Individual members could still attend division meetings and participate in debate, but only elected delegates could vote on business before the assemblies.[6] This reform made the divisions more accountable to their members and ensured fairer representation at the local level. This model was adopted by many IEA divisions.

Organizing Local Associations

Democratic reform within the divisions, by itself, would not necessarily increase membership involvement to a significant degree. In the late 1930s, IEA began to encourage organizing local associations. Lake Shore division president George Wells best summarized IEA's vision: "I believe in a thoroughly organized and unified profession beginning with local teachers' councils which make up the divisions, the divisions closely affiliated with the state, and the state educational associations united into one great national organization."[7]

IEA already had some local associations in large cities. Besides Chicago, IEA had chartered locals in Rockford, Decatur, Evanston, Pekin, Joliet, and East St. Louis in the 1920s. By the late 1930s, Champaign, Peoria, Galesburg, Danville, and Quincy had organized locals in response to Depression-era layoffs, shortened school terms, and salary cuts.[8] Most small districts, especially in rural areas, did not have locals until much later. In reporting about the chartering of IFT, Robert C. Moore argued the necessity for IEA to organize teacher locals: "If IEA does not have the sense to do these things, then some other organization must." Moore added that teachers and administrators in high-paid districts "should not discourage plans and efforts made by teachers in poor communities and in the lower salary scales." Instead, they should "lead the fight for fair wages, adequate pensions, and secure tenure for the many poorly paid and insecure classroom teachers in Illinois. If more fortunate teachers do not lead such a fight, they should not condemn or criticize teachers who form unions and look to organize labor for help."[9]

Having thousands of small districts was a major impediment to teacher involvement. In October 1940, IEA established a committee on reorganization to suggest reforms that could strengthen the association. The committee report recommended that locals serve as the "organic connecting link" between the individual members, divisions, and state association. Locals should meet frequently to promote teacher involvement in the association. Division delegates, as well as delegates to the annual meetings of IEA and NEA, should be elected by and responsible to the local members. Locals could build political support for education in their communities through public events and publicity.[10] They should also promote a "professional *esprit de corps* and good fellowship" among teachers, principals, and superintendents. Divisions should serve "as the clearinghouse between the state association, its local units, and individual members."[11] In 1940, eighteen large locals organized the Affiliated Teachers Association (ATA). ATA served as the advocate for classroom teachers' concerns within IEA, in much the same manner as other affiliated

SUSAN SCULLY

Susan Scully, born in 1894, graduated from Chicago Normal with a two-year teaching degree in 1912. When Scully asked for special permission to teach at the age of seventeen, Ella Flagg Young said, "my child, you should be home playing with your dolls, instead of wanting to teach school." The following year she began her teaching career. Over time, she earned a PhD at Loyola University Chicago. In 1919, Scully was elected treasurer of the Chicago division. She held that position until 1935. After serving two terms as division president, Scully was elected IEA president in 1938, the sixth female teacher elected to that position. She was also active in CTU; she lost a close race for president in 1943.[15] In 1948, she became principal of Henderson Elementary School. In 1950, the Chicago division and CTU endorsed her as a candidate for the CPS pension board. She served on the Chicago pension board for many years: "more than anyone else, [she] did the mathematics and wrote the laws that give Chicago teachers the best pension system. Many pension problems were left for her to settle."[16]

groups did for superintendents, higher education, county superintendents, and principals.[12]

Chicago provided the best example of teacher participation. It had a long history of teacher activism dating back to the founding of the Chicago Teachers Federation (CTF) in 1897. IEA's Chicago division was the largest education organization in the city. In 1938, 70 percent of Chicago Public Schools (CPS) teachers were members of the IEA division. The majority of CTU members joined, as did those from CTF, the Chicago Principals' Club, and the Association of Chicago Teachers.[13] The Chicago division was appealing to them since it was focused on the legislative agenda in Springfield. Division meetings were well attended. Elections for division officers were held in the school buildings. In 1940, a majority of its officers were classroom teachers, and eight of the twelve were women.[14] Such a high level of teacher involvement in the community made the Chicago division a powerful force in the city and in Springfield.

CTU and the Chicago Division

Like CTF, CTU was primarily a teacher welfare organization focused on local issues such as salary schedule, teaching load, sick leave, and teacher councils. It was created to deal with problems unique to Chicago. CPS stood apart from other districts in Illinois not only in size but also in its teacher certification standards, tenure law, pension system, and taxation powers. The mayor appointed the school board, which effectively gave city hall control over the school system. Increasing the ability to deal with municipal politics was the impetus for organizing CTU. The Chicago Federation of Labor (CFL) was a natural ally for the union. Through this affiliation, CTU conducted weekly broadcasts on the CFL radio station, WCFL (the "Voice of Labor"), and contributed articles for its newsletter, *Federation News*, which was read by thousands of union members across the city and suburbs. CTU's membership in CFL was crucial in its efforts to improve the lives of CPS teachers.[17]

CTU worked closely with IEA and its Chicago division on the legislative agenda in Springfield. The Chicago division was also an important ally in dealings with CPS administration; many CPS principals and administrative staff were division members. There was a general understanding between CTU and the division that they had separate but mutually compatible roles in Chicago education politics. While CTU focused on teacher welfare, the division would serve as its legislative voice in Springfield.[18] This arrangement made perfect sense given the size and resources of the division and IEA. The Chicago division maintained an office in the city and sent a representative to the General Assembly to lobby for legislation affecting city teachers. Moreover, with its 44,475 members statewide as of 1940 (about 90 percent of Illinois teachers), Springfield headquarters, and full-time professional staff, IEA was a powerful force in securing education legislation.[19] As the largest IEA division, Chicago built support across the state for its program by standing in solidarity with the "downstate" concerns of the other seventeen divisions, on such issues as pensions, tenure, and the equalization formula. CTU encouraged its members to join the Chicago division because it was a valuable ally. For as little as seven dollars, a teacher could join both organizations. IEA annual dues were between two and four dollars based on income; CTU annual membership cost five dollars. A majority of CTU members joined IEA.[20]

In 1938, the Chicago Board of Education attempted to take control of the Chicago division in a bid to weaken the newly organized CTU. Superintendent William H. Johnson, a protégé of the corrupt Kelly-Nash machine, temporarily gained control over the Principals' Club through the demotion of his critics and the appointment of principals beholden to him. A former executive of the Principals' Club claimed: "The organization has deteriorated from a club dedicated to guarding the best interest of the school children to one whose members lick the boots of Superintendent William H. Johnson in the hope that they may gain personal advancement."[21] Superintendent Johnson packed the annual division meeting with patronage appointees and had the support of CTF, which had previously controlled the election of division officials through the nominating committee. Backed by the Principals' Club, the nominating committee slated school board supporters for division offices, but, with several thousand teachers in attendance, an opposition slate backed by CTU won the election.[22] IEA president Susan Scully, who had previously served two terms as Chicago division president, joined CTU and played a key role in electing the CTU-backed slate for the division.

To ensure fair representation in future meetings, a resolution was passed providing for the apportionment of delegates based on the membership of participating organizations. The next year, Scully served as a CTU delegate at a meeting of the newly organized IFT. In 1939, IFT reported that "it is vital that the Chicago Division and the Chicago Teachers Union work harmoniously if the schools and the teachers of Chicago are to be protected."[23] Throughout the 1940s, Scully continued to serve in various association capacities, including as an IEA representative on the NEA board of directors. Scully also served on the CTU board. In 1943, she led an opposition slate of candidates for CTU office against the official slate nominated by the union's leadership, arguing—just as she had done in the 1938 Chicago division election—for "democratization." Even though she lost the 1943 election, she received 48 percent of the vote and several members on her slate were elected.[24]

CTU maintained an organizational membership in NEA. CTU representatives actively participated in the 1941, 1943, and 1944 NEA RAs. CTU activists were also invited to speak before IEA division meetings downstate. IEA executive secretary Irving Pearson, who succeeded Moore, contributed articles to CTU publications. When CPS superintendent Johnson announced his candidacy for NEA president in 1941, CTU successfully blocked his election at the annual NEA RA. Mary Herrick wrote: "Until 1948, candidates supported by the Union were elected to leadership in the Chicago Division."[25]

The close ties between CTU and the Chicago division are best illustrated by the fact that two key leaders of the division, Edward Keener and Susan Scully, joined CTU and served as union delegates at the 1939 SFL convention. Keener, a Principals' Club activist, was division president from 1940 until 1945 and NEA vice president from 1946 to 1948. In 1943, Keener urged NEA to investigate the corruption of CPS under Superintendent Johnson's leadership. Donald Du Shane, chairman of the NEA Commission for the Defense of Democracy through Education, supported Keener's request. Mary Herrick wrote that CTU "supported a request of the NEA and made available all of its records to the NEA Committee under Donald Du Shane, paid $1,000 to have the NEA report printed, and urged its distribution by members."[26] After the report went public, NEA expelled Superintendent Johnson for "unprofessional conduct." The NEA investigation fueled political support for reform. In 1947, reform mayor Martin Kennelly was elected. Herald C. Hunt replaced Johnson as CPS superintendent, and Keener was appointed director of the department of personnel, ending the corrupt patronage appointments of the Johnson years.[27]

Membership in both organizations dropped during World War II. By 1950, CTU losses were minimal, but the Chicago division never recovered its numbers. Membership in the Chicago division declined precipitously, from a high of 10,054 in 1939 to 3,538 in 1950. CTU membership never fell below 7,000. The union slowly increased its membership in the 1950s, reaching 12,669 by 1960, while the division hovered just over 3,000 members throughout this period. Almost all of IEA's membership losses in the 1940s can be attributed to the Chicago division. Outside

Table 6. Total Membership of CTU, the IEA Chicago Division, and
the State IEA

Year[*]	CPS teachers	CTU	Chicago division	IEA[**]
1938	13,435	8,199	9,652	44,475
1939	14,121	8,171	10,054	45,987
1940	14,134	8,015	7,478	43,796
1945	12,504	7,051	4,285	39,956
1950	13,287	7,993	3,358	41,265
1955	14,622	9,008	3,079	47,649
1960	17,753	11,067	3,038	58,273

Sources: IFT, unprocessed collection, box 1, Walter P. Reuther Library, Wayne
State University, Detroit; CTU, "Membership in the Chicago Teachers Union
from 1937 to 1963," 1963, author's collection; *Illinois Teacher* 28, no. 7 (March
1940): 223; *Illinois Education* 29, no. 7 (March 1941): 221; 34, no. 1 (September
1945): 16; 39, no. 1 (September 1950): third cover; 44, no. 1 (September 1955):
second cover; 49, no. 1 (September 1960): second cover.
* Fiscal year ending June 30.
** Includes active members, retirees, and others.

of Chicago, IEA membership ballooned in the 1950s as the postwar baby boomers
increased school attendance (see table 6).

The CTU focus on local concerns explains its success among CPS teachers. With
help from CFL and progressive allies, the union won concessions on issues such as
class size, a ten-step salary schedule for elementary teachers, and pay increases.
In doing so, the union established credibility as the voice of Chicago teachers.
CTU would continue to work closely with IEA into the early 1950s, when pressure
mounted from the American Federation of Teachers (AFT) and its local unions in
Illinois to publicly condemn the association as a "company union."[28]

Illinois Federation of Teachers

Outside Chicago, AFT had very little success in Illinois until it chartered IFT. From
1916 to 1922, AFT organized seventeen local unions outside Chicago. Most of these
unions were relatively small, averaging thirty-one members; one local only had
five members, while the largest local numbered fifty. Only three survived into the
1930s. AFT did not charter another Illinois local until 1933. In December 1936, a
group of locals discussed organizing IFT; it held its founding convention in Springfield that spring. Following the establishment of IFT, the number of AFT locals
steadily increased. By 1940, IFT reported that twelve of the twenty-six largest Illinois cities had local unions. The federation's organizing strategy focused on large
urban centers and coal mining towns, using American Federation of Labor (AFL)
union contacts to help organize local chapters. Even so, most of these locals had
relatively few members, and they often served as a militant caucus within districts

BENLD TEACHERS ORGANIZED

In 1934, amid the Great Depression, teachers in the Illinois coal mining town of Benld (Macoupin County) organized the Progressive Teachers Local, affiliated with the Progressive Trades and Labor Unions of America. The Benld union successfully bargained one of the first teacher contracts in the nation. The one-page agreement included seniority rights, a grievance clause, the right to join a union, and language on salary, layoffs, and a "closed shop." Soon afterward, Illinois attorney general Otto Kerner declared the contract unconstitutional. This ruling was based on the widely held argument that school boards could only sign individual contracts with private vendors, not collective bargaining agreements with employees. Years later, AFT chartered a teacher local in the town that superseded the Progressive Teachers Local.[29]

where the IEA was the dominant teacher organization. IFT did have sizable locals in East St. Louis, Rockford, Quincy, Belleville, Granite City, and several other large urban districts.[30] For a summary of chartered AFT locals from 1916 to 1960, see table 7.

Though Illinois had more AFT locals and members by 1946 than any other state, AFT membership outside Cook County remained small. In 1955, the union had 10,300 members. Of that total, 7,700 were CTU members, 700 were from the West Suburban Teachers Union, Local 571, and the remaining 1,900 members were scattered in small locals across Illinois. The entire IFT budget for that school year was only $10,000. It had no full-time staff. With few exceptions outside Cook County, IEA was the dominant organization. In Springfield, the IFT local even paid the dues for its president to join the IEA local.[31] It was not until the 1960s that IFT seriously began to challenge the association's leadership in districts across the state. According to Oscar Weil, an IFT executive director hired in the late 1950s, there was "little evidence early leaders planned to bargain all economic benefits and working conditions for teachers into signed union contracts." Instead, the local teacher organizations were mainly involved in meet-and-confer discussions with the administration over teacher welfare and grievances.[32]

Table 7. AFT Local Unions Excluding Chicago

Years	Chartered locals	Continuing locals*
1916–22	17	1
1923–32	0	0
1933–36	10	3
1937–45	39	27
1946–60	53	33
Total	119	64

Source: AFT, "Statistical Report by States: Illinois, 1916–1976," author's collection.

* Fifty-five of the 119 locals chartered since 1916 had disbanded by 1960.

Tenure: IEA and IFT Working Together

IEA first proposed a tenure law in 1913. It forcefully opposed the firings of CTF leaders prompted by the 1915 Loeb Rule, and it supported the 1917 Otis Bill, which established tenure rights for Chicago teachers. IEA continued to support similar tenure legislation for teachers statewide. In 1934, the association arranged to have Dr. Donald Du Shane address the NEA RA on tenure. After Du Shane's speech, the Illinois delegation successfully supported the naming of an NEA committee on tenure for teachers. Du Shane became chair of the committee and later served as NEA president. In September 1938, Dr. Du Shane and fellow committee members met with the IEA tenure committee and representatives of IFT locals to discuss tenure legislation. In December, a second meeting was held at IEA headquarters, this time with CTU and seven other IFT locals, to plan legislation.[33] IEA executive secretary Irving Pearson praised IFT and SFL for "giving effective assistance to this—perhaps the most united effort the profession of teaching in Illinois has enjoyed."[34]

In May 1939, a tenure bill jointly sponsored by IEA and IFT was introduced in the Illinois Senate. IEA also urged all its divisions to establish tenure committees and to send a member of this committee to a meeting with the IEA tenure committee. IEA argued that the passage of a tenure bill would require the "co-operation of all members of the teaching profession and of all divisions," pointing out the strong opposition of the Illinois Association of School Boards (IASB) to the law.[35]

Meanwhile, just as the tenure bill was introduced in the General Assembly, the Proviso High School board in Maywood fired West Suburban IFT Local 571 leaders Mary Wheeler and Ralph Marshall, without consulting the superintendent, on the grounds that their union was involved in school board electioneering. The firings became a cause célèbre in the fight to get a tenure law enacted. IEA and NEA launched a joint investigation into the firings.[36] Backed by IEA, CTU, and CFL, Wheeler and Marshall were reinstated in January 1940. As part of the settlement of the case, the *Illinois Union Teacher* announced that the Proviso school board had signed a "collective bargaining agreement with Local 571." The agreement, just a few paragraphs long, outlined the future relationship between the board and the union. It was not a comprehensive labor contract covering salary, benefits, and working conditions. It stipulated that faculty would not participate, except for voting, in the election of school board members or conduct union activities during school hours. In exchange, the board agreed to meet regularly with the union to discuss teacher welfare issues and to allow union representation in any future disputes between a teacher and the board.[37] Local 571, in effect, became the exclusive bargaining representative of Proviso teachers.

The IEA issued its investigation report that May. It praised the agreement between the parties, sharply criticized the board for acting unilaterally on teacher employment issues, and supported the right of teachers to join education organizations.[38] The Proviso firings undermined the opposition to a statewide tenure law. IASB finally agreed to support the tenure bill after securing a few minor changes to the proposed legislation in 1941. The tenure law provided for "sufficient cause" as grounds for dismissal and ensured the right of the teacher to receive a hearing, if requested, before the school board. If the employing school board upheld the dismissal, the teacher could appeal the decision to a committee appointed by the county superintendent of schools. This review committee could not include any members of the school board involved in the firing. Either side had the right to appeal the decision to the state courts.[39]

The new tenure law had its shortcomings, but it opened the door for IEA to test the language in the courts and to amend it in the legislature. The law stated that a teacher could be dismissed for "incompetency, cruelty, negligence, immorality, or any other sufficient cause," as well as in cases when, "in the opinion of the board of education, he is not qualified to teach, or . . . the interest of the schools requires it." The law also provided that the reason for dismissal must be "specific."[40] Following the adoption of the law, the IEA tenure committee investigated cases involving decisions by school boards to not rehire teachers based on vague passages in the law. One district refused to rehire its teachers on the grounds that it did not want them to "come under the Tenure Law." Several districts refused to rehire teachers without providing any reasons for their dismissals. IEA pointed out that the law made "sufficient cause" the grounds for firing and sharply criticized the districts for failing to specify why the teachers were not renewed. IEA won these cases.[41]

IEA committed itself "to assist all worthy cases and help to finance legal action . . . where the ultimate decision is vital to the teaching profession." IEA supported cases to ensure that "sufficient cause" be the standard for all dismissals and that specific reasons be included with the decision.[42] Although "sufficient cause" addressed firings based on teacher incompetency, it did not specifically address other grounds for dismissal. Some newly organized districts (created as a result of school consolidations) did not recognize the tenure of the teachers earned in the districts being consolidated. Married and pregnant teachers also faced dismissals in some districts, despite tenure. In all these situations, IEA supported teacher tenure rights, mainly through legislation and, at times, legal action. In 1948, nonrenewal of a married teacher became a violation of tenure rights. By 1956, IEA had reviewed over seven hundred tenure rights cases.[43] In the 1967 school year, it reported receiving more than two hundred inquiries about tenure rights. In addition to providing requested information or meeting with the individuals involved, IEA conducted a formal investigation in twenty of these cases. Two cases led to school board hearings, and one was settled by the circuit court.[44] As late as 1970, IEA won the reinstatement of a pregnant teacher who had been let go after requesting maternity leave. IEA successfully argued that the teacher could continue to teach as long as she was not sick, and was entitled to return when physically able. Laws were eventually enacted covering pregnancy, tenure rights in school consolidation, and other issues.[45]

In 1972, IEA budgeted $135,000 for legal services. From July 1971 through March 1972, it handled 554 consultations with attorneys, and 221 members received legal aid. In 1975, Governor Dan Walker signed the IEA-sponsored Senate Bill 1371, which established ground rules for an independent hearing officer to decide dismissal cases involving tenure. This law ended the county review process for final decisions on firing tenured staff. After its enactment, the only recourse left for either side was an appeal in the state courts.[46]

World War II

The US entrance into World War II diverted attention away from two of IEA's most important goals: a significant increase in state funding and school consolidation. Addressing these issues would involve a huge commitment of money and resources that the state was not willing to consider during wartime. Though action on these issues would be delayed until Germany's surrender, the war reinforced the importance of public education as a national priority and as a founding principle of American democracy. With the outbreak of the war, *Illinois Education* ran a series of articles calling for long-term planning for education reform after the war. According to the 1940 US Census, only 73 percent of Illinois children sixteen years or older were enrolled in school. In addition, the curriculum being offered, especially in many small rural schools, did not prepare students for the industrial economy. Lester Grimm wrote: "This present war emphasizes the dependence of our civilization upon technology. It is a struggle of complicated engines of war, assembly line production, streamlined transportation, the speed of communication and scientific machinery, and of thorough, technical training of man power."[47]

Public education was critical to national security. Inadequate schooling and poor health care were the primary reasons for rejecting young men drafted into the US Army. A Selective Service System study reported that of the first one million men rejected by the military draft, about 10 percent lacked the equivalent of a fourth-grade education. An additional 20.9 percent were rejected because of dental defects, and another 13.7 percent for poor eyesight. The rest had other physical or psychological problems.[48]

Investment in public education could improve the situation. Grimm stressed the importance of expanding the school curriculum in science, technology, and vocational training. Schools must also promote physical education programs, conduct medical screenings at an early age, and teach personal hygiene. Every student should take classes on government, citizenship, and democratic values. Students needed "a keen understanding of the rights and obligations of the individual in a democracy."[49] He wrote: "Our Nation's leaders have always emphasized the importance of widespread public education to the survival of democracy. Now technology and war accentuate and multiply education's responsibilities. Reaffirming our faith in the democratic way of life should include a more liberal support of our schools."[50] Such improvements were not possible in small, fiscally strapped rural districts. The overreliance on local property taxes to fund education undermined school improvement in property-poor, rural districts. In Illinois, six thousand districts had school terms of eight months or less. Sixty percent of teachers in these districts did not have a college degree.[51]

School Consolidation

Consolidating schools into larger districts was critical to reform. Consolidation had been a high priority of the association as far back as the late nineteenth century. In 1924, IEA appointed a large unit committee to make suggestions for school consolidation. But, despite its unrelenting push for consolidation, very little was accomplished in reducing the number of school districts. In the late 1930s, IEA "launched an all-out drive to reduce the number of school districts in the state."[52] There were 10,719 one-room schools in 1900; 9,700 were still operating in 1944. At that time, Illinois had the largest number of school districts in the nation. In an *Illinois Education* article, University of Chicago professor Floyd Reeves wrote that "small school districts served well when the nation's economy was primarily agrarian, but the complexity of modern life requires a much broader education than the small schools are providing."[53]

As farming became more mechanized and the number of small farms decreased, average attendance in one-room schools declined significantly, from twenty-nine students in 1907 to only fifteen students thirty years later. In 1937, 2,733 one-room schools had fewer than ten students.[54] Besides these one-room schools, many small elementary and high school districts offered inadequate educational programs. In 1946, 107 high schools had operated for less than four years. The Pike County superintendent of public instruction reported that the county had 170 schools serving 5,732 pupils, for an average school size of 34.7 students. The vast majority of its schools (145) were one-room facilities. He stated that the situation would be "funny or laughable if it were not such a serious matter."[55]

After the attack on Pearl Harbor, the focus on the war effort delayed action on consolidation, but in 1945, the General Assembly finally enacted meaningful legislation to incentivize schools to reorganize into larger districts. The County School Survey Law encouraged school boards to appoint county study committees to develop plans for consolidation. A state advisory commission was established to assist counties that created planning committees. The state paid half of all expenses incurred by these committees. The law required that any reorganization plan developed by the county committees be submitted as a referendum for voter approval in the affected districts.[56] A Community Unit Law enacted in 1947 simplified the legal process for unit district consolidation.[57]

Illinois greatly increased state aid to education during this time. From 1943 to 1951, the total biennial state funding increased by 267 percent, from just over $41 million to nearly $151 million. Besides general state aid, funding included transportation, vocational education, school lunch programs, and aid for disabled students.[58] By 1960, the state paid over 25 percent of the total funding for K–12 education. Such large increases in funding provided the state with considerable leverage in prodding local communities to support consolidation. Although school boards were not required to establish survey committees, the state provided a host of economic incentives to act. The state enacted stringent requirements to qualify for state aid. Poorly funded districts, especially those with one-room schools, were major targets of the legislation. State aid was withheld from districts that averaged fewer than seven students in daily attendance for two consecutive years, unless the state superintendent granted a waiver due to "special circumstances." A $1,200 minimum teacher salary was finally enacted to pressure poor districts into consolidation.[59] IEA successfully lobbied for higher teaching standards, equal pay regardless of sex, paid sick leave, and a provision that marriage could not be used to dismiss a woman from teaching.[60] Any new high school district was required to have a minimum funding level to ensure that it could afford to provide students with an adequate secondary education. The state increased transportation aid as an inducement for creating larger districts. Kindergarten was included in the state aid formula for the first time. Legislation encouraged the creation of unit districts (K–12 grades) by lowering the minimum local property tax levy required for unit districts to receive state aid. Voters in poor downstate communities were more likely to support unit district consolidation if the state required a lower levy to qualify for aid.[61] Eventually, every county in the state conducted a school survey and made recommendations on consolidation. These reforms and others enacted in later years greatly reduced the number of operating school districts.

In 1940, Illinois had the largest number of school districts in the nation. From 1945 to 1956, it consolidated 9,937 (83 percent) of its K–12 school districts (see table 8). Most of this was accomplished by closing small rural districts. Today, it is third in number of districts, surpassed only by California and Texas. Across roughly the same years, from 1945 to 1960, the number of one-room schoolhouses in the state declined from 9,680 to 126. The last one-room schoolhouse in the state was McAuley School District 27 in DuPage County.[62] It was consolidated in 1993 with West Chicago Elementary School District 33.

Table 8. Decreasing Number of K–12 Districts as a Result
of Consolidation

Year	Elementary	Secondary	Unit	Total
1945	11,210	646	99	11,955
1949	4,194	442	315	4,951
1956	1,389	291	338	2,018

Source: Propeck and Pearson, *The History of the Illinois Education Association*, 148–49.

School consolidation increased investment in school buses and rural road-building projects. Larger school districts increased the size, duties, and power of the administrative staff. In the past, many superintendent and principal positions were part time. Administrators taught alongside teachers. Consolidation meant full-time management positions and a growing disconnect between classroom teachers and central office administrative staff. This development manifested itself in the 1960s as teachers organized local associations and pushed for collective bargaining.

Progressive Education

The New Deal and the victory over the racist ideology of the Axis powers inspired IEA to promote a progressive education. In 1945, IEA articulated a platform that centered its long-term educational vision for public education as the "inalienable right of every American." It further explained: "Every child as a member of the American Democracy—regardless of race, religious belief, economic status, residence, or handicap—should have the opportunity for fullest development—mentally, morally, socially, and physically—and for training in the attitudes, knowledge, habits, and skills that are essential for individual happiness and effective citizenship in a democracy."[63]

A public school system would instill democratic values, independent thought, citizenship, a sense of national purpose, and the skills to adapt to a rapidly changing world. Recognizing the diversity of the American people, the platform called for "enrichment curriculums that prepare the child for his cultural, vocational, recreational, social, and civic responsibilities and that take into account his individual interests, needs, and abilities."[64] Schools should provide a broad selection of classes and programs such as home economics, consumer education, vocational education, guidance counseling, art, band, and theater so as to appeal to the particular interests and talents of the entire student population. Public schools must prepare students for life in an ever-changing industrial democracy. The platform pointed out that for schools to be successful in fulfilling this mission, some basic social conditions must exist. It called for school lunch programs; instruction on health and hygiene; and a staff doctor, dentist, and nurse to ensure that all children had proper medical care.[65]

Highly qualified and motivated teachers were essential. Standards for teacher certification should be raised. The platform supported salaries and retirement benefits high enough to attract and to hold capable teachers in the profession. Class size should be limited to thirty students. Male and female teachers should be treated equally. Effective tenure laws should protect teachers against unjust dismissals. Academic freedom must be protected. Teachers should be free to teach all points of view without fear of reprisals. They should also "participate in the determination of courses of study, in the selection of textbooks and other educational materials, and in decisions relating to the ways and means of school organization and of school management." Adult education should include literacy classes, English language classes for immigrants, and parenting classes, and should encourage "life-long learning." Adult education would provide opportunities for people to pursue cultural interests and develop their talents.[66]

Such a school system would require a major investment by states and the federal government. While state and federal agencies could set minimum standards to qualify for funding, control over school programs must remain at the local level. IEA believed that public education from preschool through the university should be free.[67] The IEA platform included much more. It was based on the philosophy of progressive education and met stiff opposition from conservatives.

Civil Rights

Since its founding, IEA had always supported the rights of all children, regardless of race, religion, sex, nationality, or social class, to a free, common school education. Except for occasional criticism of the unjust treatment of African Americans in the South and of religious intolerance, IEA did not directly confront issues of racial injustice or school segregation prior to World War II. The outbreak of war in Europe and Japanese expansionism resulted in a large increase in federal military spending prior to the December 1941 attack on Pearl Harbor. The military buildup encouraged the Second Great Migration, as African Americans escaped Jim Crow oppression in the South in search of a better life in Chicago and other northern industrial centers. In June 1941, A. Philip Randolph, Bayard Rustin, and others organized a march on Washington to protest job discrimination in federal government hiring and defense industries. The march was canceled, but only after Franklin D. Roosevelt issued executive order 8802, creating the Committee on Fair Employment Practice. As the size of African American communities and their organizational strength developed in cities across Illinois, pressure mounted on school districts to address racial inequality.

The Second Great Migration continued through the 1960s. By 1970, about five million African Americans had moved to cities mainly in the Northeast and Midwest. After World War II, IEA took a stand against school segregation and racism. In 1948, the IEA platform endorsed "the principle of non-segregation of groups because of race, color, or creed within the public schools" and called on "responsible authorities rigidly to enforce the laws of the state prohibiting such segregation."[68]

Despite this platform, segregation was common in Illinois schools in the postwar era. School boards in at least eleven counties in southern Illinois maintained racially segregated schools into the 1950s. Edwardsville (like several other municipalities) had a four-year high school for white students and a three-year school for Black students until 1950. Tamms School District bused its forty-five Black students, along with children from nearby Elco, Sandusky, and Unity, to a segregated school in Cairo, twenty-five miles away. Pressure mounted to end compulsory segregation. In 1951, the legislature threatened to withhold state aid from any district that operated segregated schools. At first, amid a bombing and cross burnings by white segregationists, Cairo refused to admit Black students to its white schools. State aid was frozen and not resumed until the spring of 1952, when Cairo finally began to desegregate its schools.

However, not all the racially segregated schools were in southern Illinois. In 1950, it took a lawsuit to force Argo, in suburban Cook County, to end compulsory segregated schooling. Segregated dual districts eventually ended in Illinois, following *Brown v. Board of Education* (1954), but one district in Madison County maintained segregated schools into the mid-1960s. Housing discrimination and racial gerrymandering of school boundaries in Chicago and other large municipalities often resulted in de facto segregation of neighborhood schools. By the late 1960s, civil rights legislation, open housing laws, and court-ordered busing had somewhat diminished segregation in many Illinois schools.[69]

IEA published numerous articles deploring racism. In 1950, an article in *Illinois Education* entitled "What Does Race Have to Do with IQ?" asserted that such tests were biased in favor of "higher socio-economic groups" and that "one of the major wastes of human resources in the United States" is the "failure to discover the able but poor children and to develop their abilities." Another article, "Merit Not Color," highlighted the success of a racially integrated elementary school in Chicago.[70]

Fascist anti-Semitism demonstrated the danger of racism to democratic institutions and world peace. In its advocacy of racial and religious harmony, IEA joined the National Conference of Christians and Jews in celebrating American Brotherhood Week. It actively promoted the conference's programs in Illinois schools. IEA suggested a broad range of school activities for the week to encourage racial and religious tolerance. It listed classroom reading materials, posters for bulletin boards, and films and filmstrips that were available through the conference and other organizations. Districts were encouraged to purchase textbooks that explained the contributions of racial, religious, and ethnic groups to American life. In-service programs and summer workshops helped teachers develop classroom activities to teach tolerance. Among the suggested activities that could expose students to the diversity and richness of American culture were art projects, plays, skits, music, and guest speakers at student assemblies. CPS superintendent Dr. Herold C. Hunt was interviewed for an editorial in *Illinois Education*: "Brotherhood Week gives us a chance to show the world that Democracy does work and that we in America are building the brotherhood of man."[71] IEA continued to celebrate American Brotherhood Week into the 1960s.

Internationalism and the Great Red Scare

In 1923, NEA organized the World Federation of Education Associations to promote world peace, international understanding, and "friendship." It met every two years. IEA actively participated in the federation until the late 1930s. Throughout this period, the *Illinois Teacher* advertised tours of the Soviet Union.[72] As political tension in Europe increased on the eve of World War II, involvement in the federation waned. Following the war, IEA supported international efforts to promote world peace through such agencies as the United Nations, UNICEF, and UNESCO. IEA also supported foreign student exchange programs. In 1946, NEA and nineteen of its state affiliates, including IEA, hosted the founding of the World Organisation of the Teaching Profession. Its purpose was to promote democratic ideals, teacher welfare, international understanding, and world peace through public education.[73] In 1951, this organization merged with several others to form the World Confederation of Organisations of the Teaching Profession. This confederation continued to work closely with the United Nations. It merged in 1988 with its AFT rival, the International Federation of Free Teachers' Unions, forming Education International.[74]

IEA's support for progressive education, civil rights, the international peace movement, and labor unions made public education a target of attacks by right-wing conspiracists. The *Chicago Tribune*, National Association of Manufacturers, American Legion, and Daughters of the American Revolution engaged in red-baiting of educators, calling for loyalty oaths, book bans, and curriculum censorship during the World War I era and the Great Depression.[75] Anti-communist hysteria reached a fever pitch during the Red Scare. The Cold War in Europe, a hot war in Korea, and the threat of nuclear annihilation created extreme anxiety and fear in the postwar period. Far-right conservatives and self-serving politicians exploited this angst to launch attacks on the New Deal, United Nations, labor unions, and public education. After the war, the National Council for American Education, led by right-wing propagandist Allen Zoll, promoted private schools as an alternative to "communist influence." A widely circulated pamphlet entitled "The Commies Are after Your Kids" alleged that public schools, colleges, and universities were hotbeds of communist teachers seeking to propagandize students.[76] In 1954, IEA listed thirteen far-right organizations that promoted "unwarranted attacks largely on the grounds that the schools were fostering subversion or failing to teach the three R's."[77]

In 1947, the Illinois Senate Seditious Activities Investigation Commission, chaired by state senator Paul Broyles (R–Mount Vernon) and backed by the American Legion, launched a probe of "communist" activities in the state. The commission focused its attention on public schools. Not surprising, the *Chicago Tribune* picked up on the Broyles Commission investigations to attack "New Dealers" and liberal educators as communist plotters. An official of the Conference of American Small Business Organizations claimed: "there isn't a decent civics textbook in Chicago. They are all tainted with statism, New Dealism, and socialism. Most of our teachers have been made unconsciously disloyal by the teachers' colleges."[78]

In 1953, state senator John Meyer (R-Danville) proposed a bill to remove books from schools that were "antagonistic to or incompatible with the ideals and principles of American constitutional form of government." Under the bill, the state superintendent of public instruction would have established a committee to investigate books that any citizens felt violated the law. The legislature did not take up the book-banning bill, but it did enact a compulsory loyalty oath.[79]

IEA's position on loyalty oaths in this era stands in sharp contrast to its outspoken opposition as articulated by Robert C. Moore in the 1930s. In large part, this difference can be attributed to the extreme level of fear generated by the nuclear-armed Cold War. The reactionary climate of fear and distrust generated by the Red Scare was politically difficult for many organizations to resist. In 1948, AFT voted to ban communists from teaching, and NEA followed suit a year later. Following the NEA vote, a vigorous debate ensued at the IEA RA over NEA's anti-communist resolutions. Instead of forcibly opposing these attacks, IEA sought to soften their impact on public schools. IEA passed a resolution that communists should not teach in public schools but also included this statement: "we condemn the careless, incorrect, and unjust use of such words as 'Red' and 'Communist' to attack teachers and other persons who in point of fact are not Communists, but who merely have views different from those of their accusers."[80]

Loyalty oaths served as a litmus test for the far-right crusade of fear and intimidation. Anyone challenging the loyalty oath became a target of red-baiting attacks.[81] The issue of compulsory oaths of allegiance was especially divisive. *Illinois Education* published numerous articles for and against loyalty oaths. CTU and the Chicago division opposed the practice, but many teachers, especially in the more conservative rural areas of the state, enthusiastically supported compulsory loyalty oaths. A teacher from Evergreen Park stated: "Personally, I feel a swelling of pride whenever I'm called upon to take an oath of allegiance to my country and its symbols."[82] A teacher from Centralia wrote: "I am very much in favor of teachers taking this oath. I think anyone who cannot swear to the oath should not be permitted to teach."[83]

IEA took the position that a loyalty oath should be a positive pledge of support for the US Constitution, and not a negative oath so broadly worded that it would subject teachers to political biases of school board members. Any required oath of allegiance should also be enacted by state or federal legislation, not by local school boards. Tenure rights must be protected. State law should govern dismissals based on cause, and those accused should have proper legal recourse to defend themselves. Irving Pearson argued that the real danger to public education was not "from subversive organizations," but rather "from the suspicions and fears engendered by promiscuous, non-professional investigations (public and private) which cause teachers to feel circumscribed and insecure in teaching the truth."[84]

Based on these principles, IEA opposed the loyalty oath legislation proposed by the Broyles Commission.[85] Democratic governor Adlai Stevenson vetoed the Broyles Bill, but in 1955, Republican governor William Stratton signed the legislation. It required all elected officials and public employees in the state to swear:

> I am not affiliated directly or indirectly with any communist organization or any communist front organization, or any foreign political agency, party, organization or government which advocates the overthrow of the constitutional government by force or other means not permitted under the Constitution of the United States or the Constitution of this State; . . . I do not directly or indirectly teach or advocate the overthrow of the government of the United States or of this State or any unlawful change in the form of government thereof by force or any unlawful means.[86]

In 1955, three Chicago teachers—Albert Soglin, Shirley Lens, and Sara Pickus—refused to sign the oath. Soglin stated: "I cannot abandon the Bill of Rights by supporting the replacement of its principles and the search for truth by fear and conformity of opinion and behavior, condone a public test for a teaching position, or open the door to intimidation of teachers and educational organizations." The American Civil Liberties Union took up the case on their behalf, but the Illinois Supreme Court upheld the law the following year. Wanting to continue teaching, both Soglin and Lens eventually signed, but Pickus refused.[87] In 1977, this oath was made "optional." It stayed on the books for teachers until 1983.

Conservative attacks on public education in the 1960s shifted to opposing federal funding. The Elementary and Secondary Education Act of 1965 and subsequent legislation tied eligibility for federal funds to district practices on minorities, women, the disabled, and other groups. As a result, racial integration, sport programs for girls, inclusion of disabled students in school programs, and other socially progressive policies were adopted by school districts across the nation. Let Freedom Ring, a right-wing organization, accused the US Office of Education of attempting "to federalize our schools in the Russian manner."[88]

Illinois Association of Classroom Teachers

IEA assisted members in organizing local associations. Executive secretary Irving Pearson urged large urban locals to create a statewide IEA affiliate. In 1940, eighteen teacher locals organized ATA to promote "educational and teacher welfare" within their communities. ATA's annual dues were initially ten cents per member. At first, ATA focused mainly on influencing IEA's legislative agenda, establishing credit unions, supporting tenure legislation, arranging insurance programs, and securing other membership benefits.[89] IEA established the Mutual Insurance Company (later becoming Horace Mann), which offered members affordable casualty and life insurance policies. Beginning in January 1957, IEA provided all members with $10,000 teacher liability insurance coverage.[90] The amount of coverage would increase over time. An early source of tension between IFT and IEA was their competing benefit systems.

ATA held its annual meetings in conjunction with the IEA RA. In 1946, IEA recognized it as the official representative of teachers' interests. ATA also affiliated with the NEA department of classroom teachers.[91] Most of the larger IEA local associations joined ATA. As more rank-and-file teachers became involved, demands for membership services and benefits grew. Teacher welfare was no longer confined to legislative efforts in Springfield, but was broadened to include direct discussions with school administration over salary and benefits. In 1946, ATA opposed merit pay programs and announced "plans to make recommendations to administrators on teaching load and class size." It went "on record favoring the participation of classroom teachers in all matters of school policy and wherever possible in the filling of vacancies in the school staff."[92] Teacher locals began dealing directly with their employers on wages, hours, benefits, and working conditions. ATA locals reported successes in establishing single salary schedules, regulating class loads, raising salaries, and improving economic benefits provided by their school districts. By 1949, ATA encompassed eighty locals. It changed its name to the Illinois Association of Classroom Teachers (IACT) and became a vocal teacher advocate with the association. It held annual meetings, sponsored workshops, and published a newsletter, *IACT in Action*.[93]

Many smaller districts tended to include superintendents and administrators in their locals and affiliated directly with IEA rather than joining IACT. IACT was a classroom-controlled teacher organization that banned administrators from holding elected positions. In September 1961, IEA reported that 132 local associations were members of IACT.[94]

By 1960, IEA was, by any measure, an influential professional organization. Membership was increasing rapidly, having risen from 1,177 in 1912 to over 58,000 in 1960. It had a large staff and a powerful presence in Springfield. It played a major role in shaping education policy, improving compensation and benefits for educators, and securing state funding for schools. Members could access numerous association services. IEA's Mutual Insurance Company offered members a variety of low-cost insurance policies, including life, home, and auto. All members received liability insurance protection. Teacher institutes and workshops were held on a regular basis. Local associations could access IEA research, and field staff had been hired to help them prepare their salary schedule and benefit proposals for the school board to address. More than 77 percent of all Illinois teachers were IEA members.[95]

Conclusion

Association leaders viewed the lack of teacher involvement in the early twentieth century as undemocratic, a weak link in the "professional unity" that they considered vital to IEA's political agenda. The organizational reforms begun in the late 1930s, which increased teacher participation in division governance and organized local associations, had unforeseen consequences for IEA. The tenure law and the rising standard of living for union families after World War II emboldened teachers to be more assertive in their demands for higher salaries and improved benefits. The dilemma for IEA was how to maintain an all-inclusive professional organization amid a rising tide of teacher activism. While IACT played a leading role in teacher advocacy within the association, many of the most militant teachers were attracted to IFT and collective bargaining. Consequently, IEA faced a growing organizational challenge from IFT by the late 1950s.

CHAPTER 6

Professional Solidarity or Professional Unionism, 1960–1970

The Illinois Education Association is the one statewide organization which invites both administrators and teachers to share alike in its membership. For almost 100 years administration and teachers have counseled together with mutual respect for the improvement of education in Chicago and the state.

—Robert D. Gregg, IEA Chicago division president

The Illinois Education Association (IEA) billed itself as an all-inclusive professional organization that best represented the interests of all public education employees. IEA membership included teachers, college faculty, administrators, and county school superintendents. After World War II, it added education secretaries, school nurses, student teachers, and retired teachers to its membership rolls. While more than 90 percent of its members were K–12 teachers, administrators constituted a majority of IEA's top leadership positions. Throughout its history, the primary focus of IEA had been on influencing public policy in the state legislature to advance the cause of education, but after World War II the increasing number of local associations pressured IEA for assistance in dealing with their school districts. The postwar baby boom created a huge demand for classroom teachers, many of whom were from working-class families educated under the GI Bill. Given the rising standard of living, many of those entering the teaching profession were inspired by the successes of organized labor and militant in their demands for higher salaries and benefits. Professional solidarity had its limits. IEA faced a growing challenge to its leadership in public education from the Illinois Federation of Teachers (IFT). By the mid-1950s, American Federation of Teachers (AFT) locals in Illinois and other heavily unionized states took the lead in organizing teachers for collective bargaining, often meeting stiff resistance from superintendents and school boards. In 1957, AFT labeled the National Education Association (NEA) a "company union" dominated by school administrators. IFT used the company union label to build support among disgruntled teachers.[1]

Professional Solidarity

IEA was an all-inclusive professional organization. While 90 percent of its members were classroom teachers, its membership included "any person engaged in educational work in public schools or colleges in Illinois," from the smallest rural to the largest urban districts. The association maintained that all employees within the public education community shared a common set of values of service to their communities and the children being taught. Since public education served every child regardless of race, sex, religion, ethnicity, or social class, IEA insisted on being an independent, nonpartisan organization strictly focused on the best interests of the children served by the school system.[2] IEA took strong positions on educational issues, but it did not endorse political candidates seeking office. While labor unions had always vigorously supported public education, IEA maintained its "professional" status and its independence from organized labor. IEA's political agenda relied on broad-based public support throughout the state, rather than on ties to any specific interest group, whether it was unions, a political party, or other organizations. This attitude, in large part, explains why the association is still not affiliated with the labor movement, despite becoming a militant union in the 1970s.[3]

In keeping with its objective of professional solidarity, IEA surmised that there were no fundamental differences within the profession that could not be settled amicably between the school administration, teachers, and other employees. Even though administrators controlled the board of directors, IEA leadership argued that it best represented the economic and professional interests of teachers. IEA consistently championed higher pay, pension benefits, tenure rights, and other issues that would improve the lives of teachers. It also maintained that the "local education association is the one place where all teachers and administrators may come together on a common level to discuss their mutual problems."[4]

A code of ethics was adopted in December 1949 and refined in subsequent years to serve as a guide for "professional conduct." The code of ethics sought to establish the ground rules for "cooperative teacher-administrative relationships." It was predicated on the belief that conflict within the profession could be resolved through "responsible criticism" carried out "through properly designated channels." This meant that disputes should be settled through the chain of command within the school district and not aired publicly, except as a last resort. The final decision on teacher welfare issues would be made by the school board, based on a recommendation of the superintendent, in consultation with the teaching staff.[5] Professional solidarity had its limits, however. The idea that all disputes, especially over teacher salaries, benefits, and working conditions, could be settled without conflict was not realistic. The Illinois Association of School Boards (IASB) adhered to the legal theory that districts could not legally bargain with their teachers over any policy matters that restricted their sovereign power to manage the schools, as granted to them by the public. Even though IEA portrayed the superintendent as the arbitrator between the local association and the school board, IASB maintained that administrators were agents of the school board and not independent professionals.[6] While teachers had tenure rights that provided them with some protection from political retribution rising out of disputes with school officials, the superintendent and other administrators did not have any such protections. They were, in essence, at-will political appointees. Their careers relied on maintaining the support of the school board. While some administrators would stand up for their teachers in a dispute, they often bent to the will of board members. Some administrators even sought to advance their own careers by being tough on teacher demands. They vigorously opposed collective bargaining as a threat to their own power and influence.

Salary Schedule "Negotiations"

Since the 1930s, IEA had supported a single salary schedule that rewarded teachers based on their years of teaching experience and level of education achievement. After World War II, local associations started urging school districts to adopt such pay scales. In some districts, fifth-grade teachers received higher pay than those teaching first grade. Junior high teachers often received higher compensation than teachers in elementary school. Unit districts frequently had two or more salary schedules for teachers at various grade levels. In some districts, male teachers received better health insurance coverage than women, based on the assumption that women were secondary income earners for their families. The association argued that a single salary schedule would be a fair and less divisive system for compensation. It would also foster a spirit of cooperation among teachers, helping create a positive educational environment for the children by reducing historical inequities between male and female teachers. As more schools consolidated into larger unit districts, a single salary schedule established a fair standard for determining compensation among high school, junior high, and elementary teachers. It also reduced divisiveness within the staff. A single salary schedule provided teachers with a reason to organize local associations, which, in turn, increased the effectiveness of the state organization in passing its political agenda in Springfield.[7]

After World War II, IEA locals began appointing salary committees to do research and to present their recommendations either to the superintendent or directly to the school board. IEA supported these discussions on salary and fringe benefits as legitimate efforts to improve teacher welfare. Often after an exchange of pleasantries, the salary committee would leave and await the announcement of the school board's decision.[8] By the early 1950s, the association hired three field representatives to assist locals in the development of salary schedules and other organizational matters.[9] The number of field staff continued to increase as locals became increasingly insistent in their posture and demanded assistance. Most districts adopted single salary schedules.

However, for many, especially in the larger urban school districts, this timid approach was not enough. By the late 1950s, some locals began to have meet-and-confer discussions with school officials involving not only salary schedule issues but also fringe benefits and working conditions. These discussions were strictly advisory and did not lead to contractual agreements with the locals. The Decatur Education Association (DEA) led the way in broadening the scope of these discussions to include school finances, salaries, benefits, and working conditions. In 1959, DEA established an educational policy committee that attended every school board meeting and represented teachers in negotiations with the superintendent. At times, these meetings included the school board.[10] This policy committee was an important step within IEA, foreshadowing the move toward collective bargaining. DEA teachers would continue to play a leading role in teacher advocacy as IEA transformed into a union.

Not surprisingly, conservatives opposed the single salary schedule, instead promoting merit pay programs. They believed that it was a management prerogative to reward individual teachers based on their perceived performance rather than having a uniform pay scale. Besides, they also feared that salary schedules would drive up labor costs, thereby pressuring school boards and the General Assembly to raise taxes. A number of conservative school boards devised merit pay schemes to modify or replace the single salary schedule, although with limited success. NEA reported that, nationally, only 9 percent of the merit pay plans adopted after 1940 were still in use by 1961.[11] In Illinois, merit pay plans gained very little traction. In 1973, only 37 (3.6 percent) of the state's 1,052 districts had merit pay programs. Forty-one years later, even fewer districts had merit pay programs. Fourteen of the nineteen districts with merit pay plans had fewer than 1,000 students. Only two districts with 6,000 or more students had merit pay.[12] Obviously, merit pay had very little support, especially among teachers and many administrators. These efforts proved to be divisive, creating tension among teachers as well as between teachers and administrative staff.[13] Nevertheless, conservative critics have continued to support merit pay as an alternative to collective bargaining.

Parochial Aid

In the late nineteenth and early twentieth century, Irish, Italian, Polish, and other Catholic immigrants established parochial schools in industrial centers across the United States. Catholic schools were the largest private school system in Illinois, and two-thirds of all parochial students attended schools in Chicago. By the late 1960s, many of these schools faced growing financial difficulties. A dwindling supply of men and women entering the clergy after World War II forced parochial schools to rely on nonclerical employees. The fact that the salaries and benefits of public school teachers were improving made it much more expensive for parochial schools to hire and retain teaching staff. Improvements in public school curriculum and programs also raised expenses for parochial schools as they were forced to respond in kind. Many Catholic schools in the racially changing neighborhoods on the West and South Sides of Chicago were forced to close as the Black population replaced white residents moving to the suburbs. While Catholic schools readily accepted Black students regardless of their religious backgrounds, most African American families were Protestant and too poor to afford the expense of a parochial school. The Catholic archdiocese and many Chicago Democrats from heavily Catholic ethnic neighborhoods supported parochial aid. They argued that parochial schools ease the tax burden by reducing public school enrollment. They called on state governments to provide funding, claiming that parents who send their children to parochial schools are, in effect, paying double by being taxed for public schools they do not use. Of course, this rationale would also call into question why anyone without children should pay taxes to support public schools.[14]

IEA had steadfastly opposed all efforts to provide any state aid to private schools, stating: "The public schools have historically provided a great equalizing force in America—a common meeting ground for affluent and disadvantaged, for able and slow, for students with racially different backgrounds, for children of varying religious beliefs. Here children learn to live together in preparation for an adult world. This strengthening fiber in the fabric of our national lives must not be weakened, particularly at a time when other factors are pulling at some of the threads which bind it together."[15] IEA organized a diverse coalition of parochial aid opponents called Public Education and Religious Liberty (PEARL). Its members included Protestant groups such as the Illinois Baptist Association and Seventh-day Adventists, whose opposition was based on the fact that Catholic schools in Chicago would be the chief beneficiaries of the aid. Americans United for Separation of Church and State and other civil libertarian organizations joined PEARL as well. The president of PEARL was the executive director of the Illinois Association of School Administrators (IASA). IEA contributed $5,000. The American Civil Liberties Union donated legal services to challenge parochial aid in the courts. Besides constitutional issues over the separation of church and state, PEARL cited the lack of regulatory oversight, the reinforcement of school segregation, and the creation of a dual school system as grounds for its opposition to parochial aid. PEARL also sponsored a public information campaign to rally support against diverting state aid to private schools.[16]

In 1970, Republican governor Richard Ogilvie included $32 million for parochial aid in his proposed budget. In a guest editorial in *Insight*, state senator Harris W. Fawell, a Republican from DuPage County, wrote: "A private school is private. It retains, and rightly so, the right to pick and choose its students." Fawell warned that public funding of private schools would create religious, social, and political division "in a society which is already pulsating with ideological polarization." He also criticized parochial aid proponents' efforts to dismantle "what they referred to as a 'monolithic public school monopoly' on education" and praised public education for all children as "a continuing and a unique American experience."[17]

The General Assembly passed the budget with $30 million for parochial schools, but the governor sent it back unsigned after the US Supreme Court struck down similar parochial aid laws in Pennsylvania and Rhode Island, declaring that "direct aid" to religious schools created "excessive entanglement" between church and state.[18]

Growing Teacher Militancy

Following World War II, there were increasing demands among teachers for greater participation in policy decisions affecting their employment. The ongoing efforts of IEA to organize local associations provided a mechanism whereby teachers could begin to assert their economic and professional interests in their school districts. School consolidation increased the size of the administrative bureaucracy and created the sense that the superintendent was no longer a colleague but rather the boss. Since the Depression, teacher salaries had lagged behind those of skilled and even unskilled workers. During World War II, inflation made the situation worse. From 1941 to 1947, worker wages increased by 97 percent, greater than the cost of living, while teacher salaries failed to keep up with inflation.[19] Over the next sixteen years, the real income of working-class families doubled. The postwar success of the labor movement in improving the standard of living among workers raised expectations among teachers that they too should share in the growing prosperity.

Increased education requirements for teacher certification also led to more demands for higher pay. By 1965, 85 percent of US K–12 teachers had bachelor's degrees. The GI Bill meant that a college education was attainable for many veterans. By the mid-1950s, there was a large teacher shortage as baby boomers entered the classrooms. The teacher shortage attracted former GIs to teaching. From

1954 to 1964, there was a 93 percent increase in male teachers, as compared to a 38 percent increase in female teachers. A large portion of these male teachers (47 percent) came from working-class backgrounds. Many of them entered the teaching profession only to learn that blue-collar union workers often received higher compensation than teachers.[20]

The struggle for civil rights and economic justice by African Americans, too, inspired men and women teachers to be more assertive in their dealings with school boards and administrators. There was a growing sense that teachers could no longer rely simply on the good will of the administration in promoting their interests. NEA pointed out that by the late 1960s, a majority of the nation's teachers were relatively young, having been hired after 1955. The radicalism of the 1960s, the militancy of its younger teachers, and the organizing pressure from IFT played a key role in pushing IEA into collective bargaining. Addressing the 1966 Illinois Association of Classroom Teachers (IACT) spring meeting, an NEA spokesperson gave this summary of the younger teachers entering the profession: "The average age has dropped several years during the past decade. . . . More than one fourth have master's degrees. . . . Men in high-schools now exceed the number of women, and one third of the elementary teachers are now men."[21]

IEA locals were more restrained than IFT in their dealings with management and school boards. Many members came from small, conservative farming communities, making them less likely to stand up to their superintendent or their neighbors on the school board. Moreover, IEA membership included all educators. Prior to the adoption of unified dues in 1971, there was no requirement for IEA members to join the local association or, for that matter, NEA. Though many locals, especially those affiliated with IACT, excluded superintendents and administrators, these individuals joined IEA through their IEA-affiliated statewide organizations. Consequently, these administrators could be active members of the divisions and could hold prominent leadership positions in the state organization. Only three teachers served as IEA presidents from 1945 to 1966; thirteen K–12 superintendents held that post, and the remaining six presidents included an assistant superintendent, a principal, a college administrator, a county superintendent of schools, and a program director for the State Office of Public Instruction.[22] More importantly, even though teachers were regularly elected to the IEA board of directors, administrators controlled the board throughout this period. This fact served as a restraint on militancy even in local associations that excluded administrators from membership. The state organization clung to its historical mission of professionalism and discouraged militant action by its locals, in effect, ceding leadership for collective bargaining to IFT.

IFT members were much less encumbered than their IEA counterparts in taking militant action to improve their lot. Teachers from working-class families were more likely to join IFT, support collective bargaining, and participate in job actions than were association members, especially those from middle-class and rural communities. The federation strongholds were heavily unionized communities, especially in Cook County and in the coal mining area of southern Illinois. Teachers controlled these organizations. Though IFT did organize a few locals of principals and their assistants, superintendents were viewed as agents of their school boards and thus excluded from membership. IFT was modeled after trade unionism and committed to exclusive representation and bargaining with school boards.

Prior to the 1960s, "bargaining" typically consisted of meet-and-confer discussions with management that, at best, produced a memorandum of understanding but not a mutually signed agreement. IFT executive director Oscar Weil explained: "During the 1940s and 1950s, IFT leaders had still not formed any clearer idea of how they were to overcome the major obstacles to building their union. The most important obstacle was what appeared to most legal and educational authorities to be the impregnable legal barriers to organizing teachers' unions and bargaining with school boards."[24]

CICERO: AN EARLY IFT COLLECTIVE BARGAINING AGREEMENT

In 1944, IFT Local 571 Cicero Elementary bargained an agreement that included many of the provisions that would become standards in contracts bargained in the late 1960s. This contract included a salary schedule, extra duty pay, seniority, use of school facilities for union activities, paid sick leave, paid bereavement leave, sabbatical leave, teacher evaluation, and a grievance process. Unlike later teacher contracts, the exclusive representation clause of the Cicero agreement covered principals and other administrators; only the superintendent and assistant superintendent were excluded. The superintendent and the union signed the contract. This agreement was the first and, for a long time, the only comprehensive collective bargaining agreement in the state.[23]

IASB clung to the theory that districts could not legally bargain binding contracts with teacher organizations. Unlike private businesses, public schools were established through the constitutional power of the people, as given to their elected representatives. Boards of education could not limit or relinquish this sovereign authority to control and manage the operation of their schools by negotiating away their authority over school policy. Answering an inquiry by IFT in 1950, AFT general counsel John Ligtenberg argued in contrast that school boards could negotiate collective bargaining agreements with a recognized representative of their employees. School boards regularly signed contracts with private companies for a broad range of services. So it would seem that a mutually binding contract with their employees was also permissible. But he admitted that it was his opinion and not yet tested in the courts. This issue remained in legal limbo until the mid-1960s and provided the rationale for school boards to oppose demands for exclusive bargaining recognition and negotiated agreements. Nevertheless, teacher organizations would conduct a limited number of job actions to pressure districts to accede to their demands.[25]

Oscar Weil wrote that prior to the 1950s, IFT was primarily "an organization of protest." Other than Cicero elementary teachers, IFT locals did not begin to bargain comprehensive contracts until the 1960s.[26] Nevertheless, in the immediate aftermath of World War II, the union engaged in a flurry of militant job actions. Even though AFT and IFT were on record as opposing strikes, federation affiliates sometimes acted otherwise. In 1947, IFT teacher locals walked out in downstate West Frankfort and Madison over disputes involving exclusive representation and salary schedules.[27] The following year, the Chicago Teachers Union (CTU) voted to strike unless the city council approved a tax levy for public schools that was within the limit established by the state legislature. The city council backed down.[28] When three tenured teachers were not hired following a school consolidation in downstate Gillespie, IFT Local 817 refused to return to work after the summer break, resulting in a two-week delay of the school year.[29]

The most widely publicized incident occurred in Oglesby School District. In 1949, IFT Local 580 initiated a work stoppage over the nonrenewal of Helen Mecum, a probationary union member. Based on a recommendation by the superintendent, the school board refused to renew her contract for a third year, which would have established tenure rights. At the behest of the IFT local, the LaSalle County Trades and Labor Council established a picket line to protest the school board's action. The teachers refused to cross, delaying the start of the school year. At the September 7 school board meeting, several hundred union members packed the assembly, demanding her reinstatement. After the board renewed her contract, the board members promptly resigned, claiming that they had been physically threatened by "an angry mob of union members." Four previous labor disputes with the district contributed to the union's reaction to her dismissal. At the behest of IEA, NEA's Commission for the Defense of Democracy through Education conducted an extensive investigation into the Oglesby incident, finding blame on all sides. It condemned "the conduct of the union teachers in relation to work stoppages by the Trades and Labor Council at Oglesby, whose picket lines at the schools American Federation of Teachers members refused to cross, although their union has a 'no-strike' policy."[30]

The NEA commission found no basis for the charge that the district was "endeavoring to break the local teachers union," but it did criticize the superintendent and board for violating "sound professional practices" in Mecum's case. Prior to her nonrenewal, she did not receive any consultation over her alleged defects by the administration. "Any teacher, even though considered incompetent, is entitled to know in what ways he is failing to meet teaching standards during the course of an employment period and is further entitled to an opportunity to remedy any alleged defects."[31]

The NEA commission concluded that Oglesby School District was "an unprofessional place in which to work" and that teachers must "give their first loyalty to the children and not to any organization of teachers, union or non-union." Only by developing and maintaining "a sound professional atmosphere . . . will it be possible to restore teacher morale and to recruit and retain high calibre teaching personnel."[32] The commission's report was apparently not well received by Oglesby teachers. They eventually became an IFT bargaining unit.

The NEA commission, in effect, sanctioned the district and criticized it for the damage done to the education system. This public shaming was intended to create local political support to pressure the school board to resolve the bitter dispute and to warn teacher applicants about the situation that they would face if they accepted a job there. IEA would use similar sanctions in the 1960s, when local associations reached an impasse over negotiations.

Even though Illinois did not have legislation that outlawed strikes, it was generally assumed that public employee strikes were illegal. Regardless, several IFT locals either threatened to strike or actually walked out in downstate locals during the 1950s. In 1957, East St. Louis teachers threatened a walkout, forcing the district to conduct a representation election that IFT won.[33] Federation locals in Madison (1954) and Cahokia (1959) conducted brief strikes over salary negotiations.[34]

As demands for collective bargaining increased across the nation, AFT president Carl J. Megel, at the 1957 American Federation of Labor and Congress of Industrial Organizations (AFL-CIO) convention, sponsored a resolution that labeled NEA and its affiliates as a "company union" that was dominated by school administrators. He introduced the proposal "so that the delegates and labor representatives understand fully the company union aspects of the National Education Association, its state, and local affiliates," as well as the "anti-labor program of this NEA company union."[35]

NEA executive secretary William G. Carr was quick to issue a press release following the AFL-CIO convention, stating that "powerful organizations in American life which oppose the NEA and organized labor on such vital questions as federal and state financial support of education will be pleased by these efforts to divide our educational forces." Carr pointed out that a company union is set up and controlled by owners or officers of the corporation so as to control its workforce and maximize its profits. Public education is a public service controlled by the citizenry through their elected school boards and not a for-profit business. School boards do not control the association. The association is a self-governing professional organization that seeks to influence the policies of the state legislature, school boards, and the public for the "common good of the profession" and the children it serves. Since public education relies on the support of the general public, the association cannot be identified as narrowly "sectarian." It must remain completely independent of political parties, factions, and any other groups, including labor unions. Only a broad-based professional organization can advance the cause of public education. It was also argued that labor affiliation would make teachers beholden to labor unions.[36] IEA executive secretary Irving Pearson responded to the company union label by pointing out IEA support for higher salaries, pension benefits, tenure rights, and other teacher welfare issues. He concluded that "teachers should not be misled by false propaganda" being promoted by IFT.[37]

CTU president John Fewkes supported Megel's resolution and predicted that IFT "is soon going to be the dominant organization throughout the entire state of Illinois."[38] This prediction was incredibly optimistic, given the relative standing of IFT and IEA. At the time, IFT had a $10,000 annual budget, only five thousand members outside Chicago, and no full-time staff. IEA, on the other hand, had a $332,700 budget, over fifty thousand members, and eleven full-time professional staff, including four field representatives.[39] Nevertheless, IFT's greatest resources were the militancy of its members and its affiliation with the labor movement.

The rivalry between IEA and IFT had slowly intensified since the 1940s. On several occasions, the *Illinois Union Teacher* published articles about overly zealous superintendents pressuring teachers to join the association or providing duty-free release time to attend association meetings at teacher institutes. The *Illinois Union Teacher* also noted that "some superintendents simply tell the teachers when interviewing them that membership in the association is expected of all teachers in the district. . . . A letter usually follows to all teachers early in the year in which they are reminded that membership in the associations is a 'professional' responsibility."[40] In 1956, IFT published an opinion by Robert W. Deffenbaugh, assistant legal advisor to the Illinois Department of Education, stating that neither the superintendent nor the board of education has the legal authority to require any teacher to join a "particular organization."[41]

Fewkes's support for Megel's resolution at the AFL-CIO convention not only ended any cooperation between CTU and the IEA Chicago division, but also signaled the increasingly bitter rivalry between IFT and IEA over representation rights and bargaining.[42] On its own, the fiscally strapped IFT might not have been able to mount a serious threat to IEA, but following the 1957 convention it received significant staff and financial support from AFL-CIO. United Auto Workers president Walter Reuther, the most progressive national labor leader of the time, believed that teacher unionism was a critical component in the advancement of unionism and industrial democracy. As director of the AFL-CIO industrial union department, Reuther committed organizers and financial support to AFT's campaign to establish collective bargaining rights in New York City.[43] Following the New York victory in 1962, Reuther dispatched his brother Victor, along with Charles Chiakulas and Karl Shier, to meet with a group of young CTU activists to pressure Fewkes to begin a drive for collective bargaining in Chicago. Among those attending the meeting was Bob Healey, a future IFT president.[44] In 1964, the industrial union department promised to match every dollar that AFT raised for organizing. By 1968, the department had given AFT more than $5 million for organizing. This support enabled AFT to challenge NEA leadership in major industrial centers across the United States. Illinois became a key target of AFT organizing since it had a powerful labor movement and the second-largest concentration of AFT members in the country. This support sent shock waves throughout NEA and its state affiliates.[45]

By 1962, IFT was poised to challenge IEA dominance in Illinois. It had local unions in almost every large city in the state. Many of these locals, such as Joliet, East St. Louis, and Belleville, eventually won exclusive bargaining rights for the federation; in many other large districts, such as Rockford, Springfield, Galesburg, Decatur, and Bloomington, IFT would remain active for years to come, though it was never able to establish exclusive representation rights. In addition, IFT hired its first full-time executive director in 1959.[46] Four years later, Oscar Weil assumed the position. Weil, a Roxana high school teacher, was a talented organizer totally committed to unionism and collective bargaining. He, more than anyone else, helped build the union into a formidable challenge to IEA dominance in the state.[47] Under his leadership, IFT hired additional staff and began an aggressive organizing campaign throughout Illinois. Critical to Weil's efforts was financial support and organizing staff from AFL-CIO.

"Denver—A Turning Point"

With the AFT victory in New York City followed by a successful strike as a backdrop, AFL-CIO vice president James B. Carey addressed the 1962 NEA representative assembly (RA) by warning that "teachers are welcoming unionism as a wave of the future." So should NEA, he said; otherwise, it will "find that it has been left behind as history marches past." He pointed out that many teachers are paid less than high school custodial employees, who "have sense enough to band together and organize."[48]

NEA executive secretary William G. Carr called the 1962 convention in Denver a turning point in the association's history. Carr praised the labor movement as a "staunch and valued ally" in support for public education, but he argued that union affiliation threatened the professional unity so critical to the future of public education, saying: "American teachers must remain free and independent of entangling alliances with any group in society." Carr claimed that NEA was "strong enough to stand on its own feet, develop its own programs and standards, in full cooperation with other interested groups, including labor, and yet remain free . . . to act independently.[49] In response, the RA adopted resolutions urging all local associations to develop written agreements on professional negotiation (PN) procedures with their school boards and to merge local, state, and national associations into a unified organization. The delegates also insisted "on the right of professional associations, through democratically selected representatives, to participate with the boards of education in the determination of salaries and working conditions."[50]

While supporting PN, the convention reaffirmed NEA's opposition to strikes. Carr ended his speech by warning of the "threat of teacher unionization" and calling on members to leave the meeting as "a militant and united force."[51] Obviously, AFT's threat to its large urban locals was a major concern prompting NEA to support PN.

NEA had good reason to be concerned. Following its success in New York City, AFT continued to win bargaining elections in other large urban centers. By 1968, AFT locals had become the bargaining agents for teachers in New York, Chicago, Philadelphia, Detroit, Boston, Kansas City, Cleveland, Newark, Toledo, St. Louis, New Orleans, and Washington, DC. These victories inspired teacher militancy and propelled NEA to take an increasingly proactive role in assisting its state affiliates in matters of collective bargaining. In 1971, an IEA membership poll indicated that 41 percent of respondents supported a more militant stand for improving teacher compensation; 51 percent were satisfied with the current degree of militancy; and only 9 percent wanted a more conciliatory approach.[52] As a teacher leader said: "The AFT is the best thing that ever happened to the NEA. If the AFT hadn't come along, NEA would have had to create it."[53]

Professional Negotiation

There was hardly any mention of negotiations in *Illinois Education*, the IEA newsletter, prior to the Denver convention. However, as far back as the 1930s, IEA had maintained that the entire professional staff should participate in formulating policy decisions with the school board (even if exactly how this was to be carried out was not clearly expressed). While the Denver convention provided the catalyst, IEA executive secretary Wayne Stoneking would later point out that the impetus for PN was "a gradual dissatisfaction of teachers as a group with unilateral decisions which affected them without their involvement."[54]

PN was intended to be an alternative to the positional and often adversarial collective bargaining developed in the private sector. It sought to maintain the broad coalition of school administration, teachers, and other education officials on which IEA had built its success in the twentieth century. It assumed that teachers, administrators, school boards, and the public shared a common interest in providing children with the best education possible. Disagreements that arose between the parties could be resolved without resorting to strikes.[55] In theory, PN also would involve teachers in collaboration with the administration in the broadest scope of decision-making. According to retired IEA UniServ director Robert Jensen, "Teachers wanted to place contractual limits on class size. Teachers also wanted a voice in matters such as the process of developing the curriculum, student discipline, and other educational policies that affected the teaching/learning environment."[56]

In reference to PN, Stoneking expressed hope that "this cooperative procedure should preclude the arbitrary exercise of unilateral authority by the Board of Education and the use of strikes by the teachers."[57] Notably, even the development of PN procedures was cooperative in nature. Since there was no legal framework to guide PN, the procedures were developed at the local level (or not at all) in a "cooperative" effort between the teachers, administration, and school board. Given the large number and diversity of school districts, PN varied greatly across the state depending on the strength of the local associations, the conservatism of the school board, or the attitude of the superintendent.

IEA prescribed five types of PN, from a recognition agreement (level 1) to a comprehensive collective bargaining contract (level 5). At a minimum, the school board would recognize the association as the bargaining agent and meet to discuss its concerns if it could demonstrate majority status among the teachers (level 1). The next type, level 2, also included written agreement on the procedures to be followed by the school board, administration, and teacher local. The procedures could include a schedule for meetings, the scope of bargaining, and the makeup of the teams. Level 3 added an agreement on resolving disputes through fact-finding and mediation. In addition to all the above, level 4 was a comprehensive, mutually signed agreement covering salary, benefits, a grievance clause, working conditions, and other teacher concerns. Binding arbitration to settle an impasse over negotiations was level 5, but very few, if any, locals achieved such agreements with their school boards.[58] In 1970, the Office of the Superintendent of Public Instruction opined that school boards might agree to binding arbitration to settle negotiation impasses, but IASB opposed this approach. Not surprisingly, Illinois teachers would increasingly conduct work stoppages by the late 1960s to settle bitter disputes over bargaining.

Following the Denver meeting, IACT, IEA, IASA, and IASB met to compare their organizational positions on PN. They agreed to work "cooperatively" in developing PN policies, to resolve disputes through "professional channels," to oppose strikes, and to recognize the legal authority of the school board to make the final decisions on education policy. Several major differences between IEA and IASB were evident. IASB wanted all administrators excluded from the bargaining unit, while

IEA sought only to exclude central office administrators. IASB also opposed a law that would mandate school boards to bargain with an organization representing a majority of the teaching staff. Instead, it held, the local school board should be able to decide whether to bargain with the teachers. Finally, it opposed binding arbitration; the final decision to settle an impasse should be the board's prerogative. Despite the efforts of the organizations to work together, school boards across the state resisted teachers' demands for a meaningful voice in determining school policy.[59] Nevertheless, PN slowly gained momentum across Illinois. By 1968, IEA reported about one hundred PN agreements, although only five of these were level 4 contracts.[60]

PN was intended to keep teacher organizations independent of organized labor and to preserve "professional unity." Unlike collective bargaining in the private sector, PN kept administrators in the IEA. Large urban locals usually, but not always, excluded principals and other building administrators from the bargaining unit. IASB, too, insisted that superintendents were agents of the school board and could not be included in a bargaining unit. But many superintendents and principals maintained IEA membership through the IASA and other IEA-affiliated administrative organizations. Their involvement in IEA enabled them to be elected to leadership positions in divisions as well as statewide offices.

Given the prominence of school administrators in IEA's top leadership positions, it is not surprising that professional solidarity was viewed by the organization as the key to successful negotiations. In their dual capacity as a professional colleague and the chief executive officer of the school board, the superintendent was considered critical to the success of PN. NEA recommended that the superintendent should serve as a neutral third party in negotiations between the teachers and the school board. Both sides could draw on the superintendent's expertise and experience to resolve their differences. NEA envisioned the "superintendent's role [as] a central one. Since he is probably in possession of more facts about school revenue and needs than anyone else, it is imperative that he is deeply and actively involved." Successful PN would need the superintendent to be the voice of reason whenever heated disagreements occurred. The superintendent must be "free to exercise independent judgment with respect to school matters, serving as adviser to both groups, and so long as free access is maintained between representatives of the staff organization and the school board, then such a procedure can be made to work successfully."[61]

If the two sides reached an impasse, the association called for fact-finding to resolve the dispute. If fact-finding too failed, IEA supported nonbinding mediation by a mutually agreed-on representative of the county superintendent or state education officials. IEA initially opposed the use of the "outside" organizations American Arbitration Association and Federal Mediation and Conciliation Service, which were used by labor unions to settle impasses.[62]

Oscar Weil labeled PN "a perverted substitute for collective bargaining."[63] According to Laird "Larry" Lawlyes, retired IEA director of program development, many teachers as well as the general public, especially in conservative suburban and rural communities, were hesitant to accept "union" collective bargaining by school districts. PN provided a positive terminology for a broad range of approaches to negotiations developed in local communities across the state. PN made the process more acceptable in the eyes of many. Lawlyes stated: "Professional negotiation was often derided by the IFT and some labor leaders (I think unfairly) as a lesser form of collective bargaining. It was used at the time to 'elevate' the notion of collective bargaining both to an audience of teachers and to the court of public opinion that had not yet accepted the idea that educators ought to be engaging in bargaining."[64] Whatever its initial shortcomings as adopted at the 1962 RA in Denver, PN quickly evolved, to the point that it differed very little from private sector negotiations by the late 1960s.

Professional Sanctions

Besides introducing PN, the Denver convention featured a wide-ranging and somewhat bitter discussion over the use of sanctions against school boards or state officials who acted in an arbitrary and unreasonable manner. The discussion ensued about the use of sanctions as an alternative to strikes as a last resort to enforce the use of PN against recalcitrant school boards. Professional sanctions were ill defined, but the delegates adopted the following resolution:

> The NEA believes that, as a means for preventing unethical or arbitrary policies or practices that have a deleterious effect on the welfare of the schools, professional sanctions should be invoked. These sanctions would provide for appropriate disciplinary action by the organized profession.
>
> That NEA calls upon its affiliated state associations to cooperate in developing guidelines, which would define, organize, and definitely specify procedural steps for invoking sanctions by the teaching profession.[65]

Sanctions typically involved an investigation by state association or NEA officials, followed by a public report and recommended actions.[66] For some, sanctions relied on moral persuasion and public censure of school district policies. The association would also notify college teacher placement services about the sanctions, so as to warn prospective teachers about the problems in the district. In the discussion of sanctions at the Denver meeting, this action was framed as a sort of boycott. Sanctions might possibly include encouraging teacher applicants "not to accept employment if the school district offered only substandard conditions. Thus, teachers might withhold their services before a school year opened (without striking and without the injury to pupils involved in a teacher strike)."[67]

Sanctions were left up to state associations to develop, but NEA had, in the past, invoked sanctions for violations of professional ethics, as was the case in the late 1940s with the expulsion of Chicago Public Schools (CPS) superintendent William Johnson for "unprofessional conduct" and the public shaming of Oglesby School District. In 1965, IEA adopted procedures for implementing professional sanctions.[68]

Immediately following the NEA convention, four hundred teachers attended a meeting of the NEA department of classroom teachers to discuss the situation. Dr. T. M. Stinnett, NEA assistant executive secretary for program development and welfare, called a teacher strike "highly questionable" as an economic weapon; however, he added that "the strike in the interest of education and the welfare of the children, as a means of dramatizing public neglect and disgraceful and dangerous conditions," could be effective "when all other appeals to reason and justice have failed." Given NEA's official opposition to strikes, Stinnett suggested that "withholding of professional services" from a school district prior to the start of the school year would not break a contract signed in good faith between the school board and teachers, and would be less disruptive to the education of children.[69] "Withholding of professional services" was a euphemism for striking that helped justify such job actions. In 1967, an IEA survey indicated increasing support among its members, especially among male and high school teachers, for the use of strikes to resolve conflicts with recalcitrant school boards. Professional solidarity was about to give way to professional unionism.[70]

The NEA department of classroom teachers was a driving force in the effort to establish formal procedures for negotiations among state affiliates. As teacher locals increased their demand for assistance across the nation, the department was reorganized, becoming the Association of Classroom Teachers (ACT), an affiliate controlled by member locals rather than NEA staff. IACT, an affiliate of ACT, became the center of teacher power within IEA, as well as the largest IEA affiliate and a major force in the movement for collective bargaining. Because of IACT's teacher advocacy focus, its bylaws barred administrators from holding any elective office in member locals. At the national level, the National Council of Urban Education Associations played a key role in pushing NEA into more militant teacher advocacy.[71]

Affiliates and Services to Members

In 1960, IEA expanded its services to affiliated organizations in an effort to strengthen its "professional family." Affiliates were offered office space and access to facilities at IEA headquarters. IEA created two new departments to provide services to its thirteen affiliates. A professional staff employee was assigned to each department. Their duties included serving as the executive secretary, consultant, and lobbyist for the department's affiliates. One department covered employee affiliates: IACT (classroom teachers), Illinois Association of School Librarians, Illinois Association of School Nurses, Illinois Association of Education Secretaries, Illinois Retired Teachers Association (IRTA), Future Teachers of America, and the Student Illinois Education Association. The other department was responsible for IASA (administrators), Illinois Association of County School Superintendents, Illinois Association of Secondary School Principals, Illinois Junior High Principals Association, Illinois Elementary School Principals Association, and Illinois Association for Supervision and Curriculum Development. During the 1960s, the Illinois Association of Higher Education, Illinois Alliance of Administrators of Special Education, and Illinois High School and College Driver Education Association became affiliates as well. The Illinois Association of Junior Colleges briefly joined but ended its affiliation soon after. Affiliates were also provided with secretarial help. In 1966, three additional staff positions were added to the affiliate services departments, increasing IEA assistance to its affiliated organizations.[72]

Faced with the challenge from IFT, the association built its appeal on "service to members." It developed a broad range of member benefits. All members received liability insurance coverage. Local associations had access to legal services, school district budget research, and PN assistance. IEA and NEA offered discounted member benefits including summer travel and various insurance policies through Horace Mann. In response to a proposal by IRTA, IEA even sponsored a self-funded retirement center in Normal for teacher members. The Shamel Manor retirement home opened in 1964 but never achieved full occupancy. It operated at a loss and was put up for sale in 1969.[73]

Despite efforts by administrators to maintain professional unity, IEA was about to undergo a complete restructuring to become a labor union. Teacher strikes across the United States were increasing in response to school boards and superintendents that resisted collective bargaining. NEA reported that teachers' support for strikes was steadily increasing. In 1965, 53.3 percent supported the right to strike mainly "under extreme conditions and after all other means have failed." By 1974, this support had increased to 79.9 percent. During the same period, teacher opposition to strikes declined from 37.8 percent to 13.9 percent.[74] There were 114 strikes nationally in 1967–68, 131 strikes the next year, and 181 strikes in 1969–70.[75] Between 1960 and 1980, the country experienced over a thousand teacher strikes.

Illinois had its share of job actions as well. During the 1960s, IFT locals engaged in forty strikes involving twenty-seven employers. Downstate East St. Louis walked out five times; Granite City struck three times. Thirty-three of these strikes occurred following an Illinois court decision by Judge Cornelius Harrington in 1966 that ended the notion that school districts could not legally bargain contracts with their employees.[76] IFT bargained some of the earliest comprehensive collective bargaining units. Such militant action raised the credibility of the federation as a progressive alternative to the administration-dominated IEA as an advocate for teachers. Many talented K–12 and higher education activists joined the federation. By the late 1960s, local association leaders were pushing IEA in the same direction as IFT.[77] The first IEA local to strike was Decatur Education Association in 1966. In 1970, IEA reported seven strikes.[78]

Conclusion

Hoping to hold together the education community, IEA leaders responded cautiously to teacher demands for negotiation assistance and the challenge posed by IFT. The 1966 Harrington decision ended the legal argument that Illinois districts could not bargain binding agreements with their employees. NEA conceived PN as an acceptable alternative to collective bargaining, but it quickly evolved into union-style negotiations in Illinois. By 1970, IEA and some of its divisions had hired full-time staff to assist locals with negotiations and contract enforcement. Here lies the basic dilemma for IEA. The very term *professional negotiation* suggested a power-sharing relationship with teacher locals that many superintendents and school boards were not ready to accept. In 1970, teachers took control and IEA became a union.

CHAPTER 7

A Radical Transformation

Teachers will join unions, whether they will be AFT locals, IEA affiliates
or independent groups; and they will follow leadership that gets results.
It is clear, also that the old company union education association will be
either changed overnight into a viable instrument to secure the rights of
teachers or it will be shunted aside in favor of a genuine union.

—IFT executive director Oscar Weil

The transformation of the Illinois Education Association (IEA) into a union was part of a national movement among public school teachers in the 1960s. The successes of organized labor in improving the standard of living for working-class families, along with the civil rights movement, inspired teachers across the nation to demand collective bargaining rights. Faced with demands from teacher activists for assistance in discussions of salary schedule and fringe benefits with school officials, as well as the threat of the Illinois Federation of Teachers (IFT) in many larger districts, IEA increased its field staff and supported professional negotiation (PN) legislation in the General Assembly. Following the 1966 Harrington decision, which said that public employees could bargain collectively with their employers, the competition between IEA and IFT over exclusive representation set in motion events that, within a few years, transformed IEA from a moderate, professional organization into a militant union. In 1974, Illinois Senate minority leader Cecil Partee (D-Chicago) congratulated IEA: "You have turned your organization around in the last three or four years. . . . I applaud you for making a conscious and determined effort to transform the IEA from a passive, status quo type association into a positive, goal-oriented action group."[1]

The Harrington Decision

The absence of any state law or court decision to define the recognition of exclusive representation created confusion for school districts. Faced with competing claims for recognition, some districts recognized both IEA and IFT as bargaining representatives and met with each organization separately to consider their concerns. Others simply refused to recognize any organization as the teachers' representative. In Chicago, the Chicago Teachers Union (CTU) threatened to conduct a strike vote unless Chicago Public Schools (CPS) agreed to exclusive representation.[2] In February 1964, the board recognized CTU as a bargaining agent, but in March, it also recognized the IEA Chicago division as a representative. CTU postponed its strike vote after CPS scheduled an election to settle the controversy. The Chicago Education Association, a Chicago division teacher affiliate, filed a lawsuit to block the election.[3] In November 1966, the *Chicago Education Association v. Chicago Board of Education* case resolved the issue when the Chicago appellate court upheld an earlier decision of circuit court judge Cornelius Harrington. The Harrington decision included the following provisions:

1. the board of education has the right to enter into a written agreement with an exclusive bargaining agent
2. it has the authority to conduct an exclusive representation election
3. written agreements covering negotiation procedures and grievances are mutually binding
4. strikes and other disruptive picketing are illegal
5. employees have a right to organizations of their choosing
6. individuals have a right to represent themselves before the board
7. items raised with the board need not wait implementation through negotiations
8. decisions must apply equally to all employees
9. the board has final decision-making authority[4]

When the Illinois Supreme Court refused to consider an appeal of the Harrington decision, it established a legal precedent governing collective bargaining. CTU easily defeated CEA in a representation election in 1967.[5] The Chicago Teachers Federation (CTF) disbanded after the CTU victory.[6]

The Harrington decision opened the floodgates for bargaining. It ended the long-standing argument that school boards could not legally bargain away their sovereign power by signing contracts with their employees. The decision allowed but did not require school boards to grant exclusive recognition to a majority local. It did not address a process for determining majority status. Faced with demands for bargaining by their teachers, some districts agreed voluntarily to recognize locals that could prove majority status or had conducted internal elections to determine majority status. In some districts, the turmoil created by the bitter rivalry between IEA and IFT locals served as an incentive for school boards to conduct an election; others, encouraged by the Illinois Association of School Boards (IASB), simply refused to bargain.

Decatur Strike

In November 1966, the Decatur Education Association (DEA) walked out for two days; it was IEA's first strike. Prior to the strike, DEA had met directly with the school board to discuss a salary index, class size, and other concerns. Superintendent Les Grant strongly objected to the meeting as an infringement of his duties as chief administrator of the staff. In response, the board adopted a salary plan that was totally unacceptable to the teachers. DEA called a meeting for six o'clock the next morning at the county fairgrounds, which almost every teacher attended. A motion to strike passed, and the strike commenced. The National Education Association (NEA) provided the local with much-appreciated assistance, but IEA, still under the control of administrators, remained neutral, much to the dismay of DEA teachers. Many teachers questioned their membership in IEA. When the board obtained a court injunction, DEA teachers returned to work, but not before receiving assurance that the district would work with DEA to resolve the issues that led to the strike.[7] According to DEA chief negotiator Earl Rudolph: "To resolve the conflict, both sides sought outside professional help. DEA retained an attorney, and the district hired an Illinois State University professor. The recommendations of the professor basically supported the DEA's position. Subsequently, the board approved a 4 percent salary index and settled several other issues."[8]

The Decatur strike not only opened the door for DEA to bargain contractual improvements over the next several years, but also served as a wake-up call to IEA about the growing support for collective bargaining. Facing strong criticism from one of its largest locals, IEA adopted a "clean hands" policy that opposed the use of court injunctions against strikes. IEA claimed that unreasonable school boards needlessly provoked strikes and disrupted public education out of desperation. Courts should not take a side in such disputes when the quality of education is at stake. IEA also announced that it would assist locals on strike even though it remained officially opposed to such job actions.[9] Nevertheless, IEA's reputation among DEA teachers was not fully restored until 1971, when DEA again went on strike.

Responding to Support for Collective Bargaining

By leaving decisions regarding collective bargaining solely to the discretion of school boards, the Harrington decision amplified the need for legislation to govern the process. Many states had already enacted bargaining laws. New Hampshire was the first state to do so, in 1955, followed by Alaska in 1959 and Wisconsin in 1962. By 1969, twenty-two states had bargaining laws covering teachers.[10]

The IEA representative assembly (RA) passed resolutions in 1967 and 1968 calling on the legislature to enact bargaining legislation. In 1969, IEA drafted its first comprehensive PN bill. Representative Gene Hoffman (R-Elmhurst), a former IEA member, sponsored House Bill 1235. It only covered teachers. Its provisions included the right to organize for bargaining, a department of employee relations in the Office of the Superintendent of Public Instruction to oversee enforcement, an unfair labor practices definition, procedures for determining exclusive representation, advisory fact-finding and mediation, and a limited right to strike.[11]

House Bill 1235 passed the House by a wide margin (115–9) but failed in the Senate by six votes. Only one Democratic senator voted in favor of the bill.[12] Opponents not only included conservative legislators and IASB, but also IFT. Executive director Oscar Weil of IFT, with the backing of the State Federation of Labor (SFL), organized union opposition to IEA's bill. IFT was engaged in a bitter fight with IEA over exclusive representation. Weil continued to label the association as a "company union," despite the association's increasing advocacy of teacher welfare. Weil opposed any law that included a state labor board to oversee bargaining recognition; he believed that such an agency would give IEA the distinct advantage of extra time to organize against IFT efforts to take over local associations. His disdain for IEA precluded any effort to compromise on legislation. Weil wrote, "I worked with conservative legislators, with legislators who were allied with Chicago's mayor [Richard J.] Daley, and with downstate legislators" to defeat the IEA bill.[13] This coalition would continue to thwart IEA's efforts to pass a law throughout the 1970s.

In response to the demand of members for assistance in negotiations and the intense rivalry with IFT over representation, IEA expanded its field services. Prior to the Harrington decision, IEA had six field staff and only one office outside of Springfield. In the two years following the Harrington decision, IEA added four new field staff positions and opened eight new regional field offices. Their stated purpose was to organize new locals and to initiate PN whenever possible. In order to encourage divisions to establish regional service centers, IEA provided stipends for divisions to hire full-time executive directors to assist their locals. Some divisions, like Lake Shore and DuPage Valley, hired their own full-time executive directors, while others pooled their resources to hire staff. By September 1969, sixteen full-time professional field staff were providing services for the twenty-two divisions. IEA also hired and trained twenty-five local leaders as part-time "negotiators" to assist locals.[14] Robert Jensen, the field representative hired by the Northwestern and Rock River divisions, stated:

Following the Harrington decision, there was a rush to establish local associations as more formal, functioning organizations prepared to represent the rights of their members. Previously, many local associations functioned more like social clubs, with membership often including the district administration. It was a step-by-step process. Depending on the strength and determination of the teachers, I would help them win exclusive representation and bargain agreements with their school boards. At first, these agreements often were very limited in scope, but [they] eventually evolved into full-blown contracts.[15]

IEA also began publishing a monthly newsletter, *Insight*, in September 1966. Unlike the journal *Illinois Education*, which tended to run forty or more pages in length, *Insight* varied from four to eight pages in length and did not include any advertisement. It kept locals informed on legislative matters, organizing, training programs, bargaining, and other important news in a concise manner. In many respects, it was IEA's version of IFT's *Illinois Union Teacher*. *Insight* was published from 1966 to 1971. That year, *Insight*, along with *Illinois Education*, was replaced by *Advocate: The Voice of Education in Illinois*.[16]

As IEA expanded its member services, graduated dues were regularly raised. In 1969, dues ranged from fifteen to forty-five dollars.[17] A debate ensued over the graduated dues provision, which had been adopted in 1938. Since individual members and every local, no matter how small, had equal access to the array of IEA expanded services available by 1970, it was deemed only fair that everyone should pay the same dues amount. In contrast, many low-paid teachers, especially from downstate districts, favored retaining graduated dues.[18] At the 1970 RA, IEA adopted flat-rate annual dues equating to 0.3 percent of the average instructional salary.[19] Though bylaws and resolutions only required a simple majority to pass, budgets with dues increases required a two-thirds majority. Dues increases were often the most contentious issue facing the RA, provoking hours of vigorous debate among delegates. Downstate members generally supported lower dues increases. The amounts supported by the leadership and the majority of delegates quite often did not pass. Compromise often resulted in lower dues increases than the amount supported by the board of directors. In 2023, IEA once again passed a graduated dues structure.

The Harrington decision marked a new stage in the rivalry between IEA and IFT over organizing, a rivalry that would last into the 1990s. Both organizations rushed to organize and win exclusive recognition. The *Illinois Union Teacher* wrote: "Every AFT local in Illinois that has not yet won a collective bargaining contract must be prepared for contests with the education associations that are certain to occur in most school districts in Illinois in the next few years for the right to be exclusive bargaining agent of teachers in their jurisdictions."[20]

Prior to the Harrington decision, IEA had only 278 K–12 local associations; 1,012 districts did not have locals. In the next seven years (1966–72), IEA chartered 362 new locals.[21] Though administrators played a leading role in many of the smaller locals, teachers controlled almost all the larger urban districts by 1970. The rapid surge in locals increased membership involvement and contributed to the emergence of leaders who transformed IEA into a union.

For its part, IFT had chartered 135 locals, excluding the CPS units, since 1916. By 1965, only 75 of these unions still existed. Though focused chiefly on public K–12 teachers, IFT chartered other groups as well. In CPS, there were locals for truant officers, school secretaries, and librarians. In 1933, the federation chartered a local at the University of Chicago—its first in higher education. Later, it chartered locals at the University of Illinois and Roosevelt College. IFT even had locals among East St. Louis principals and Catholic schools in the Archdiocese Chicago and Diocese of Joliet.

Although many of its locals collapsed, the number of local charters does not accurately reflect IFT's organizing successes. Some IFT locals that disbanded, such as Benton Elementary, Granite City, and East St. Louis, would later reorganize and thrive. In addition, IFT chartered three "federated" (multi–bargaining unit) locals in the Chicago area. West Suburban Local 571 was its largest federated local, with councils (i.e., bargaining units) in thirteen school districts. In the seven years following the Harrington decision, IFT organized forty-four new unions. By 1972, the federation had local unions competing against IEA in about one hundred K–12 Illinois districts (see table 9).

Teachers in urban locals outside Cook County, including Champaign, Urbana, Decatur, Rock Island, Rockford, Elgin, and DeKalb, provided the impetus for the movement that transformed IEA into a union. These efforts began at the division level. Joe Pasteris of the DeKalb Classroom Teachers' Association explained: "Teachers in the Chicago suburbs were very well paid compared to the rest of the state. For the most part, they were relatively timid; school administrators controlled

Table 9. New Locals Chartered by IEA and IFT, Excluding CPS, 1920–1972

Years	IEA		IFT	
	K–12	Higher ed.	K–12	Higher ed.
1920s	9	0	1	0
1930s	5	0	15	0
1940s	62	0	20	0
1950s	83	0	23	1
1960–65	119	0	16	2
1966–72	362	18	44	13
Total, pre-1965	278	0	75	3
Total, all years	640	18	119	16

Sources: AFT, "Statistical Report by States: April 15, 1916-February 1, 1976," 1976, author's collection; *Affiliated Local Associations—Illinois: 1973–74*, 237–44.

Note: These figures do not include IFT locals that had disbanded by 1972 or IFT charters for Catholic schools in Chicago (1967) and Joliet (1971).

the IEA suburban divisions. We realized that if the situation was going to improve, we needed to be in charge. So we started attending Rock River division meetings, and, by the late 1960s, teachers were in control."[22]

By 1970, a majority of division presidents were either classroom teachers or other nonsupervisory employees. Of the twenty-two division presidents, there were eleven teachers, a school librarian, a guidance counselor, and a department chair. Only one superintendent was a president; the seven other division presidents included an assistant superintendent, four principals, a director of guidance, and an elementary coordinator.[23]

The growing rift between locals and school boards over bargaining made working within "professional channels" to settle disputes less productive. IEA supported the use of the American Arbitration Association, the Federal Mediation and Conciliation Service, and other such "outside" organizations to mediate impasses.[24] IEA continued to redefine its position on negotiations, to the extent that by 1970, PN differed very little from the collective bargaining advocated by IFT. In 1967, the Illinois Association of School Administrators (IASA) hired a full-time executive secretary rather than relying on IEA staff for services, clearly indicating the growing tension between administrators and teachers over collective bargaining. In 1970, IEA conducted seven strikes. IASA, at the time a thousand-member organization, dropped its affiliation, moved out of IEA headquarters, and established its own Springfield office that year.[25]

IEA's Constitutional Convention

The 1970 RA set the stage for the official transformation of IEA into a union. The RA adopted a resolution calling for a constitutional convention to completely reorganize IEA. Con Con, as it was called, was the final step in transforming IEA into a union.

At the 1970 RA, IEA local leaders revolted against the school administrators who controlled the association's board. Despite the fact that nine of the eleven board members were administrators, teachers were clearly in control of the annual meeting. The RA delegates "flatly rejected" a report by the ad hoc committee on governance and structure that included a proposal to replace the annual RA, attended by over seven hundred delegates, with a forty- to sixty-member board of governors. This proposal was roundly criticized as undemocratic and in "direct opposition to the concept of teacher control." Instead, the RA adopted a resolution mandating a statewide constitutional convention, charged with "creating a new structure of organization and operation."[26] This resolution authorized each division to elect three delegates by May 1 (two months after the RA), with at least two being teachers, to meet in August to draft new bylaws. The resolution also established a nonvoting advisory board consisting of three field staff, a representative from each affiliated organization, and an executive-level staff member.[27] Elgin junior high teacher Mel Swiedarke chaired the Con Con meeting. A preliminary draft of the bylaws was published in the October issue of *Insight*, after which open hearings were held around the state for input from members. A final draft was published two weeks prior to the 1971 RA.[28]

The 1970 RA delegates also passed a unified dues amendment that required all members to belong to their local association, IEA, and NEA. Previously, IEA members had the option (but were not required) to join NEA and the local teacher associations, and only two divisions and thirty locals had unified dues, even though a majority of IEA members did join NEA.[29] In addition, many school administrators joined IEA through professional organizations affiliated with IEA rather than through locals. Most large urban locals excluded superintendents, principals, and supervisors; the unified dues amendment effectively ended their IEA membership. Besides IASA, five other administrative affiliates representing principals and school supervisors eventually ended their ties to IEA, resulting in the loss of over three thousand members.[30]

The 1970 RA budget also provided for a full-time release president. Although a handful of teachers had previously served as president, they could not devote the time that administrators could to the job. The presidency had been largely a ceremonial position. The term of office was just one year. Creating a full-time release presidency meant that teacher leaders would take direct oversight of the daily operations of the organization and the management of IEA staff in Springfield.[31] Ironically, the first full-time president of the emerging teacher union was a Glen Ellyn principal, Dwight Knous. He was the president-elect and next in line to assume the presidency as provided in the IEA bylaws. Knous was the last school administrator to serve as president.[32] Throughout the 1970s, elected leaders would increasingly assert their authority over management. In 1974, the presidential term of office was increased to two years (effective 1975); a vice presidency was also created, replacing the positions of past president and president-elect. Officers could serve a maximum of two terms.[33] These changes significantly increased the power of IEA governance over the day-to-day operations of the headquarters staff. In 1980, an elected secretary-treasurer position was created. Initially, only the president was a full-time release officer. Today, the president, vice president, and secretary-treasurer are full-time, paid positions. They can serve two three-year terms.

Finally, the 1970 RA authorized the hiring of Morris Andrews as assistant director of field services and coordinator of negotiations. Andrews had previously worked for the Michigan Education Association, one of the earliest NEA affiliates to engage in bargaining. He also served as a negotiation specialist in the NEA

Midwest Office prior to being hired by IEA. Andrews was a talented organizer and totally committed to expanding collective bargaining in Illinois. He worked closely with Mel Swiedarke, Blanche Erst, Joe Pasteris, and other key leaders in planning a strategy to pass the bylaws at the 1971 RA.[34]

The New IEA

In February 1971, the RA approved the new bylaws without any amendments, but not without some drama.[35] The delegate credentials of twenty school administrators, including some affiliate presidents and a member of the IEA board, were challenged on the grounds that they were not qualified under the new unified dues rules. In a ruling by the president, they were seated on the second and third days of the meeting, since their elections occurred prior to the adoption of unified membership. The new board of directors sent a letter to the challenged delegates explaining the situation and apologizing for the confusion. In April, all members received mailed ballots that had to be returned to their respective divisions. In May, the divisions counted the ballots and the bylaws were ratified, becoming effective on July 1, 1971.[36]

The new bylaws put teachers clearly in control of the association. The bylaws replaced the twenty-one divisions with forty region councils. The new board of directors was increased from eleven to fifty-one members. Besides the forty region council chairs, the board included the three IEA officers, four NEA directors, two directors at-large, and the presidents of the Student Illinois Education Association and the Illinois Association of Classroom Teachers (IACT). All but two of the board members were classroom teachers. An executive committee was established to meet prior to the board meetings to prepare the agenda. The executive committee included the president, president-elect, an NEA director, and five members elected by the board.[37]

The region councils greatly expanded membership involvement in all levels of decision-making. Having almost twice as many regional bodies made traveling much easier for members to attend meetings. IEA provided each region with an annual reimbursement based on its full-time equivalent membership. Region councils used this money to conduct leadership trainings, reimburse members for official business, pay for social events, and fund other programs for their locals.[38] The councils served as a two-way conduit between the locals and the state organization. Each local elected delegates to serve on the region council, based on proportional representation. Every local, no matter how small, qualified for at least one delegate. Local association members elected a region chairperson to conduct monthly council meetings and to serve on the board in Springfield. To ensure a measure of continuity on the board, the terms of office were staggered over three years in 1971, so that only one-third of the region chairs would be elected each year. After that, all region chairs served two-year terms.[39] Since most members of the board were elected directly by the membership in their respective regions, the new bylaws ensured that state officials could not handpick the governing body. Instead, regional leaders wielded considerable power in their dealings with IEA management and state leaders.

Grassroots democracy was further advanced when IEA adopted the NEA Unified Service (UniServ) program.[40] NEA created this program in 1970 to incentivize state and local associations to adopt unified dues by providing financial assistance for hiring professional field staff. Under the program, any local or state affiliate with unified dues and at least 1,200 members received an annual $7,500 grant and $1,500 in training funds to hire a UniServ director. Once the new IEA bylaws were ratified, IEA joined the UniServ program and each region council qualified for a UniServ director. Rather than the state organization assigning UniServ staff to the regions, local leaders, for the most part, controlled their hiring and supervision. Executive secretary Wayne Stoneking explained that locals "will supervise, direct, participate in employment of, and participate in the disemployment of the UniServ director."[41]

Even though the state organization was responsible for their compensation and expenses, UniServ directors were hired and held accountable by the locals they served. To fill a vacancy, local association presidents would form hiring committees and select candidates from a hiring pool to interview for the position. Candidates in the hiring pool were vetted by management and approved by the board, but the region hiring committee would decide which candidates to interview and make a hiring recommendation to the board. Approval of the region's recommendation was a mere formality. Subsequently, the region council leaders regularly evaluated the performance of the UniServ staff. UniServ director John McCluskey dubbed this process "decentralized polity."[42]

The bylaws established a strict division between staff and governance. IEA employees were prohibited from voting at the RA, seeking elected positions, and participating in other governance activities. Consequently, most leaders, hired for staff positions, did not continue their IEA membership. Instead, they organized unions. In 1971, IEA voluntarily agreed to negotiate contracts with two staff unions: the IEA Staff Organization (IEASO, for professional staff) and the IEA Secretaries Association (IEASA, for associate staff). Managerial staff and their administrative assistants were excluded from these bargaining units. A staff union protected the members from arbitrary or vindictive action by management and governance. These unions also gave the staff a mechanism to influence governance policies through contract negotiations. IEASO affiliated with the National Staff Organization (NSO), which, today, has over four thousand members employed by NEA and its affiliates. NSO is the largest union representing union staff in the United

States. The two IEA unions merged under the IEASO banner in 1987, but they still remain separate bargaining units due to the managerial role of UniServ directors in supervising associate staff. Since 1989, a single team of professional and associate staff have bargained both IEASO contracts. As a result, most but not all the language and benefits of the contracts are the same.[43]

About half of the forty professional UniServ positions created under the new bylaws included staff who had been hired by divisions under the old bylaws and IEA field staff previously assigned to offices across the state. About twenty other UniServ directors had to be hired soon after the ratification of the bylaws. Many of the teachers hired for the expanded field staff had limited organizing and bargaining experience outside of their own school districts. In the rush to fill so many positions, some of these initial UniServ directors proved to be inadequate for the job.[44] Morris Andrews used NEA training funds to provide extensive and ongoing UniServ training on negotiations, grievance/arbitration, organizing, and other servicing needs. Some UniServ directors viewed themselves primarily as negotiators and as a resource to help locals enforce their contracts, but failed to appreciate the importance of organizing as an integral aspect of their work. Organizing skills were especially important to meet the threat posed by anti-union school boards seeking to undermine IEA locals. Without organizing, dysfunctional locals floundered, opening the door for IFT raiding. To remedy the situation, Andrews contracted Saul Alinsky's Industrial Areas Foundation (IAF) to train staff in confrontational organizing techniques. IAF taught staff how to mobilize union and community members to confront intractable superintendents and school boards. IAF training was especially helpful in crisis management and strikes.[45] IEA had a growing number of strikes in the 1970s. Ironically, IFT, which had been so critical of IEA's lack of militancy in the 1960s, criticized the association in its campaign literature on the grounds that "they out strike us." IFT circulated a flyer that claimed IEA had 209 strikes compared to only 40 by IFT from 1976 to 1983.[46] This criticism is somewhat misleading, given the fact that IEA had three times as many teacher bargaining units as IFT (see table 10).

Wayne Stoneking retired soon after the 1971 RA. In April, IEA hired Curtis Plott as executive secretary. Plott had previously, as assistant executive secretary, helped reorganize the California Teachers Association as a union. He was described as a charismatic personality, someone self-assured and always well dressed, and a "forthright public speaker for teacher rights."[47] His forceful management style would eventually lead to conflicts within the board of directors and the staff unions, but he provided solid leadership during the implementation of the newly adopted bylaws.[48] In April 1971, Plott wrote a six-page report describing his proposals to reorganize IEA in accordance with the new constitution.[49]

Table 10. K–12 Teacher Bargaining Units

	1973–74	1980–81	1986–87	1992–93	2013–14
IEA					
Elementary	117	129	204	237	229
High school	47	49	72	71	63
Unit	157	188	347	336	295
Total	321	366	623	644	587
IFT					
Elementary	24	59	90	93	92
High school	14	19	27	27	24
Unit	12	23	53	61	57
Total	50	101	170	181	173
Other*					
Elementary	27	12	18	15	5
High school	9	4	5	4	1
Unit	16	4	10	6	3
Total	52	20	33	25	9

Sources: Superintendent of Public Instruction, "Illinois Teacher Salary Schedule Study: 1973–74"; Superintendent of Public Instruction, "Illinois Teacher Salary Schedule and Contract Provision Study: 1980–1981"; ISBE, *Teacher Salary Study*, for years 1986–87, 1992–93, 2013–14.

* Includes independent unions, IEA/IFT confederations, and unions affiliated with organizations other than IEA or IFT.

Plott's most immediate task was reorganizing headquarters management to meet IEA's needs. Besides Stoneking, there were at least eight other retirements of IEA staff as a result of the radical changes under the new bylaws. Programs that assisted its school administrator affiliates were eliminated; most staff working with these affiliated organizations retired or took positions with other organizations. Plott created five departments: field services, legislative and political action, public relations, business services, and professional development. The responsibilities of each department were clearly defined. Assistant executive secretaries managed each department. Field services, by far the largest department, included two field coordinators to assist in the supervision of field staff.[50] As manager of field services, Andrews maintained a positive working relationship with the UniServ staff. However, the relationship between Plott and Andrews was strained from the beginning. Plott did not trust him; he believed that Andrews, who had applied for the executive secretary position, was behind the opposition he faced among UniServ staff. Andrews left IEA in 1972 to become the executive secretary in Wisconsin.[51]

IEA completely restructured its affiliate program. Previously, there had been fourteen organizations that "coordinated their activities through the services of IEA," with many of their members also joining IEA. Under the new system, the Illinois Association of Higher Education (IAHE), though not attached to a geographic region, became the forty-first region council. IAHE included twenty-four higher education locals. The Student IEA and IACT became departments, which had to maintain 100 percent unified IEA membership and were given seats on the IEA board of directors. IACT membership declined from 2,457 in 1970 to 1,139 the next year. It had outlived its purpose once teachers controlled the organization, and so it disbanded in 1972. The other statewide organizations had one year to decide whether to be an affiliate or an associated organization. The new affiliate classification required at least 50 percent IEA membership. The Illinois Association of School Librarians, the Illinois Association of School Nurses, and the Illinois Retired Teachers Association (IRTA) became IEA affiliates. The third classification, associated organizations, required no IEA membership. It included the Illinois Association of Administrators of Special Education and the Illinois High School and College Driver Education Association. The 2,700-member Illinois Principals Association (IPA) was created when three organizations representing high school, junior high, and elementary principals merged.[52] IPA was closely tied to IRTA. Both organizations eventually severed their ties with IEA, as did the Association of Administrators of Special Education.

Reorganizing the Regions

According to Wayne Stoneking, IEA was committed to "equaliz[ing] services for the members."[53] It soon became apparent that many inequities existed in terms of service. Regions 1 and 2 in the northwest part of the state covered 9 counties, 89 locals, and 3,900 members. Rockford, the largest urban district in the area, was a separate region unto itself. In the sparsely populated downstate regions, servicing locals was especially difficult. Regions 36–39 encompassed 32 southern counties and 274 school districts.[54] A UniServ research committee was appointed by the board of directors to make recommendations on realigning the regions. The reorganization took over two years to achieve. In 1973, four new regions were created and some locals were moved into neighboring regions with lower membership to achieve a more equitable balance.[55]

Having hundreds of small- and medium-sized locals necessitated extensive leadership training programs. Plott established collective bargaining conferences in the fall to help locals prepare for upcoming negotiations in the spring; he also expanded the annual four-day Summer Leadership Academy for emerging leaders and officers. Academy workshops were designed to improve leadership skills of local officers, increase membership involvement, and organize strong locals. Hundreds of members across the state attended these statewide conferences. Such trainings were a major responsibility of the IEA staff. Field offices also held workshops throughout the school year. UniServ directors often coordinated training programs with other locals in their office or even pooled their resources with other offices for regional conferences. Plott started the development of training manuals covering model contract language and crisis organizing.[56]

Support for Human Rights: Minorities and Women

As far back as the Civil War era, the association had consistently supported equal educational opportunities for all children, regardless of race, creed, sex, or national origin. In the twentieth century, IEA remained relatively silent about racial injustice until World War II. After the war, IEA publicly condemned Jim Crow, supported school integration, and took a stand on human rights at home and abroad. In the late 1960s, many high schools began to experience racial unrest as integration increased. In response, IEA established a human relations committee chaired by John Capocy, a Downers Grove teacher, to champion "just and equal treatment of all people." According to Capocy, "The focus of attention in the development of human relations programs can include, among many others, such topics as curriculum change, training teacher trainers, in-service education for present staff of teachers, recruitment of minority staff personnel, racially isolated white schools, crisis situations in the schools and community."[57]

After teachers took over, IEA became more outspoken in its commitment to human rights causes. The board of directors adopted the following policy statement: "Education associations must be about the business of helping school systems design the kind of cross-cultural, multi-ethnic, multi-racial experiences which will produce mutual understanding and respect among children of different races and cultural backgrounds. This is an essential element of an education for a productive happy life in a complex, changing society."[58] IEA established a Center for Human Relations (as had NEA) and hired Albert Raby as its full-time director.[59] Raby, a former Chicago teacher and civil rights activist, had played a leading role in the fight against CPS superintendent Benjamin Willis's policy to maintain racial segregation in the city's schools in the 1960s. Segregated housing in Chicago's Black neighborhoods meant overcrowded schools. To remedy the situation, CPS set up mobile classrooms, called "Willis wagons," rather than enrolling Black students in underutilized white schools. Working with the Chicago Urban League and parent groups, Raby organized protests. Willis was forced to resign, and the use of mobile classrooms to relieve overcrowding was reduced significantly.[60]

As IEA's director of the Center for Human Relations, Raby worked with civil rights groups, government agencies, local associations, and community organizations "to improve human relations in the classroom as well as within the education profession and the community." Progress in human rights required the center to "take the abstract idea and make it concrete."[61]

At the annual RA, IEA "honored individuals who have made significant strides towards improving interracial relationships affecting education and their communities" with a Human Relations Award.[62] The IEA endorsed the lettuce boycott and contributed $500 to the United Farm Workers. It was outspoken in its support of the Equal Rights Amendment, bilingual education, and minority representation in its governance. In 1974, it adopted a bylaw provision that provided that four ethnic-minority candidates be elected to the board of directors. IEA later added a bylaw that provided for each region to elect at large one ethnic-minority delegate to the annual RA. These at-large delegates were in addition to any ethnic-minority delegates elected by the local associations in the regions. Ethnic minority was defined as American Indian/Alaska Native, Asian/Pacific Islander, African American, or Latino.[63]

Encouraged by Plott, Reg Weaver, Pearl Mack, Anne Davis, Patty Brown-Barnes, Patricio Perez, Tony Vasquez, and other activists organized a minority caucus in 1972 to address the concerns of ethnic-minority members within the mostly white association. Though largely composed of African Americans, the caucus included Asians, Latinos, and Native Americans. It encouraged minority teacher involvement, agitated for appointments to statewide committees, urged IEA to support civil rights legislation, and encouraged the election of friendly candidates to public office. It also worked with the Center for Human Relations on programs to improve educational opportunities for minority students and combat racism. The caucus was instrumental in electing minority candidates to region council chairs and statewide office.[64] In 1973, Region 19 chairman Reg Weaver from Harvey lost a runoff election for president to Woody Lee.[65] From 1977 to 1981, Weaver served as IEA's vice president. He became IEA's first African American president in 1981. Anne Davis became IEA's first female African American president in 1999.[66] By 1990, eleven members (20 percent) of the board of directors were ethnic minority.[67]

Responding to criticism about the failure to hire minorities, IEA created an intern program to identify, train, and hire minority staff in 1974. Patty Brown-Barnes was the first female African American UniServ director hired under the program. A few years later, NEA set up a national intern program modeled on the IEA program. By the late 1970s, Brown-Barnes and several other minority staff from Illinois and Indiana began meeting at her house to discuss the difficulties facing minorities being hired. Similar discussions among minority staff occurred in other states. A National Black Staff Network (NBSN) soon emerged. The main focus of this network was to encourage states to hire interns from the NEA program and to serve as a mentoring system for African American staff. Brown-Barnes regularly provided trainings at the network's conferences. In 2003, the network recognized her "outstanding contributions to NBSN and advocacy on behalf of African American employees of NEA and its affiliates."[68]

IEA hiring of minorities slowly improved. By 1990, legal services had hired two minority attorneys—Sandra Holman (African American) and Feliz Berlanga

(Latino). Four of the IEA staff's ten organizers were African American, but Brown-Barnes was still the only African American UniServ director. None of the eleven managers were minorities. In all, seven members (8 percent) of the IEA professional staff were ethnic minority. Ever since, progress has been made.[69] By 2020, eighteen members (23 percent) of the professional staff were minorities—thirteen African American, five Latino, and one Asian American.[70]

Since the association's founding in the mid-1800s, IEA leadership had always been overwhelmingly male. This pattern continued even after the adoption of the new bylaws. While Blanche Erst was a key leader in IEA's transformation into a union and served as president in 1972, she was the only woman on the executive committee. Seventy-seven percent of all K–12 teachers were female at the time, but just seven of the forty region chairs were women. Even more striking, all but two of the forty original UniServ directors were men, as well as all the managers in Springfield.[71]

In 1972, a women's caucus was organized to address women's rights and encourage female involvement in IEA. Illinois was critical to efforts to pass the Equal Rights Amendment. The caucus lobbied unsuccessfully for the passage of the amendment and targeted for defeat legislators who opposed it. In 1974, the caucus hosted its first dinner during the RA. Marline Rennels, president of the Illinois chapter of the National Organization for Women and an Elgin Teachers Association member, was the honored speaker.[72] Over the next ten years, the number of women elected to leadership positions increased significantly. In 1983, twenty-five of the fifty-one members of the board of directors were women, including eighteen region chairs. Change came much slower in hiring women staff. In 1983, only one of the ten managers was female; seven of the thirty-eight UniServ directors were women. Just ten of the fifty-six professional staff members were women. By 1990, the number of female UniServ directors had increased to twenty-six. In 2020, 53 percent of the professional staff was female, including seven of the thirteen managers (see table 11).

Table 11. Women in IEA Leadership Roles

| Year | IEA board of directors | | Professional staff | |
	No. directors	No. women (%)	No. staff	No. women (%)
1972	51	8 (16)	57	3 (5)
1983	51	25 (49)	55*	9 (16)
1990	54	29 (54)	88	26 (30)
2020	88	61 (69)	118	62 (53)

Sources: Illinois Education 60, no. 1 (September 1971): 24; NEA, "Profiles of State Associations," for years 1982–83, 1989–90; IEA Department of Business Services Membership, 2020.

* Two regions were eliminated as a result of declining membership.

Illinois Political Action Committee for Education (IPACE)

In IEA's early years, prior to the adoption of the new bylaws, each division would elect a representative to serve on the IEA legislative committee. This committee's primary purpose was to prepare a report and make recommendations regarding IEA's legislative agenda at the RA. IEA did not endorse candidates for office. Lobbying was left largely to staff in Springfield. After the new bylaws were adopted, in contrast, IEA began endorsing, contributing to, and campaigning for candidates, and mobilizing members for political action.[73]

At the 1971 RA, a group of delegates led by James Bernier of Pekin announced the creation of EDPAC, a political action committee independent of IEA. It had three levels of membership: $25 sustaining, $10 contributing, and under $10 friend. It collected $3,900 in voluntary contributions.[74] EDPAC was short lived, but it prompted IEA to create the Illinois Political Action Committee for Education (IPACE) to manage its electoral efforts and legislative agenda. At first, IPACE had no dedicated revenue stream, relying instead on contributions from individual members. In 1972, the RA assessed each member $5 for the IPACE fund. Individual members could opt out of paying this fee upon written request, but few bothered to do so. As recalled by Larry Lawlyes, lobbyist Robert Burgess noted that IPACE "harnessed the forces of apathy."[75] Local associations could receive, upon written request, a rebate of between $1 and $2.50 per member for their own political action fund, depending on their needs. The IPACE dues assessment generated over $300,000. In addition, a $50 per plate dinner at the RA that year generated $20,000, giving IEA a sizable war chest to pursue its political agenda. IPACE funds were kept in a separate account as required by law. IEA reorganized its central office staff to manage legislation and political education, and to supervise lobbyists assigned to IPACE activities.[76]

When not dealing with Springfield politics, lobbyists helped locals establish their own political action committees. The rebate provided an incentive for locals to get politically involved. Locals could use their IPACE rebates to interview and endorse candidates for their school boards. IEA lobbyists conducted political action workshops to train local activists. IEA also assisted locals with school board elections, bond campaigns, and tax referenda. The chairperson of each local IPACE committee became a member of the legislative district committee, which interviewed candidates for the General Assembly and made endorsement recommendations to the board of directors. The state IPACE committee consisted of the three officers and thirteen members of the board of directors. Its responsibility was to make endorsement recommendations for governor and other statewide offices to the IEA board.[77]

IEA made membership involvement in political affairs a high priority. IPACE sponsored legislative breakfasts for members to meet legislators. It arranged school tours for legislators to learn about member concerns and the problems facing schools in their legislative districts. At the end of each school year, IPACE held Lobby Day. As many as two thousand members from across the state arrived in Springfield to lobby their representatives in support of public education. Lobby Day connected rank-and-file members to their representatives in the legislature. IEA lobbyist Larry Lawlyes stated: "The association took the position that it wasn't enough to just represent members to the legislature. [It needed] to raise members' level of awareness of political issues affecting public education and to involve members directly in the political processes. We always felt our greatest power was in the numbers of members we had in virtually every legislative district in the state rather than just the money we could raise. Few organizations have members who can vote and who can be active in all parts of the state."[78]

IPACE became a political powerhouse. It had local associations in all 102 counties in the state.[79] Though IEA leaned more toward the Democratic camp, it maintained close ties with moderate Republicans. In heavy Republican areas in the Chicago suburbs and downstate, IEA actively supported pro-education Republicans in the primary, knowing that the winners would be elected in the general election. With support from both parties in the legislature, IEA was able to get IPACE legislation enacted. In 1974, Chicago Democrat Cecil Partee, minority leader in the state Senate, stated: "This organization is widely acknowledged to be a major lobby force for education: a lobby that has power and influence. To ignore or slight education means to incur the IEA's wrath and, if you are a legislator, it could well spell doom on Election Day."[80]

IEA also had full-time lobbyists working both sides of the aisle in the General Assembly. At that time, Dave Elder lead the legislative and political action department, which included Ken Bruce and Bob Burgess. Elder did not ideologically fit in with the new IEA. He left IEA and became a staff member for the Republican Party in the Illinois Senate. He spent the rest of his career opposing much of IEA's efforts. Bruce became the director of the department. Bruce primarily worked the Democratic side, while Burgess lobbied the Republicans in the General Assembly. Democrat Terry Bruce, Ken's brother, was the chief sponsor of the IEA bargaining bills in the state Senate.[81] Ken Bruce was a master at the kind of wheeling and dealing that epitomized Illinois politics. He kept a tight rein over IPACE activities and controlled a large political war chest. In a 1974 memo, UniServ director Larry Phillips stated that IPACE managers "operate in limbo, probably responsible directly only to the executive secretary."[82] IPACE was often referred to as the "other IEA," given Bruce's limited interaction with the field staff. According to the *Chicago Tribune*, Bruce was one of the top lobbyists in the state. "He has gotten teachers' locals involved in legislative elections and built up the chest for political contributions to $180,000 per campaign year. . . . The IEA is regarded among lawmakers as one of the stronger labor groups, particularly in Chicago suburbs and downstate."[83] IEA's bipartisan strategy has become increasingly less effective in recent years, as the Republican Party has moved to the far right, backing privatization and evangelical conservatism.

In 1972, Senate Bill 1112, a comprehensive bargaining bill, was introduced in the state Senate. The bill had the support of IEA and was a product of a report by the Labor Laws Commission established by Governor Richard Ogilvie. Senate Bill 1112 covered all public employees. It protected the right of employees to organize, set procedures for establishing exclusive recognition, required school boards to conduct representation elections based on a "showing of interest," mandated grievance arbitration to settle contract violations, and defined the scope of bargaining. The bill required mediation and fact-finding to be conducted before a strike could take place, and established a state agency to enforce the law. The American Federation of State, County and Municipal Employees (AFSCME) supported the bill. IFT and the Illinois Federation of Labor opposed it.[84] Instead, they supported House Bill 1, introduced by Rep. Thomas Hanahan (D-McHenry), a carpenters union business agent. This bill shared some features with the Senate bill but did not include a state labor board to oversee procedures for establishing exclusive representation or any regulations on withholding services (i.e., striking).

IFT executive director Oscar Weil called Senate Bill 1112 "a sham negotiations bill." He advocated what he termed "free collective bargaining," the approach guiding Hanahan's bill. Rather than having oversight by a state labor board, collective bargaining should be left up to the local unions and school boards. He opposed any regulation on the right to strike, including fact-finding and mediation as a precondition of walkouts. Weil believed that a labor board would slow down the process of establishing recognition, giving the association an important advantage.[85] Many early IFT activists shared Weil's views about IEA and organizing. In referring to the collective bargaining law that was eventually enacted, Bob Breving, who served as assistant executive director in the early 1970s, said, "a lot of us feel that the 1984 law was not a benefit to the IFT." Without a law to govern how exclusive recognition was determined, IFT could contact IEA local presidents who were having problems in an effort to persuade them to consider IFT as an option. After meeting with the federation, a number of IEA locals held votes at membership meetings to switch affiliation. IEA might not even learn of the situation until it was too late.[86]

IEA strongly supported the enactment of a comprehensive bargaining law. In a publication addressed to Chicago teachers, IEA wrote: "Uncontrolled negotiations in the public sector can only lead to increased disruption. The reality of public employee negotiations is simple. Negotiations is, and will continue to be, a fact of life for public employees. The question then becomes will the 'law of the jungle' prevail or will bold legislative action be taken to regulate public employee negotiations."[87] IEA further argued that Weil's position would, in effect, leave the right to strike up to local school boards and the courts, perhaps setting legal precedents that would undermine collective bargaining. A number of school boards fired teachers who went on strike. Illinois courts regularly issued injunctions and jailed teachers who defied court order. Often facing intimidation and threats, teachers in small school districts were especially at a disadvantage when they tried to organize a union without legal protection. Going public, IEA ran a media campaign around the theme: "There Ought to Be a Law."[88]

A powerful coalition of disparate interests defeated Senate Bill 1112. IASB had become increasingly hostile to IEA once teachers gained control of the association. IASB strongly objected to any law that mandated bargaining with a union that could verify its majority representation status.[89] Chicago machine Democrats opposed the law as a threat to their patronage system. Teachers had tenure protection from political intrigue, but thousands of other school employees were not so fortunate. CTU also opposed the bargaining bill. It viewed IEA as a rival; furthermore, it did not need a law to force CPS to bargain a contract. It conducted three strikes in five years (1969, 1971, and 1973). The sheer size of the school system precluded CPS from hiring strikebreakers or firing strikers en masse. Moreover, CTU needed the support of the mayor, who controlled the Chicago Board of Education through his appointments. This political control of the board was critical in reaching CTU contract settlements and attaining funding in Springfield. Oscar Weil wrote: "[CTU president Bob] Healey thwarted this effort in a major way when he opposed the legislation to allow free collective bargaining by teachers. . . . I've been promised that the bill had the blessings of the Chicago Democrats, and, implicitly, of Chicago's Mayor Daley, since it was universally believed that the Chicago Democrats would not vote for anything as important as collective bargaining for teachers without the blessing of the mayor."[90]

Given this situation, AFSCME formed an alliance with IEA to pass a bill covering all public employees.[91] Opposition to a public employee law came from the Chicago Building Trades Council and the contractors' associations, which were closely aligned with the Daley machine. SFL had its own reasons for opposing the bill. The building trades unions that dominated the state federation worried that public employee unions would undermine their influence in the state organization.

The House passed both Senate Bill 1112 and House Bill 1, only for them to die in the Senate Labor Committee, which took no action on either bill. IEA bills introduced later in the 1970s faced a similar fate. The first bill to pass the Senate was Senate Bill 646 in 1979, introduced by Democrat Vince Demuzio from southwestern

Illinois. It was a comprehensive bargaining bill that included the right to strike. Democrats from Chicago blocked the bill in the House Labor Committee.[92] Referring to union opposition to IEA-backed legislation, IEA lobbyist Larry Lawlyes wrote: "None of them could afford a public posture of opposition. Each found a strategy to align its private needs with a public image. By publicly supporting an uncompromising, wide-ranging, comprehensive bill for all public employees that could not possibly pass the Illinois General Assembly, they literally loved collective bargaining to death. The intricacies of the legislation process allowed them to achieve the comfort of the paradoxical position, that is no law and no stigma."[93]

IEA's funding for its political action program was something that IFT could not hope to match. In May 1972, Oscar Weil published a report in the IFT newsletter, *Capitol News Roundup*, where he accused IPACE of "offers of money, staff assistance and other support in return for votes" on Senate Bill 1112. Though *Roundup* was meant for IFT staff and leadership, the memo leaked out and created a firestorm in the General Assembly. Legislators demanded an investigation. A joint legislative investigation committee was commissioned. Weil could not produce any evidence to support his charges. He admitted that his accusations were based on "loose talk by the IEA." Weil added: "I have not and am not accusing anyone of a crime."[94]

IPACE opened its books for the investigators, but they found no evidence to support Weil's claims. The committee report concluded that it "strongly deplored" and "found no basis whatsoever for Weil's charges." The committee cited him for "unpardonable irresponsibility and extremely bad judgment," concluding that Weil was "stupid."[95] He later wrote that his source was Norm Swenson, IFT president of Cook County College Teachers Union. The controversy prevented any action on a bargaining bill. Weil later claimed that the incident accomplished some good; it buried "the collective negotiations bills for good that session—which was more than I could have hoped for."[96] However, his reputation in the legislature was permanently damaged. This embarrassing episode opened a rift between him and CTU president Healey. Healey wanted to enhance CTU influence in Springfield by building a statewide organization. Healey, who was elected IFT president in 1972 while also serving as CTU president, chastised Weil for being a "purist."[97] Healey also believed that Weil played downstate teachers against Chicago. He was not about to leave Weil in charge. As IFT president, Healey "reorganized" the union, removing Weil as its executive director in 1975. Weil accepted a position of IFT legislative director, but his influence in the federation was greatly diminished.[98] IEA claimed that "the Illinois Federation of Teachers is really the Chicago Teachers Union run by Bob Healey from the Chicago Office. His concerns are the Chicago teachers and only to Chicago teachers—not the 3/4 of the Illinois teachers in suburban or outstate districts represented by IEA."[99] In the legislature, CTU, closely aligned with Chicago Democrats, was the voice of Chicago teachers. With support in the General Assembly on both sides of the aisle, IEA was widely recognized as the representative of the rest of the state's teachers.

Conclusion

The transformation of IEA into a union was a direct result of a policy adopted in the 1940s to increase teacher involvement through local associations. By the 1960s, many of these locals were demanding a greater voice in decisions affecting their employment. Following the Harrington decision, organizing of locals intensified as a result of the rivalry between IEA and IFT over exclusive representation. Even though the IEA board of directors was controlled by administrators, teacher activists in the late 1960s increasingly asserted their influence. At the 1970 RA, local association delegates rejected moderate reforms supported by the board and effectively ended administrators' influence within IEA. The bylaws adopted in 1971 greatly increased the power of local associations in the governance of the state organization. Not only did locals, through their region councils, elect the majority of the IEA board, but they also controlled the hiring of UniServ field staff. No longer having influence within IEA, many superintendents and school boards vigorously resisted efforts by local teachers unions to bargain a contract. Without a law to govern collective bargaining, school boards had legal power over decisions. But local associations had organizing power to force districts to meet their demands, setting the stage for bitter struggles between IEA and school management.

CHAPTER 8

Bargaining without a Law

These strikes simply would not have occurred if Illinois had a law that tells school boards that they shall bargain collectively contracts at the request of a legitimate bargaining agent and that the contract shall be with such and such guidelines and, when impasse occurs in the bargaining, such and such steps shall be taken to resolve the dispute.

—IEA executive secretary Curtis Plott

The adoption of unified dues effectively ended the influence of administrators within the Illinois Education Association (IEA). No longer able to moderate IEA policies from within, many superintendents and school boards sought to limit the range of issues covered in negotiations, while other districts even refused to bargain. District officials responded in various ways to union demands, but without a law, the decision on bargaining rested with school boards. Many districts worked out agreements with their teachers limiting as much as possible the range of issues covered in the contracts. Others set preconditions for negotiations, including a deadline to achieve a final settlement, at which point they would declare an impasse and impose a "take it or leave it" offer.[1] Even when the local clearly had majority support, some districts refused to negotiate, there being no comprehensive collective bargaining law requiring them to do so.

Local associations, on the other hand, sought to expand the scope of bargaining into areas that the Illinois Association of School Boards (IASB) considered management's prerogative, such as class size, student discipline, grievance arbitration, and curriculum development. Many early "contracts," especially in smaller districts, covered little more than salary and fringe benefits—but this would change over the years. Though districts retained the legal power to establish the terms and conditions of employment, unions relied on teacher solidarity backed by mass action, community pressure, and, as a last resort, strikes to achieve their goals. The threat of a strike convinced many boards, but not all, to bargain in good faith.

Union Busting

Districts' efforts to stop unionism varied greatly. In several wealthy Chicago-area high school districts, superintendents convinced their teachers to end their affiliation with IEA with the promise that the board would maintain their salaries among the top five in the metropolitan area. This meant that salaries bargained by high school unions in the area would determine their raises. District 214 Education Association (Palatine) and District 113 Education Association (Highland Park–Deerfield High School) voted to end their affiliations with IEA and become independent bargaining units. Oak Park and River Forest High School teachers agreed to a faculty senate, which would meet and confer with the administration. As a result of such changes, IEA membership steadily declined in the 1970s.[2]

Some districts tried intimidating teachers to break their unions. In the summer of 1971, Oswego District 308 issued individual contracts and threatened to fire any teacher who refused to sign by the first day of the fall term. The superintendent of public instruction prevented the enforcement of this action, declaring it a violation of continuing employment under the tenure law.[3] Although it eventually agreed to meet with the Oswego Teachers Association, the board set a deadline to reach an agreement; if an agreement was not reached by the predetermined date, the board would break off negotiations and impose its "best and final offer."[4]

In 1971, according to then Decatur Education Association (DEA) president Vern Thistlewaite, a right-wing school board tried to break the DEA during a strike. Racial politics played an important role in the events leading up to the walkout. African Americans made up about 10 percent of the city's population. Most Black students (along with many lower-income white students) attended schools in the older, working-class neighborhoods. These schools were low achieving and poorly equipped, and they offered fewer enrichment programs compared to the newer schools in the affluent areas of the city. African American leaders organized the Community Commission on Integration, calling on the district to integrate. They believed that integrating the schools would provide their children with improved educational opportunities and pressure the district to upgrade facilities in the older buildings. They also wanted the district to hire more Black teachers. The commission worked collaboratively with the school board and administration on a plan that would integrate the schools. The plan called for busing students to achieve more racial balance in the district. DEA, too, firmly supported these integration efforts.[5]

In response, conservative white citizens formed the Neighborhood School Coalition, which demanded that the district maintain the "neighborhood schools." Using subtly racist appeals to white voters, the coalition successfully elected its candidates to the board. By 1971, when DEA took up the call for expanded bargaining rights, the conservative coalition had a five-to-two majority. Board president John Fick, who was closely aligned with the right-wing USA Party and the John Birch Society, publicly disparaged the teachers union. *American Opinion*, the John Birch Society newsletter, widely circulated in the city, accused the National Education Association (NEA) of being a "dictatorship of the educariat" with ties to communism.[6]

The board majority depicted DEA as a labor union only interested in higher teacher salaries. It hired the reputedly hard-nosed Jack Taylor to represent the board in negotiations. The board was willing to meet and confer with DEA on salary and fringe benefits but opposed any agreement that limited its management prerogatives, including curriculum, evaluation, class size, transfer policy, and assignment of extra duties.[7]

The board proposed ending the salary index that DEA had achieved in the 1966 strike, the grievance procedure, and paid personal leave. It proposed adding eight days to the school year and giving itself the unlimited right to assign teachers extra duties. It even proposed eliminating the payroll deduction for DEA dues. Not surprising, DEA declared an impasse in June.[8]

Joel Seidman of the American Arbitration Association served as mediator over the summer. He issued a report with recommendations favorable to the board on eleven of its fourteen positions. The report only offered to teachers the previous year's salary index, with no salary increase. The board accepted the recommendations, except for the three that favored the union. DEA members voted four to one to withhold services.[9] IEA and NEA provided staff as well as legal and organizational assistance to support the strike. In response, Fick blamed the walkout on the union and not the teachers, claiming, "The National Education Association, the Illinois Education Association and the Decatur Education Association staff are duping our teachers into holding this illegal strike. The teachers are good people, it's only the NEA-IEA-DEA combined."[10]

The strike lasted fourteen days. More than seven hundred teachers (80 percent) walked out, including many nontenured teachers. Fourteen nontenured teachers (four of them African American) who refused to return to work despite threats of dismissal were fired. The board briefly opened three of its thirty-eight schools. IEA supported a parent lawsuit demanding the closure of the remaining schools on the grounds that their being open was a violation of equal opportunity for all students to attend school under the Illinois Constitution. A court injunction closed the schools. The board also filed a lawsuit against striking teachers, seeking to nullify their tenure rights as a prelude to firing. This threat did not break the union. The district withdrew the lawsuit when the strike ended.[11]

The DEA fought back. It produced a daily newsletter, *GLUE: The Paper for Teachers Who Stick Together*. It also organized parents, canvassed neighborhoods, and distributed literature throughout the community.[12] DEA president Vern Thistlewaite recalled: "Community support for the teachers was critical. The DEA not only had to address the needs of teachers, but it raised the concerns of parents and students for educational improvement. DEA published its proposals to improve the school buildings and [make] curriculum reforms."[13] Parents joined teachers on the picket line and attended mass rallies with teachers from other districts. The rallies drew more than three thousand people. DEA organized a boycott of businesses associated with the anti-union board members. Local newspapers and television editorials called for binding arbitration of the dispute. The board rejected these overtures.[14]

The board retaliated against the DEA spokesperson for the bargaining team, Dorothy Morris, who was a former DEA president and an outstanding elementary teacher widely respected by her colleagues, students' parents, and the community. Her measured but sharp criticism of the board rallied the teachers and many parents behind DEA. After the strike, the board obtained a court injunction from a politically connected judge, forcing Morris to undergo a psychiatric examination. This action further incensed faculty, parents, and many in the community against the board.[15]

Finally, state superintendent of public instruction Michael Bakalis and his aides tried to mediate the impasse. When no agreement was reached after twenty-six hours, Bakalis obtained an injunction against the strike and recommended a contract settlement. DEA accepted Bakalis's recommendations and returned to work without any assurances that the settlement would be enforced. The board rejected the Bakalis settlement and proceeded to fire the fourteen nontenured striking faculty. Only one of the Decatur 14 was rehired as a teacher, several years later; another was eventually hired as a teaching assistant. The strike ended on the board's terms. In the short run, the board won. But the board was unable to break the union. Vern Thistlewaite concluded: "The Board wanted to destroy all efforts of teachers to act collectively. . . . We are better people and stronger teachers because we stood tall for valid professional principles."[16]

After the strike, DEA announced a boycott of Christmas shopping in Decatur stores. Local associations in the area encouraged people to do their shopping elsewhere. DEA also organized a "Save the 14" campaign. It established a special fund to pay their salaries for the year. Decatur teachers contributed $15,000. On January 15, 1972, IEA and DEA jointly sponsored a $100 a plate Save the Decatur 14 dinner. Civil rights activist Julian Bond was the keynote speaker. Decatur was inundated with accusations that Bond was a communist. Nevertheless, the dinner was a huge success. More than six hundred teachers from locals across the state attended.[17] The strike hardened the determination of the teachers to remove the right-wing ideologues from the board. In the following elections, DEA worked with parents and community members to elect acceptable board members. DEA would not be involved in another strike until 1989.[18]

Once again, DEA had played a leading role in the fight for collective bargaining. The strike came immediately following the adoption of the new bylaws that transformed IEA into a union. IEA's robust support for the strike redeemed its reputation with Decatur teachers, which had been badly tarnished in the 1966 strike. Schools were closed for almost three weeks, making it IEA's longest strike up until that point. DEA faced a right-wing board majority that was determined to enforce its will on the teachers at all costs. The board prevailed on most issues, but it failed to destroy the union. Decatur teachers came out of the strike more unified than ever. The strike caused a major disruption to the Decatur community, convincing many downstate school boards and community leaders of the need to deal more reasonably with their unions.[19]

Hired Guns

Sensing a lucrative business opportunity, freelance negotiators offered their services to boards and superintendents with the promise of undermining teacher solidarity. Anti-union school boards employed these so-called hired guns in Decatur, East Aurora, and elsewhere to break teacher unions.

When East Aurora negotiations failed in the spring of 1971 and a strike seemed imminent in the fall, Roy O'Neil, the assistant superintendent for research and development, issued individual contracts over the summer, with a salary schedule that included a pay increase. Teachers were instructed to sign these contracts before the start of the fall term; otherwise, they would work under the previous year's schedule. Seven nontenured teachers who refused to sign the contracts were fired.[20] IEA filed a lawsuit on their behalf (reaching a settlement years later), but O'Neil's tactics caused a serious rift among the faculty. Many signed the contracts, effectively destroying teacher solidarity and the IEA local.[21] As a guest speaker at an IASB meeting, O'Neil was acclaimed as "the man who broke the Aurora teachers."[22] Following up on his success, O'Neil established a consulting firm, Countersearch Inc.[23] School boards in Gillespie, Cahokia, and Mascoutah hired him to bargain their teacher contracts after he promised that he could break the power of their unions. He made negotiations painful by threatening to give bonuses to teachers who signed individual contracts, impose a settlement, and decertify the bargaining unit, but these tactics failed to break the unions in these districts.

In 1977, O'Neil was elected to the Sandwich school board on the promise that he "wouldn't be involved in negotiations in the district." Once elected, he became the board's chief negotiator. While engaged in contentious negotiations with the Sandwich Classroom Teachers' Association, he offered teachers individual contracts with an $800 raise and a clause promising not to strike. He employed the same tactic that he had used to break the East Aurora union, but no one in Sandwich signed his contracts. In August, O'Neil broke off negotiations with the teachers.

The association walked out in September. Teachers who stayed in their classrooms received the $800 pay raise. Almost all tenured teachers supported the strike; most nontenured teachers crossed the picket line. Many Sandwich High School students joined the teachers on the picket lines. On September 9, the school board fired sixty teachers and ended the association's representation rights.[24]

The board hired substitutes and bused in strikebreakers from neighboring towns to keep the schools open. The local newspaper printed unsubstantiated rumors conjured up by the administration and the board, which did their utmost to turn the community against the strikers.[25] On September 17, the fired teachers began returning to work without a contract; they signed a no-strike clause at this time. However, four tenured teachers who refused to sign the no-strike clause were not rehired. IEA filed a complaint against the district for violating the tenure law. The district hired Reid, Ochsenschlager, Murphy and Hupp, an anti-union law firm with ties to right-wing politicians, to handle the case. IEA won the case on the grounds that teachers could not be required to sign O'Neil's "yellow-dog" contract as a condition of returning to work; the teachers were reinstated with back pay. Teachers were particularly rankled by the fact that administrators received pay raises averaging $2,000 after the strike.

Sandwich Classroom Teachers' Association leadership held together and rallied teachers to organize community support against the board; they elected two school board members in the spring, which enabled the teachers to reestablish bargaining with the district.[26] The fired nontenured teachers left the district, except for Mary Ann Beil, who picketed the district every morning. She became known as the "lone picket of Sandwich Schools." She had a hearing before the school board on November 8. IEA attorney Ralph Loewenstein handled her case. Despite Loewenstein's excellent representation, the board confirmed its earlier decision to fire her. Afterward, IEA hired Beil as a political intern. She later became a lobbyist for the Illinois Nurses Association, Milwaukee Public Schools, and Dane County, Wisconsin.[27]

A close associate of O'Neil's was the attorney Richard Zweiback, who served on the East Aurora board. Like O'Neil, he marketed his expertise in bargaining contracts based on school board terms. In 1973, the Charleston board paid him $8,900 to negotiate the teachers' contract. After months of "surface bargaining" by Zweiback—that is, raising issues that had no bearing on the teachers' proposals—the teachers voted to strike. The board fired Zweiback and reached a settlement with the union in one twelve-hour session.[28]

Small Districts

Teachers in districts with fewer than one thousand students were at a major disadvantage in establishing bargaining rights. These districts were typically in small towns, where personal relationships often tempered teacher militancy. Teachers in these districts were often too intimidated or themselves too conservative to question the authority of the administration. Once teachers took over IEA, some administration-dominated locals disbanded, as was the case in Franklin Park. Elsewhere, politically conservative teachers who believed that unionism was not compatible with the teaching profession dropped their memberships. Local associations were never organized in many smaller districts, both rural and suburban. Hillside, Forest Park, Rhodes, Sunnybrook, Union Ridge, and others in Cook County did not organize unions until after the 1984 comprehensive bargaining law took effect. In other districts, school administrators pressured teachers to join independent organizations as the price for agreeing to meet. In 1974, there were fifty-two independent teacher bargaining units in the state, most of which were former IEA locals that dropped their affiliation following the new bylaw changes.[29] These locals tended to be little more than "company unions" controlled by the superintendents.

By 1974, 423 (40 percent) of the state's 1,052 K–12 districts had recognized teachers unions. Of that total, 321 (76 percent) were IEA locals. Only 19 percent of the 607 districts with under 1,000 students had exclusive representation. Elementary districts under 1,000 students were the least likely to bargain; only 42 (14 percent) had bargaining rights. Unit and high school districts under 1,000 students fared somewhat better; 75 (25 percent) had signed agreements. School boards in most large districts, albeit at times reluctantly, agreed to bargain collectively. In the 445 districts with 1,000 or more students, 306 (69 percent) were bargaining units. Locals in large high school districts were the most successful; 55 (84 percent) of 67 locals had exclusive recognition (see table 12).

Strikes to force small districts to bargain were very risky. Districts could open schools with strikebreakers and fire the teachers who walked out. Such threats were real. In 1972, school districts in Berkeley, Dolton, Belvidere, and Bensenville hired strikebreakers during strikes.[30] That same year, Queen Bee District 16 (Du-Page County) fired seventy-four teachers during a fifty-eight-day strike. Forty of the teachers were eventually rehired as nontenured teachers, losing several weeks

Table 12. K–12 Teacher Unions with Exclusive Recognition as of June 1974

District size	Elementary	High school	Unit	Total districts
Fewer than 1,000 students				
No. districts	304	68	235	607
No. recognized unions (%)	42 (13.8)	14 (20.6)	61 (26.0)	117 (19.3)
1,000 or more students				
No. districts	172	67	206	445
No. recognized unions (%)	126 (73.3)	56 (83.6)	124 (60.2)	306 (68.8)
Total districts	476	135	441	1,052
Total recognized unions (%)	168 (35.3)	70 (51.9)	185 (42.0)	423 (40.2)

Source: Superintendent of Public Instruction, "Illinois Teacher Salary Study: 1973–74," 5–6, 26–72.

of pay. The local association collapsed, and it took ten years and the enactment of the bargaining law for Queen Bee teachers to reorganize.[31]

The threat of firing strikers in small districts, however, did not always work. In 1972, the forty-two-member Sesser Education Association in the heart of the southern Illinois coal mining region walked out. The board threatened to fire any teacher who did not report to work the next day. Not a single teacher crossed the picket line. Union coal mining families supported the teachers. Only 10 percent of students showed up on the second day of the strike. The strike ended with all the teachers, tenured and nontenured, fully exonerated, and a satisfactory bargaining agreement ratified. Teacher solidarity and community support won the day.[32]

Lake Park Education Association: A Sixteen-Year Struggle with the Board

The most protracted struggle in IEA's history involved Lake Park High School in DuPage County. District 108 did not have a standard salary; instead, in 1968, superintendent Carl Forrester developed a differentiated merit pay system that concentrated power in his hands. Lake Park Education Association (LPEA) activist Steven Fischer described how it worked: "the Superintendent initiated a system called 'Differentiated Staffing' where teachers were given various responsibilities in return for extra pay; only 'known-non-trouble makers' were given such higher paying contracts and people who began trouble making (e.g. talking of forming a union) suddenly lost their higher pay levels on the five level differentiated scale—leading teachers to rename the system 'Differentiated Shafting.'"[33]

Teachers who received an "outstanding" evaluation were given a plaque and a meager bump in their merit-based remuneration. Forrester appointed department chairs; they were on the highest pay grade and served on the faculty senate. Others appointed to the faculty senate were placed on the next highest pay level. First-year teachers were on the lowest pay grade. All of the assignments that determined a teacher's pay grade depended on maintaining the good will of the administration. Teachers who criticized the system were demoted. According to Fischer, even with the pay incentives, the average Lake Park teacher salary was the lowest of the surrounding high school districts and among the lowest in DuPage County.[34]

LPEA was chartered in 1972. At first, the district did not overtly oppose the new local; it even allowed the association to hold meetings at the high school. However, in 1975, when LPEA leaders pressed demands for bargaining, the superintendent took actions to undermine the union. LPEA was denied further use of the building; the administration made threats of layoffs and increased workloads. Forrester made it clear that LPEA membership was incompatible with the differentiated staffing system. Administrators created a climate of fear about joining the union. Teachers were removed from a higher pay grade unless they ended their LPEA membership. LPEA president Larry Studt stated: "When the administration started restructuring and ordering new job descriptions (1975), our membership dropped off dramatically. I think some people were scared and intimidated by it."[35]

LPEA, backed by IEA's legal services, sued District 108 and school officials in federal court under the Civil Rights Act, arguing that the administration was engaging in a "blatant attempt to keep the local Association from organizing," clearly in violation of citizens' rights under the US Constitution. According to the 1981 US District Court of Northern Illinois decision: "In August and September 1975, members of the Association were told that they were prohibited from talking to each other about Association business on the school premises between 7:15 a.m. and 3:15 p.m. (except during lunch hour) even when no students were present on the premises; were reprimanded for placing a memorandum relating to this suit in the teachers' mailboxes, a previously permitted practice, and for being suspected of talking to each other on the telephone about Association activities."[36]

The federal court ruled in favor of LPEA and ordered the district to pay $45,000 in compensation, to be divided among thirty LPEA members (and former members no longer teaching in the district). LPEA also received an additional $28,000, won earlier with the lawsuit.[37] Superintendent Forrester retired in the late 1970s, but his policies continued under his successor, George A. Gogo. The district continued to refuse to bargain with LPEA until the 1984 bargaining law took effect.[38]

Southern 45

Small rural locals were not powerless if they banded together. The most successful organizing efforts occurred in southern Illinois. In the early 1970s, region council leaders and UniServ directors in the seven downstate regions held a series of meetings to discuss the problems that they faced in dealing with unyielding superintendents and school boards. They agreed that progress depended on organizing on a regional basis. In 1974, seventy locals representing 8,500 teachers from forty-five counties in southern Illinois decided to coordinate their bargaining. They called themselves the Southern 45.[39] They adopted the slogan "We mean Business," along with a logo of a .45-caliber pistol that they proudly displayed on buttons, T-shirts, and other paraphernalia. Most of the locals ranged in size from fewer than twenty up to two hundred teachers. In addition, a number of education support professionals (ESPs) participated in Southern 45 activities.[40] IEA board member Roberta Hickman stated in an address at a Southern 45 meeting that "the lesson was learned long ago in the private sector labor movement that collective bargaining in a geographical area within the same industry could realize the maximum success only through common goals, concerted effort, coordinated strategy, constant communication, and a centralized negotiations discipline."[41]

Ahead of the Saturday meetings of the Southern 45, region council chairs and UniServ directors would meet jointly for dinner on Friday evenings to plan the agenda. Region leaders always chaired the Southern 45 meetings. Those UniServ directors in attendance served in an advisory capacity, providing valuable input, but the final decision on actions rested with the elected leadership. This cooperation between staff and governance was critical to the Southern 45's success. Southern 45 meetings built friendships, trust, and mutual support that transcended district borders throughout the region.[42]

The first step toward bargaining was to win exclusive representation. School boards and superintendents in the Southern 45 that adamantly refused to bargain faced recognition strikes. A widely publicized strike occurred in Waterloo Community Unit School District 5. That district had four strikes in the 1977–78 school year. In the fall, teachers and ESPs formed an alliance. They agreed not to return to work until the district recognized and bargained with both unions. Negotiations commenced soon after the recognition strikes ended, but the district dragged its feet over basic contract language. In the spring, both IEA locals walked out again to get their first contracts. Throughout the strike, other members of the Southern 45 lent assistance. The district settled. These first contracts were only three to four pages long, but they started a process on which the two unions eventually developed comprehensive agreements.[43]

The Southern 45 negotiation teams held joint meetings at which they shared information about their local efforts, prioritized goals for upcoming negotiations, and developed strategies to assist locals that did not have exclusive recognition. UniServ directors provided training programs in the Edwardsville, Effingham, and Marion offices that were easily accessible for member locals. Besides hosting workshops on school finance and negotiations, they worked with the Industrial Areas Foundation (IAF) to train local leaders in community organizing. Knowing that superintendents were in regular communication with one another to undercut negotiations, the locals agreed to common language and strict timelines prior to settling on salary and other high-priority issues. They wanted the best settlements to set the bar for those still bargaining. The local bargaining teams continued to meet regularly to share information about the progress of negotiations.[44]

Southern 45 locals assisted one another in a variety of ways when school boards were unreasonable at the negotiation table. Observers from other districts were invited to attend bargaining sessions. If bargaining reached an impasse and a strike seemed imminent, members from other locals joined the teachers on the informational picket line and attended rallies. IAF trained locals in analyzing the community power structure, which involved identifying influential leaders, businesses, and community organizations with ties to the school board. This information was used to pressure boards to be more reasonable and settle. Meeting with community decision-makers, picketing businesses, and writing press releases were some of the tactics used. Teachers also invited parents and community leaders to their homes for coffee. Retired UniServ director Dave Sneddon explained: "We had to rely on building community support; it was crucial to our success in achieving our bargaining goals."[45]

It was a well-known fact that, as a prelude to a strike, IEA would send someone from headquarters to assess the situation. A rather amusing tactic to indicate that IEA meant "business" was to have a teacher activist from another district dressed in a dark suit and carrying a briefcase visit a local bank to ask about establishing a $50,000 account for the local association. Another tactic was to have a teacher from another district attend board meetings. This unfamiliar visitor would sit with local leaders and take notes during the meeting in order to raise concern among board members.[46]

The Southern 45 continued into the 1980s. After the 1984 comprehensive bargaining law took effect, establishing rules for recognition, negotiations, and strikes, the Southern 45 ceased to operate. The success of the Southern 45 demonstrated the advantage of locals working together in the absence of a bargaining law. About the same time, unified bargaining councils were organized in DuPage County, Kane County, and elsewhere, with varying degrees of success.[47]

Unified Bargaining Councils: NSUBC and MBC

It was widely known that superintendents were in regular communication with one another about bargaining. They used the information gathered through these informal networks to their advantage at the bargaining table and with the media in their communities to undermine teachers' bargaining position by citing other contracts with weaker language, less fringe benefits, and lower salaries than that being discussed.

In 1974, UniServ directors Clay Marquardt and Jo Anderson proposed a plan to organize suburban Cook County districts that did not have locals or that had struggling local associations vulnerable to Illinois Federation of Teachers (IFT) raiding. IEA executive secretary Curtis Plott received board approval for this plan, dubbed the Belt Line Project; Marquardt and Anderson were hired as organizers. Though the project organized only one teacher local—the North Suburban Special Education District—it did organize several support staff unions.[48]

The Belt Line Project's most important accomplishment was the North Suburban Unified Bargaining Council (NSUBC). IEA had many small, ineffective locals that were, on their own, too weak to bargain good contracts. NSUBC was intended to turn this weakness into a strength by transforming a network of small locals into a large, powerful entity. Anderson explained: "IEA locals had the numbers but did not work together. [NSUBC] was intended as a demonstration of what an organizing-for-power strategy might look like."[49] He further explained:

> The results were not just the cohesiveness of a new organization that bound together a number of locals so that in a unified way they could bargain better contracts. But the NSUBC also created a presence . . . in the metro Chicago media as a power actor, capable of [creating] a power analysis of the dynamics of school funding, the politics of underassessing shopping centers and banks that cost school districts revenue, and [of] taking action to disclose these realities, including the connection between lower assessments and campaign contributions to Cook County assessor Tom Tully. One of the reactions was that the Cook County Democratic machine reached out to us to try to work out some of these issues.
>
> Another key aspect of the strategy was to show the power of what IEA could do for internal consumption. No amount of creative PR can replace the strategy of actually publicly demonstrating power so that locals, leaders, and members see the value of being part of such a powerful larger organization.[50]

In 1975, eight locals held a convention for hundreds of teachers to adopt a constitution and a "battle plan"—that is, a strategy to guide the organization. The intent of the battle plan was to rally the teachers behind the NSUBC goals, to inform the public about the issues, and to pressure the boards to address their concerns at the table. One of NSUBC's top priorities was a $10,000 base salary. To promote this priority, teachers wore buttons calling for salary parity, supporters distributed flyers at the commuter train stations, and parents were invited to attend coffee sessions. The council solicited support from real estate agents, police, banks, and community organizations. The bargaining teams met regularly to monitor progress at the table. In the end, all eight locals settled without a strike. The base salary settlements in these affluent districts ranged from $9,500 to $10,060. The total increase in the contracts ranged from 9.5 percent to 11.7 percent. Teacher leader Claire Hyman said: "We have never shared much of anything before. But we were tired of being used against one another as had happened so often in the past. We found that we could depend upon each other."[51]

In 1975, La Grange High School leader Ken Lumb and UniServ director Bruce Lund undertook a similar strategy, organizing the Metro Bargaining Council (MBC) in the western Chicago suburbs to coordinate negotiation efforts. Besides La Grange, MBC included the high school districts in Riverside-Brookfield, Hinsdale, Downers Grove, Wheaton, Lisle, and Glenbard. MBC invited IFT high school districts to participate as well. Several federation locals attended a few MBC meetings, but none became members.[52]

Coordinated bargaining was made possible by the fact that contracts, at the time, were bargained on an annual basis, typically beginning in late May and continuing over the summer. Using their research on suburban high school contracts, MBC locals established the bargaining goal that all members propose similar language at the table, covering topics such as early retirement, fringe benefits, longevity pay, extra duty compensation, class size, reductions in force, recall rights, and agency shop. Timelines were set to maintain these bargaining positions so as to prevent locals from undermining one another by withdrawing language early in the bargaining process. The MBC teams met on a regular basis to debrief and to refine their strategy. Though not all locals adhered strictly to these guidelines, this coordinated approach to negotiations led to improvements in contracts for member locals.

The comprehensive bargaining law that went into effect in 1984 ended MBC and other unified bargaining councils by requiring that both sides negotiate in "good faith" and not have preconditions with other teams that prevented the settlement of issues at the table.[53]

Expanding Organizing Efforts

Although IEA focused its organizing mainly on K–12 teachers, it expanded its efforts to many other groups. Most of IEA's higher education members joined through the Illinois Association of Higher Education (IAHE), which had 1,038 members (many of them college administrators) in 1968. At the time, IAHE did not have any faculty locals (unlike IFT, which was by then organizing on eight campuses). In 1969, IEA chartered its first higher education locals, at Sauk Valley and Lakeland Community Colleges. By 1971, it had ten faculty locals, none with bargaining agreements. Additionally, separate from both IEA and IFT, many university faculty were members of the American Association of University Professors (AAUP).[54]

In 1973, several faculty at Southern Illinois University Edwardsville (SIUE), including English professor John McCluskey, organized the Faculty Organization for Collective Bargaining (FOCB). The new organization included IEA, IFT, and AAUP supporters. To avoid organizational infighting, FOCB members agreed that they would support whatever organization received the most votes in an internal election. In December 1974, IEA hired McCluskey as the UniServ director for Region 89 (higher education). A few months later, in early 1975, 250 FOCB members voted to affiliate with IEA, defeating IFT and AAUP. NEA's commitment of $100,000 to the organizing project was a key factor in winning support for IEA. At the urging of a state senator friendly to FOCB-IEA, the faculty senate agreed to fund a study on the impact of collective bargaining on academia at other state universities. McCluskey and fellow English professor Jules Zanger conducted the study, visiting Illinois State University, Northern Illinois University, the University of Illinois Urbana-Champaign, the University of Illinois Chicago, and Sangamon State University. They reported positive findings to the faculty senate, which was sharply divided over the issue of collective bargaining. It did nothing.[55] FOCB-IEA decided to conduct a collective bargaining election among the faculty. IEA hired Peat, Marwick, and Mitchell, a prestigious Chicago accounting firm, to supervise the election. A majority of the faculty voting supported collective bargaining. A faculty-authored history of SIUE explains: "Of the 546 ballots distributed, 376 (69%) had been returned, and of these, 230 (61%) approved collective bargaining." Although FOCB-IEA easily won the election, the board of trustees voted six to one to reject FOCB-IEA's request to hold a representation election since there was no law requiring the university to bargain.[56] FOCB-IEA continued to agitate for bargaining without success; in 1979, IFT supporters took over the organization, renaming it FOCB-IFT. Bargaining for SIUE faculty would not occur until after the passage of the 1984 collective bargaining law.[57]

In 1976, McCluskey, Mike Cook, and other IEA staff began organizing the civil service employees at Southern Illinois University Carbondale (SIUC), creating in the process a union called the Civil Service Bargaining Organization (CSBO), which included sixty-four classifications. Under the rules of the Illinois Civil Service Commission, salaries of employees were meant to be equal for comparable work. The Civil Service Commission created a cumbersome appeals process for employees to redress inequities in salary, promotion, and employment. In reality, appeals varied greatly depending on the department's administrator. In effect, the Civil Service Commission opened the door for bargaining. Unlike with the faculty, the university would be required to address employment concerns if CSBO won an election. The campaign took thirty months. McCluskey coordinated the campaign while Cook was its key organizer; other IEA staff occasionally helped the campaign.[58]

The university already had a Civil Service Council as an advisory board for the group's concerns. IEA recruited council president Lee Hester and a core of talented council leaders to spearhead the organizing campaign. Mike Cook described Hester as a "legend on campus for his fearless advocacy of civil service employees in dealing with the administration." He became CSBO's key spokesperson. Prior to the CSBO elections, McCluskey accepted a UniServ position in Lake County Region 6. He continued to work with CSBO and the organizers. CSBO won the elections, covering over one thousand employees in 1978. McCluskey served as chief spokesperson for the new local at the bargaining table. The CSBO contract was IEA's first university agreement.[59] In subsequent years, the number of CSBO employees steadily declined due to budget cuts, reductions in force, and the reclassification of job responsibilities due to changing technology. In 1999, CSBO changed its name to the Association of Civil Service Employees. By the early 2000s, this association covered about six hundred to seven hundred employees.[60]

Organizing K–12 Support Staff

Prior to the passage of a bargaining law, organizing support staff unions was particularly difficult, especially among transportation, food service, and custodial workers, since large service companies regularly solicited school districts to subcontract their jobs. IEA did not have any support staff locals until the mid-1970s. In 1974, District U-46 Transportation Union (DUTU) in Elgin became IEA's first transportation union.

The Elgin Teachers Association (ETA) went on strike five times against Elgin Unit District 46 (i.e., U-46) between 1971 and 1981. Upset over a meager pay raise and poor working conditions, the Elgin U-46 transportation employees contacted ETA and the Teamsters Union about organizing a union in the fall of 1973.[61] U-46 transportation management urged the drivers to appoint a committee to meet with the administration to air their grievances, rather than seeking "outside help." The resultant bus drivers committee met with the administration over the course of five months but achieved nothing. In April 1974, the committee met with ETA leadership. Subsequently, 96 of the 102 drivers signed an ETA representation petition. The school board agreed to conduct an election. Even though 88 drivers voted for ETA on May 17, the board voted three to two not to recognize the union. The board vice president explained: "We don't want you people to think we're arbitrary. It's very clear what you want, but we don't have to abide by it. A bargaining law for public employees would be a good thing; but until we have one, we don't have to recognize anyone we don't want to." Incensed, the drivers walked out on May 21. ETA fully supported the drivers; teachers joined them on the picket line and provided refreshments. On May 27, the district agreed to recognize the transportation union as DUTU. ETA's chief negotiator helped them bargain a contract. Ten months later, DUTU ratified a comprehensive agreement.[62]

ETA had a bitter strike in 1975. In the spring, U-46 laid off 119 teachers, about 10 percent of the staff, without consulting ETA as required under the contract. This large staff reduction meant increasing class size and raised the ire of the teachers. ETA filed a grievance. At the bargaining table, the board refused to rehire the laid-off teachers. ETA walked out in September, and the board obtained an injunction against it. Since the two sides were only $100 apart on the negotiations over base salary, ETA reached a settlement to strengthen its reduction-force language, but it did not withdraw its grievance. In December, ETA won its grievance, calling on U-46 to rehire all the teachers with back pay. Since there was no law requiring binding arbitration, however, U-46 rejected the arbitrator's decision. Nevertheless, the district rehired with back pay everyone save for a few nontenured teachers. For ETA, this episode reinforced the importance of electing favorable candidates to the U-46 board and of building political alliance among district support staff employees.[63]

A 1978 strike ended on terms favorable to ETA's position. DUTU drivers supported the teachers' strike, closing down the transportation department and blaming their sympathy strike on "yellow fever." When the U-46 board voted on a motion to obtain an injunction against the strike, two board members, elected with ETA support, blocked it and pushed the board to reach a fair settlement. Success in 1978 illustrated the importance of ETA's political involvement in school board elections.[64]

In 1981, the board obtained an injunction against ETA, but, at a mass membership meeting, the teachers voted overwhelmingly to continue their strike. After giving the two sides time to resolve the impasse, the judge ordered the arrest of the union leadership—president Edward Schock, vice presidents Rupert Searcy and Kathy Thomas, and UniServ director Robert Jensen—for violating the injunction. These four individuals spent twenty-four hours in Kane County jail. The next day, the judge ordered both sides to his courtroom to oversee negotiations between the parties. Jailing the union leadership backfired. It greatly strengthened teacher support for the strike and led to a favorable contract settlement. The solidarity between DUTU and ETA during these strikes inspired Elgin secretarial and clerical staff to organize the District U-46 Secretarial Association in 1981.[65] U-46 custodial/maintenance and teaching assistants would organize IEA locals after passage of the bargaining law a few years later.

Following DUTU's success, other support staff unions were organized in the 1970s. Organized in the mid-1970s, the Urbana Custodians Association was IEA's oldest custodial union.[66] Blue Island High School secretarial staff organized in 1976 and went on strike two years later.[67] Waterloo support staff organized in 1977. The next year, custodial/maintenance employees in East Maine District 63 and Crete-Monee District 201-U organized.[68] In 1979, Champaign support staff joined IEA.[69] By 1981, IEA had 1,333 support staff members in fourteen locals. Despite these successes, IEA did not begin organizing large numbers of support staff unions until the comprehensive bargaining law went into effect in 1984.

Organizing in the Private Sector

IEA's success in organizing sparked interest in union representation among private sector school employees. In 1975, after winning reinstatement of three drivers fired for union organizing, Bee Line bus drivers of Danville voted overwhelmingly for IEA representation. Their local successfully bargained a one-year closed shop agreement that included a 10 percent raise, a grievance arbitration clause, paid sick leave, holiday pay, and other provisions.[70] In the next year, the district contracted its transportation services with the American Transportation Corporation. IEA maintained its bargaining rights, but the company created divisions among the drivers and broke the union shortly thereafter.[71]

In 1975, IEA won a National Labor Relations Board (NLRB) representation election among forty-five lay teachers at Quigley North and South, high schools in the Chicago Catholic school system. The next year, IEA won an election at another Catholic high school, Gordon Tech. In response, the Archdiocese of Chicago refused to bargain and appealed the elections to the NLRB on grounds that the federal government had no jurisdiction over religious schools. In 1979, the US Supreme Court ruled in favor of the archdiocese. IEA never bargained at these schools.[72]

In 1976, the drivers of Soy City Bus Service, which served Decatur District 61, organized an IEA union. The bus company was a subsidiary of Kankakee Auto Leasing (KAL Inc.). After threatening to strike, Soy City Drivers Association successfully bargained a first contract.[73] As the contract was about to expire (in August 1979), KAL Inc. sold Soy City Bus Service to R. W. Harmon and Sons of Belton, Missouri, and the Teamsters Local 279 petitioned the NLRB to represent the bargaining unit. Alma Robinson, the chief negotiator for the Soy City Drivers Association, said that the drivers "are split down the middle" on the issue of representation. She was reported to say that the Teamsters petition was not prompted by the change in company ownership or dissatisfaction with IEA. "I think some of the members were just shopping around. Maybe what the Teamsters have gotten elsewhere enticed them. The IEA has worked very closely with us and very hard."[74] IEA lost the election.

Conclusion

In the absence of a bargaining law, districts—and especially smaller districts—used their legal authority to limit or block bargaining rights. Except for tenure, school boards had at-will legal authority to set unilaterally the terms and conditions of employment. This power was inhibited, especially in larger school districts, as long as teachers unions remained determined, united, and organized politically in their communities. Though some school boards and superintendents succeeded, in the short run, in their efforts to thwart unionism, 428 districts representing 79 percent of full-time K–12 teachers in the state were covered by negotiated agreements by 1976.[75] IFT made impressive gains, winning bargaining rights in Cahokia, Kankakee, Granite City, Belleville, and other cities, and increasing its membership by 8,200 from 1973 to 1977. During these years, IEA added 7,200 members, despite the school boards' opposition and IFT organizing victories. IEA gains, however, were short lived, as a power struggle developed within IEA among the elected leadership, central office management, and staff, resulting in huge membership losses.

Charles C. Hovey, ISTA president, 1856.
Courtesy of IEA Archives.

Richard Edwards, ISTA president, 1864.
Courtesy of IEA Archives.

ISNU campus and the nearby Normal community, 1861. Courtesy of IEA Archives.

Ella Flagg Young, first female president of
ISTA, 1910, and NEA, 1911. Courtesy of IEA
Archives.

Robert C. Moore, ISTA/IEA executive secretary, 1915–38. Courtesy of IEA Archives.

Rural schoolhouse, 1940. Courtesy of IEA Archives.

Merit pay cartoon, 1956. Courtesy of AFT publication collection, box 61, Walter P. Reuther Library, Wayne State University.

IEA Annual Lobby Day in Springfield, 1989. Courtesy of IEA Archives.

Striking teachers picketing, 1974. Courtesy of IEA Archives.

ETA officers and UniServ director arrested for violating court injunction to end the 1981 Elgin teacher strike. Courtesy of IEA Archives.

Governor James Thompson signs the IELRA at IEA rally, 1983. Courtesy of IEA Archives.

President Reg Weaver celebrates the signing of the IELRA, 1983. Courtesy of IEA Archives.

IEA Equal Rights Amendment rally, 1980.
Courtesy of IEA Archives.

Collective bargaining cartoon, 1983. Courtesy of IEA Archives.

Delegates attend an IEA representative assembly, 2023. Courtesy of IEA Archives.

Protest against subcontracting school services to a private, for-profit, company, 1990. Courtesy of IEA Archives.

CHAPTER 9

Internecine Warfare and the IFT Challenge

The current IEA staff reflect the divisiveness that exists within the membership and in many cases the same internecine warfare that is currently being waged by leaders is paralleled by factions within the staff. The conflict and disagreements between headquarter staff and field staff has followed a pattern similar to other states who have experienced a rapid philosophical change and large expansion of staff.

—IEA executive secretary Curtis Plott

Following the ratification of the new bylaws in 1971, the Illinois Educational Association (IEA) embarked on an impressive organizing campaign. By 1977, IEA had increased the number of chartered K–12 teacher locals from 640 to 807. Only 355 of these locals had signed agreements. IEA also began organizing support staff, higher education, and private sector bargaining units. Its active membership increased from 54,192 in 1973 to 61,408 in 1977. IEA achieved these gains despite the fact that it faced stiff opposition from school districts, superintendents, and the Illinois Federation of Teachers (IFT). However, during this period, a power struggle developed within IEA among the elected leadership, central office management, and the staff. The internecine warfare led to a disastrous lockout of the professional staff in 1977, followed by a professional staff strike in 1980 that resulted in huge membership losses. By June 1983, IEA had just 51,232 active members.

Merger Discussions

By the late 1960s, the National Education Association (NEA) was clearly on the path to becoming a progressive teachers union. Speculation swirled around the possibility of a merger with the American Federation of Teachers (AFT), which would, if undertaken, create the largest union in the nation. In 1968, David Selden was elected president of AFT on a platform of a merger with NEA; he initiated discussions with NEA president George Fischer the following year. These talks continued intermittently for the next four years. Meanwhile, some NEA locals and state affiliates engaged in talks with their AFT counterparts; these discussions led to merger agreements under the "United Teachers" banner in Los Angeles; Flint, Michigan; and New York state. In 1972, the NEA representative assembly (RA) passed a resolution that prohibited affiliates from any further mergers with AFT while talks continued at the national level.[1]

IFT reacted negatively to Selden's merger proposal. In January 1969, Stan Stover, president of the Galesburg Local 1491, listed four major objections to a merger:

1. Administrative membership in teacher organizations is not conducive to efficient collective bargaining. (NEA members will never agree to exclude administrators!)
2. Labor organizations were instrumental in free public education in the United States; the AFT would lose labor affiliation in the merger.
3. The reasons for AFT's tremendous success is that its members are a special breed who will, if necessary, rebel against the status quo and fight for a new era of education. Those teachers who cannot or will not lead nor follow belong in the old, stable education associations.
4. There is nothing repulsive about a "two-party" system. I will never forget (nor forgive) the years of complacency that I spent in my profession before joining the union movement.[2]

IFT had competing locals in all of the larger IEA districts. Galesburg was just one such local challenging IEA for exclusive representation. For leaders like Stover, a merger would likely result in their locals being absorbed by the much-larger association. The rivalry in Illinois over exclusive representation continued unabated, despite the ongoing discussions at the national level. In 1970, IFT adopted the following resolution: "The IFT executive board is opposed to any kind of so-called merger talks between the AFT or independent groups at the national, state, or local levels."[3]

IEA was less interested in a merger than in an end to the intense rivalry with IFT that threatened so many of its locals. The 1971 IEA RA adopted a resolution directing its leadership "to begin discussions with the Chicago Teachers Union and the Illinois Federation of Teachers towards resolving organizational rivalries and competition for membership."[4]

IFT staff and leaders took great pride in being part of the "House of Labor" and had a profound antipathy for IEA, dating back to the years when school administrators controlled the association. IFT responded that there would be no merger talks unless IEA first committed to affiliation with AFL and the Congress of Industrial Organizations (AFL-CIO): "The Illinois Federation of Teachers shall not enter into negotiations towards merger with the Association until the Association demonstrates clearly its intent to lead its members into the House of Labor."[5] While the labor movement always supported public education, IEA opposed any IFT merger that would require AFL-CIO membership. IEA believed that an AFL-CIO affiliation would undermine its efforts to build support for public education among businesses, rural communities, and other constituencies.

At the national level, merger discussions lingered until 1974; talks were never held between IEA and IFT. As an alternative to a merger with IFT, IEA supported a confederation of public employee unions.

An Alternative to Merger

In March 1971, IEA began working closely with an NEA coalition that included the American Federation of State, County and Municipal Employees (AFSCME) and the International Association of Fire Fighters to oppose the Nixon administration's wage and price freeze, which was enacted in August 1970. Local and state governments responded not only by freezing negotiated cost of living increases for the upcoming school year but also by denying employees salary schedule increments already allocated under existing agreements. This 1.87-million-member labor alliance pressured the federal government to backtrack. By early 1972, negotiated salary schedules including annual increment increases were restored retroactively. In March 1973, following this success, the three national unions organized the Coalition of American Public Employees (CAPE) to work together on legislation, litigation, political action, and public relations on behalf of public employees at the national and state levels. NEA opposed a merger with AFL-CIO, but it viewed CAPE as an important bridge to an alliance with the labor movement. NEA encouraged state affiliates to organize similar coalitions.[6]

In 1974, IEA organized Illinois CAPE, "to provide a vehicle through which they and other public employee organizations may work cooperatively for the mutual benefit of their members." Besides IEA, Illinois CAPE included AFSCME Illinois, the Associated Fire Fighters of Illinois, and the Illinois Nurses Association. IFT was invited to join but refused, charging that it was a violation of AFL-CIO's policy against "dual unionism." A major focus of Illinois CAPE was a comprehensive bargaining law that would protect the rights of all public employees to unionize. It also opposed conservative organizations over issues involving school funding, union rights, and privatization of public services.[7] CAPE had some impact at the local level. Larry Lawlyes recalled that "we organized VPEC (Vermilion County Public Employees Coalition). We supported each other in various ways, including school board elections, city elections, candidate endorsements, fighting against residency requirements for police and fire, and other issues."[8]

An important reason for IFT's opposition to merging with IEA or joining CAPE was its confidence that it would prevail against the association. In late 1970, IFT announced that its "answer to merger—conquest—is the only way to true collective bargaining and dignity for all teachers."[9] IFT hired five full-time staff and a number of teacher leaders to work as part-time organizers. Leaders, especially in the large, federated locals, actively recruited members and organized locals in neighboring districts.[10] IFT was making inroads into IEA's dominance and was not about to give up these advances by merging with the much-larger association.

By the early 1970s, IFT had already won exclusive representation in fifty K–12 districts. About thirty of these districts had no IEA locals prior to the 1971 IEA constitutional convention; others, including Granite City, East St. Louis, Cahokia, Niles High School, Kankakee, Morton High School, Proviso High School, and Cicero Elementary, had well-established IFT unions organized prior to 1970.[11] During the 1971–72 school year, IFT won representation elections against IEA locals in Lyons, Park Forest, Reavis High School, and Chicago Heights. Other organizing victories included Lockport, Argo High School, Oak Lawn–Hometown, and several other districts where neither organization had exclusive recognition.[12] IFT's biggest victories that year involved the consolidation of dual districts, for example, in Valley View and Waukegan, where IFT represented the high schools and IEA had the elementary schools. After the schools merged, IFT won representation elections of 520 and 750 teachers, respectively, in these newly consolidated districts.[13] Finally, in 1973, the federation won another school consolidation election, this one involving the IFT high school and two IEA elementary districts in Elmhurst, covering 781 teachers. IFT won just two elections against small IEA locals: Summit Hill and Spring Valley. Teachers in Tinley Park, Skokie-Fairview, and several other small districts voted internally to switch affiliation to IFT. IEA successfully fended off IFT raids in Springfield, Rock Island, Dolton, Berkeley, Urbana, Galesburg, and Moline.[14]

IFT was especially successful in organizing higher education. The successful strike and contract fights by Cook County College Teachers Union (Local 1600) against the City Colleges of Chicago in the 1960s contributed much to its credibility among college professors. Local 1600 organized faculty units at Chicago State University, Prairie State College, and Moraine Valley Community College, and support staff units in urban and suburban Cook County.[15] Local 1600 councils led strikes against the City Colleges of Chicago, Chicago State University, and suburban Prairie State College in the early 1970s. Norman Swenson, president of the IFT Local 1600, spent time in jail twice for violating court injunctions, after refusing to call off the City Colleges faculty strikes in 1966 and 1975.[16] Local 1600's successful strikes and Swenson's brief imprisonment proved to be a public relations boon, contributing to IFT's reputation as an advocate of faculty rights. Local 1600 eventually organized the full-time faculty in six suburban community colleges and nine other higher education bargaining units in Cook County.[17]

IEA sought to reestablish its presence in Chicago in the wake of the Chicago Teachers Union (CTU) winning the 1967 representation election and the IEA Chicago division collapsing. By 1971, IEA had lost more than 2,800 members and no longer had an organization in the city. At the time, IEA locals were under attack by IFT across the state. Being labeled as a "professional association" dominated by school administrators hampered IEA's ability to respond effectively to the militant appeal of the federation. Once teachers took over the association, however, IEA organized the United Teachers of Chicago (UTC), under the leadership of Albert Raby, as a progressive alternative to CTU. The association's motivation was, in part, a desire to counteract IFT organizing, but it also reflected a genuine commitment to civil rights and educational improvement. CTU had been receiving mounting criticism for its perceived focus on teacher welfare, with little regard for the quality of education in minority neighborhoods. Raby argued that educators must "relate to community people" and offered this critique of CTU leadership: "Parents are not damn fools. If kids can't read and write, then somebody's at fault, and if teachers can't share the real problems with parents, then the parents are going to hit out irrationally at the teachers."[18]

Raby had close ties to the Chicago Urban League, Jesse Jackson's Operation PUSH, and African American communities in the city. He modeled UTC on the community organizing formula of Saul Alinsky's Industrial Areas Foundation. Raby explained the plan:

> UTC wants to build a vehicle for educational leadership, the kind of leadership that will come from teachers willing to stand up for bold new programs, not educational policies of moral bankruptcy.
>
> UTC wants to build a coalition of teachers and parents that have a conscience. Teachers and parents that have a common dream of quality education.
>
> UTC wants to build an education lobby that will unite downstate and upstate politicians into a children-first force with a conscience.[19]

UTC was highly critical of CTU's reliance on the Daley machine, which dampened civil rights, integration, and collective bargaining for nonteaching public employees. Raby cited the "massive education crisis" in the city: Black and Spanish-speaking students were graduating from high school with a fourth- or fifth-grade level of education, and the high school dropout rate was as high as 60 percent in some schools. Raby argued that improvement in public education in minority neighborhoods was only possible through a community organization approach. Teachers must organize alliances with parents and community groups in order to improve education. UTC published a periodic newspaper, tried unsuccessfully to form an alliance with the Teacher Action Caucus (a dissident organization within CTU), and received a friendly reception at the Operation PUSH Expo.[20] After two years, it had recruited fewer than one thousand members; it never seriously challenged CTU dominance in the city.

Who Runs the Show?

The restructuring of IEA left unsettled how management, governance, and staff would interact in the new organization. In the old IEA, the executive secretary managed the day-to-day operations of the association in accordance with policies established at the annual RA, and under the limited oversight of the board of directors at its monthly meetings. The fact that IEA had only three executive secretaries over fifty-eight years indicates its ability to manage effectively without major disruptions. The transformation of IEA into a union under the 1971 bylaws added a complex dimension to decision-making within IEA. For the first time in its history, IEA had a full-time release president to oversee management at headquarters. In 1973, the term of office was increased to two years, greatly enhancing the power of the president. In addition, expanding the board of directors from eleven to fifty-one members made consensus decision-making difficult. Having region council leaders directly involved in the hiring and supervision of UniServ staff meant that Springfield had much less influence over field staff. Further complicating the situation, both the professional and the associate staff organized unions and bargained agreements with IEA. The executive secretary's ability to manage IEA was much more difficult than it had been prior to the reorganization. Infighting among board members, management, and staff resulted in two executive secretaries being forced out in just ten years. IEA president Joseph Pasteris (1973–74) was critical of executive secretary Curtis Plott for overstepping his authority. Pasteris later recalled: "We were inexperienced in running an organization. Neither the elected leaders nor the UniServ staff seemed to know how to conduct themselves. Plott's approach was top-down; he wanted to be in charge as were past executive secretaries but did not know how to build a team."[21] Pasteris and many board members resented Plott's management style, which undermined their authority in governing IEA. They did not want to have Plott running the show.

Plott was especially concerned about the "bilateral" supervision of UniServ staff, which was shared by region council leaders and headquarters management. UniServ directors worked with the region leaders on a daily basis, with little direct supervision from Springfield. Much to the chagrin of management, a UniServ director who enjoyed the support of the region leader could act with impunity. Conversely, when the relationship between the region leader and the UniServ director broke down, management was expected to address the situation, potentially ending in a grievance/arbitration with the IEA Staff Organization (IEASO). Plott wrote that the supervision and evaluation of UniServ staff "creates confusion (real or imagined) about who is responsible for administrating the UniServ staff. The current arrangement, while designed to provide for local involvement and control, has the liability of offering the individual staff member the opportunity to hide behind either the executive secretary or the regional council chairperson."[22] Plott wanted management to have more authority over the field staff. Having only two field supervisors involved with local leaders to evaluate forty UniServ directors was ineffectual. He proposed that IEA create as many as six UniServ area coordinators, who would remain part of the IEASO bargaining unit, continue to service a region, and receive release time from their UniServ duties as well as additional compensation. The executive secretary and the director of field services would hire these area coordinators in consultation with the staff in their assigned areas. The coordinator would provide assistance and "participate in evaluation of program but would not have the authority to hire, fire, transfer, or suspend [UniServ directors]."[23]

Plott's proposal received mixed reactions at a professional staff meeting. Some viewed it as an opportunity for additional pay and possible career advancement into management. Others saw it as a divide and conquer strategy by management to undermine IEASO solidarity while increasing the power of headquarters management. Plott considered the lack of consensus among the UniServ staff as "a symptom of many of our problems." He believed that it was "unrealistic to expect staff to arrive at a consensus for a plan to increase coordination, control, and follow up of statewide programs."[24]

Some region chairs also objected to the proposal, viewing it as a power grab by Springfield management to undermine the power of regions. Plott's UniServ area coordinator proposal was never implemented, but it sowed seeds of distrust among IEASO members and some region leaders over IEA's management. Eventually, two more field coordinators were hired; they were not in the IEASO bargaining unit.[25]

Although Plott maintained majority support on the board, his forceful management style rankled some leaders. Joseph Pasteris later recalled of Plott: "Curt was it. He wanted me to be a mouthpiece, not a leader." Pasteris was further angered by the fact that despite being president, he was not informed about a meeting of the central office professional staff. Pasteris showed up uninvited anyway. After his presidential term, Pasteris was elected NEA director. He also served a term on the Illinois Teachers Retirement Board, with IEA support. Yet he became increasingly dissatisfied with IEA. President Woody Lee, his successor, particularly angered him. When Pasteris's DeKalb local was having problems with its school board, Lee met with board members without notifying him. Pasteris found out about the visit after the fact, commenting that "Lee committed the biggest sin that you can commit." As infighting increased in IEA in the late 1970s, he led his DeKalb local to disaffiliate. It became an independent union in 1979 and affiliated with IFT in 1983.[26]

Governance Infighting

Infighting on the board over Plott's leadership took a bizarre turn. President Lee and his supporters resented Plott's influence among board members and criticized Plott's failure to share information with standing committees. In April 1976, region chair Gary Randolph complained that Plott consistently ignored suggestions in his board evaluations to be responsive to the leadership. Plott "isn't supportive, either because it is intentional not to be supportive, which is interference in politics . . . or he is not supportive because he does not know how to be supportive, which is incompetence. This has been true for several presidents, not just Woody." Randolph concluded: "In summary, I would say that he has kept none of the promises he has made to me, the Executive Committee, and this Board when we extended him a contract a year ago for two years. I think he has outlived his usefulness and should be replaced."[27]

In 1976, IEA was deep in debt, forcing the sale of its Horace Mann stock. Plott's critics blamed him for the fiscal problems. After the board ousted Region 10 chair John Zaremba (Barrington), a Plott critic, from the budget committee, President Lee and his supporters tried to fire Plott. In June, Plott narrowly survived a vote of twenty-seven to twenty-one.[28] Plott suspected that some UniServ directors instigated the push to have him fired, in collaboration with their region chairs. Nevertheless, Plott's support on the board improved significantly over the summer, as "friendlier" region chairs were elected, replacing Randolph and several other critics. After the failure to fire Plott, Lee and Zaremba filed a lawsuit against IEA to enjoin the board from making committee assignments, on the ground that they were made in violation of the bylaws. President Lee's behavior severely undermined his support on the board. When the lawsuit was filed, Zaremba stated: "there's a kind of disillusionment that a lot of us feel. It just seems like the teachers are getting pushed back further and further in a nebulous network of the IEA."[29] In September, the board voted thirty-four to ten that Lee and Zaremba should withdraw their lawsuit. The lawsuit was eventually settled out of court.[30]

In the meantime, Zaremba began circulating a "referendum" among the regions to terminate Plott's employment. In September, the board adopted by a vote of thirty-one to eight a resolution that declared the Zaremba petition to be a violation of IEA bylaws. The board ordered: "that in the event the drafters of the proposed petition go ahead with their intent to distribute the petition, that the local members who may receive the petition be informed it is a violation of the IEA Bylaws."[31] Some regions circulated Zaremba's petition, despite being asked by field office staff not to use IEA equipment or money to print and circulate it.[32]

IEA's financial problems, dues increases, and infighting threatened membership losses and encouraged IFT to raid locals. Following the 1977 RA, the District 211 Education Association (Cook County), the largest high school district in the state, appointed an independence committee to research an alternative to IEA affiliation. The committee considered whether the district local should become independent, as had happened in the neighboring high school District 214 five years earlier, but it ultimately rejected that option, recommending instead an IFT affiliation. The teachers voted 373 to 111 to join IFT. Linda Bailey, the local's president, claimed that the Plott administration was concentrating power in Springfield and increasing state dues to create "a more powerful state organization at the expense of the local organizations." She added, "We feel teachers have lost control of IEA."[33] The loss of District 211 further undermined IEA's support in a number of locals.

Conflict with Staff Unions

Besides infighting on the board of directors over Plott's leadership, tension increased between IEA management and the staff unions. The IEA Secretaries Association (IEASA), the associate staff union, accused the Plott administration of bad-faith bargaining and conducted a one-day walkout in September 1975. IEASA filed an unfair labor practice (ULP) charge with the National Labor Relations Board (NLRB), charging Plott with threatening discipline up to and including firing in retaliation for the walkout. Since there was no disciplinary action taken against the staff, IEASA later withdrew the ULP charge and reached a contract settlement.[34]

By the mid-1970s, Plott's relationship with IEASO, the professional staff union, was also seriously strained, as indicated by its newsletter, *Oh Shit!*, which typically included sarcastic diatribes against managers, along with updates of numerous contract grievances filed by staff. In 1976, the newsletter offered tongue-in-cheek advice to staff: "Just because management makes you sick, don't consider retiring."[35]

IEASO was not immune to its own infighting. In February 1977, UniServ director Edward Kalish filed a ULP charge against IEASO, claiming that he "was illegally removed from the office of Vice President of IEASO [and that] the President of IEASO threatened to inflict great bodily harm on Edward Kalish if he pursued whatever legal remedies were available to him in order to restore himself to the Vice President." The NLRB hearing officer refused to issue a complaint, on the grounds that Kalish was legally removed from office by a vote of the membership. Following this decision, Kalish and five other UniServ directors sued IEASO in

Lake County over his removal. The court dismissed the lawsuit.[36] IEASO president Charles DesEnfants recalled that "everyone in IEA was fighting over everything during this period."[37]

The conflict with IEASO reached a climax in 1977. The board believed that the staff was out of control, IEASO salary demands were exorbitant, and IEA dues were already too high. Plott encouraged this sentiment so as to shift the board's acrimony away from himself to IEASO. IEASO gave early indications that it was prepared to strike, discussing that possibility at the very onset of bargaining in February. With the IEASO contract about to expire on June 30, Plott surmised that IEASO was trying to maximize its leverage at the bargaining table: purposely holding up a contract settlement until mid-August, just prior to the start of the new school year, when locals entered the critical stage of negotiations. Rather than wait, Plott sought to preempt a strike. IEASO depicted his thinking as: "We have to get them, before they get us."[38]

Newly elected IEA president Mel Smith and the board voted forty-four to one on July 5 to lock out IEASO unless they reached a contract settlement by July 11. The lockout came to pass. IEA managers collected staff keys to the offices, leased automobiles, and IEA credit cards.[39] In a letter to local presidents, Mel Smith explained that IEA's lockout strategy was intended to preempt a strike beginning in late August: "Past history indicates that the vast majority of our UniServ personnel take their vacations during the months of June and July. Further, the strike season has consistently taken place during September and October." He concluded: "the Board of Directors made their determination that it would be better to lose service now than to face the crisis season without our UniServ staff."[40]

Region chairs were urged to take over UniServ work. IEASO called those region chairs "scabs." The wedge between parties deepened when two UniServ directors, James Penca and Mike McNally, trashed the Peoria IEA office during the lockout, painting swastikas and four-letter words on the walls and vandalizing telephones, the postage meter, and other office equipment. Penca and McNally were arrested, but IEA dropped the charges after receiving apologies and restitution for the damage.[41]

Penca and McNally continued to work for IEA while privately meeting with IFT officials about employment with the federation. They were talented organizers with inside information about districts that were vulnerable to IFT raiding. In January, IFT hired them and created the Central Illinois Project. Before leaving IEA, Penca and McNally took copies of membership lists from the Peoria office, which they later used to raid IEA locals. AFT contributed $88,917 to fund an organizing project for two years. IFT provided $46,222.[42] McNally stated: "It is our opinion that the IEA management has in fact deserted the cause of teachers and teaching."[43] Penca and McNally were successful in raiding IEA locals. Penca explained their strategy:

You call up and say this is who we are and we would like to meet with you. No strings attached. We want to explain our program and see what you say. And that's basically how we started. It was a very simple process. We use very little paper because paper can't talk back to you, can't answer questions. We build our nucleus on the local hierarchy to the building reps. From the building reps, we went to the buildings, had meetings and would have dinners in some instances depending on what would bring the best turnout. And it worked 99% of the time.[44]

Dubbed "Plott's plot" by IEASO, the lockout was a disaster. Many of their former IEASO colleagues considered Penca and McNally's actions a betrayal.[45] In 1979, NEA provided IEA with a grant to hire three full-time organizers to fend off IFT raids.

Plott thought that the lockout would force IEASO to settle the staff contract by August 1, prior to the most intense period of negotiations between school boards and locals. Instead, the lockout did not end until August 16, almost five weeks after it began. It was a disaster for IEA, magnifying dissatisfaction with IEA across the state. A number of locals disaffiliated from IEA, and independent organizations more than doubled between 1977 and 1979, from ten to twenty-one. Besides leading to disaffiliations by DeKalb, North Chicago, and others, the lockout opened IEA up to IFT raiding across the state. With the defection of the District 211 Education Association to IFT already underway, the lockout doomed any hope of reversing course. IEA lost this six-hundred-member teacher local to IFT in a fall representation election; it was the beginning of a series of losses that continued into the early 1980s. Penca and McNally engineered numerous successful organizing campaigns against IEA locals in central Illinois, including North Greene, Quincy, Carrollton, Champaign, and Peoria. IEA suffered huge membership losses, worsening its fiscal condition.[46]

The lockout was a bitter pill for staff to accept, as the IEASO newsletter described: "We who were true believers are saying, we came to this job because we saw the teachers' plight and decided to change the order so teachers could make decisions instead of superintendents, and the teachers were so vicious under the leadership of Plott that they engaged in a lockout, something no school superintendent would do."[47]

After the lockout, most IEASO members continued to do their best to provide services for IEA members and their locals. However, at least ten UniServ directors left IEA for jobs with other state associations. A few pursued other careers. UniServ director John Aurand, a former school administrator, resigned and established a business as a school board negotiator. Several staff started selling real estate as a side business. One UniServ director even arranged for his region to pay for classes for him to pursue a law degree; another was fired for stealing money.

Within IEASO, a small but vocal minority wanted revenge. Following the lockout, IEASO leadership gave each member an axe handle with "Never forget" printed on the side. IEASO members were urged to hang their axe handles on their office walls for everyone to see. IEASO was divided into those who clung to their axe handles and those who did not.

Larry Lawlyes, elected IEASO vice president after the lockout, stated, "IEASO was divided. Many members, while unhappy with management, were also unhappy with what they thought was ineffective union leadership. Some were not pleased with naming the union newsletter *Oh, Shit*, feeling that it projected a negative image of the union and pushed their region chairs and local leadership to support management rather than IEASO." Later the newsletter was renamed *IEASOlidarity* by new union leadership. Some union members felt that a strategy of constant belligerence would keep IEA in the downward spiral. They felt that what was needed was a union that was assertive in its defense and promotion of members but was also willing to work with those in management and governance who wanted to find a better way forward.[48]

In 1977, IEA suffered another major setback, this time in Lake County. Joseph Triolo, Region 5 chair, strongly objected to a management decision to move the IEA office from Waukegan farther south to Deerfield. Region 6, also served out of the Waukegan office, supported the move. Unable to get management to back down, Triolo withheld IEA dues and filed a lawsuit against IEA to stop the move. Eventually, in 1979, Triolo resigned from the board and organized the Independent Teachers Association.[49] This association included four school districts: North Chicago High School, North Chicago Elementary, Warren High School, and Gavin Elementary. It never added any other locals. Ironically, Triolo's North Chicago High School local was the first to leave the Independent Teachers Association; it affiliated with IFT in 1983.[50] Gavin rejoined IEA, while the other two locals ended up with IFT by 1988.

IEASO Strike

The 1977 IEASO lockout was a harbinger of even more turbulent events, which would lead directly to an IEASO staff strike three years later. Though anger over the lockout forced IEASO leaders to take a hard line on some issues, the decisions of President Smith and his management team were the major cause of the 1980 strike. In April 1978, Plott resigned, effective June 30. Smith announced that he would take over the responsibilities of the executive secretary until a replacement could be hired. The board set June 15 as the deadline for applications, but it took seven months to fill the vacancy. Smith was in no hurry to hire. He wanted to run the show.[51]

As IEA continued to lose members and problems mounted with the staff, Smith found a replacement whom he thought would take control of the staff. In December 1978, IEA hired William Stoltz as executive secretary. Prior to his appointment, Stoltz was the director of field services for the Ohio Education Association. In his first meeting with the board, prior to being hired, Stoltz launched a diatribe against IEA staff, referring to them as "cowboys." He promised to "be tough on the staff." In the spring of 1979, IEA hired Stoltz's close associate from the Ohio association, Glen Darr, as assistant executive secretary of UniServ operations.[52]

At the 1979 RA, Smith sought to extend his career as IEA president by changing the term limit provision in the IEA bylaws. This effort met with stiff opposition among governance. Jim Nagle, a Danville Community College leader, ran for president, opposing the bylaws change backed by Smith. Two amendments were introduced by delegates. The first completely eliminated term limits, while the other would have allowed Smith to seek a third two-year term. Nagle, a progressive activist, vigorously campaigned against the "extend" bylaw proposals. Both bylaw amendments were defeated at the RA. Smith barely won reelection to a second (and final) term, defeating the relative newcomer Nagle. Before adjourning, the RA delegates elected Nagle to fill a newly created elective office of secretary-treasurer. Jan Stutts, Region 36, questioned Nagle's appointment as a violation of the bylaws, arguing that the new position was not properly elected. Subsequently, Mel Smith and William Stoltz filed a complaint with the US Department of Labor, which eventually vacated Nagle's election. Nagle was elected as secretary-treasurer in accordance with the bylaws the following year.[53]

The situation between IEA and IEASO further deteriorated following the 1979 RA. Stoltz and Darr were determined to establish control over the staff. At region council meetings around the state, Stoltz criticized IEASO members for violating the terms of their employment, citing the very few incidents of "double-dipping" of expense vouchers and other abuses.[54] In the field, Darr either ignored or narrowly interpreted the IEASO contract, which resulted in numerous grievances over compensatory time, paid leave time, and relatively minor issues. Due to the strained relationship between the leadership and professional staff, President Smith ordered UniServ directors not to attend the 1980 RA. The few UniServ directors who did attend received reprimands. IEASO filed a grievance, noting that several staff had the right to attend on their own free time because they had maintained their IEA membership while others had been directed by their regions to attend. IEASO surmised: "IEA management actions, in the larger context, can be seen as efforts to assert centralized authority over the local direction of staff and to divide the membership from their employees. In so doing, they have ignored the contractual rights and obligations, as well as constitutional rights.[55]

Stoltz and Darr's confrontational management style earned them the nickname the "Ohio Mafia." They were generally despised, not only by UniServ staff but also by other managers. An IEASO strike seemed imminent. Contract negotiations stalled. Communication between the staff and management had completely broken down. Stoltz did not hold a general staff meeting in over nine months.[56] Hoping to avoid a strike, the IEASO executive committee proposed a general staff meeting to rebuild the "broken communication and the deteriorating relationship between staff and management." Stoltz agreed to consider this proposal. Middle management and IEASO leaders met "with some trepidation on both sides" and hammered out an agreement for a June 4 staff meeting. The proposed agenda included discussions of IEA goals and objectives in light of declining membership, IFT's organizing offensive, budget cuts, and other problems facing the association. Stoltz canceled the meeting after the agreement was announced. In response, IEASO asked these questions:

Can Bill Stoltz ever work with the IEA staff?
Can he work in a democratic manner?
Can he delegate real authority to anyone?
Does he envision programs and goals for Illinois teachers?
Is he capable of planning for them and accomplishing them?[57]

After Stoltz canceled the staff meeting, *IEASOlidarity*, the union's newsletter, published a tongue-in-cheek contest, "Guess the Date of the Next Staff Meeting." The contest rules included that "guesses must be confined to the 20th Century" and that "when hell freezes over" was not an acceptable response.[58]

The final blow to the Smith-Stoltz administration was the disastrous 1980 staff strike. After both sides rejected binding arbitration, IEASO walked out in August. The two sides were far apart on money.[59] The United States was undergoing a period of double-digit inflation; the 1980 rate of inflation was 12.5 percent. IEASO sent members for several weeks to picket NEA headquarters in Washington, DC, during the strike. The purpose was not only to have NEA put pressure on IEA to settle but also to solicit support from NEA staff unions.[60] IEASO also maintained picket lines at IEA headquarters and the field offices. Almost all associate staff honored the picket lines. In one incident at headquarters, UniServ director Patty Brown-Barnes asked Glen Darr, "When are we gonna settle this?" Darr replied: "When you guys cave!"[61]

On September 5, IEASO president Jay Hammer sent a letter to IEA teacher leaders accusing Stoltz of "skimming" and hiding $700,000 from regional budgets over the past two years, without the knowledge or approval of the leadership. Hammer wrote that the executive secretary's behavior raised "both ethical and legal questions of law and the adherence to the bylaws and constitution of the IEA." Since the staff strike involved $138,000, Stoltz made "IEASO less sympathetic at the table to arguments of impoverishment."[62]

Hammer's letter was published in newspapers across the state. In response, IEA threatened to sue Hammer and IEASO unless they retracted the accusation that Stoltz was personally pocketing money. Secretary-treasurer Jim Nagle began an investigation of IEASO's charges with business manager Bob Daniels and IEA accountant Terry Thomas. A lawsuit against IEASO was not filed.[63]

The Night of Rage

In mid-October, dramatic events ended the strike. While IEASO and IEA bargaining teams were meeting in Chicago, the IEA executive committee met in Springfield. Secretary-treasurer Nagle reported that Stoltz had indeed misappropriated IEA funds without authorization and that he had used some money for unauthorized personal expenses. When confronted with the evidence, Stoltz and Smith immediately called a recess. When the meeting resumed, Stoltz broke down, admitting that he had redirected funds without authorization. He did not apologize for his actions; instead, he condemned teacher leaders for not appreciating his efforts on their behalf. The executive committee created an audit committee and hired an outside attorney to investigate IEA's financial records.[64]

Meanwhile, the anger and frustration of the striking staff reached a boiling point outside the boardroom. A large, rowdy group of IEASO members and UniServ staff from neighboring states picketed the executive board meeting in the parking lot at headquarters. As the protest continued and beer was liberally consumed, Stoltz's car became the object of the protesters' ire. The car was keyed, radio antennae broken, empty beer cans glued to the vinyl roof, door locks glued, and a number of other outrageous acts perpetrated that disabled his car. Several other automobiles suffered lesser damage. Stoltz's maleficence and the shocking behavior in the parking lot convinced IEA and IEASO of the need to end the strike that was tearing IEA apart. On October 18, the strike was settled. Stoltz's brief career with IEA was about to end.[65]

Shortly after Stoltz's resignation, Darr left IEA for a job in Ohio; Mike Butera, a field coordinator closely aligned with Stoltz, left IEA the following year. The strike reinforced the perception that chaos reigned in IEA. IFT used the strike in its organizing campaigns to discredit IEA. IFT secretary-treasurer Ken Drum commented: "When one organization (IEA) is constantly fighting internally, it harms the image of teachers, offends the community, hurts the influence of the teachers in the legislature and makes teacher representation more difficult."[66]

The Smith presidency hit a low point. Even after the strike was settled, Smith remained hostile to IEASO, rejecting its request to participate on the search committee to replace Stoltz. His support on the board declined. Most region chairs and staff realized that the infighting had to end. Leadership, management, and staff needed a conciliatory approach to resolving disagreements if IEA was going to stop the membership losses and budget cuts. NEA was increasingly alarmed by the situation. IEA was losing locals to IFT, while others disaffiliated and became independents. NEA strongly encouraged IEA to hire John Ryor, a former NEA president, as the next executive secretary. Unlike Stoltz, Ryor was politically astute, even-tempered, and congenial. He helped mollify much of the bitterness within IEASO.

John Ryor's hiring in 1980 marked the beginning of a resurgence of IEA. Under Ryor, IEA management was reorganized. Bruce Lund, a UniServ field staff coordinator, was hired as the deputy executive secretary. This new position combined three departments: field services, public relations, and professional development. In effect, Lund became responsible for managing much of the staff operations. He reported directly to Ryor. Business services and government relations remained, as before, separate administrative entities. Clayton "Clay" Marquardt was hired as a field coordinator. Carol Bland was hired to manage public relations, and Ron Pierce headed professional development. Pierce and Bland were also assigned as part-time field coordinators to cover the responsibilities of a position that was cut in the budget. NEA "loaned" John White, one of its field staff, to assist IEA management with its field operations. Despite five years of chaos, Mel Smith left office on a high note, with the hiring of Ryor and the new management team.[67]

IEA Membership Losses, 1978–1983

IEA suffered large membership losses during this period. Between 1977 and 1980, the number of IEA K–12 teacher bargaining units declined from 355 to 348. IEA active membership declined from 61,406 to just 53,747. Membership hit a low point two years later, at 51,232 (see table 13). These losses were, in part, due to declining student enrollment as the baby boomers graduated high school, entered college, or joined the workforce.

To make matters worse, the internal strife within IEA led to local disaffiliations in DeKalb, North Chicago, and elsewhere. By far, the most significant losses amid the chaos of the lockout and strike were to the IFT. IFT membership in large districts increased at the expense of IEA. From 1978 to 1983, IEA lost twelve teacher units to IFT, including locals in Palatine High School 211, Harlem, Champaign, Orland Park, and Peoria (although it also successfully defeated IFT raids in many large locals, including Dundee 300, Palatine 15, Pekin, Rock Island, and Galesburg).[68] These were formal elections conducted by arbitrators, county superintendent officials, or other independent third parties. The association also lost dozens of small- to medium-size bargaining units to IFT through a less formal process conducted internally by the locals. Since there were no state laws governing how exclusive

Table 13. Active Union Membership, 1972–1984

Year*	IEA membership	IFT membership
1972	54,490	31,085
1973	54,192	31,679
1974	56,623	33,765
1975	58,360	37,000
1976	60,416	39,477
1977	61,406	39,928
1978	57,267	40,697
1979	53,403	42,296
1980	53,982	42,825
1981	53,747	42,466
1982	51,951	44,017
1983	51,232	45,785
1984	52,437	45,266

Sources: Box 12 (1981) and Box 26 (1981–88), IFT collection, Walter P. Reuther Library, Wayne State University; "IEA-NEA Membership Services Activity: 1988–1989," IEA, 1989, author's collection.

* Fiscal year ending June 30.

representation was established prior to 1981, a bargaining unit could simply "flip" its affiliation to IFT by a vote at a general membership meeting. In many cases, IFT would contact local association leaders in hopes of initiating discussions about affiliation with them. If this contact was successful, the local leaders would propose a general membership meeting to consider IFT affiliation. At times, both UniServ directors and IFT representatives would be invited to make presentations prior to a vote on affiliation. In some cases, IEA staff did not find out about these votes to switch affiliation until just prior to the meeting. By that time, IEA had little, if any, chance of keeping these locals.[69]

IFT also relied heavily on its ties to AFL-CIO to recruit family members and friends who taught in IEA districts. UniServ director Gerry Gordon related a story about how when he was president of the Sycamore Education Association (SEA), he was invited to dinner by Tony Viron, a steelworkers union business agent he knew from his earlier time as the machinist union shop chair at Barber-Greene in DeKalb. "I expected a casual get-together, I was surprised that the dinner included IFT staffer Ed Morrissey, the Harlem District 122 federation president, and AFL-CIO Rockford council members." So began an intense but failed effort by IFT to "flip" SEA. After this initial meeting, Gerry attended a meeting between the SEA board and IFT. He later arranged a meeting with IEA staff to air the SEA members' concerns. At this point, SEA decided to remain with the association.[70]

Illinois Union Teacher, the IFT newsletter, regularly published a growing list of IEA locals that switched affiliation. Its "IFT score card" in fall 1983 claimed that seventy-five IEA teacher locals had joined IFT.[71] While the list was fairly accurate,

Table 14. K–12 Districts with Signed Collective Bargaining Agreements

Year[*]	IEA	IFT	Other[**]	Total
1975	308	58	22	388
1976	354	64	10	428
1977	355	65	10	430
1978	348	76	14	438
1979	342	82	18	442
1980	348	87	21	456
1981	355	95	18	468
1982	366	101	20	487
1983	370	102	21	493
1984	378	109	20	507

Sources: Superintendent of Public Instruction, "Illinois Teacher Salary Schedule and Contract Provision Study: 1980–1981," 14; ISBE, "Illinois Teacher Salary Schedule and Policy Study: 1984–1985," 17.

[*] Fiscal year ending June 30.

[**] Includes independent unions, an IEA/IFT confederation, and unions affiliated with organizations other than IEA or IFT.

some of the locals on the list, like the Illinois State Archivists and State Librarians, were not teachers; others were never IEA bargaining units. IFT claimed Indian Prairie 204, a former IEA local, but, as was the case under IEA, it failed to get the district to agree to bargain. When District 204 teachers actually voted for exclusive representation in 1984, IEA won. In some districts that joined IFT, IEA did not have a chartered local. Nevertheless, IEA did lose majority status in at least sixty of the seventy-five locals on the list.

After defeating IEA in a Peoria representation election in 1983, IFT claimed to be the majority teacher organization in the state.[72] It never actually achieved that goal, and it dropped the claim several years later. Peoria was the last significant loss of bargaining rights to IFT (see table 14).

Conclusion

The turning point for IEA was 1981. Though some leaders and staff continued to cast blame at each other for years to come, IEA and IEASO realized that the infighting must end. At the 1981 RA, Reg Weaver was elected president in a three-way race, beating Glen Schneider and Gary Elmen. Weaver had been vice president during the strike, but he had avoided most of the rancor of Smith's presidency. As president, Weaver was adept at fostering a positive, conciliatory atmosphere within the organization. Even though its membership losses continued until 1983, IEA made a dramatic turnaround under the leadership of Weaver and Ryor and was finally able to get a comprehensive bargaining law passed in 1983, to go into effect in 1984.

CHAPTER 10

President Weaver and Bargaining Legislation, 1981–1984

Knowledgeable observers speculate that the confrontation between
the IEA staff, the IEA management and the IEA elected leadership was
actually a symptom of an organizational malady that five years of fighting,
reorganizing and restaffing have not been able to overcome.

—*Illinois Union Teacher*

Following the chaos of the 1977 lockout and the 1980 strike, the situation seemed dire for the Illinois Education Association (IEA). Membership had plummeted. By 1983, IEA had lost over ten thousand members in six years. As the number of baby boomers attending K–12 schools declined by 1980, districts cut the size of their teaching staff. This reduction in force was a major reason for IEA's membership losses in the early 1980s. Adding to the declining K–12 enrollment, the Illinois Federation of Teachers (IFT) successfully challenged representation rights over numerous association locals. IEA lost two large districts, Champaign and Peoria, to IFT raids in the early 1980s. Clayton Marquardt recalled, "Given all the internal strife of the staff lockout and the strike, it was a miracle that the IEA survived."[1] Despite this grim picture, the election of Reg Weaver as president at the 1981 representative assembly (RA) marked a turning point for IEA. Though IEA continued to lose members until the end of the 1982–83 school year, Weaver successfully reached out to all factions within the association to resolve their differences. His presidency laid the foundations for the passage of collective bargaining legislation and continuous growth that would last well into the twenty-first century.

President Reginald "Reg" Weaver

Reg Weaver was a charismatic and personable leader. He was widely admired by rank-and-file members, elected leaders, and staff. He was a gifted public speaker who could rally a crowd to action. He was also a good listener, always positive and hopeful. During his six-year presidency, Weaver helped calm the bitterness of the 1970s and paved the way for a lasting IEA resurgence.

In his first year as president, IEA lost just under 1,800 members, in part due to IFT raids on IEA locals, but also as a result of districts cutting the size of teaching staffs as student enrollment declined. The Illinois State Board of Education (ISBE) reported that K–12 public school enrollment dropped from 2.31 million in 1974 to 1.82 million (21 percent) by 1984.[2] Economic turmoil in the early 1980s also contributed to layoffs. Double-digit inflation in 1979–80 was followed by a recession in 1981–82. High interest rates caused by the Federal Reserve's tight monetary policy discouraged school districts from borrowing. Out of extreme caution, given the economic uncertainty, districts often issued more reduction-in-force notices than they actually anticipated. In April 1983, IEA reported over 6,000 "riffed" employees, mostly teachers and teaching assistants.[3] More than half of these employees were hired back by August, even though school budgets for the upcoming year were finalized in late June. President Weaver said: "It's a sad state of affairs when the lives of individual members are disrupted to the point where extreme stress, anxiety, anger, frustration, and hostility set in, all because of the callous inhumane, arbitrary, capricious action on the part of some boards of education." He further stated, "There is no reason for it."[4] After 1983, reductions in force steadily declined, in response to an economic recovery.

After taking office, President Weaver set as his highest priorities rebuilding the tattered relationships within the association, increasing membership, and restoring IEA to fiscal health. Weaver knew that UniServ directors worked closely, on a daily basis, with local leaders and region chairs. "If I could build trust among the UniServ Staff, it would go a long way in improving relationships among the members of the Board of Directors."[5] Soon after his election, he initiated individual meetings with some of the most outspoken board members and IEA Staff Organization (IEASO) individuals to discuss their concerns. In early 1982, all board members, IEASO staff, and management were invited to a statewide membership recruitment meeting. Weaver later explained: "To be successful in membership recruitment, IEA needed first to build understanding and trust among the leadership, staff, and management." At the start of the meeting, participants were encouraged to air their differences and to share their feelings about the problems facing the association. Weaver stressed the negative impact of infighting on IEA membership and finances. He told the attendees, "Bring me some members."[6] A joint staff/governance membership task force was subsequently established to encourage each region to devise a strategy for increasing membership. The task force compared membership in locals to the number of teachers in districts they represented as reported in ISBE's annual Teacher Salary Schedule Study. This information helped IEA identify areas of potential membership growth in each region. By September

REGINALD "REG" WEAVER

Reg was raised in a working-class family in Danville, Illinois. He earned a BS at Illinois State Normal University in special education for the physically handicapped and an MS at Roosevelt University in education administration. Weaver was a founding member of the IEA Minority Caucus, which played an instrumental role in increasing minority involvement in IEA governance and staff. In 1981, Reg, a science teacher in Harvey District 152, became the first African American to be elected IEA president. In 1989, he was elected to the nine-member NEA executive committee. Four years later, he was elected NEA vice president, after which he served six years as NEA president. Reg is often invited by various organizations to speak about education and social justice issues. He has served on the boards of the Tom Joyner Foundation, People for the American Way, and FAME. Over the years, he has received numerous awards, including three honorary doctorate degrees for his service to public education.[8]

1982, more than half of the region councils had developed membership plans.[7]

By 1984, IEA began a dramatic recovery. A comprehensive collective bargaining law was enacted, and membership increased. President Weaver's support among governance was so strong that the RA readily adopted a bylaw amendment that enabled the president to serve as many as three two-year terms. A similar amendment had been defeated in 1979 when Mel Smith was president. After Weaver's presidency ended in 1987, it was widely expected within IEA that Weaver would someday be the National Education Association (NEA) president.

IEA's Political Strategy

By the early 1980s, the political climate was changing. Numerous teacher strikes had disrupted communities, forcing many school boards and superintendents to accept (if begrudgingly) collective bargaining as a part of school district management. From 1970 to 1981, IEA locals engaged in more than two hundred strikes. Many of these walkouts were "recognition strikes" intended to force school boards to recognize and bargain with the local associations. Very few districts were successful in breaking their teacher unions, and those that did paid a painful price. Support for a law that would formalize collective bargaining procedures increased in the General Assembly. The IEA department of government relations pursued a bipartisan political strategy that enabled it to build support for its legislative agenda on both sides of the aisle. IEA enjoyed strong support within the Illinois Democratic Party. In addition, it had local associations in every county throughout the state; many IEA members lived in conservative communities and voted Republican. This fact provided IEA with the opportunity to develop political support in communities that were solidly Republican. IEA lobbyists used their connections in these communities to seek out moderate Republican candidates who supported issues of importance to public school employees. The Illinois Political Action Committee for Education (IPACE) would endorse these candidates in the primary, providing funding and campaign assistance, knowing full well that the winners in these legislative primaries were going to win the general election. As a result, IEA could always rely on support from IPACE-endorsed Republicans in the legislature.[9] IPACE's endorsement of four-term Republican governor James Thompson was another critical component of its victories. In 1982, IEA noted: "In the six years that Thompson has held the title of Governor, IEA-NEA has been more successful than ever before in passing into law pro-teacher and pro-education legislation."[10] Thompson signed into law early-out retirement benefits, which allowed many senior teachers to retire early, thereby opening up new jobs in school districts across the state. He also supported nearly every significant piece of IEA legislation, including hearings for reductions in force (teacher layoffs) and retired teacher medical insurance.[11]

Membership in IFT, conversely, like the state American Federation of Labor and Congress of Industrial Organizations (AFL-CIO), was concentrated in heavily unionized, Democratic counties. IFT did not have any K–12 locals in a majority of Illinois counties. More than half its locals were concentrated in five counties—Cook, Lake, Will, St. Clair, and Peoria. It did not have any locals in over 50 of the 102 Illinois counties.[12] As a result, its political outreach was largely limited to the Democratic Party. In 1982 in the General Assembly, it endorsed forty-one Democrats and only five Republican candidates for the state Senate; only two Republicans received IFT endorsements for the 118 House seats that year. IFT endorsed only Democrats for statewide office, including Adlai Stevenson III, who ran against incumbent governor Thompson.[13] Thompson defeated Stevenson by about 5,500 votes.

IEA—which unlike IFT had a "history of endorsing candidates of both parties"—likely made the difference in the election by endorsing Thompson. Consequently, IEA, and not IFT, would be the critical player in securing passage of the comprehensive bargaining bill, which required support from both sides of the aisle and the signature of the Republican governor.[14] According to IEA lobbyist Larry Lawlyes, "the federation's liking or not liking our bills did not move Democratic legislators. We endorsed those Democrats as well. They would not carry the IFT's water over our interests."[15]

Public Act 82-107: The "Mini" Bargaining Law

Throughout the 1970s, IEA achieved numerous legislation victories that benefited school employees, including attaining a hearing officer for tenure cases, improved paid sick leave, seniority rights in layoffs and recall, early retirement provisions, a minimum teacher salary, and board-paid retirement. However, despite its large war chest, talented lobbyists, and politically active membership, IEA was unable to get bargaining legislation enacted. Aligned with the conservative wing of the Republican Party, the Chicago Democratic machine regularly blocked legislation in Springfield in order to protect its patronage system. As Larry Lawlyes remarked, "The interests of the political machine guided Chicago Democrats' voting in the General Assembly."[16]

In the 1970s, tension over political corruption, police brutality, and racial injustice in Chicago increased. A coalition of white, middle-class reformers and African American activists emerged, demanding change. In 1976, Mayor Richard J. Daley died in office. Daley's successors, Michael Bilandic and Jane Byrne, were unable to maintain party discipline. As a result of litigation by reformer Michael Shakman that challenged the patronage system, the federal court issued a series of orders, the Shakman Decrees, in 1972, 1979, and 1983, effectively stymieing Chicago's patronage system.[17]

Ken Bruce, the director of the IEA department of political action, recalled: "Politics is all about being at the right place at the right time. IEA was perfectly positioned to pass bargaining legislation. Our endorsement and continued support of Governor James Thompson, a moderate Republican, in 1977 was key to our legislative success."[18] Bruce surmised that "the election of Harvey teachers Reg Weaver (IEA president), Pearl Mack (NEA executive committee), and Ann Davis (Teacher Retirement Board member) to top leadership positions in the early 1980s greatly enhanced our influence among the emerging African American leadership elected to the General Assembly, especially on Chicago's South Side and in the south suburbs."[19]

Though Illinois did not have a law requiring collective bargaining, 80 percent of all K–12 teachers were working under negotiated agreements by 1981. Many districts, especially those in large urban centers, voluntarily agreed to bargain. School boards that refused to bargain often faced recognition strikes to force them to the table. Nevertheless, the majority of K–12 districts (542 of 1,010) did not bargain in 1981; 449 of these were small districts with fewer than 1,000 students.[20] While most K–12 teachers as well as many higher education employees and school personnel had negotiated agreements, the decision to bargain rested exclusively with the employer. Not only was there no requirement to bargain, but, if they did agree to meet, the boards could dictate the ground rules for the meetings, decide what issues would be discussed, and impose a "last and final offer" if an agreement was not reached by a certain date. Without a bargaining law, the legal relationship between employers and employees was one sided.

In 1982, the General Assembly enacted Public Act 82-107 (House Bill 701), Illinois's first K–12 collective bargaining law. Often referred to as the "mini" bargaining law, Public Act 82-107 created a process for establishing exclusive representation. A union could petition for a representation election at any time, as long as at least 30 percent of the employees signed union authorization statements. However, if a bargaining agreement existed, a union could only petition for representation against an incumbent union from January 15 to February 15 in the final year of the contract. Petitions were filed with the regional superintendent of schools, who conducted a secret ballot election among the proposed bargaining unit members. "No representative" was always a choice on the ballot. A third union could be included in the election by filing an intervening petition signed by at least 15 percent of the eligible voters. A simple majority of ballots cast determined the outcome of the election. If none of the ballot choices received a majority, a runoff election was held between the top two choices to determine a winner. A tie vote preserved the status quo. If a majority of an unorganized group signed the union petition and no other organization intervened with 15 percent, the union could ask the district for voluntary recognition, forgoing the need to conduct an election. Voluntary recognition was solely at the discretion of the employer. Public Act 82-107 did not require an employer to bargain, however, even if a union won the election. If the employer agreed to negotiate, the law allowed the exclusive representative to bargain a provision to collect agency fees ("fair share") from nonmembers to cover the cost of negotiations and contract enforcement.[21]

IFT sharply criticized Public Act 82-107 as totally inadequate since it did not require school boards to bargain.[22] The law also made it much more difficult for IFT to "flip" IEA locals. Exclusive representation was no longer the prerogative of school boards. The act established procedures for exclusive representation petitions and oversight by the regional superintendents of education that required an election between the incumbent union and the challenger. This process gave time for the incumbent union to prepare a defense. When asked whether the law was a benefit, IFT organizer Jim Penca answered: "No it wasn't. It slowed down the process and gave everyone somewhat of an equal footing, which is somewhat to our disadvantage. We like to sneak in the door in the night. And before we knew it, here we were. We lost two huge elections because of the law."[23]

Public Act 83-1014: Illinois Educational Labor Relations Act

By early 1983, passage of a comprehensive bargaining law seemed imminent. IEA had used Public Act 82-107 very effectively. IEA focused on organizing new locals and petitioning for exclusive representation. Confident that a comprehensive bargaining law was about to be enacted, IEA won 134 representation elections in 1983, anticipating that school boards would be required to bargain once the law went into effect on January 1, 1984.[24] By mid-1982, IEA had chartered more than 825 locals, the highest total in its history, and had 366 bargaining units.[25]

IEA wrote the bill that eventually became the Illinois Educational Labor Relations Act (IELRA). IEA hired attorney Robert Stine to help draft the legislation based on previous IEA bills introduced in the General Assembly. As a former employee of the Illinois Legislative Reference Bureau, Stine had extensive experience in drafting legislation for state assembly members. IEA lobbyists met with NEA general counsel Bob Chanin to review the proposed legislation prior to it being introduced in the legislature. Knowing the pitfalls that other states had experienced with bargaining laws, Chanin provided valuable suggestions that improved the language of the bill.[26]

In early 1983, Larry Stuffle (D-Charleston) submitted House Bill 249, a comprehensive collective bargaining bill, to the General Assembly. Stuffle's bill covered all school employees from kindergarten through the university level. It served as the basis for the bill that was eventually signed into law. After more conversations with IEA, Jim McPike (D-Alton), Stuffle, and other representatives made revisions in the bill and introduced it as House Bill 1530. In April, Terry Bruce (D-Olney), Ken Bruce's younger brother, introduced the bill in the Senate. IEA reported: "Many of the provisions outlined in HB 1530 stem directly from HB 249, the Association's original collective bargaining bill which was introduced earlier this year."[27]

Prior to the House vote on House Bill 1530, Speaker Michael Madigan (D-Chicago) held a meeting in his office with all interested parties. Besides IEA, representatives from IFT, the Illinois Association of School Boards (IASB), the Illinois Association of School Administrators, the Illinois Principals Association, and the American Federation of State, County and Municipal Employees (AFSCME) attended. The purpose of the meeting was to give the organizations an opportunity to air their concerns about the pending legislation. The school boards' and school administrators' representatives expressed opposition to binding arbitration of grievances and several other provisions in the bill. When Madigan asked the labor representatives about their concerns, IFT representative Margaret Blackshere said that they could agree to exclude binding arbitration in the bill to accommodate management concerns. IEA lobbyist Larry Lawlyes strongly objected. The bill remained intact. Following this meeting, Madigan and IFT announced their support of House Bill 1530. Political considerations may have been behind Madigan's support for the bill. Lawlyes suggested that Madigan's support for House Bill 1530 reduced Chicago mayor Harold Washington's power over patronage. With a weakened Chicago mayor, Madigan would be the most powerful Democrat in Illinois.[28]

On May 26, the House passed the bill without any major changes. The bill won Senate approval on June 27. When the General Assembly recessed for the summer, two bargaining bills were sent to the governor's desk. House Bill 1530 covered all public education employees, while Senate Bill 536 covered all public employees, including those in education. Governor Thompson item vetoed both bills. Over the summer, IEA president Weaver, executive secretary John Ryor, and director of political action Ken Bruce met with the governor at his Chicago home to finalize item veto amendments for House Bill 1530. Bruce arranged an official signing ceremony with Thompson in September. The public school employee section was deleted from Senate Bill 536, ensuring that there would be a separate labor board exclusively covering public education.[29] In 1985, professor Martin H. Malin, Chicago-Kent College of Law, explained the thinking behind having a separate Educational Labor Relations Board: "This separation of public education from the rest of the public sector 'recognizes that substantial differences exist between educational employees and other public employees as a result of the uniqueness of the educational work calendar and educational work duties and the traditional and historical patterns of collective bargaining.'"[30]

On September 23 at a signing ceremony in Chicago, before a cheering crowd of nine hundred IEA members and staff, Governor Thompson, with his daughter, Samantha, at his side, signed the amended House Bill 1530. Standing behind him at the podium were IEA president Reg Weaver, vice president Lee Betterman, secretary-treasurer Jim Nagle, John Ryor, Ken Bruce, and the sponsors of the bill, Senators Terry Bruce and Earlean Collins and Representatives Jim McPike and Al Greiman. House Bill 1530 became law on January 1, 1984.[31] The *Chicago Tribune* wrote that the bill gives "teachers official VIP status among all public employees, with their own statewide mechanism for getting their problems solved. . . . It seems to take a lobby as muscular as the Illinois Education Association to create a separate special set of laws for them.[32]

Major Provisions of the IELRA

The IELRA is the most comprehensive bargaining law for public education employees in the nation. It covers all full-time and part-time K–12 and higher education employees in Illinois. Supervisory, managerial, student, confidential, and short-term employees are excluded from bargaining, but these categories are narrowly defined. Managerial and supervisory employees are defined as those "who devote a preponderance of their employment time to such exercising authority." In other words, employees such as department chairs, head custodians, administrative secretaries, and others who perform some managerial or supervisory tasks may be included in a bargaining unit. Most graduate students hired as teachers or research assistants by universities as well as employees working in state agencies that provide educational services can also organize under the act.[33]

The range of issues that can be bargained is extremely broad. Educational employers are required to bargain with the exclusive representative in good faith and in a timely manner, "policy matters directly affecting wages, hours, and terms and conditions of employment as well as the impact thereon upon request by employee representatives." The "impact" wording gives the union a powerful voice. Management rights such as budget establishment, hiring/firing, employee evaluations, layoffs, curriculum, and class size invariably affect wages, hours, and the terms and conditions of employment. Impact bargaining provides union employees with the potential to influence much of management's decision-making.[34] A union can even bargain in the midterm of an agreement if an issue arises that was not considered during the contract settlement. For this reason, districts often try to bargain a so-called zipper clause, which waives the union's right to bargain such issues midterm. Under the act, employees through their unions can have a major input on education policy.[35]

All collective bargaining agreements must include three provisions. First, a contract must have a recognition clause describing the employee groups covered by the agreement. An "appropriate bargaining unit" under the act must share an undefined "community of interest," which, in effect, allows a broad mix of professional and nonprofessional employees to be covered under a single contract. Second, all agreements must include a grievance clause, with the last step ending with binding arbitration by a neutral third party. Any individual in the bargaining unit or the union has the right to file a grievance to settle a dispute over a violation or misinterpretation of the agreement by the employer, but only the union can take a grievance to binding arbitration. To encourage both sides to settle grievances early in the process and avoid arbitration, the employer and the union must share the cost of binding arbitration. Finally, all contracts must include a no-strike clause. Strikes are only allowed after the expiration date of the contract, and only under prescribed conditions. Negotiations must begin within sixty days of either party issuing a demand to bargain. Bargaining must proceed for at least sixty days; within ninety days of the beginning of the school year either side may petition the Illinois Educational Labor Relations Board (IELRB) for mediation; or, if both parties agree, they may use the Federal Mediation and Conciliation Service, American Arbitration Association, or other bona fide organization. The employer and the union equally share the costs of mediation. If both parties mutually agree, the outstanding issues on the table may be submitted to binding arbitration.

In the original language of the law, if mediation failed, the union could file a five-day strike notification prior to a walkout. In 1998, the act was amended to include a ten-day strike notice. In 2011, an additional step was added before a strike can occur. After fifteen days of unsuccessful mediation, the mediator, employer, or union can initiate a public posting process, whereby both parties have seven days to submit their final offers on outstanding issues to the mediator and the IELRB. Seven days after these offers are received, the labor board shall post the final offers of both parties on its website for fourteen days. After that, the union can strike, provided that its ten-day strike notice has been given and the ten days have elapsed.[36]

The IELRA protects the individual rights "to organize, form, join, or assist employee organizations or engage in lawful concerted activities for the purpose of collective bargaining . . . through representatives of their own free choice." Employees also have the right not to participate in all such activities. The employer, as well as the union, is prohibited from "restraining or coercing employees . . . in the exercise of their rights guaranteed under the Act." In effect, any employee can file an unfair labor practice (ULP) charge against the employer or the union, if the individual's rights to participate or refrain from participation in union activities are violated.[37]

The union contract applies equally to all members in the bargaining unit. The union has a duty to provide "fair representation" for all bargaining unit members, whether they join the union or not. It is illegal for the union to discriminate against nonmembers. "Fair representation" means that even in a worst-case scenario such as a nonmember accused of child abuse, the union must provide at least a minimum of representation. The union is not required to defend the person's actions or support a grievance, but it cannot refuse to investigate the case and offer advice. Otherwise, it risks being charged with a ULP.[38]

Since the union is legally required to bargain and represent all members of the bargaining unit, the IELRA originally allowed the union to bargain fair share agreements, which required nonmembers to pay a percentage of membership dues that the union spent in negotiations and enforcement of the contract.[39] In 2018, however, the US Supreme Court in *Janus v. AFSCME* ruled that fair share clauses in public employee contracts violate the First Amendment, reversing the 1977 decision in *Abood v. Detroit Board of Education*, which upheld fair share agreements. The National Right to Work Foundation and other anti-union groups believed that many employees signed union membership forms only because they were faced with the option of paying fair share fees or joining the union. With fair share eliminated, these anti-union organizations expected many union members to discontinue their membership. IEA was concerned that the National Right to Work Foundation and other anti-union organizations would launch a direct mail campaign to achieve that goal.[40] In 2019, Illinois enacted post-*Janus* legislation that increased the union's access to new employee information, ensured the right of the exclusive representative to use building premises for meetings, and restricted the employer from releasing union membership information to outside, third-party organizations. Ultimately, IEA did not experience a significant loss of active membership as a result of the *Janus* decision, though it did lose 5,205 fair share fee payers in 2018. IEA mobilized its leaders and staff to sign up fee payers prior to the expected announcement of the *Janus* decision. The loss of these fee payers was offset, in part, by a 1,248 increase in active membership. Many of the former fee payers joined.[41]

Disputes such as ULPs or representation petitions are resolved through IELRB hearings. After reviewing the evidence, a labor board hearing officer renders a decision based on the act and legal precedence. Either party can appeal the hearing officer's decision to the full labor board. Any appeal of the labor board's decision begins in the state circuit court.[42]

Implementation of the IELRA

IEA was conscious of the fact that the implementation of the IELRA was critical. Governor Thompson appointed a three-member board acceptable to IEA. Edna Krueger, a Republican and Elgin Teachers Association (ETA) activist, was the union appointee to the labor board. Wes Wildman, a management attorney for school boards, was considered a reasonable appointment. Professor Gerald E. Berendt, a legal scholar, was the neutral, third appointee to the labor board.[43] When the act was passed, Clay Marquardt, then the associate executive director of membership services for IEA, noted that other state associations had passed good bargaining laws prior to Illinois's, "only to have them eventually watered down by the labor boards that were established as part of the bills. Key protections and rights were lost." IEA planned "to do everything we could to keep that from happening."[44] Knowing that the early decisions of the IELRB would set legal precedents for future cases before the board, IEA retained Winston and Strawn LLP and hired two staff attorneys, Sandra Holman and Feliz Berlanga, to manage cases brought before the labor board. Berlanga explained that "the IEA legal department has made a concerted effort to carefully screen the merits of each case to enable it to impact the establishment of sound, well-reasoned labor law to clarify, protect and enforce our locals' and members' rights." As a result, "IEA cases have established the majority of critical and important standards in the enforcement of the IELRA."[45] In the five years following the enactment of the law, IEA reported that the IELRB decided about 206 cases, approximately 113 of which involved IEA. These decisions do not include the hundreds of decisions of the IELRB hearing officers and executive director that never reached the three-member labor board. Nor do they include cases that were resolved by the parties prior to a formal labor board determination.[46]

While state labor board decisions and legislative actions in states controlled by anti-union conservatives (such as Michigan, Indiana, and Wisconsin) have undermined public employee bargaining rights, the IELRA has not only remained intact but also been enhanced by subsequent legislation. In 2003, the IELRA was amended to allow a union to forgo an election via a majority interest petition (MIP). An MIP requires a majority of employees to sign individual statements in support of union representation so that a union can be certified by the labor board as a new bargaining unit or add employees to an existing unit without conducting an election. With the election forgone, employers cannot mount a campaign against the union. An MIP petition can be challenged if there is convincing evidence of "fraud or coercion" in signature gathering. To avoid any question of having enough valid signatures, IEA's legal department recommends that at least 60 percent of the group sign union authorization statements prior to filing an MIP. A rival union can force an election if it files an intervening petition with at least a 30 percent showing of interest during the required thirty-day posting period in which the MIP is announced in the workplace.[47]

Subcontracting of public services has always been a threat to school employees seeking to unionize. In 2007, the legislature amended the Illinois School Code to establish stringent requirements on districts seeking to subcontract employment services to vendors. These requirements include:

- There can be no subcontracting during the life of a collective bargaining agreement.
- Employee benefits provided by the private company must be comparable to the benefit package provided by the district to the employees who previously provided the services.
- Employees must be given a ninety-day notice prior to the implementation of subcontracting work.
- A subcontractor must provide evidence of liability insurance equivalent to that required by the school code and provided by the school board.
- Any contract with the private company must include a detailed, three-year cost projection in the bid that cannot be increased.
- The board of education must provide a detailed cost comparison of its in-house services and the outsourcing bid.
- The subcontractor must provide information regarding sexual misconduct, substance or alcohol abuse, Department of Children and Family Services (DCFS) complaints and investigations, traffic violations, and licensure problems and revocation of employees who may perform the services.
- A review and consideration of bids must take place in an open session of the regularly scheduled school board meetings.
- Two public hearings must be held before two regularly scheduled board of education meetings to discuss the issue. Public notice of the first hearing must be posted six months in advance of that hearing.
- The subcontractor must offer available positions to district employees who are terminated due to the contract.

In addition, if employees have union representation, the employer must negotiate in "good faith" as required under the IELRA any decision to outsource jobs. It is illegal to threaten outsourcing as a means to oppose unionization.[48]

Conclusion

Following the 1977 staff lockout and subsequent 1980 strike, most IEA leaders and staff wanted an end to the destructive internecine warfare that plagued the organization. The election of President Weaver in 1981 ended the bitter political infighting within IEA and set the stage for forty years of progress. Having a talented department of government relations led by Ken Bruce enabled IEA to pass what many consider to be the best public education bargaining laws in the nation. The IELRA includes provisions lacking in the laws of many other states. It provides a major incentive to organize unions since it guarantees public education employees a major voice in all decisions that affect their employment. By 2010, virtually all K–12 teachers had union representation. In addition, IEA, IFT, and other unions organized thousands of education support personnel. Almost all community college full-time faculty have organized unions, as have the faculty and staff at many state universities. By 2021, IEA active membership had increased almost 250 percent since 1983, making it the largest union in Illinois, with 124,349 members.[49] On numerous occasions, President Weaver called on IEA members and staff to "bring me some members." His call was answered.

CHAPTER 11

Organizing K–12 under the Act

When we realized that we might be able to pass a comprehensive collective bargaining bill, we began to think about our organizing strategy under the new law.

—Clay Marquardt, IEA executive director

Passage of the Illinois Educational Labor Relations Act (IELRA) marked the beginning of twenty-seven consecutive years of membership growth for the Illinois Education Association (IEA). In 2010, IEA reported 130,158 active members, a 254 percent increase from 1983.[1] While the bargaining law provided the incentive for education employees to organize unions, IEA's success would not have been possible without some major changes within the organization. Even though IEA continued to suffer membership losses until 1983, the election of Reginald "Reg" Weaver as president and the hiring of competent field managers under executive secretary John Ryor enabled a positive turnaround in the organization. Organizing local associations became a top priority with the passage of the bargaining laws. The National Education Association (NEA) provided organizing funding once the IELRA was adopted, and IEA hired Clayton "Clay" Marquardt, an astute manager, to direct field operations.

The NEA Organizing Project

Anticipating the enactment of the bargaining law, NEA provided valuable funding and staff to assist IEA's implementation of the law. Ted Tunison, NEA Midwest office, was assigned as coordinator of the Illinois organizing project. The NEA grant enabled IEA to hire ten full-time organizers to assist UniServ directors in organizing unions; over twenty teacher leaders were also hired part time to organize support staff units. While the organizing project funding slowly decreased, IEA secured additional NEA UniServ funding as a result of its membership increases. IEA retained its full-time organizers into the 1990s. Six organizers were assigned to offices across the state to assist locals facing internal problems, to ward off raids from the Illinois Federation of Teachers (IFT), and to generate election campaigns among the unorganized school employees and IFT locals. The other four organizers worked on the Southern Illinois University campuses at Edwardsville, Carbondale, and East St. Louis. IEA was positioned to take full advantage of the bargaining law, embarking on a major organizing campaign in 1983.[2]

The organizing campaign began prior to the signing of the bargaining law. Knowing that boards of education would be required to bargain once the IELRA went into effect on January 1, 1984, IEA staff and leaders won 134 K–12 exclusive recognition elections from August to December 1983 following procedures established under the 1982 recognition law (Public Act 82-107). The locals that won these elections began preparing for negotiations immediately, knowing that bargaining would begin soon after January 1. IEA had another seventy-two elections from January through June 1984.[3] Many of these elections were also handled under the procedures of the 1982 recognition law, while the Illinois Educational Labor Relations Board (IELRB) was in the process of hiring staff and adopting its operating rules and regulations. From September 1983 to July 1986, the number of IEA K–12 teacher contracts increased from 370 to 606, resulting in over 7,600 new members (see table 15).[4]

As the director of field operations, Marquardt kept the focus on organizing and membership growth. He believed that "data was crucial in identifying organizing targets."[5] His department regularly published detailed analyses of IEA membership and of labor board petitions filed by IEA, IFT, and other unions.[6] He began semiannual field staff meetings with updates on election activity, fair share contract settlements, IFT activity, and IEA membership. He encouraged leaders and staff to bargain fair share provisions in contracts. By 2001, over 60 percent (611) of IEA

Table 15. K–12 Teacher Bargaining Agreements

Year[*]	Districts[**]	No. contracts (%)[***]	IEA	IFT	Other[****]	No agreement
1983	1,008	493 (49)	370	102	21	515
1986	996	807 (81)	606	162	39	189
1991	950	854 (90)	645	179	30	96
2001	892	856 (96)	653	190	13	36

Sources: ISBE, "Illinois Teacher Salary and Contract Provision Study: 1983–84," ii, 15–16; ISBE, *Teacher Salary Study*, for years 1990–91, 9–10, 24; 2000–2001, iii, 9–10.

* Fiscal year ending June 30.

** The number of K–12 districts steadily declined due to school consolidations.

*** The figures in parentheses represent the percentage of total districts with contracts.

**** In 1983, Woodstock District 200 teachers had an IEA-IFT confederated bargaining unit. In 1984, IFT won exclusive representation rights in the district.

contracts would have fair share clauses.[7] Marquardt, in effect, fostered a sense of accomplishment and confidence among the field staff that encouraged organizing, in sharp contrast to the anger and frustration of the Stoltz-Darr administration.

The rapid increase in local unions resulting from organizing added greatly to the workload of UniServ directors. As a result, IEA management was concerned that the situation could result in a reluctance to organize new locals. To address this situation, Marquardt devised a flexible staffing plan. This plan established 1,300 members (slightly higher than the 1,200 required for NEA UniServ funding grants) as the baseline for regional membership. When the membership of a region reached 2,600 members (twice the baseline), it qualified for an additional UniServ director. If two or more regions in a field office had a combined membership in excess of this amount, they also qualified for an additional UniServ director. For example, in June 1987, Palatine office Regions 34 and 35 together had 4,071 members. Under the plan, the two regions hired a UniServ director to provide assistance for seven of their locals totaling 1,319 members in a new service area. Region 34 was left with eight locals with 1,303 members, and Region 35 ended up with four locals and 1,449 members for servicing. Service areas for region councils were created across the state, as IEA membership increased after the passage of the IELRA. In many cases, new region councils with representation on the board of directors were created. In 2024, IEA had sixty-nine region councils.[8] Having fewer locals in a region also meant less traveling time for UniServ directors, especially in rural downstate regions. Knowing that additional staff would be hired to handle the increased workload, region leaders and staff encouraged locals to organize. The flexible staffing plan incentivized organizing. Marquardt served as the IEA executive director from 1993 to 2005.[9] According to Larry Lawlyes, Clay's leadership in "handling growth through organizing" contributed greatly to IEA's long-term success.[10]

In addition to K–12 teachers, IEA had 263 education support professional (ESP) unions by 2010. All but 14 of these bargaining units were organized after the passage of the IELRA. K–12 ESP membership ballooned from just 1,365 in 1983 to 29,433 by 2010.[11]

As suburban sprawl reached west of Cook County, IEA preeminence in DuPage County and the Fox River Valley school districts resulted in large membership increases. In DuPage County, IEA represented K–12 teachers in forty of the forty-three districts. In Kane, Kendall, and McHenry Counties, IEA had teacher bargaining units in all but two of the thirty-four K–12 districts. IFT represented only Woodstock and East Aurora in these three counties. IEA also represented the Plainfield teachers in Will County.[12] By the mid-1980s, baby boomer families started moving in ever-increasing numbers to the suburban collar counties. As the population of these suburban counties increased, so too did the number of

Table 16. IEA Membership Increases in West Suburban Counties

County/District	1974 Teachers	1983 Teachers[*]	2020 Teachers	ESPs
DuPage County				
Naperville	540	564	1,409	592
Indian Prairie	65	128	2,109	556
Wheaton	548	436	1,132	198
Kane County				
St. Charles	280	285	1,007	343
Geneva	149	90	460	70
Elgin	1,414	1,079	2,512	1,233
West Aurora	458	353	884	248
McHenry County				
Huntley	41	40	719	283
Dundee	692	495	1,545	660
Kendall County				
Oswego	179	185	1,359	711
Yorkville	94	88	448	167
Will County				
Plainfield	198	160	1,988	847
Total	4,658	3,903	15,572	5,908

Sources: Superintendent of Public Instruction, "Illinois Teacher Salary Study: 1973–74"; ISBE, "Illinois Teacher Salary Schedule and Contract Provision Study: 1982–1983"; IEA Membership Processing, membership data provided January 5, 2021.

* In 1983, IEA did not have any ESP units in these districts except for Elgin U-46. Elgin had two IEA support staff unions in 1983; today it has four.

students, teachers, and support staff. Except for Elgin, the support staff employees in the twelve suburban districts shown in table 16 were not organized until after the enactment of the IELRA. Consequently, organizing a relatively small group of support staff employees in these suburban districts resulted in a large membership increase over the years. For example, when the Huntley support staff union organized in 1996, there were only 48 eligible voters; by 2020 the union had 283 members.[13] Across the twelve districts shown in table 16, IEA gained more than 17,000 members between 1983 and 2020.

From 1984 to 2013, IEA won 648 of 849 (76.3 percent) representation elections, with a potential membership of 35,265. During this same time, IEA filed 124 voluntary recognition petitions approved by the labor board, covering 4,319 employees. Many of these voluntary recognition petitions involved adding job categories to existing bargaining units rather than creating new locals.[14] In 2003, the IELRA was amended to allow a union to forgo an election if a majority of the employees in the proposed bargaining unit signed statements for union representation.[15] From 2003 to 2013, IEA filed 158 majority interest petitions, covering 4,989 employees (see table 17).

Once the IELRA became law, the vigorous opposition to collective bargaining in many districts, such as Oswego, Belvidere, Bensenville, and Sandwich, ebbed.

Table 17. IEA Representation Petitions, 1984–2013

	Election	Majority interest	Voluntary recognition
No. petitions	849 (648)*	158	124
No. employees	35,265	4,989	4,319

Source: "Activity and Membership Data: September 1, 2012–August 31, 2013," IEA Field Services Series, 2013, 36, 38–39.

* Figure in parentheses represents the number of elections won.

Collective bargaining became the norm throughout the state, but some districts continued to resist.

School District Resistance

In Queen Bee District 16 (Glendale Heights), superintendent Joseph Kariotis, who had fired seventy-four striking teachers in 1972, vowed that "bargaining with the teachers union will be over my dead body." As it turned out, he had good reasons for not wanting a teacher association to oversee how District 16 was spending its money.[16]

In July 1979, my wife, Barbara, and I moved to Glen Ellyn Countryside, where our children attended District 16 schools. Barbara was hired as a full-time secretary and became good friends with many of the district's teachers. In 1983, I was president of the Geneva Education Association and had been hired as a part-time organizer. When District 16 teachers petitioned the labor board for exclusive representation under Public Act 82-107, I was asked to help with the election. Barbara and I encouraged teachers to vote for the Queen Bee Education Association (QBEA). After the union won the election, the superintendent announced major cuts in staff and programs effective July 1, 1984. The budget cuts seemed to be a prelude to hard bargaining that might result in another teacher strike, but events led District 16 in another direction.

QBEA president John Mazur, Barbara, and I, along with many parents, attended the next school board meeting, where the budget cuts were publicly announced.[17] We raised some critical questions about the district's finances and spending. Three days later, Barbara was fired, even though her job was not included in the announced cuts. Kariotis gave her ten minutes to gather her belongings and leave the school or face arrest. IEA filed a federal lawsuit on Barbara's behalf, charging the district with violating her freedom of speech.[18]

In the meantime, we organized the Concerned Parents of Queen Bee Schools to pressure the school board to pass a referendum and restore the budget cuts. The parent group exposed the fact that the superintendent had, for years, been doling out favors to some school board members and misappropriating district funds. As the scandal came to light, school board members resigned and the parent group filled the vacancies.[19] In 1985, the superintendent was fired and faced a sixty-count felony indictment. We settled out of court soon after his firing.[20] He eventually pleaded guilty and was fined $14,868, given a six-month of weekend nights in jail sentence, and ordered to do five hundred hours of community service.[21] Subsequently, QBEA reached an excellent bargaining agreement with the new board, and the support staff employees joined QBEA, creating a wall-to-wall union.

Like with Queen Bee, many districts across the state did not have local associations until after the bargaining laws were passed in the early 1980s. Other districts did have well-established teacher locals but refused to bargain until they were mandated to do so by the IELRA. Such was the case with Lake Park High School. Throughout the 1970s, the Lake Park administration did its utmost to undermine the Lake Park Education Association (LPEA). It refused to bargain with the local, even though most teachers were LPEA members. Having no choice, Lake Park reluctantly commenced negotiations with LPEA in 1984, but the teachers threatened a strike to force the board to settle a first contract. For LPEA, the first contract was about power. To secure its rights, LPEA prioritized contract language over salary. It bargained a modest salary increase and secured some of the best contract language in the state. A salary schedule based on education and teaching experience replaced merit pay and the differentiated staffing system. A separate salary schedule was bargained for coaches and those who oversaw extracurricular activities. Parental leave for the birth of a child or for adoption, teacher evaluation, discipline, medical benefits, and other contract language ended much of the discretionary power of the administration. Future negotiations focused on achieving salary equity with other high schools in the county. The LPEA's second agreement, signed in 1986, included all ESP employees. Along with the QBEA agreement, it was among the first IEA wall-to-wall contracts.[22]

Strikes

Prior to the 1984 act, strikes were widely considered illegal, and participants faced possible court injunctions, fines, firings, and arrest. Usually, such threats did not dissuade strikes. IEA locals engaged in more than two hundred strikes from 1971 to 1983. Importantly, the 1984 act established a legal framework not just for strikes to take place but also for school employers and the union to bargain collectively, and it provided for the filing of unfair labor practice (ULP) charges to redress violations of the law. Boards could no longer assert raw power over the unions. Even though the law upheld the right to strike, then, the number and duration of strikes steadily declined (see table 18).

Negotiations could be especially difficult even with the protections of the IELRA. Such was the case in Homer, a small central Illinois town. After months of bargaining, the Homer Association of Teachers and the school board reached an impasse,

Table 18. IEA Strikes

Years	No. strikes	Total days	Average days/strike
1984–93	115	1,192	10.4
1994–2003	46	418	9.1
2004–13	31	193	6.2
2014–23	10	76	7.6

Sources: "Activity and Membership Data: September 1, 2012–August 31, 2013," IEA Field Services Series, 2013, 34; "IEA Strike History: 2014–2023," IEA Field Services, information provided to author, 2022.

mainly over salary. Twenty-seven teachers, including eleven nontenured, walked out on October 17, 1986. Citing a large budget deficit, the school board refused to budge on its salary offer. As the strike dragged on, IEA research specialist Harry Van Houdnos exposed the fact that the district had asked the Champaign County treasurer to withhold $250,000 in tax revenue in order to support its deficit claim.[23]

In January, the Homer board began hiring substitute strikebreakers at $92 per day, a higher daily pay rate than many of the striking teachers received.[24] This action hardened feelings on both sides. Colleen Brodie, a sixth-grade teacher and president of the local association, explained: "If that had not been done, things would have progressed differently." As the strike dragged on, legal expenses mounted. Brodie demurred: "The thing that sticks with me is that the School Board spent more money on legal fees than it would have taken to settle with the teachers."[25] The strike polarized this tightly knit community. Some families moved out of town. Property values declined. Others paid out-of-district tuition to enroll their children in neighboring school districts.[26] Bruce Miller, a junior high teacher, said: "It was sad. It tore the town apart. Some awfully good people left Homer and never moved back. I don't think Homer ever fully recovered. It was discouraging to see how people that I thought were my friends turned against me. I would wave at somebody, and he or she wouldn't wave back to me."[27]

In January, IEA asked its thirty-eight regions to each raise $800 per month in support of the Homer teachers for the duration of the strike.[28] IEA ultimately raised $225,000 in support of the "Homer 27." President Weaver made numerous visits to Homer; he reported: "I remember the nastiness. Even though they started back the next year, it wasn't the same. There were a number of excellent teachers who had gone somewhere else to teach. The whole town suffered."[29]

The strike became a lockout in April, when the board refused to rehire the striking teachers.[30] Ten ESP employees voted to join the teacher bargaining unit, and the union was renamed the Homer Association of Teachers and Support Staff.[31] A two-year contract was signed on June 23, ending the strike. All striking employees were reinstated. Brodie stated: "The teachers and the support staff are very pleased. The ratification vote was unanimous. The terms of the settlement are fair and reasonable."[32] The strike lasted 147 school days. It was the longest education strike in Illinois history.

In the aftermath of the strike, the region's UniServ director resigned his position and moved to Peoria to work in his father's business. More than half of the teaching staff left the district. In 1989, Homer consolidated with Allerton-Broadlands-Longview. Homer High School was closed as part of the consolidation agreement.[33]

While a teacher strike in a small town like Homer could be especially difficult for all involved, an Elgin secretarial strike in 1987 demonstrated the power of a support staff union in a large school district. The strike lasted just three days. On the first day, the district hired temporary replacements from Kelly Girl Services. It turned out to be a disaster. The Kelly secretaries did not know how to fill out attendance sheets, arrange for substitute teachers, distribute medication required by some students, prepare timesheets for the upcoming payroll, or handle most other duties of the striking secretaries. The striking secretaries purposely hid office materials so that many of these temporary secretaries could not even find filing cabinet keys, phone numbers, or other work-related materials. Not knowing the students, staff, or daily routine, the Kelly replacements proved to be a total waste of money. In addition, the principals were concerned that their relationship with the secretaries would be permanently damaged. They urged the administration to settle the strike quickly.[34]

The strike took place in the dead of winter; 100 percent of secretaries walked out. Their picketing in the bitter cold raised a great deal of sympathy within the community. Some principals provided hot chocolate to the secretaries on the picket line. Teachers joined them on the picket line and flooded the schools with various requests that the replacements could not fulfill. Community members, especially parents, demanded that the board settle the strike. On the second day, the teachers union threatened to file a grievance against Elgin Unit District 46 (U-46) unless the payroll checks arrived on time. On the third day, U-46 "surrendered" and reached a fair settlement with the secretaries union. UniServ director Gerry Gordon, who assisted the union during the strike, observed: "In organizing school secretary unions, I would refer to my experience [in Elgin]. Secretaries are critical to the operation of a school district. I would explain to the secretaries that they could achieve much if they organize a union."[35]

In 1988, U-46 custodial/maintenance union employees switched their affiliation from the Service Employees International Union (SEIU) to IEA; teacher assistants organized with IEA the following year. IEA represented five unions in U-46—all the district's employees except the SEIU food service union.[36] In Elgin, school boards would ebb and flow politically, sometimes working cooperatively with IEA and sometimes taking an aggressive stand in negotiations with IEA locals. Despite occasional efforts by superintendents and board members to undermine these unions, IEA locals in districts like Queen Bee, Lake Park High School, and Elgin have survived and thrived over the years.

Organizational Rivalry between IEA and IFT

Since the 1960s, IEA had been engaged in a bitter contest with IFT over teacher representation rights. Prior to the passage of the IELRA, IFT was on the offensive in raids against IEA bargaining units. IFT won fifteen representation elections against IEA teacher locals from 1977 to 1983, including the large districts of Champaign, District 211, Harlem, and Peoria. In addition, IFT "flipped" dozens of smaller IEA locals. Without a law establishing procedures for exclusive representation, IFT organizers convinced a number of IEA locals to switch their affiliation to the federation without conducting a formal election. During this same period, IEA won only four elections against small IFT locals. After the passage of the IELRA, however, IEA did not suffer any major losses to IFT. In the spring of 1984, IEA won thirteen of fourteen elections involving IFT challenges of IEA locals; the only local that IEA lost was West Harvey, a district that IEA had taken from the federation in 1982.[37] IEA reported:

> IFT activity, especially challenges, was a standoff this year and is an important benchmark for IEA. We view this year as the end of a cycle where we corrected problems to hold off challenges to only Bloomington and had our organizers working on take-backs. This is the first year we could direct our attention from challenges to our existing locals. The cycle will be reversed if we can challenge them in more districts and they challenge us next year.[38]

In fact, IEA did somewhat reverse the course with the federation. IEA not only stopped any major losses to IFT after 1983, but actually gained more potential members than did IFT as a result of raiding (see table 19).

Table 19. Raiding Involving IEA and IFT Incumbent Unions

Year*	Elections	IEA Wins	PMs**	Elections	IFT Wins	PMs
1984	0	0	0	8	1	135
1985	2	0	0	2	0	0
1986	5	1	86	5	0	0
1987	2	0	0	1	1	43
1988	2	1	24	3	2	191
1989	2	1	102	3	1	67
1990	2	0	0	5	0	0
1991	2	2	430	5	2	88
1992	1	0	0	1	1	29
1993	1	0	0	4	3	120
1994	3	2	388	2	2	71
1995	0	0	0	1	0	22
Total	22	9	1,030	40	13	766

Sources: IEA, "Election and Voluntary Recognition Activity," 1991–92, 1994–95.
* Fiscal year ending June 30.
** PMs refers to potential members.

After 1988, Decatur and Rock Island were the only large IEA locals to face a challenge from an IFT local. Fair share agreements in Galesburg, Collinsville, and other large locals made it more difficult for IFT to maintain minority locals.

Turmoil in Decatur

The Decatur Education Association (DEA) fought representation elections against the Decatur Federation of Teachers (DFT) in 1986, 1989, and 1991. DFT was organized in 1946 and remained a small but vocal critic of DEA. Its membership varied from ten to fifty-three members. In 1984, the Decatur Federation of Teaching Assistants filed a petition with the labor board to represent 143 employees. IEA filed an intervening petition in order to be included on the ballot but was decisively defeated in the representation election. This victory gave IFT a solid foothold in the district. Consequently, IFT committed more resources to DFT.[39]

In March 1986, DFT filed an IELRA petition to represent Decatur teachers. At the time, DEA had 587 members, while DFT had fewer than 100 members. Surprisingly, DFT made a very credible showing in the election. In April, DEA defeated DFT by a 147-vote margin (493 to 346). Over 92 percent of eligible voters cast ballots in the election.[40]

UniServ director James Williams had provided effective service for DEA since 1971; however, he became the target of DFT derision by the mid-1980s. Williams purchased and remodeled a Frank Lloyd Wright mansion in an exclusive neighborhood in Decatur. His large social events at his home were widely known. This extravagance did not go over well with many Decatur teachers. To make matters worse, Williams increasingly spent less time attending building meetings with members. His aloofness undermined support for DEA. In 1986, Williams agreed to retire, and Mike Gibler, a talented UniServ director out of the Peoria office with extensive experience in dealing with IFT, agreed to assist DEA with negotiations.[41]

DEA committed itself to an ambitious bargaining package. Its demands included a significant salary increase to lift the average teacher pay to the median of comparable large school districts. It also wanted contract language on class size, seniority rights covering transfer policy, teacher evaluation, and student discipline. Soon after, DEA initiated negotiations.[42]

Negotiations did not go well. Sensing a sharp division among the teachers as evident by the April election, the school board decided to take advantage of the situation. The board refused to bargain class size, claiming that this was solely a management right and that it was not legally required to address the issue. It also opposed including language on teacher evaluation, involuntary transfer, and student discipline in the DEA contract. The board indicated a willingness to discuss these language issues with DEA after the contract was ratified.[43] The Decatur *Herald and Review* reported: "The Board thinks its administrative policies are sufficient, but the teachers want the issues addressed in their new contract."[44]

In September, DEA filed ULP charges against the district for refusing to bargain in good faith over class size and other language items.[45] After the district rejected binding arbitration offered by DEA, the teachers walked out on September 12.[46] DFT members fully supported the strike. In a show of solidarity, DEA promised, for the first time, that nonmembers would be allowed to vote on ratification of the new agreement.[47] Hoping to avoid the long-term bitterness generated by the 1971 strike, the district did not attempt to open any school buildings or require non-tenured teachers to report to work.[48] Ironically, Jeanelle Norman, the school board president, had been one of the "Decatur 14" nontenured teachers fired during the 1971 strike.[49] Jane Deininger, the director of personnel and board chief negotiator, had been DEA's chief negotiator in 1979.[50]

As the strike dragged on, the board offered a one-year contract with a 9.2 percent increase in the total cost of the salary schedule, including step and lane advancement and movement on teacher evaluation language, with the knowledge that a one-year contract would expose DEA to another challenge by DFT in the spring. James Hendren, the district's director of business affairs, acknowledged that DEA faced a predicament: "they're having problems with their membership. If there is the perception that they did not make a good settlement, there could be a problem with the (Decatur) Federation of Teachers."[51] Instead of rejecting a one-year deal outright, DEA countered with a 16.5 percent increase in the cost of the salary schedule. Joe Opitz explained: "We gave them a one-year proposal to demonstrate what it would take to get us up to the average pay in the state."[52] The strike continued with little progress at the table. The board publicly declared that there would be no makeup days, even though other districts that faced long teacher strikes made up most, if not all, of the missed days. DEA president Cole Williams countered: "We need to make up as many of those days as we can for the students. It makes a difference in the amount of curriculum covered and state aid received."[53]

On October 7, the eighteenth day of the strike, both sides had two-year proposals on the table. Teacher evaluation was now addressed, but there was no movement on class size, student discipline, or seniority rights. DEA asked for a 10.6 percent increase in the cost of the salary schedule the first year, followed by 6.8 percent the next, and makeup days for those lost during the strike. The board proposed 9.2 percent followed by 4 percent for the second year, and no makeup days.[54] Frustrated with the lack of progress, DEA asked IEA area coordinator Larry Lawlyes to meet with board attorney Jack Taylor in an attempt to reach a settlement. Joe Opitz explained: "We had reached a point where Jane (Deininger, the board's chief negotiator) and I simply wouldn't get it done."[55]

Later in the afternoon on October 7, Lawlyes met with Taylor. After several hours of discussion, Lawlyes presented to the DEA negotiating team an offer from the board to settle the strike on the condition that the schools must open the next morning. Following Lawlyes's presentation, DEA negotiators met with the board team to discuss the offer. At two o'clock in the morning, they reached a settlement. DEA notified all teachers to attend a meeting at five thirty that morning at the Lincoln Theater to consider ratification of the offer. If the contract passed, they were to resume classes at eight thirty that morning.[56] According to Lawlyes, the board's insistence on teachers returning to classes that same day as a condition of the settlement was revenge:

> The board wanted to punish the teachers. That was their "ounce of flesh." They were adamant about it. I knew from my meeting with the board's representatives that they were willing to move on several issues (makeup days was a major one). It was clear to me they wanted a settlement, but the board's representatives knew that to get five votes on the board, they had to get their little revenge. I concluded that a settlement was not possible if we didn't give the board that win. I knew that the forced timeline was going to be unpopular, but I reasoned that getting a long-term settlement with substantial contract improvements and ending a long tough strike was more important than a short-term inconvenience.[57]

The board agreed to a three-year contract with a 9.2 percent salary increase in the first year, followed by 4.75 percent and 5 percent in the next two years. The board also offered to make the 9.2 percent salary increase retroactive to the start of the school year. Just six of the eighteen strike days would be made up. Class size would be reopened for negotiations if the labor board ruled in favor of DEA's ULP. The contract included language on teacher evaluation and seniority rights for reductions in force. Involuntary transfer based on seniority was not covered. A letter of intent was included that committed the district to establishing a joint committee to discuss the problem of student discipline. Finally, in a surprise move, the board offered a fair share provision and increased association leave time.

The contract passed with an 89 percent vote of those attending the five thirty meeting. Classes resumed that morning.[58] Superintendent Robert Oakes pointed out that there was "less animosity out there today than there was at the end of the 1971 strike . . . this time a decision was made at the very onset, that if there was a work stoppage, the schools would be closed to all staff, and I think that helped to prevent the staff from getting angry with one another."[59]

But all was not quite so peacefully resolved. The crack-of-dawn ratification meeting time created a major problem for DEA. Leara Evans said that the ratification meeting was "just awful." At the time, she was a nontenured teacher and

DEA member. In 1984–85, she worked as a teaching assistant and was the vice president of the Decatur Federation of Teaching Assistants. Since the meeting was mere hours ahead of its early start, teachers with young children scrambled to get babysitters. A few were even out of town. Many were unable to attend. DFT also vociferously opposed the settlement. The fact that fair share was not on the table until the night that the tentative agreement was reached fed into DFT's narrative that DEA had sold out on salary, class size, and other issues in exchange for fair share, half-time release of the DEA president, and association leave time.[60]

The rush to settle left confusion over teacher evaluation. DEA understood that its ULP on the issue would not be withdrawn, whereas the district said it expected the matter to be settled since it agreed to include language in the contract outlining evaluation procedures. This disagreement delayed the signing of the contract until mid-November and further damaged DEA's reputation. DFT claimed that it could do better if teachers just gave it a chance.[61]

The 1986 strike became a rallying cry for DFT amid representation challenges in 1989 and 1991. IFT committed money and staff to the project. It viewed Decatur as a key link between its two large urban locals in Champaign and Peoria. With Decatur, it would be in a strong position to challenge IEA locals across central Illinois. IFT hired Dennis Zinn, the president of its Mt. Zion local, to lead the organizing efforts in neighboring Decatur. He received assistance from staff in Peoria and Champaign. In March 1989, DFT filed a petition to represent Decatur teachers; an election was scheduled for April 13.[62]

DEA had reason to be confident that it would prevail in the April election. It had won the 1986 election by 147 votes. Now, with fair share, 812 of the 949 teachers joined DEA.[63] It also had a solid core of activists in most district buildings. In spring 1987, DEA hired Mike Gibler to replace the retired James Williams as UniServ director. In sharp contrast to his predecessor, Gibler regularly visited school buildings, especially during lunch hours, to meet with teachers. These visits established his credibility among many teachers. In the 1987–88 school year, Ann Chambliss, a highly respected leader among teachers and someone well known throughout the community, was elected DEA president. Over the years, she had held leadership roles within the Black community and in various civic organizations.[64] Chambliss and Gibler provided strong leadership at the top of DEA. Chambliss stated: "We have the votes to win if we can get the teachers to vote."[65]

The April election was, however, a near disaster for DEA. Not only did DEA fail to get out the vote, but many teachers decided to give DFT "a chance to do better." Voter turnout was down from 92 percent in 1986 to 86.4 percent. More importantly, DEA received 87 fewer votes in the 1989 election than it did in 1986, while DFT's vote total increased by 62. The initial vote count indicated that DFT won the election by one vote: 407 to 406. On the next day, April 14, the labor board announced a corrected tally that gave DFT a two-vote margin (407 to 405); two votes were cast for "no representative," and six ballots were challenged.[66]

DEA filed an objection to the conduct of the election, citing the unauthorized closure of the polls at McArthur High School for a fifteen-minute break. DEA produced testimony of Jane Spires that "she went to the polls during the time. They were temporarily closed. Upon learning that the polls were closed, Spires stated that she decided not to wait for the polls to reopen because she had several appointments that afternoon. Spires further testified that because of her appointments, she was unable to return to the polls before they closed at 6 PM."[67] Based on this testimony, the labor board's executive director set aside the April 13 election results and scheduled a new election for May 24. On May 10, DEA filed a "limited exception" to the executive director's decision to schedule the new election without providing the required thirty-day campaigning period. Two days later, DFT filed a response to DEA's motion to stay the May 24 election. In response, the labor board canceled the May 24 election and ordered a hearing on the issue raised. In June, the hearing officer concluded that the unauthorized closure of the polls for fifteen minutes could have affected the outcome of the April election. An election was scheduled for September 28.[68]

IEA assigned five of its organizers to work with DEA leadership to stave off the DFT raid.[69] For the five weeks leading up to the election, IEA organizers assisted DEA building representatives in identifying supporters and organizing for the election. DEA also made a major concession on the issue of fair share. Ever since 1986, DFT had promised that it would eliminate fair share from the contact once it became the bargaining agent. In response, DEA promised that all teachers would again be allowed to vote on ratification of the successor agreement. But unlike in 1986, once the contract was ratified, there would be a separate vote on the implementation of the fair share provision. Turnout was key; 95 percent of eligible voters cast ballots. DEA won the election by sixty-four votes, 475 to 411. DFT gained only four more votes over its April election count, while DEA's support increased by seventy votes.[70]

DEA successfully bargained a two-year contract. As promised, once the contract was ratified, a vote to implement the fair share clause was taken. It failed to pass, and remained an unenforced provision of the DEA contract. DFT continued its efforts to oust DEA. In 1991, DFT again petitioned for a representation election. IEA assigned the same organizers to assist DEA. On April 24, DEA won by a wider margin than in 1989, 473 to 382. The turnout of eligible voters was 91.1 percent. DFT president Carole Sue Bean indicated that this challenge was probably DFT's last against DEA, stating: "We tried our best and brought issues to the forefront. The vote shows there are still a significant number of teachers who are dissatisfied. Perhaps, it will always be that way." The fair share clause was ratified in a separate ballot of the 1991 agreement.[71]

Rock Island Education Association

Though several large locals such as Collinsville, Galesburg, and Palatine success-fully fended off attempts by IFT insurgents to switch union affiliation in the 1980s, no IEA local faced more IFT challenges than did the Rock Island Education Asso-ciation (RIEA). From 1968 to 1993, RIEA defeated the IFT local union in ten rep-resentation elections.[72] All the victory margins were relatively close. In 1973, RIEA won by just six votes, 260 to 254; the last election was held in 1993, just prior to a no-raid agreement between NEA and the American Federation of Teachers (AFT).[73]

Rock Island was an important target of IFT not only because of its size but also because of its location in the heavily industrialized Quad Cities area. The school district hired over five hundred teachers in the 1970s. International Harvester, John Deere, J. I. Case, and other local manufacturers were unionized, giving the Rock Island Federation of Teachers (RIFT) a strong base from which to challenge RIEA over exclusive representation. Throughout the 1970s, RIFT membership steadily increased. Dues were much lower than for RIEA so as to encourage teachers to join RIFT. By 1981, 205 teachers (44 percent) had joined RIFT. In the 1981 elec-tion, RIEA won 223 to 214.[74] In nearby Moline—and in Davenport, Bettendorf, and other school districts on the Iowa side of the Mississippi River—AFT affili-ates made little headway against the NEA unions. Rock Island remained the focal point of IFT-AFT's efforts. If Rock Island teachers affiliated with the federation, it was believed that other districts would follow suit in the Quad Cities area.[75]

RIEA's greatest advantage in these elections was its strong local leadership and UniServ staff. George Dodd was hired in 1971 as the RIEA UniServ director. Pat Bihn, who replaced Dodd in 1984 after he retired, stated: "RIEA had some very strong women activists. They along with George Dodd were the glue that held the RIEA together in the face of a continuing RIFT onslaught."[76] In 1983, Dan Miller was elected RIEA president. Miller was a strong union advocate. He and Bihn worked well together, defeating RIFT challenges in 1984, 1989, 1990, and 1993.[77] Bihn recalled:

> Any mistake we made, RIFT would exploit to the hilt; and we made some mistakes. Perhaps the biggest mistake was trying to include the support staff employees in a wall-to-wall union with the teachers. We imagined how powerful a union of eight hundred teachers and support staff would be. In 1988, we petitioned for the support staff represented by AFSCME [the American Federation of State, County and Mu-nicipal Employees]. In doing so, we opened the door for RIFT. Many teachers were opposed to an all-inclusive wall-to-wall union. Not only did we withdraw our peti-tion against the AFSCME unit, but we almost lost the teachers 178 to 172 to RIFT.[78]

After 1988, the margin of wins over RIFT increased. In 1990 RIEA won by twenty-nine votes (216 to 187); RIEA's final victory over RIFT, in 1993, was 225 to 181.[79] The strong leadership of President Miller and the effective service provided by Bihn were crucial to RIEA's ability to fend off the RIFT threat.

The victories in Decatur and Rock Island marked the last attempt by IFT to challenge the bargaining rights of large IEA locals. After 1993, many of RIFT's leaders who had continued the fight over the years had retired.[80]

By the early 1990s, NEA and AFT initiated merger discussions because, in part, the competition between the two unions over representation of K–12 districts had largely been settled, not only in Illinois but also throughout the nation. Neither organization could hope to gain much from the K–12 organizing rivalry; more importantly, the unions shared common political interests and had been faced with growing attacks on public education and unionism from conservative anti-union groups since the 1980 election of President Ronald Reagan. While merger discussions continued at the national level, IEA entered a no-raid agreement with IFT in 1995. The national leadership of NEA and AFT drafted a merger agreement entitled "Principles of Unity." When the merger agreement came up for a vote at the 1998 NEA representative assembly (RA), however, only 42 percent of delegates supported it. Though the merger failed, it paved the way for IEA, the Chicago Teachers Union (CTU), and IFT to work together on educational reform and to address the growing right-wing threat to education unionism.

Conclusion

The IELRA paved the way for a remarkable turnaround in IEA's fortunes. The NEA organizing project, coupled with insightful leadership, resulted in a major increase in membership. NEA funding enabled IEA to hire staff who organized thousands of teachers and support staff employees. The rapid growth of suburban school districts outside Cook County where IEA locals represented many K–12 teachers and support staff employees also contributed greatly to membership increases. IEA membership more than doubled from 1984 to 2001. The IELRA also effectively limited efforts by superintendents and school boards to oppose unionism. Most districts, often reluctantly, reached contractual agreements with their unions. The number and length of strikes steadily declined, even though they were legal for the first time. Following the passage of the IELRA, almost all the membership increases of IEA and IFT were a result of organizing the unorganized. Very little was gained by raiding the other's bargaining units. While the two unions competed, at times, in organizing new unions, the no-raid agreement marked the growing cooperation between IEA and IFT in addressing the threat to public education and unionism by the political right.

CHAPTER 12

Organizing Higher Education

Today, university faculties are faced with a new threat to their academic freedom—one which does not come from zealots outside the university, but from the university bureaucracy itself. . . . It has to do with administrative interference with the management of classrooms and research activities, and with administrative retaliation against faculty members who express opposition to managerial decisions of the university bureaucracy.

—Donald J. Keck and Marcus Albrecht

Besides funding K–12 organizing efforts, the National Education Association (NEA) organizing project provided the Illinois Education Association (IEA) with significant resources to organize at state universities. In 1984, IEA staff visited universities across the state to measure support for collective bargaining. IEA decided that Southern Illinois University (SIU), where IEA already represented civil service employees through the Civil Service Bargaining Organization (CSBO), offered the best organizing opportunities among faculty and staff at Edwardsville (SIUE) and Carbondale (SIUC). When the Illinois Educational Labor Relations Act (IELRA) was enacted, IEA had just five full-time faculty units, all at community colleges: McHenry, Lewis and Clark, John L. Logan, Carl Sandburg, and Southeastern. As was the case with K–12 districts, organizing community college employees was the responsibility of IEA organizers, UniServ directors, and leaders in the areas served by the colleges. In 1983, IEA reported 590 higher education members; by 2021, it had 4,377.[1]

Organizing at Universities

The first step in this effort was to identify potential organizing targets. UniServ director John McCluskey, who played a key role organizing efforts at SIU in the 1970s, had conversations with faculty at Northern Illinois University and reported back that there was very little interest in collective bargaining on the campus.[2] In May 1984, IEA hired David Rathke to scout potential targets at other campuses. His visits at Sangamon State University and Illinois State University were not productive. Rathke spent seven months of intensive work at SIUE and SIUC, meeting with faculty and identifying potential leaders. Rathke recruited Sheila Ruth, a faculty member in the SIUE philosophy department, to lead IEA's faculty organizing effort at SIUE. At Carbondale, he found guidance and educational psychology professor Michael Altekruse to lead the effort.[3]

In January 1985, NEA organizing project director Ted Tunison hired Marcus Albrecht and David Vitoff for the SIUE and SIUC campaign. NEA higher education specialist Don Keck was assigned as its coordinator; he worked both campuses. Albrecht wrote: "Keck was a brilliant strategist and brought decades of higher education experience, commitment, and insight to the SIU campaigns. He inspired the IEA higher education organizing staff and directed the campaigns to completion of the first elections in 1988."[4] IEA also hired SIUE cross-country coach John Flamer. He had been the late John Rendleman's special assistant for the president for affirmative action. Flamer was well known on campus and especially effective in convincing professional staff to sign IEA's authorization cards for a representation election. After Rathke accepted a Region 5 UniServ position, IEA hired Illinois American Association of University Professors (AAUP) executive secretary Charles Zucker as a fourth organizer. In addition, IEA president Reginald "Reg" Weaver, vice president Lee Betterman, secretary-treasurer Jim Nagle, board of directors member Pearl Mack, and other elected leaders as well as UniServ directors worked with the organizers to gather faculty signatures on authorization cards needed to petition the Illinois Educational Labor Relations Board (IELRB) to conduct a union representation election. President Weaver was especially helpful; he made numerous visits to the SIUE and SIUC campuses throughout the campaign.[5] In 1985, IEA filed five representation petitions for SIU faculty and staff.[6]

Complicating the situation, the Illinois Federation of Teachers (IFT) and AAUP launched their own campaigns for representation at the university. AAUP filed representation petitions for separate units of faculty and professional staff at SIUC. IFT petitioned for combined faculty/staff units at SIUC and at SIUE. All the union faculty petitions included department chairs. IEA was the only union to file a petition for the faculty at the School of Dental Medicine in Alton, Illinois.[7]

SIU vigorously opposed the unions' organizing efforts. It hired Seyfarth, Shaw, Fairweather and Geraldson LLP, an anti-union law firm based in Chicago, to help it fight the petitions and assist its campaign against the unions. SIU paid over $335,580 for the firm's services by 1989.[8] SIU challenged the composition of the proposed bargaining units, and it objected to the inclusion of department chairs.

It also wanted a single, system-wide bargaining unit for all faculty and a single system-wide unit for all professional staff, rather than separate units at SIUE and SIUC as proposed by IEA.[9] SIU's strategy was to have bargaining units that would be most likely to lose an election. It also used the legal process to create long delays, giving it time to campaign against the unions. System-wide bargaining units would also concentrate power in the chancellor's office, rather than with the campus presidents.[10]

Labor board hearings lasted forty-one days. After the hearings, each party wrote briefs explaining their legal arguments. In October 1987, the hearing officer rendered an opinion on the composition of the bargaining units as IEA had proposed.[11] However, the university appealed the decision to the three-member labor board, causing further delays. Finally, in early September 1988, IEA threatened to seek a writ of mandamus to force a labor board ruling on the petitions. On September 30, the labor board upheld the hearing officer's decision.[12] Jim Nagle noted, "The ruling was a complete victory for IEA. We insisted on five separate campus bargaining units and the inclusion of the department chairs—and we won!"[13] After more than three years of labor board hearings and appeals, five elections were scheduled for November 16, 1988.

During this long period of delay, IEA established a Faculty Organization for Collective Bargaining (FOCB) and a Professional Staff Organizing Committee (PSOC) at SIUE and SIUC. These committees organized the filing of grievances under the university's employer-friendly grievance policy. These grievances, related to employment issues, lent credibility to IEA among the faculty and staff on each campus. Academic freedom was a major concern among faculty. As enrollment rapidly increased in the 1960s, so too had the size of the administration and the bureaucracy under its control. Association staff organizers Don Keck and Marcus Albrecht wrote: "During the past 15 to 20 years the new managerial bureaucracy has continued to expand its claims to a newfound managerial authority which entitles it to interfere with teaching and research functions of the faculty."[14] Decision-making became increasingly top-down. IEA cited examples of administrative actions that violated academic freedom, such as:

- changing students' final grades without consulting their instructors
- denying tenure to faculty critical of the administration
- interfering in classroom instruction/research and removing faculty from positions for opposing administrative planning
- threatening *Alestle,* the SIUE student newspaper, for publishing stories critical of the administration
- systematically downsizing the tenured faculty at SIUC by hiring non-tenure-track instructors.[15]

David J. Sill, SIUE associate professor, explained the need for collective bargaining: "The Administration and faculty have a parent-child relationship; the all-wise, benevolent, and protective administrators take care of us, give our work direction and meaning, and make major decisions, having final authority over all the decisions. . . . Through collective bargaining, we have the power to establish a PARTNERSHIP BETWEEN THE FACULTY AND THE ADMINISTRATION."[16] IEA's organizing committees also raised issues that affected all SIU staff, including asbestos exposure, minimal or no salary increases for faculty/staff, excessive salary increases and perks for administrators, the replacement of full-time staff positions with short-term and part-time employees, and the inadequacy of the university's internal grievance policy, which left the final decision on disputes to the administration.[17]

In September 1987, IEA released a report exposing discrepancies in hiring practices based on race and gender at SIUE.[18] The report indicated that the percentage of African Americans on the faculty and in administrative positions had declined since 1979 (see table 20).

PSOC at SIUE arranged with Rep. Helen Satterthwaite (D-Urbana), chairwoman of the Illinois House Committee on Higher Education, a public hearing to collect information on hiring practices of faculty and staff. Fifty people attended.[19] A major issue raised at the hearing involved the SIUE staff working in Head Start and child development programs at SIUE's East St. Louis Center. Leonard Long, political action chair of the SIUE PSOC, reported that:

> SIUE Professional staff who work at SIUE East St. Louis center are primarily black women who work on term contracts [of] one year, renewable at the discretion of the university, generally do not receive annual raises, and make significantly less than professional staff at the Edwardsville campus.
>
> Professional staff working at the Edwardsville campus are primarily white, evenly divided between male and female, the majority work on continuing contracts (permanent employees), generally received annual raises, and that female professional staff make significantly less than the male professional staff working in the same positions.[20]

The average annual salary of employees in East St. Louis was almost $7,000 less than that of employees in Edwardsville, where women also received lower salaries

Table 20. African American Faculty and Staff at SIUE

	All faculty		Administration	
	1979	1987	1979	1987
No. employed	535	436	183	194
No. African American (%)	44 (8.2)	18 (4.1)	24 (13.1)	18 (9.3)

Source: "Affirmative Action Problems Plague SIU-E Faculty, Staff, Administration," *Alestle* (SIUE), January 21, 1988, 1, 12.

Table 21. SIUE Employment Data, 1988

	Edwardsville campus	East St. Louis Center
Men	49%	15%
Women	51%	85%
White	88%	1%
African American	12%	99%
Continuing employment	65%	4%
Annual employment	35%	96%

Source: "Affirmative Action Problems Plague SIU-E Faculty, Staff, Administration," *Alestle* (SIUE), January 21, 1988, 1, 12.

than their male counterparts.[21] The IEA report presented at the hearing included these staff employment statistics (see table 21).

Several SIUE officials attended the hearing, but not SIUE president Earl Lazerson.[22] Lazerson later blamed the employment disparity at the two sites on the funding sources. Annual contracts and lower pay in East St. Louis, he said, were a direct result of the uncertainty of federal funding year to year. Head Start was funded by "soft money" federal grants, while the child development programs were funded by state aid grants. Edwardsville relied on a relatively secure source of student tuition and state aid. IEA responded that nothing prevented the university from providing additional funding for the East St. Louis programs to address job security and salary concerns of the staff.[23]

PSOC also challenged the firing of Fannie Jones from the East St. Louis Child Development Center. Jones was a fourteen-year employee with above-average evaluations, a civil rights activist, and a union leader. After a parent filed a complaint, Jones was suspended with pay in June 1987 and notified that her annual contract would not be renewed on July 1. Jones was denied a copy of the parent complaint. In accordance with existing university policy, IEA filed a grievance, charging that SIUE had denied Jones due process and just cause. Shortly thereafter, her husband suffered a stroke. PSOC organized several benefits on her family's behalf and appealed to local political leaders and churches to support her reinstatement. The NAACP, Child Development Center parents, East St. Louis mayor and city council, and East St. Louis Human Rights Commission called on President Lazerson to reinstate her with full back pay.[24] In January 1988, Lazerson denied her grievance, after which SIU chancellor Lawrence Pettit rejected her appeal.[25] Jones responded: "I am disappointed in the chancellor. I had hoped for justice. My case demonstrates how much SIU employees need collective-bargaining." In April 1988, Fannie Jones graduated with honors in computer programming at a local vocational center and found a good-paying job.[26]

Censorship of *Alestle*, SIUE's student newspaper, was another organizing issue. On a number of occasions, university officials sharply criticized the newspaper over articles about the IEA union organizing campaign. In December 1986, *Alestle* ran a story about an investigation into missing funds at the newspaper, despite an administrator's order not to print it. In retaliation, the administration withheld commission payments for the student advertising staff. In April, the Illinois House Committee on Higher Education scheduled a subcommittee hearing on the issue. The next month, *Alestle*'s editor, Deborah Pauly, charged that about two thousand copies of the newspaper at four campus buildings were removed before students could access them.[27] At a press conference, IEA president Weaver said: "We are not going to go away. We are not going to allow those things that we believe are wrong to continue."[28] The House subcommittee never met. Instead, several legislators met with Pauly, two PSOC leaders, and IEA staff. A follow-up meeting of state legislators, IEA representatives, and President Lazerson resolved the issue in favor of Pauly and the newspaper staff.[29]

By acting on these issues, the IEA organizing committees became the leading advocates for faculty and staff. Their efforts helped them recruit a core of highly credible leaders for the emerging SIU unions. Realizing that IEA had the lead, IFT and AAUP resorted to a merger and consolidated their petitions in August 1988. They campaigned as a single organization, AAUP-FOCB/IFT. Soon after the labor board set the date for the elections, tenured faculty opposed to unionism organized the Committee on No Agent to garner support for "no representative." IEA purchased ads in *Alestle* to make its case for collective bargaining.[30] The Committee on No Agent also purchased ads in the two months leading up to the November election.[31]

On November 16, 1988, IEA lost three of the elections. A majority of both faculty and professional staff employees at SIUC voted against representation, as did the faculty at the School of Dental Medicine. The majority of SIUE faculty voted for representation, splitting their votes between IEA and AAUP-FOCB/IFT. "No representative" received the largest number (42 percent) of votes cast. IEA came in second, with 28 percent, and AAUP-FOCB/IFT received 27 percent. The result was a runoff between IEA and "no representative." The SIUE professional staff election results were not counted. The labor board impounded the professional staff ballots due to an AAUP-FOCB/IFT motion challenging the ballot configuration. Instead of having all employees vote on a single ballot, AAUP-FOCB/IFT argued that the staff at the East St. Louis Center did not fit the IELRA's definition of professional employees and therefore should receive separate ballots.[32]

Rather than face long delays in hearings at the labor board, IEA agreed to have another election, this time with Edwardsville and East St. Louis voting separately. Two questions were asked: (1) whether to combine the two subgroups of professional staff into one bargaining unit, and (2) whether to have union recognition. For the IEA-backed SIUE Professional Staff Association (PSA) to win, it needed to receive a majority of the votes cast on both questions, and to do so among voters at both sites. This agreement made it more difficult for a union victory. The runoff elections for SIUE faculty and professional staff were held on February 22, 1989. Despite several leaders of the AAUP-FOCB/AFT faction urging their supporters to vote for representation, the SIUE Faculty Association lost by thirteen votes (220 to 207) to "no representative." The SIUE PSA, however, won the election at both sites, 129 to 85.[33]

PSA's bargaining was a slow and tedious process. With so many different job categories scattered across the Edwardsville campus and the East St. Louis Center, it took PSA a considerable time to develop and present its initial proposal to SIUE. But PSA, with the assistance of UniServ director Mike Cook, put together and trained a bargaining team that included representatives from both sites and that had instructional services lecturer LaDonna Holshouser as chief negotiator.[34]

PSA made its initial proposal for a comprehensive contract in the late spring of 1990. Contract negotiations began shortly thereafter and continued until October 1990, whereupon the parties mutually called a temporary pause in the negotiations and established an interim agreement containing a recognition clause, a grievance procedure ending in binding arbitration, and a "maintenance of standards" clause that would remain in place as negotiations toward a comprehensive contract continued later. Negotiations resumed in the spring of 1991. The contract, which took over a year to complete, resulted in a retroactive, three-year agreement covering the period from July 1, 1990, through June 30, 1993. It was ratified by PSA membership.[35]

In 1991, SIUE faculty voted again for "no representative," this time by a larger margin than in 1989.[36] Despite this loss, IEA's organizing efforts made progress. In 1995, an American Federation of State, County and Municipal Employees (AFSCME) technical staff bargaining unit at SIUE voted to join IEA.

SIUC Organizing

In 1996, SIUC tenure and tenure-track activists assisted by IEA organizer Dave Vitoff jumped on administration missteps and filed a representation petition. Unlike with the 1988 election, department chairs and non-tenure-track faculty were intentionally excluded from the petition, due to their low level of union support. Consequently, the SIUC Faculty Association won a decisive 63 percent of the vote. For NEA, this was the first four-year public university tenure-line faculty win in decades.[37]

Following the election, IEA UniServ director Jim Clark assisted the faculty unit at the bargaining table. It took over eighteen months of intensive negotiations—supplemented by the picketing of SIUC president Ted Sanders's office and other high-profile organizing actions—to achieve a first contract, retroactive to 1998. Clark explained: "Everything at the university goes really slow."[38] Nevertheless, the SIUC Faculty Association bargained successor agreements in 2000, 2002, and 2006. Throughout this period, the SIUC Faculty Association successfully lobbied to get friendly trustees appointed to the university's board. It even discovered that a hostile board member was no longer living in Illinois. As a result of its organizing activities, the union made steady progress at the bargaining table.[39]

The SIUC Faculty Association's success encouraged other university employees to organize. Clark continued to serve the local and assisted Vitoff in efforts to organize at SIUC. In 2004, the SIUC Non-Tenure Track Faculty Association (NTTFA) won representation rights in a vote of 109 to 58.[40] Once the SIUC Graduate Assistants United (GAU) organized in 2005, IEA had three unions at Carbondale. In 2010, all the IEA contracts expired. Bargaining of successor contracts began that spring.[41]

In early 2010, Illinois asked all its state agencies, including the universities, to implement unpaid furlough days to offset projected revenue shortfalls for the 2010–11 fiscal year. SIUC decided to impose four furlough days, representing roughly a 2 percent salary cut for its nonunion employees. American Federation of Labor and Congress of Industrial Organizations (AFL-CIO) unions on campus, including the plumbers, operating engineers, and AFSCME, reluctantly accepted the furlough days. Since the IEA contracts were about to expire, however, IEA locals refused to accept the furlough days and instead addressed the issue in bargaining. GAU was the exception; it had not received any furlough days.[42] After almost a year of bargaining with the unions, the university declared an impasse and imposed a one-year contract for 2010–11 that included the four furlough days. In response, IEA filed three unfair labor practice (ULP) complaints, charging the university with failing to bargain in good faith.[43]

Bargaining for the 2011–12 fiscal year began almost immediately. GAU and NTTFA settled their contracts, but the SIUC Faculty Association, failing to reach a settlement, went on strike in November 2011 after eighteen months of bargaining. The other IEA locals and many students supported the walkout. After six days, a tentative agreement was reached on all issues except the furlough days. According to professor Dave Johnson: "This new proposal represents a marked improvement over where we were just a few days ago, before the strike began."[44] A side letter signed by both parties acknowledged the refusal of IEA locals to drop the ULPs related to the imposed 2010–11 contract. IEA attorney Gene Holt consolidated the three ULPs charging SIUC with bad faith bargaining. In filing evidence for the ULP hearing, SIUC inexplicitly included notes of secret administrative meetings. Holt used this evidence to prove that the university's goal was to reach an impasse as quickly as possible in order to impose the furlough days on the unions. The evidence included such statements as "We want to get to impasse quickly. . . . We just have to get them to a point where they aren't proposing and they aren't agreeing to our proposal—need to box them in."[45]

In 2014, the IELRB upheld the hearing officer's decision that SIUC had engaged in bad faith bargaining. The labor board awarded the 1,500 employees of the three affected IEA unions $1.7 million in back pay. There was no economic remedy for GAU, since furlough days did not apply to graduate assistants; instead, the SIUC administration had to post a cease and desist statement that acknowledged its bad faith bargaining.[46] SIUC Faculty Association president Rachel Stocking stated: "This decision represents a victory not only for the unions that filed the unfair labor practice charge and the employees they represent, but also for the principles and practice of good faith collective bargaining."[47] Subsequently, SIUC decided to pay another $1.3 million to the other employees affected by the furlough days, to avoid potential legal action by other unions not party to the IEA ULP.

IEA's victory on the furlough days further enhanced IEA organizing efforts at SIUE. In 2016, the SIUE Faculty Association filed a majority interest petition (MIP) with the labor board. The MIP did not require an election, as long as the association could demonstrate majority support on individually signed forms among those covered by the proposed bargaining unit. The university never saw the signatures and could not mount a campaign against the union as it had done in the past. Since the labor board had already determined the appropriateness of the faculty bargaining unit, the union was certified soon after a required thirty-day posting period.[48]

University of Illinois Urbana-Champaign Coalition Organizing

In 1991, Larry Lawlyes and Jim Nagle convinced Gene Vanderport, their old friend from Danville, to apply to a UniServ director position in the Urbana-Champaign office. Vanderport left his job as the national director of organizing for the American Federation of Government Employees and accepted the UniServ director position. At the time, K–12 school employees were, by far, the largest group of unionized employees in the community, but there were ten thousand largely unorganized employees at the University of Illinois Urbana-Champaign (UIUC). Here was a great opportunity to have an impact.[49]

Vanderport convinced his IEA teacher and education support professional (ESP) locals of the importance of developing ties with other unions in the area. In 1991, his region council affiliated with the Champaign County Central Labor Council, the first IEA affiliation with an AFL-CIO central labor body. Meanwhile, the Graduate Employees' Organization (GEO), having close ties to other AFT graduate assistant unions, voted to organize as an IFT affiliate. IEA, along with AFSCME and the

Service Employees International Union (SEIU), supported GEO's efforts in its long and bitter battle with the university for bargaining rights. Eventually, other unions, including laborers, stagehands, and operating engineers, joined in the fray. GEO and its union allies organized a campus labor coalition named UIUC Unions United (UUU). UUU held regular strategy meetings and organized protests in support of GEO. In 2000, Vanderport, fifty-six graduate students, and a prominent minister conducted a highly publicized sit-in at the office of the board of trustees. The next year, GEO organized a strike that threatened to paralyze the university. In response, UIUC dropped its legal opposition and agreed to a representation election.[50]

GEO won the election, but bargaining with UIUC was tough. Throughout 2005–6, campus unions organized almost-daily rallies, building occupations, informational picketing events, and other public actions in support of GEO. GEO reached a settlement with UIUC that year. It is the largest union on the campus, representing more than 2,700 graduate assistants. The success of the labor coalition rested on union solidarity, in contrast with the union rivalries so prevalent in Illinois over the past forty years. The UUU coalition became a powerful force on the UIUC campus.[51]

The GEO victory had several important payoffs for IEA. The union's struggle served as a "boot camp" for union organizers and activists. IEA hired two talented GEO activists—Peter Miller and Steve Vaughan—after they graduated. Dan Chambers, a third organizer, was also hired by IEA. Chambers was not a GEO member but was politically active in the university community while his wife attended veterinary school. It should be noted that other unions ended up hiring, at least, seven GEO activists.[52]

Another payoff was the IEA's first union at UIUC. Vanderport organized a group of visiting academic professionals—about 350 employees—and bargained an agreement with the university in November 2006. Steve Vaughan organized staff at the UIUC Laboratory High School and the non-tenure-track faculty at Illinois State University.[53]

Vanderport's coalition building was not limited to unions. In 2006, he organized a central Illinois Mother Jones Chapter, affiliated with Jobs with Justice. The Mother Jones Chapter reached out to faith-based and community organizations. It brought labor unions, university workers, and community activists together to work on a living wage, privatization, health care, and other social justice/labor issues.[54]

The Champaign County Central Labor Council, UUU campus labor coalition, and Jobs with Justice chapter each conducted monthly meetings. The leadership of these three organizations overlapped, ensuring constant communication. Vanderport, for example, was a co-chair of UUU and Jobs with Justice. This coalition of unions and community organizations produced results. The Champaign County Central Labor Council and UUU endorsed and helped elect State senator Mike Frerichs, a progressive Democrat, over a tough Republican opponent. Senator

Frerichs, eventually elected as state treasurer, regularly attended UUU meetings and joined Jobs with Justice on the picket line about privatization at a community hospital. The union coalition was instrumental in introducing legislative initiatives and lobbying in Springfield for legislation. It also lent its support to A-Plus Illinois, a statewide effort to reform education funding. The goal of A-Plus was to create a more equitable funding system across the state while assuring wealthy school districts that they would not suffer revenue losses as a consequence.[55]

The funding issue opened the lines of communication with UIUC. Obviously, the university had an interest in state funding, especially in light of the fact that higher education had received a significant reduction in state aid over the past six years. UIUC president Joe White met on a regular basis with the labor coalition, and they worked together on lobbying efforts in Springfield.[56]

Contingent Faculty Organizing in the Chicago Metropolitan Area

As higher education attendance rapidly increased beginning in the 1960s, the percentage of full-time, tenure-track faculty steadily declined as a portion of the teaching staff. The abundance of college-educated baby boomers created a plentiful supply of labor to fulfill the growing demand for higher education teachers. According to Joe Berry, a cofounder of the Illinois chapter of the Coalition of Contingent Academic Labor and a member of its international advisory committee, contingent faculty today teach a substantial majority of all higher education classes. For employers, hiring contingent faculty provides a great deal of flexibility in scheduling classes, increases management control over faculty, and is an inexpensive source of labor.[57]

Contingent faculty include a wide variety of temporary, non-tenure-line teachers in public and private higher education institutions. There is a long list of terms used to describe these contingent faculty, but, in Illinois, large universities that have doctoral programs generally rely heavily on graduate assistants and non-tenure-track faculty to teach undergraduate classes. Graduate assistants normally teach one or two classes per semester, whereas non-tenure-track faculty often teach as many as four classes per semester. Though paid considerably less per semester hour than tenured and tenure-track faculty, contingent faculty at large universities typically receive higher pay than part-time faculty at community colleges and small, four-year institutions. In some cases, large universities even provide basic health-care benefits for contingent employees. At Illinois community colleges and institutions without doctoral programs, the part-time faculty are typically referred to as adjuncts. Community colleges and small private institutions like St. Xavier University and Columbia College hire adjunct instructors to teach a majority of their credit and noncredit (adult education) courses. These adjunct faculty typically teach one or two classes per semester, are paid at a much lower rate per class than tenure-line faculty, and receive little else. Private for-profit institutions generally hire the highest percent of adjuncts for teaching; these faculty are the lowest paid and have the highest turnover rate of any adjuncts.[58] While adjunct employment is temporary in that these instructors have no job security, some of them have taught classes at the same institution for over a decade.[59]

Adjunct faculty represent a complex and mobile workforce. Many work second jobs. For some, teaching supplements their full-time employment. Others hold several teaching positions on two or more campuses. Adjuncts also include graduate students working on their dissertations, moonlighting K–12 teachers, retirees, and private-sector professionals. Their teaching schedules vary just as widely as their working experiences do. Many teach classes late into the night. Most adjuncts spend very little time on campus other than teaching and have few opportunities to get acquainted with one another, making it difficult to act in a concerted manner around their common interests.[60]

Many adjuncts refer to themselves as "road scholars," traveling long distances to teach classes at several institutions in what amounts to a full-time faculty position, as they try to cobble together enough money to pay their bills, with the hope of eventually being hired full time. In 1998, for example, the *Chicago Tribune* reported that "Bob Lorek, a philosophy teacher, juggles as many as seven or eight classes at as many as five schools a week," making less than $33,000 and receiving no health insurance.[61] In effect, Lorek was teaching the equivalent of two full-time faculty positions. Low pay, few if any benefits, lack of any assurance of continued employment, and anger at being exploited have spurred unionism among contingent faculty. Liesl Orenic, a leader of the Roosevelt University union, stated, "you get overwhelmed with a sense of exploitation. Anyone who does this amount of work that requires so much skill and dedication deserves proper compensation. We are sort of invisible. We are there but we really don't exist. We could be gone at any time."[62]

Prior to the passage of the IELRA, contingent faculty remained unorganized. In 1986, IEA organized its first adjunct faculty union, at Oakton Community College.[63] In 1991, Harper College challenged an IEA petition to represent adjunct faculty teaching six semester hours; the college's argument was that they were "short-term" employees, had "no assurance of continued employment," and were, therefore, excluded from bargaining under the law. The case dragged on for two years but ended with a labor board decision favorable for IEA. Harper adjuncts won the election in 1994.[64]

In the 1990s, the General Assembly made two important changes to the IELRA that paved the way for contingent faculty in the public sector to organize unions. Instead of six semester hours being the threshold for unionization, the law was amended to cover part-time faculty teaching three hours per term. In addition, the General Assembly amended the "reasonable assurance of reappointment" as a standard for inclusion to read "reasonable expectation of reappointment." This modification of the law made it more difficult for employers to argue that contingent faculty were ineligible as "short-term" employees from coverage under the act.[65] While these legal encumbrances to organizing public-sector unions were removed, it was the organizing of private-sector adjuncts at Columbia College that sparked organizing drives among contingent faculty in the Chicago metropolitan area.

When the Part-Time Faculty Union at Columbia (P-Fac) voted 379 to 80 for IEA representation in 1998, it was widely reported in the media. P-Fac's first contract increased salary for a three-credit-hour class from an average of $1,600 (some adjuncts received only $1,350) to between $2,000 and $3,000, depending on seniority.[66] Some adjuncts nearly doubled their salaries. This achievement prompted adjuncts at Roosevelt University, two city blocks north of Columbia College, to organize in 2001. The Roosevelt Adjunct Faculty Organization, affiliated with IEA, easily won the election. Four years later, Columbia College staff voted for IEA representation.[67]

Though the IFT-affiliated Cook County College Teachers Union, Local 1600, represented full-time faculty in the majority of Cook County community colleges, it was reluctant to organize adjunct faculty. In fact, part-time adult educators in the city colleges organized with AFSCME after Local 1600 twice rejected their overtures. In 2003, IEA organized the part-time faculty at the City Colleges of Chicago. I worked with the three newly hired organizers on the seven campuses recruiting adjunct activists. Even though Local 1600 had represented the city's full-time faculty since the 1960s and was able to gather enough signatures to petition for a position on the ballot, IEA's City Colleges Contingent Labor Organizing Committee easily won the representation election.[68] Over the next eight years, IEA organized part-timers at College of DuPage, McHenry County College, and six community colleges in the Chicago area at which IFT represented the full-time faculty. Local 1600 eventually organized adjuncts at Moraine Valley Community College and South Suburban College. IFT Local 504 organized Lake County in the early 2000s. IEA also had six other elections that added part-time librarians, counselors, and three-credit-hour instructors to its existing part-time locals.[69]

Organizing for Power

In April 2007, IEA convened an Organizing for Power Conference to discuss how the growing number of adjunct locals in the Chicago metropolitan area could coordinate their efforts to improve salaries, benefits, and working conditions.

Fifty-five activists from ten IEA locals in the Chicago area attended. AFSCME and IFT locals were invited but did not attend; both unions indicated a willingness to participate in future conferences. The conference ended with a consensus on the following goals:[70]

- continue organizing part-time faculty at community colleges and private institutions in the Chicago area
- establish a Chicago higher education region that would provide adjunct locals with a voice on the IEA board of directors and be a focal point for help coordinating bargaining efforts
- create an online hiring hall where members could post their professional credentials accessible to colleges, universities, and other institutions; employers could post ads for part-time and full-time jobs
- post on a website a detailed spreadsheet that summarizes the provisions of each contract as well as the contracts that bargaining teams could easily access
- meet on a regular basis to develop bargaining goals and strategies
- establish a political action committee to promote contingent faculty's legislative interests on health insurance, pension and other matters
- explore ways to provide access to health-care benefits for members needing them

Even though a majority of all higher education faculty in Illinois are part time, the City Colleges of Chicago was the only employer as of 2007 to allow its part-timers access to its HMO group plan. Even so, part-time faculty and staff who elected to participate in the HMO had to pay almost all of the HMO premiums. While many had access to insurance through second jobs or spouses, a substantial number had no health insurance. One idea discussed at the time was a multi-employer health benefit plan similar to those established in the building trades. Colleges would contribute a prescribed amount to health benefit plans based on the hours taught, and those adjuncts in need could buy insurance at an affordable price. The success of such an ambitious program would depend on organizing unions throughout the public- and private-sector colleges in the metropolitan area, recruiting activists, and building a strong multicampus organization.[71] This idea has yet to be realized. This discussion about health insurance preceded the election of President Barack Obama and the 2010 passage of the Affordable Care Act.

Saint Xavier University's Opposition to Adjunct Organizing

By 2011, all the community colleges in the Chicago area had adjunct faculty unions. IEA next turned its attention to the not-for-profit Saint Xavier University (SXU), a religiously affiliated institution in Chicago. If successful at SXU, IEA planned to target other religiously affiliated schools such as Lewis University, the University of St. Francis, and Concordia University Chicago.

The big issue among SXU adjuncts was salary. Even though college tuition had increased 39 percent since 2006, adjunct salaries had remained frozen since 2003.[72] One adjunct activist explained:

> I was hired to teach a psychology class at SXU in the spring of 2006. I love teaching and the university was located only a few minutes away from my home. I like the faculty, administration, and staff. The only hitch was that Saint Xavier paid its adjuncts very little. We were receiving a pittance of what I felt adjuncts should be paid for the essential service of teaching students. In 2009, I decided that perhaps it was time for the adjunct faculty to have a union. The Illinois Education Association (IEA) seemed the perfect choice because it was doing a fine job representing adjuncts at Roosevelt where I also taught at the time.
>
> With the help of an IEA higher education organizer, we recruited several colleagues to be part of our organizing committee to reach out to fellow adjuncts to explain the need to unionize. We met as many as we could before and after classes to tell them about the benefits of collective bargaining.[73]

In 2010, the adjunct faculty at SXU petitioned the National Labor Relations Board (NLRB) for representation. The university, led by Christine Wiseman, a newly hired secular president, sought to have the NLRB dismiss the petition, claiming: "We are here because it's a question about jurisdiction . . . and not about the natural rights of workers. The Catholic Church has long supported the moral right of workers to organize and bargain collectively. But, under the First Amendment, Catholic colleges and universities must have the freedom . . . without excessive government entanglement."[74]

SXU did not consider public funding to be "excessive government entanglement." It had accepted grants from the state and federal governments. From 2005 to 2010, SXU received over $8.5 million in government support. In 2010, it received money from the Illinois Board of Higher Education, Illinois State Board of Education (ISBE), and Illinois State Treasurer's Office. In addition, many low-income students receive federal grants to help pay their SXU tuition. SXU's objection to federal jurisdiction raised questions about its voluntary recognition of the independent full-time faculty union under the NLRB jurisdiction in 1979, and the building engineers organized by the International Union of Operating Engineers Local 399. The SXU president publicly admitted that the university's chief objection to an adjunct union was its affiliation with IEA.[75]

The NLRB regional office in Chicago ruled that even though SXU was affiliated with the Sisters of Mercy, it provided a secular education, and that an adjunct union would not infringe on the free exercise of religion. The NLRB conducted a union representation election among the adjuncts. SXU appealed the election to the NLRB national office in Washington, DC, however, and so the ballots were impounded until a decision on the appeal was rendered.[76]

SXU's legal argument rested largely on case law decided more than thirty years prior. However, much had changed in Catholic education since then. In the 1960s, small Catholic colleges such as SXU recruited most of their students from Catholic high schools. These colleges continued the students' religious education. In the Chicago area, schools such as Rosary College (now Dominican University), Lewis University, St. Procopius College (now Benedictine University), and Saint Xavier's College for Women served that purpose. But declining enrollment over the years forced many Catholic high schools to close down and led others to accept non-Catholic students. This fact meant fewer Catholic recruits for the Catholic colleges and universities. At the same time, enrollment in higher education was rapidly increasing, largely funded by government grants and federal-backed student loans. This situation provided a golden opportunity for these schools to recruit outside the Catholic education system. SXU changed. It dropped the "for Women" from its name. It adopted a "diversity" policy—accepting students regardless of religious affiliation, dropping any required Catholic training, and recruiting students from the general population. Diversity also meant that faculty members were no longer screened for their religious views. As a result, SXU's enrollment had increased significantly since the 1960s and its education program became secular.[77]

Besides SXU, there was a similar case before the NLRB involving a New York Catholic institution, Manhattan College, which drew national attention since it could open the door to unions for religiously affiliated school employees. Conservative religious organizations such as the General Conference of Seventh-day Adventists and the Association of Christian Schools International expressed support for SXU's position. Speaking of the case, Patrick J. Reilly, president of the Cardinal Newman Society, stated: "It's a clear violation of religious liberty for a federal agency to even be asking the question whether an institution is sufficiently Catholic. That's a question for the Church to answer, not the National Labor Relations Board." He continued, "Every Catholic needs to be engaged in this fight."[78]

Liberal church groups stood behind the "natural rights of workers to unionize as a fundamental principle of social justice and democracy." Arise Chicago, an interfaith workers' rights organization, reached out to SXU to encourage it to drop its opposition to the adjunct union, with no success.[79] In 2016, after years of delays, the NLRB in Washington, DC, upheld the regional office decision and counted the votes. The IEA-affiliated Saint Xavier Adjunct Faculty Organization won the election.[80]

As the union prepared for bargaining, the SXU president announced that the university would not recognize the adjunct unit (or a newly organized SEIU custodial unit), citing the fact that the labor board did not have a fully constituted majority when it voted. After Donald Trump took office, he appointed anti-union candidates to the labor board. In June 2020, the majority reversed the earlier NLRB decision, ruling instead that federal law did not have jurisdiction over religiously affiliated institutions. That decision upheld SXU's continued refusal to bargain with the adjunct union. After forty years, SXU also withdrew its recognition of the independent, full-time faculty union.[81]

The Catholic Labor Network in June 2020 published a sharp rebuke of SXU for its "busting" of the full-time faculty union: "This NLRB decision has left Catholic college employees in a labor rights desert, but the test will be for college administrators: do they intend to manage their institutions in accordance with Catholic Social Teachings or not?"[82]

Conclusion

IFT began organizing higher education locals long before the passage of the IELRA. In the 1960s, Local 1600 organized full-time faculty unions in the city college system, Chicago State University, and several suburban community colleges. IEA locals did not have any higher education contracts until the late 1970s; IEA had only six bargaining units when the IELRA was enacted in 1984. The passage of the IELRA, NEA's organizing project, and the desire of college and university employees for a meaningful voice in decisions affecting their employment enabled IEA to organize thirty-nine additional higher education unions at both public and private institutions.

UIUC GEO directly contributed to IFT's success in organizing graduate students and full-time faculty at the University of Illinois Chicago, in 2004 and 2012, respectively. IFT also organized full-time faculty unions at Northern Illinois University in 2016, and at Illinois State University in 2024.

By 2024, all full-time faculty at Illinois community colleges and tenured or tenure-track faculty at all Illinois state universities except UIUC had union representation. In addition, IEA and IFT organized part-time, contingent faculty—adjuncts, adult educators, non-tenure-track teachers, graduate assistants, adult education teachers, and others—at public as well as some private institutions. Besides IEA and IFT, other unions including AFSCME, SEIU, and the International Union of Operating Engineers organized higher education staff employees across the state.

In 2012, IEA's active higher education membership, including fee payers, peaked at 7,295. Several factors contributed to subsequent declining membership.[83] In

Table 22. IEA Higher Education Active Membership
and Fee Payers

	1983	2012	2021
University members	148	834	1,055
College F-T faculty	342	961	998
College classified staff	0	1,303	695
College adjuncts	0	1,753	1,629
Total IEA members	590	4,851	4,377
Fee payers	0	2,444	54*

Source: "Higher Education Locals: 1983 and 2021," provided
by Donald Jordan, IEA Membership Processing, June 1, 2022;
"Higher Education Locals: 2012," provided by Dawn Hall, IEA
Membership Processing, July 25, 2024.
* The fifty-four fee payers in 2021 worked in private-sector
locals at Colombia College and Roosevelt University and are
not counted in the membership totals.

2014, P-Fac ended its ties with IEA, becoming an independent union, largely as a result of a dispute with the Columbia College staff union over teaching classes. Long before the staff organized a union, some staff members also taught classes. This practice became an issue as college enrollment began to decline in 2008, leading to layoffs of adjunct faculty. Diana Vallera, elected P-Fac president in 2011, complained that the IEA was "advocating for full-time staff to teach, in opposition to our contract. They couldn't represent both groups." In 2015, P-Fac changed its name to the Columbia College Faculty Union and affiliated with IFT.[84] In addition, the prolonged legal battle with SXU stalled efforts to organize other religiously affiliated universities and colleges that employed thousands of adjuncts. Donald Trump's NLRB decisions to rescind federal labor board jurisdiction over religiously affiliated schools forestalled other organizing campaigns. The Supreme Court's *Janus* decision, too, resulted in the loss of a large number of higher education fee payers. Finally, the COVID-19 pandemic impeded higher education organizing campaigns. In 2021, IEA had forty-five higher education unions with 4,377 members (see table 22).

Trump's labor board and the *Janus* decision are part of a national movement on the Right that gained momentum after the election of President Reagan in 1980. Privatization of public education and the undermining of unionism have been a major focus of this movement.

CHAPTER 13

School Reform

Public schools are at the center of the manufactured breakdown of the fabric of everyday life. They are under attack not because they are failing, but because they are public.

—Henry Giroux

By the early 1980s, academic studies reported a steady decline in standardized achievement test scores.[1] In sharp contrast to studies that pointed out that changes in achievement testing and society at large had contributed to the decline in test scores, Ronald Reagan, in his 1980 presidential campaign, blamed public education and teachers unions for the declining test scores; he backed "free market" privatization to address the issue. While Reagan's election marked a major shift within the national Republican Party to the conservative right, Republican leadership in Illinois continued to support much more moderate policies. As a result, the Illinois Education Association (IEA) endorsed Republican candidates in five of the six gubernatorial elections held from 1982 to 1998. The move to the conservative right in the state Republican Party was more gradual, but with the 2014 election of Governor Bruce Rauner, the Reagan wing took control of the party, backing policies to undermine public-sector unionism and to promote tuition vouchers and tax credits for private schools.

Reaganism

The 1980 Republican Party platform called for reducing federal aid to education, curtailing bilingual education, eliminating the Department of Education, and urging states to require merit pay for teachers based on performance evaluation. Federal aid declined from 12 percent to 6 percent of the total spending on public education during Reagan's presidency.[2] Reagan claimed that the decline in college entrance exams, especially in science and math, meant that America was losing its competitive advantage to Japan, Germany, and other high-performing economies. He argued that the public school system was a monopoly that stifled parental choice, blamed teachers unions for their alleged indifference to student achievement, and advocated voucher programs and tuition tax credits that would redirect public funding to private schools. These proposals appealed to his political base of anti-union conservatives and evangelical Protestants. Vouchers and tuition tax credits would enable parents to send their children to private and religiously affiliated schools.

As public schools became more secular largely due to the nation's increasing racial, religious, cultural, and ethnic diversity, many evangelical congregations established their own private religious schools.[3] Evangelicals also turned to homeschooling over concerns that "Christian values" and Bible education were no longer taught in public schools. Vouchers could help pay tuition at religiously affiliated schools or be used to purchase books and cover other expenses incurred by parents homeschooling their children. Reagan solidified support among evangelical Protestants by supporting "voluntary" school prayer.[4] To lend credence to this privatization agenda, Reagan's secretary of education, Terrel Bell, appointed an eighteen-member National Commission on Excellence in Education to focus on the "quality of teaching and learning" in the nation's schools.

In 1983, the commission produced the report *A Nation at Risk*, which concluded that in education there was "a rising tide of mediocrity that threatened our very future as a Nation and a people." The report urged state governments and local districts to adopt a more rigorous curriculum, higher standards for measuring student achievement, teacher accountability for student progress, a longer school year, and merit pay rather than salary schedules (which determine pay by level of education and years of teaching experience).[5]

Though most of Reagan's education agenda—such as school prayer, tuition tax credits, merit pay, and an end to the US Department of Education—made little headway during his presidency, *A Nation at Risk* inspired studies by the RAND Corporation (1984), the Carnegie Foundation (1986), and the Holmes Group (1986) that criticized the quality of education currently being provided, especially for inner-city minority students, and suggested reforms to transform "teaching from an occupation into a profession." These studies generally agreed on the need for more rigorous curriculum standards, higher expectations for student learning, and teacher accountability. They also called for raising standards for entry into the teaching profession, improving teacher education programs, upgrading the professional competency of principals, evaluating teachers based on performance, developing a collaborative relationship between schools and universities to foster mutual learning, and raising salaries to attract the best students to the teaching profession. Unlike the Reagan administration, these three reports did not blame unions for failing schools. Instead the problems facing public education were viewed as endemic to the school system in a rapidly changing world.[6] Following the release of these reports, IEA took steps to address the growing concerns about education reform.

Interest-Based Bargaining

After reading *A Nation at Risk*, UniServ director Jo Anderson said that IEA must take the issue of school reform seriously. He explained that public schools in Chicago, New York, and other large urban centers were in deep trouble. As educators, we must be concerned about the problems facing inner-city schools. It is not only a moral imperative; public education will be defined by the performance of schools in these major media markets. Doing nothing means that others, including anti-union conservatives, will set the reform agenda, much to the detriment of IEA members and public education.[7]

Anderson became an IEA manager and took the lead in its reform efforts. He proposed a grassroots approach, whereby locals would work collaboratively with school boards and administrators to develop programs to improve education. The first step in this process was interest-based bargaining (IBB) for contract negotiations. IBB is a collaborative approach to negotiations based on the notion that the union, school board, and administration share many common interests, such as efficiently managed schools, sufficient funding, and public support.[8]

IBB begins not with each side presenting positions on the issues but, rather, with the formation of joint committees of board representatives and union negotiators to discuss salary, fringe benefits, and other major issues. These joint committees discuss their "interests" and seek to establish an understanding of each other, to build trust, and to find solutions based on their common interests. Ideally, the committee reports become the basis of the contract settlement. IBB does not end once a contract is settled. Instead, it creates ongoing communication structures between the union and the district to address problems that arise amid the term of the contract. At its best, such collaborative communication includes the union in decisions that go far beyond issues covered in the collective bargaining agreement.[9]

One of IEA's earliest efforts at IBB was in Wheaton District 200. Wheaton-Warrenville Education Association (WWEA) went on strike in 1980 and again in 1982. Clearly, something needed to change. In 1985, WWEA tried an interest-based approach developed by professor Irving Goldaber called Win-Win. Unfortunately, the process failed, and a third strike ensued. District 200 superintendent Ronald MacNicholas sardonically stated, "Win-win, it was not."[10] Others called it

"Win-Win, Lose-Lose."[11] Despite the WWEA setback, IEA continued to refine and expand IBB in Illinois using the Harvard University "Getting to Yes" model. IBB was not a panacea to end the existing hostility between the district and the union. It only worked if there was a genuine commitment to improving the relationship between the parties through open and honest communication. If successful, IBB increased respect and trust between the parties, which, in turn, could enable the local association to have a meaningful role in efforts to improve teaching and learning.[12]

At first, some leaders and staff were skeptical about IBB efforts. Would the employer use IBB to weaken the union's influence? Would collaboration undermine collective bargaining and employee rights? These concerns sparked a vigorous debate within IEA. Nevertheless, IBB would not have survived without widespread support among local leaders, officers, field staff and administrators. By 2013, about 130 IEA locals used IBB. For IEA, collaborative decision-making at the bargaining table would lead to ongoing discussions with school officials on improving education outcomes and other subjects not normally discussed during negotiations.[13]

Collaboration and the Consortium for Educational Change

In 1986, the College of Education at the University of Illinois Chicago established the Chicago Area School Effectiveness Council, which created work-study groups on reform with school districts and the university. Jo Anderson proposed to Garry Griffin, dean of the College of Education, a work-study group on the reforms suggested by the Carnegie Report. In February 1987, fifty-one participants from sixteen suburban IEA districts that had negotiated IBB contracts met under the auspices of the effectiveness council. The group included local leaders, IEA staff, school administrators, and school board officials. In September 1987, the group changed its name from the Carnegie Workgroup to the Consortium for Educational Change (CEC). It included twelve school districts, IEA, the National Education Association (NEA), the University of Illinois Chicago, and National Louis University.[14]

CEC was an outgrowth of the collaborative labor-management relationships that came about through the IBB process. In fact, IBB was an essential first step in building trust and collaboration among stakeholders in order to create change. At first, only teachers participated in CEC district leadership teams. As IEA organized more support staff locals, CEC teams became more inclusive.[15]

Anderson believed that teachers collectively should fully participate through their unions in decisions shaping policy. Unions—working together with school boards, administration, and parents in improving teaching and learning—were the vehicle for transforming education. Without abandoning traditional, bread-and-butter unionism, CEC sought to expand the union's participation in educational policies that typically were the prerogative of school boards. CEC was predicated on the ideal that a democratic school system will improve student learning. According to CEC's mission statement: "The mission of the Consortium for Educational Change, a network of school districts and professional organizations, is to enhance student learning by bringing together teachers, administrators, and board members to stimulate and promote change in school structures and relationships through collaboration."[16]

By the mid-1990s, IEA leadership was using the collaborative decision model to reduce long-simmering tension within the organization. In 1993, the newly elected IEA president, Robert Haisman, was alarmed by the strained relationship between IEA and the IEA Staff Organization (IEASO) during negotiations over staff contracts. Obviously, the bitterness and distrust of the 1977 lockout and the 1980 staff strike lingered, especially among some board members and staff. Following the settlement of professional and associate staff contracts, Haisman vowed, "We are not going through that again." Determined to change the culture within IEA, Haisman sought to develop a collaborative decision-making model. The first step was a retreat for the board of directors and the management team to discuss how to improve communication and trust within the association. The retreat ended with a decision to meet with IEASO.[17]

In August 2003, the IEA executive committee, IEA management, and IEASO executive committee met at the Hotel Marriott Hickory Ridge Conference Center in Lisle to discuss norms of behavior that would build mutual respect and understanding among the leaders in attendance. Following lengthy discussions among the participants, President Haisman, Jo Anderson, and IEASO president Lynn Adler were charged with writing a proposal to accomplish this goal.[18]

At the August meeting, those in attendance signed the Hickory Ridge Commitment, which stated: "We believe that a strong and effective IEA depends on our ability to work well together, and we further believe that a strong and effective IEA is critical for the preservation and improvement of public education in Illinois." In the Hickory Ridge Commitment, the parties pledged to observe thirteen norms, including: "respect one another . . . communicate with honesty and candor . . . [engage in] active listening with one another . . . seek information before drawing conclusions . . . build a shared vision" and "focus on the future not the past."[19] Following this group's signing of the document, the entire IEA board, managers, and staff were invited to attend a meeting in Bloomington to review and sign the Hickory Ridge Commitment. Virtually everyone who attended the Bloomington meeting signed the pledge. Subsequently, the IEA executive committee, IEA management, and IEASO executive committee met regularly to discuss their concerns, and they re-signed the pledge annually. Like IBB and CEC, the Hickory Ridge Commitment was based on a collaborative decision-making model. Only through resolving internal disputes within IEA among governance, management, and staff could the association be effective in its education reform agenda.[20] The Hickory Ridge Commitment expanded the collaborative decision-making model throughout the association and greatly increased support for IBB and CEC within IEA.

In 2000, CEC had no paid staff and a $175,000 budget. As the school reform movement gained momentum, CEC's participation increased, from a handful of districts in the Chicago suburbs to over one hundred districts throughout Illinois. By 2010, CEC had raised over $2.9 million and hired four full-time employees. The Illinois Association of School Boards (IASB), Illinois Principals Association (IPA), and Illinois State Board of Education (ISBE), along with the University of Illinois, National Louis University, Northern Illinois University, Illinois State University, and Governors State University, became CEC partners. A number of Illinois Federation of Teachers (IFT) unions participated in CEC, including large locals in East Aurora, Joliet, Woodstock, Valley View, and Peoria. The CEC thirteen-member governing board included IEA teachers and education support staff leaders as well as school board members and administrators. Since 2010, CEC's influence has reached far beyond Illinois, including partnerships with such reform groups as the national Teacher Union Reform Network and the California Labor Management Institute. From 2010 through 2018, CEC received more than $11.5 million in grants from the Bill and Melinda Gates Foundation, as well as much smaller donations from NEA and other organizations to hire full-time staff and to sponsor training programs, not only in Illinois but with its partners in other states.[21]

From the beginning, some IEA leaders and staff were critical of CEC, but the IEA board had been unwavering in its support of CEC since the mid-1990s. As CEC expanded its presence in the early 2000s, its critics, especially among UniServ staff, complained that CEC was directly contacting superintendents about its programs without first notifying them. According to CEC administrator Jo Anderson, the involvement of local associations was a prerequisite for any district's participation in CEC programs. While some UniServ directors readily participated in CEC programs, they did not have veto power over a joint decision of the local association and the district to work together.[22]

Jo Anderson had a long-term relationship with IEA, dating back to the mid-1970s. Over the years, he served in IEA management positions including a stint as executive director. In June 2020, Anderson retired from CEC, and co-executive director Mary Jane Morris returned to a full-time IEA staff position. Under the leadership of the new IEA executive director, Shelley Taylor, IEA amicably severed its ties with CEC. CEC moved out of the IEA Lombard office, changed its name to Catalyst for Educational Change, and restructured its governing board. There were no IEA members on its new six-member board. Nevertheless, CEC continued to work with IEA school districts.[23]

School Choice: Magnet Schools and Charter Schools

Leaders in both political parties supported a variety of school reform measures in an effort to improve public education, especially in low-income, minority communities of Chicago and other large urban centers. Public schools in many of these neighborhoods had high dropout rates and low scores on achievement tests. Student performance lagged far behind higher-income suburban districts, prompting some education reform proponents to argue that parents should have a "choice" where to send their children, especially if they live in a neighborhood with a failing school.[24]

Magnet schools were created and managed by K–12 districts to provide parents with a choice of schools outside their neighborhoods. Magnet schools adhere to state standards, including existing collective bargaining agreements, and operate under the direct authority of the school districts creating them. The curricula of magnets are designed to attract students with particular academic interests, such as science, technology, engineering, and math (STEM), the fine and performing arts, international studies, and world languages. Magnet schools are open to all district students but are selective. Applicants are screened to confirm that they have the academic ability and interest in magnet school curriculum. Since parental and student interests motivate attendance, magnet schools are among the highest performing schools in the state. There are twenty-three public magnet schools in Illinois, with over half in Chicago.[25]

Charter schools were originally championed as a reform that would empower teachers in their buildings to improve education with minimal interference from central office management and state mandates. Charter schools are publicly funded but privately managed schools. Unlike magnet schools, charters operate mostly outside the purview of school district management and state mandates; they have broad discretionary powers to set the curriculum and manage school operations, as long as they remain consistent with the guidelines of their contracts with the school districts or governmental agencies issuing the charters.[26]

Charter schools opened the door for for-profit business interests, anti-union conservatives, and other entities to privatize schools. Forty-four states and Washington, DC, have charter school laws. Charter school legislation varies widely, depending on the politics of the state. Only Hawai'i and Maryland require collective bargaining as a condition for receiving a charter. About 90 percent of charter schools operate without collective bargaining agreements. Twenty-four states permit private, for-profit companies to manage charters. Charter teachers typically do not have tenure rights; state certification of teachers is often not a hiring requirement; and salaries are generally lower and turnover rates higher than for

K–12 districts. In many charters, the school day and the school year are longer than in K–12 districts.[27]

In effect, charters privatize K–12 teaching and support staff positions, making them especially attractive to anti-union conservatives. In a 2007 *Harper's Magazine* article, Jonathan Kozol warned of the danger to public education posed by vouchers and charter schools. After having received from a Wall Street friend a stock market prospectus written by a group of banking analysts describing the benefits of privatization of public education, Kozol quoted the analysts' report: "The education industry represents, in our opinion, the final frontier of a number of sectors once under public control." Public education has "either voluntarily opened" or been forced" to open up to private enterprise. "The education industry represents the largest market opportunity" since health-care services were privatized during the 1970s. One analyst enthusiastically stated that "the K–12 market is the Big Enchilada."[28]

Charter school organizations have vigorously opposed unionism. About 11 percent of charter schools have unionized. Without the basic protections of just cause dismissal and grievance arbitration that are provided by a collective bargaining agreement, employment rights and practices for charter employees are governed by charter policies and management decisions. As a result, rather than empowering teachers, many charter schools have top-down business models of management.[29]

In the 1994 general election in Illinois, Republicans swept into power, reelecting Governor James Edgar and capturing control of the General Assembly. A number of hard-line conservative legislators including Albert Salvi (R–Lake County) and Peter Roskam (R–DuPage County) proposed legislation that would weaken the bargaining law, including a ban on strikes. Despite the Republican majority, they were unable to muster enough support to pass any legislation that significantly limited bargaining rights, due to IEA's bipartisan support in the legislature. Instead, Governor Edgar and the Republican majority passed, with Mayor Richard M. Daley's support, the 1995 Chicago School Reform Amendatory Act, which concentrated power in Chicago Public Schools (CPS) and limited the bargaining rights of the Chicago Teachers Union (CTU). The law gave CPS broad discretionary power to manage the system, making issues such as subcontracting, class size, and reductions in force permissive rather than mandatory subjects of bargaining. CPS was no longer required to bargain these decisions with CTU. Strikes by CTU employees were prohibited for eighteen months, giving Paul Vallas, Daley's handpicked CPS CEO, a relatively free hand to impose major changes in how the school system operated.[30] Many low-performing schools, mostly in low-income, minority neighborhoods, were closed and replaced with magnet schools and, after the passage of the state charter school law, with charter schools. According to professor Theodore Williams of the City Colleges of Chicago, "Rather than immediate sanctions, these schools required greater support. They did not receive it. Many of the recent reform efforts [as of 2013] have involved expansion of selective enrollment high schools. These schools are high achievers and consistently rank in the top of the nation. The problem is they only serve 10.1% of the CPS students and are 43.5% non-low income, which makes them substantially better off than the general CPS population."[31]

While IEA was concerned about the restrictions that the Chicago reform law placed on CTU's bargaining rights, it did not actively oppose these changes. Nevertheless, it realized that it needed to work together with IFT and CTU to maximize its influence on education legislation and to counteract conservative efforts to undermine the unions. With NEA and the American Federation of Teachers (AFT) involved in merger discussions, IEA increased its cooperation with CTU/IFT on public relations and legislative matters.[32]

In 1996, the General Assembly enacted charter school legislation. Republicans under Governor Edgar and many liberal Democrats supported charters "to create opportunities within the public school system of Illinois for development of innovative and accountable teaching techniques."[33] Unlike states like Arizona, Wisconsin, and Texas, which have very loosely regulated charter schools, Illinois took a cautious approach in creating charter schools. The Illinois law prohibited private for-profit, religious, and sectarian charters. It also established a cap on the number of charters in Chicago and the rest of the state.[34] In Chicago, there are forty-three charter schools serving 57,119 students on 122 campuses. Outside the city, there are fifteen charters with 5,460 students. Eight of the fifteen charters outside Chicago are in districts where IEA represents the teachers. All but three of the fifteen are in large, urban centers with low-income communities. Statewide, over 96 percent of charter school attendees are minority students.[35]

In 1997, Carl Ball (owner of Burpee Seed Company) and Springfield District 186 agreed to create a not-for-profit charter school. The Springfield Education Association actively participated in the planning stages of the charter. Initially, Ball Charter teachers did not have a union, but in 2003, they organized under the Illinois Educational Labor Relations Act (IELRA).[36] In 2007, IEA petitioned the Illinois Educational Labor Relations Board (IELRB) for union representation at Cambridge Lakes Charter School (Dundee District 300). After the labor board ruled in IEA's favor, Cambridge Lakes Charter won a state appellate court decision dismissing the petition on the grounds that the National Labor Relations Act (NLRA) and not state law covered privatized charter schools.[37] As a result of this case, charter school unions must be organized under the federal law.

In Chicago, IFT organized unions at 35 (26 percent) of the 122 CPS charter campuses under the NLRA. In 2018, the Chicago Alliance of Charter Teachers and Staff, an IFT affiliate, conducted a successful four-day strike over class size, hours, and salary negotiations at fifteen Acero schools. The strike was the first ever at a charter school in the nation. After the strike, the 1,200-member alliance voted to join CTU as an affiliated bargaining unit.[38]

According to ISBE, student achievement at charter schools has been a "mixed bag." ISBE data shows that some charters outperform their home districts in language arts and math, while others do not meet the district norms. The most successful charters are those that have collaborative decision-making procedures that engage parents and teachers in the operations of the school. Evidence suggests that student achievement in charter schools varies within the range of public schools in their home districts. There is a direct correlation between student achievement and the economic background of the communities in which students reside. Unless the problems associated with systemic poverty and racism in low-income communities are addressed, education improvements—whether at traditional neighborhood schools or at charters—will be limited.[39]

Support for charters among liberal Democrats has waned as the charter school movement has become increasingly anti-union.[40] Speaking before the NEA representative assembly (RA) in 2017, President Lily Eskelsen García stated: "Charter schools were started by educators who dreamed of schools in which they would be free to innovate, unfettered by bureaucratic obstacles. Handing over students' education to privately managed, unaccountable charters jeopardizes student success, undermines public education and harms communities. This policy draws a clear line between charters that serve to improve public education and those that do not."[41]

Performance Evaluation Reform Act

Beginning in 2005, Illinois leaders from businesses, unions, education organizations, and government held a series of meetings to discuss ways to improve student achievement. This group, known as the Education Policy Dialogue Group, developed the Burnham Plan, a program that included many reforms eventually enacted into law, such as improved data collection to measure student performance, a streamlined process for removal of poor-performing teachers and principals, mentoring programs, and training programs for school board members. Though it received widespread approval in the media, the Burnham Plan languished in the General Assembly.[42]

In 2009, the Obama administration's Race to the Top legislation presented Illinois with an opportunity to apply for federal grants to implement reforms in the following areas:

- development of rigorous standards and better assessments
- adoption of better data systems to provide schools, teachers, and parents with information about student progress
- support for teachers and school leaders to become more effective
- increased emphasis on and resources for the rigorous intervention needed to turn around the lowest performing schools[43]

The state superintendent of education organized a task force to draft reform legislation to apply for a Race to the Top grant. Led by state senator Kimberly Lightford (D-Maywood), the group included several members of the legislature as well as representatives from the governor's office, IEA, IFT, CTU, the Illinois Statewide School Management Alliance, CPS, and Advance Illinois, a local reform organization. As a result of these efforts, Governor Pat Quinn signed the Performance Evaluation Reform Act on January 15, 2010. Illinois received $42.8 million in Race to the Top grant money.[44]

The reform act obligated all districts to include student growth as a "significant" factor in their teacher evaluations. It required districts to establish "a joint committee composed of equal representation selected by the district and its teachers or, where applicable, the exclusive bargaining representative of its teachers" to develop an evaluation plan.[45] The act specified what a minimum student growth evaluation plan must include, so that, in case the district's joint committee did not reach an agreement, the state plan would apply. The law also required that all evaluators successfully complete an ISBE program certifying their qualifications to conduct valid evaluations. Each school district must include the following major components in its performance evaluations for teachers in contractual continued service (i.e., tenure): (1) a description of each teacher's duties and responsibilities and the standards to which the teacher is expected to conform; (2) an evaluation of each tenured teacher at least once in the course of any two school years and probationary teachers once every school year; (3) personal observation of the teacher in the classroom by an evaluator, unless the teacher has no classroom duties; (4) consideration of the teacher's attendance, planning, instructional methods, classroom management, where relevant, and competency in the subject matter taught; (5) specification as to the teacher's strengths and weaknesses, with supporting reasons for the comments made; (6) a rating of the tenured teacher on a scale of either *excellent—satisfactory—unsatisfactory* or *excellent—proficient—needs improvement—unsatisfactory*; and (7) inclusion of a copy of the evaluation in the teacher's personnel file and provision of a copy to the teacher. Additionally, the act stipulates that within thirty school days after a tenured teacher is rated as "needs improvement" or "unsatisfactory," the teacher must receive a ninety-day remediation plan; upon completion of the remediation plan, a tenured teacher who does not receive a "proficient" or better rating must be dismissed.[46]

Senate Bill 7

The Great Recession of 2007–9 caused huge deficits in the state's 2010 budget. Teacher pensions are funded by a combination of individual contributions and state revenue. For years, the state failed to contribute the full amount required by law, leaving pensions in serious debt. In response to the crisis, the state slashed education funding and Governor Quinn, Speaker Michael Madigan, and Democratic leadership spearheaded legislation to reduce teacher pension benefits. Despite opposition by education unions, a bipartisan bill was passed by the General Assembly and signed by Quinn in April 2010. The law created a two-tier pension system. Benefits remained unchanged for current members (tier 1) but were restructured for teachers hired after January 1, 2011 (tier 2). Tier 2 raised the age requirement for full benefits from sixty-two to sixty-seven, capped the annual retirement salary benefit, and increased vesting eligibility from five to ten years.[47]

In response, IFT cut off campaign contributions to any legislators facing reelection in November who voted for the pension law. The rift between Democratic leaders and the unions created an opportunity for corporate-funded education reform. In September, Bruce Rauner, a conservative Republican venture capitalist, recruited Jonah Edelman's Stand for Children to establish a chapter in Illinois. Based in Portland, Oregon, Stand for Children had raised millions from corporate donors. Rauner, billionaire Ken Griffin, and other wealthy Illinois donors contributed to the cause, as did the Illinois Chamber of Commerce, Business Roundtable, and the Chicago Commercial Club.[48] In the fall election, Stand for Children contributed $600,000 to nine targeted legislative races. All of its endorsed candidates—six Democrats and three Republicans—won reelection. Following the November election, Edelman raised $3 million.[49] Stand for Children backed Performance Counts, a proposal targeting teachers unions that called for tying performance evaluation to student testing, streamlining tenured teacher dismissal to four months with little legal recourse, ending tenure as the basis for reductions in force, restricting CTU bargaining rights, allowing districts to impose their decision when negotiations reached an impasse, and effectively ending the right to strike.[50]

Stand for Children and its corporate supporters hoped to "ram" an act based on Performance Counts through during the postelection session of the General Assembly in January, but the act was never introduced.[51] Long before Stand for Children arrived in Illinois, IEA, IFT, and CTU had been involved in discussions with the School Management Alliance, CPS, and state officials over school reform proposals, many of which subsequently became law. On January 3, 2011, the unions introduced their own legislative package, entitled Accountability for All. After months of negotiations under the leadership of Senator Lightford, an agreement over school reform was reached between the parties: Senate Bill 7.[52]

Senate Bill 7 made a number of changes in the IELRA and the Illinois School Code. It improved data collection on student learning, required training for school board members, and established procedures to address incompetency among teachers and administrators. In addition, seniority would no longer be the sole determining factor in layoffs. Instead, teachers were grouped into four layoff categories, based primarily on their last two evaluations and their seniority. Under this system, tenured teachers receiving unsatisfactory or "needs improvement" evaluations could be laid off ahead of nontenured teachers receiving proficient or excellent ratings. The law provided that a joint committee with equal representation of administrators and teachers could modify the plan to address local concerns. Senate Bill 7 also streamlined the procedures for dismissal of K–12 tenured teachers to avoid long and expensive legal delays. It provided specific timelines and dismissal procedures in cases involving misconduct or unsatisfactory performance. Unlike the proposals of Performance Counts, the burden of proof for removal remained on the district. Finally, K–12 contract negotiations were made more transparent when the parties reached an impasse with a possible strike looming. The district and the union were required to publicly post their "best and final offers" when an impasse was reached. In addition, a union could not strike until a ten-day strike notice had been issued and the final offer had been posted for fourteen days. In negotiations between CPS and CTU, Senate Bill 7 required fact-finding if the groups reached an impasse, which would delay a possible strike for several months. The law specifically required a 75 percent vote of support among all bargaining unit members to authorize a strike. Having the approval of IEA, IFT, and CTU, Senate Bill 7 received almost unanimous bipartisan support in the General Assembly. It passed 59 to 0 in the Senate and 112 to 1 in the House, and it was signed into law in June 2011.[53] It did stir much criticism among some union members and staff over the limits on seniority, tenure, and the right to strike. However, union leadership decided to support Senate Bill 7 as a much better alternative to Performance Counts.

Though Stand for Children certainly influenced the course of events, it did not play the central role in legislative negotiations that Edelman had claimed it would. Nor did it ensure that CTU would never be able to strike again.[54] At the Aspen Institute Ideas Festival in June 2011, Edelman bragged that Stand for Children had outsmarted the unions to force them to accept concessions over school reform. Edelman announced that "the union cannot strike in Chicago. . . . We did our homework; we knew that the highest threshold on any bargaining agreement that was voted on, one way or another, was 48.3 percent." Based on these figures, he surmised that CTU "will never be able to muster 75 percent threshold necessary to strike." Since issues including the length of the Chicago school day and school year were permissive rather than mandatory subjects of bargaining, CPS could impose its "best and final offer" on CTU without facing a possible strike. Edelman was surprised that CTU president Karen Lewis readily accepted the 75 percent strike vote proposal. He said that Lewis must have agreed "misunderstanding or probably not knowing the statistics" related to contract ratification history.[55]

What Edelman did not know was that a successful teacher strike required overwhelming support from its members. Only 75 percent was generally considered not enough to support a strike. One year later, CTU walked out after a 90 percent strike vote.[56] Even though CPS was not legally required to bargain the length of the school day and other permissive bargaining issues, it had little recourse but to negotiate them when faced with a CTU strike. Edelman would later apologize to the teachers unions for his "arrogant" remarks in Aspen; his apology was not accepted.[57]

The 2012 strike signaled that after years of privatization efforts emanating from city hall, a progressive caucus had ousted CTU's "old guard" and organized efforts to fight back.[58] In 2019, CTU teachers and Service Employees International Union (SEIU) Local 73 support staff conducted a joint fourteen-day strike walkout.[59] These CTU strikes received widespread attention and inspired a growing militancy throughout Illinois, particularly in higher education. In 2023, IFT unions at Chicago State, Eastern Illinois, Governors State, and the University of Illinois Chicago walked out. In addition, the part-time faculty union at Columbia College conducted a four-week strike.[60]

Illinois Policy Institute and Governor Rauner

Privatization of public education has been a major goal of conservative business interests and right-wing ideologues committed to "free market" anti-union policies. The Illinois Policy Institute (IPI), a libertarian think tank, has promoted subcontracting of public services, for-profit charter schools, tuition vouchers, cuts in education funding, and gutting of public-sector collective bargaining rights. In 2014, the IPI-endorsed Rauner, a wealthy private equity investor, was elected governor in a low-turnout election—less than half of registered voters cast ballots. The Republican governor was openly hostile to unionism and filed a federal lawsuit on behalf of Mark Janus, a state employee, challenging the fair share provisions in Illinois's public bargaining laws. In 2018, the US Supreme Court declared that fair share provisions in public employee contracts were unconstitutional.[61] The US Supreme Court's *Janus* decision in 2018 resulted in the loss of over 6,500 fair share fee payers. Anti-union conservatives expected that many members would drop their membership now that they were no longer required to pay fair share, yet IEA signed up more than 1,500 new members in 2018.[62]

Following the *Janus* decision, IPI hired plaintiff Mark Janus to tour "the country to make sure workers understand their rights and to share with workers and other people interested in his Supreme Court case what the *Janus* win means."[63] Knowing that IPI, the National Right to Work Committee, and other anti-union organizations would launch a campaign urging school employees to drop their union memberships now that there was no requirement to pay fair share fees, IEA and other unions successfully lobbied for legislation to thwart these efforts. The post-*Janus* legislation included the following provisions:

- requires public employer to provide the exclusive bargaining representative (EBR) with unit employees' names, home addresses, phone numbers, worksite, dates of hire, job titles, and other pertinent information in a timely manner
- provides the EBR with access to worksites to meet with unit employees during their duty-free time
- gives EBR access to use employer mailboxes, bulletin boards, and emails to communicate with unit employees
- requires employers to provide payroll deduction of union dues upon request
- prohibits employers from discouraging union membership among unit employees or working with any outside groups to do so
- prohibits public employers from providing outside organizations with the names, home addresses, telephone numbers, email addresses, and other personal information of bargaining unit employees
- prohibits outside organizations from using employers' internal email systems to communicate with unit employees[64]

In 2017, Governor Rauner, with the support of Speaker Madigan (D-Chicago), passed the Invest in Kids Act (Public Act 100-0465), which allowed any individual or business to donate up to $1 million to a state-approved, nonprofit scholarship granting organization and receive in return a 75 percent tax credit for the amount contributed. These contributions were not really charity, since the donors could also write off the remaining 25 percent from federal income taxes. The state tax credit was capped at $75 million. Once contributions reached this annual cap, donors did not receive any state tax credit.[65]

The Invest in Kids Act redirected $75 million in state funding to pay tuition for students attending private, primarily religious-based schools. The scholarship granting organizations managing these funds provided "scholarships" for families to send their children to approved private schools. There were six such state-approved organizations; these managed the contributions and awarded the scholarships to students in households with an income under 300 percent of the federal poverty rate ($90,000 for a family of four). In 2021–22, 9,029 students received an average of $8,390. According to Laura Welch, president of the Illinois chapter of the National Organization for Women, "about 95% of the receiving students attend religious schools" that "can legally discriminate against . . . students with disabilities, of different religions, and non-English language learners."[66] After the initial scholarship award, students remained eligible as long as their household income did not exceed 400 percent of the poverty rate. The law expired on January 1, 2024. IEA, IFT, and State Federation of Labor (SFL), along with their political allies, defeated efforts to extend the act beyond that year.[67]

Conclusion

IEA and its union allies have been largely successful in fending off right-wing efforts to undermine public education and unionism. IEA quickly responded to *A Nation at Risk* and subsequent studies calling for reform. In 1987, IEA established CEC on the premise that education employees, collectively through their unions, should play a major role in developing a reform agenda. CEC brought together teachers unions with school board members, administrators, and parents in a collaborative effort to improve student performance. Several years later, CTU created the Quest Center for Professional Learning and Teacher Leadership. IEA, IFT, and their union allies supported reforms that muted the more extreme efforts of the conservative right to undermine public education and unionism.

In 1996, Illinois passed a modest charter school law that limits the number of charters, prohibits for-profit and religious-based schools, and maintains local school districts' control over the approval process. IEA also achieved a major victory in providing job protection for all K–12 support staff employees with the passage of Public Act 095-0241 in 2007. The act established detailed ground rules that companies and school districts considering subcontracting of support staff services must follow. Illinois enacted the Performance Evaluation Reform Act and Senate Bill 7 with bipartisan and union support, defeating more extreme corporate-backed attacks on unions and teacher rights. Following the *Janus* decision, IEA and its allies secured legislation that limited IPI and other "outside" groups from obtaining personnel information from governmental bodies and defeated efforts to extend the Invest in Kids Act beyond January 1, 2024.

Nevertheless, the threat to public education is ongoing. Libertarian conservatives are well organized and financed in their efforts for publicly funded, non-union charters and for-profit schools. The evangelical right wants public funding for homeschooling and sectarian, religious schools. To deal with these threats, IEA and its allies must educate the public on the democratic mission on which public education was founded over 170 years ago and continue to organize politically against right-wing groups seeking to undermine unionism and privatize education.

Epilogue

Public education has always been one of the most contentious issues facing Illinois politics. From the earliest days of statehood to the present, issues related to taxation, race, religion, social class, gender, labor unions, and privatization have shaped education policies. Since 1853, the Illinois Education Association (IEA) has played a major role in the creation and development of the state's public school system. Today, it is one of the largest and most successful state affiliates of the National Education Association (NEA).

IEA's Union Democracy

IEA's success is a direct result of its membership involvement in the association. IEA has 919 local bargaining locals in 67 region councils across the state. At a minimum, each local elects officers and has a bargaining team. Larger associations have building representatives that serve on the local's governing board. Each local elects, at least, one region council delegate. Local members also elect delegates to the annual IEA and NEA representative assemblies (RAs). IEA has local associations in every county in Illinois. A major reason for so much membership involvement is the fact that public education in Illinois is decentralized. As of 2023, there are 852 K–12 school districts, 40 community colleges, 9 public universities, and numerous private schools.[1] With so many locals scattered across the state, IEA could not function without this democratic governance structure at the local level. All contracts are bargained directly between the districts and their local associations. This means that IEA locals manage their own affairs and decide what issues to bargain, without interference from the state organization. IEA's greatest strength is its internal democracy, which generates a great deal of involvement and ownership in the union. Education employees generally share a belief that they are serving the common good by educating the state's children. It is this educational ethos on which their union solidarity rests.

Region councils are also an important part of IEA's democratic governance structure. Each local association elects at least one delegate to their region council; local presidents participate in the hiring and evaluation of the UniServ staff, who provide assistance in bargaining, contract enforcement, training, and organizing. Unlike many other unions, the hired staff cannot run for or hold any elective office.

The chairs of the region councils are elected by the membership in their respective regions and constitute the majority on the IEA board of directors. Hence, IEA's power structure begins at the local level and works its way up through the state organization. The board of directors is the governing body that oversees the operations of the state organization, in accordance with the policies established at the annual IEA RA. The RA is structured to ensure representation for the diverse constituencies within the state organization. Since a large majority of members are K–12 teachers, IEA has constituent councils for its higher education, support staff employees, students, and retirees that elect representatives to the board of directors and address the concerns of their members. To ensure racial diversity, there are elected ethnic-minority representatives on the board. Under the 1959 Landrum-Griffin Act, any member can run for these ethnic/racial minority positions as long as they are representing minority concerns, but the intent is clear to have these positions filled by minorities. While this is not a guarantee, minority members almost always fill these positions.[2]

The eighty-eight members of the board include:

three state officers (president, vice president, and secretary-treasurer)
sixty-seven region council chairs
four ethnic-minority members
three education support professionals (ESPs, support staff employees)
two higher education members
one aspiring educator (teacher education student)
one retired member
seven NEA directors (who also represent IEA on the NEA board of directors)[3]

IEA board members can serve two terms of three years each, after which, if desired, they can then run for a different position on the board. For example, a former IEA president might be elected as an NEA director, but only after the presidential term of office has expired. IEA has only three full-time paid officers, but it has thousands of unpaid local union activists serving in various governance roles throughout the organization. Though some of its larger locals like Rockford, Naperville, and Elgin have either full-time or part-time release presidents, most leaders are full-time school employees who volunteer their time to serve their locals' needs.

Based on their membership, local associations also elect delegates to the annual RA. As many as 1,200 delegates from across the state attend the meeting each spring. As with the IEA board of directors, ethnic/racial minorities have representation at the RA. Ethnic-minority representatives, elected by each of the sixty-seven region councils, are also delegates to the annual RA, which is IEA's highest decision-making body. The RA passes the annual budget, amends bylaws, adopts the legislative platform, elects state officers and NEA directors, and enacts policies that govern IEA for the following year. It takes a two-thirds vote of the delegates to pass the annual budget, which includes the dues for the next year. Since wages for members outside the Chicago area are generally lower than those in the metropolitan area, proposed dues increases are often contentious. The two-thirds vote requirement ensures that dues increases are relatively modest and that the state organization is frugal in its spending. After nineteen previous efforts, the RA finally passed a graduated dues structure in 2022, to be phased in over several years.[4] On the final day of the RA, delegates vote by secret ballot to elect officers and NEA directors when any of their three-year terms have expired. IEA locals also elect delegates to the NEA RA, which meets annually in early July. As many as 8,000 delegates from across the nation attend this meeting.

In all, thousands of members are actively involved in IEA governance, and as a consequence, it has wielded significant power in Illinois politics. In 1983, it was instrumental in the passage of the Illinois Educational Labor Relations Act (IELRA), the most comprehensive collective bargaining law in the nation. The bargaining law covers all full-time and part-time public school employees, broadly defines the topics that can be bargained (including management decisions that affect wages, hours, and working conditions), legalizes strikes, and provides for a state labor board to oversee enforcement of the law. IEA has also been successful in supporting legislation that has further improved the law, such as Public Act 095-0241 of 2007, which tightly regulates the conditions under which districts can subcontract school services to an outside vendor. Following the 2018 US Supreme Court *Janus* decision, IEA also procured legislation that prevents school boards from providing information to outside organizations seeking to convince school employees to drop their IEA membership now that they can no longer be required to pay fair share fees. IEA did not suffer huge membership losses due to the *Janus* decision as the Illinois Policy Institute (IPI) and other anti-union organizations had expected. In 2022, IEA and union allies helped pass the Workers' Rights Amendment, which codifies existing labor legislation in the Illinois Constitution. The amendment will prevent the General Assembly from enacting legislation like the 2011 Wisconsin Act 10, which repealed collective bargaining laws in Wisconsin under Governor Scott Walker.

While IEA has been very successful in its legislative agenda, it faces an ongoing threat from for-profit business organizations, anti-union libertarians, and religious fundamentalists seeking to privatize public education through vouchers, tuition tax credits, and, to a lesser degree, charter schools.

Higher education provides the best examples of why funding for-profit companies to take over schools is a bad idea. For-profit colleges have been rocked by scandals involving the abuse of federal student loan programs, grants, and veteran education benefits. Many for-profit schools have open enrollment policies and spend a large portion of their budgets on recruitment of students in low-income and minority communities, with promises of a college education and high-earning prospects after graduation. These colleges assist students in securing federal tuition loans and grants but often do little to help them after they are enrolled. For-profit colleges rely almost exclusively on adjunct faculty to teach classes. Adjunct pay at these schools is typically the lowest in the area. The turnover rates for faculty and students are much higher than at private (not-for profit) and public institutions. Many students at for-profit colleges spend only a year or two before dropping out and are saddled with huge debts.[5]

For-profit colleges also recruit heavily among veterans, who qualify for federal aid under the GI Bill. Federal investigations of deceptive marketing practices have led to large fines and closures of a number of for-profit colleges. For example, the University of Phoenix, the nation's largest for-profit school, paid a $191 million fine; DeVry paid a $100 million fine. Corinthian Colleges and IIT Technical Institute closed. In 2021, the Federal Trade Commission filed notices of penalty offenses regarding deceptive marketing practices with seventy of the largest for-profit institutions in the nation. These scandals involving for-profit colleges suggest that the profit motive takes precedence over the quality of education being sold to students.[6]

School vouchers and tuition tax credits are, by far, the most serious threat facing K–12 public education today. In 1955, University of Chicago libertarian economist Milton Friedman first proposed tuition vouchers to give parents a choice whether to send their children to public or private schools, including those with religious affiliations. Eventually, Friedman projected that private schools would replace much of the public school system. By the late 1970s, support for Friedman's privatization proposals had increased among conservatives, as public school employees unionized and bargained higher wages and improved benefits.[7] Tuition voucher programs (sometimes referred to as education savings accounts or opportunity scholarships) are intended to undermine education unions, contain spending, reduce taxation, and open K–12 education to for-profit business enterprises.

There is plenty of evidence that the raison d'être of for-profit schools would place their bottom lines ahead of quality education. This has often been the case in subcontracting of for-profit colleges. In addition, private schools—whether they be for-profit, nonprofit, or religiously affiliated—operate with much less oversight than the public system. Unlike public schools, private schools are not required to teach all students. They can exclude students based on religion, English fluency, gender, or special needs.

Most importantly, voucher programs could undermine the nation's social fabric by financing a myriad of sectarian, religiously affiliated schools. Today, the United States is more diverse than ever in terms of race, religion, and cultural identity as a result of increasing immigration from the Middle East, Latin America, Africa, India, and China and other East Asian nations. Vouchers, especially for religiously affiliated institutions, could lead to the creation of a multitude of sectarian Christian and non-Christian schools. A private religious-based school system would segregate children and encourage mistrust among children of differing social and religious backgrounds. Friedman even acknowledged this danger, stating: "A stable and democratic society is impossible without widespread acceptance of some common set of values and without a minimum degree of literacy and knowledge on the part of most citizens."[8]

I attended Catholic schools from elementary through high school. My friends were all Catholic schoolmates. I hardly knew any students in the neighborhood who attended the local public school. We referred to these kids as "publics." My point here is that a state-sponsored private school system tends to segregate students based on their economic, religious, ethnic, and racial backgrounds and will exasperate social tension given the ever-increasing diversity of American society. Privatization runs counter to the concept of a democratically controlled "common" school, on which the public education system was founded over 170 years ago. In the inaugural issue of the NAACP magazine the *Crisis*, W. E. B. DuBois wrote: "Human contact, human acquaintanceship, human sympathy is the great solvent of human problems. Separate school children by wealth, and the result is class misunderstanding and hatred. Separate them by race and the result is war. Separate them by color and they grow up without learning the tremendous truth that it is impossible to judge the mind of a man by the color of his face." DuBois argued that segregation was "an argument against democracy."[9]

Though IPI and other right-leaning organizations have had little success up to this point in undermining IEA, they are well organized and well funded. They are part of a national effort that is not going away anytime soon. If IEA is going to survive and thrive, it must maintain its democratic, grassroots culture, continue efforts to improve the quality of public education, organize around the concerns of its members, and work closely with its labor allies on reform and political issues. It needs to publicly promote the historical mission of a "common" school system that, amid America's increasing diversity, teaches students the democratic traditions of our society.

IEA's success has always been a direct result of the high level of membership involvement in its local associations. As school districts turned to remote learning during the COVID-19 pandemic, there was a breakdown of the school community in which local associations thrived. Locals did not meet to recruit and train new building reps and others to replace those who retired.[10] Newly hired teachers were not introduced to their colleagues on the first day of school; in many cases, they were not personally asked to join the union. Union organizing is an ongoing process that involves one-on-one relationship building. The COVID-19 pandemic disrupted the school community and weakened the effectiveness of many IEA locals. Strong local associations are critical to IEA's success and require a major effort by local leaders and staff to build solidarity within the school community. When I worked as an IEA organizer, our slogan was: "Organizing is the heart of a healthy union!"

Notes

Chapter 1. Democratic Ideals and the Creation of the Illinois Public School System

The epigraph is quoted (with silent corrections) from Propeck and Pearson, *The History of the Illinois Education Association*, 24; it originally appears in *History of Boone County, Iowa* (Des Moines, IA: Union Historical, 1880), 431.

1. Spring, *The America School*, 92.

2. Tyler, *Freedom's Ferment*, 239.

3. Foner, *Free Soil, Free Labor, Free Men*, 65.

4. Stampp, *The Peculiar Institution*, 29–32.

5. Goldstein, *The Teacher Wars*, 52.

6. Winslow, "Education Reform in Antebellum America." For a description of education in Louisiana under Union occupation during the Civil War, see *Illinois Teacher* 11, no. 6 (June 1865): 189–93.

7. "Historic Home Hid Slaves," *Southern Illinoisan* (Carbondale), January 16, 1966. Besides Roots, many other ISTA members were abolitionists, most notably Newton Bateman and Richard Edwards. See Douglas, *Jim Crow Moves North*.

8. Tyack and Hansot, *Managers of Virtue*, 23, 31–33, 83–86; Stampp, *The Peculiar Institution*, 425–29; Foner, *Free Soil, Free Labor, Free Men*, 64–65, 87–90.

9. Wikipedia, s.v. "List of Most Populous Cities in the United States by Decade," last modified March 3, 2024, https://en.wikipedia.org/wiki/List_of_most_populous_cities _in_the_United_States_by_decade.

10. Foner, *Free Soil, Free Labor, Free Men*, 41.

11. *Illinois Teacher* 12, no. 4 (April 1866): 107.

12. *Biennial Report of the Superintendent of Common Schools*, 1851, 10. Gregg served as the ex officio superintendent of common schools. See also *Illinois Teacher* 1, no. 7 (August 1855): 193–94.

13. *Illinois Teacher* 3, no. 12 (December 1857): 405.

14. *Prairie Farmer*, January 11, 1941, 13.

15. *Biennial Report of the Superintendent of Common Schools*, 1851, 12; see also Herrick, *The Chicago Schools*, 27–32.

16. Cook, *Educational History of Illinois*, 38; Freed, *Educating Illinois*, 27; Propeck and Pearson, *The History of the Illinois Education Association*, 20–23.

17. Freed, *Educating Illinois*, 28; see also Bone, "Education in Illinois before 1857," 120–29.

18. Cook, *Educational History of Illinois*, 43.

19. *Illinois Teacher* 12, no. 6 (June 1866): 172–73.

20. *Prairie Farmer*, January 11, 1941, 8; Propeck and Pearson, *The History of the Illinois Education Association*, 27–30.

21. *Illinois Teacher* 12, no. 6 (June 1866): 171–78; Cook, *Educational History of Illinois*, 369–74.

22. Cook, *Educational History of Illinois*, 516–17.

23. *Prairie Farmer*, January 11, 1941, 14.

24. Marshall, *Grandest of Enterprises*, 9–10; *Prairie Farmer*, January 11, 1941, 8–9, 13–14.

25. *Prairie Farmer*, January 11, 1941, 13.

26. Propeck and Pearson, *The History of the Illinois Education Association*, 38.

27. Reproduced in Cook, *Educational History of Illinois*, 373.

28. *Illinois Teacher* 1, no. 1 (February 1855), 5–6, 26; Propeck and Pearson, *The History of the Illinois Education Association*, 32–34, 129–30.

29. Propeck and Pearson, *The History of the Illinois Education Association*, 33.

30. Cook, *Educational History of Illinois*, 113–14.

31. Propeck and Pearson, *The History of the Illinois Education Association*, 135. Powell was the only president to serve two consecutive one-year terms until the 1970s.

32. Cook, *Educational History of Illinois*, 53–58; Freed, *Educating Illinois*, 29.

33. *Journal of Proceedings of the Illinois State Teachers' Association*, 1869 meeting, 103.

34. Bone, "Education in Illinois before 1857," 135–37.

35. *Illinois Teacher* 5, no. 1 (January 1859): 7. For a good discussion of Protestant support for public education, see Tyack and Hansot, *Managers of Virtue*, 4–21.

36. *Illinois Teacher* 6, no. 1 (January 1860): 2.

37. *Illinois Teacher* 6, no. 1 (January 1860): 2.

38. *Illinois Teacher* 6, no. 1 (January 1860): 5. Horace Mann's position on Bible reading was to let it "speak for itself." Tyack and Hansot, *Managers of Virtue*, 4–21, 75.

39. *Illinois Teacher* 6, no. 2 (February 1860): 66–68.

40. Herrick, *The Chicago Schools*, 61; Tyack and Hansot, *Managers of Virtue*, 74–75.

41. Marshall, *Grandest of Enterprises*, 7–18; Propeck and Pearson, *The History of the Illinois Education Association*, 58–62. Despite its university designation, ISNU was basically a teachers college until the 1960s, when it was renamed Illinois State University. Freed, *Educating Illinois*, 12–13.

42. *Illinois Teacher* 24, no. 2 (October 1935): 41–43.

43. Marshall, *Grandest of Enterprises*, 24, 30–32; *Illinois Teacher* 9, no. 6 (June 1863): 18–20.

44. Cook, *Educational History of Illinois*, 377.

45. West, *The National Education Association*, 1.

46. According to the 1860 US Census, there were 7,628 "free colored" among the 1,711,751 residents living in Illinois. Thirty-two Native Americans were reported in the total count. *Population of the United States in 1860; Compiled from the Original Returns of the Eighth Census* (Washington, DC: Government Printing Office, 1864), 87. See David Roediger's *The Wages of Whiteness* on the role that racism played in undermining class solidarity. Early union leaders drew an analogy between southern slavery and the competitive labor market of capitalism, what they termed "the new system of wage slavery," which impoverished and oppressed workers in the United States. Following the Civil War, local union meetings often started in song with a labor rendition of "John Brown's Body." Opposition to southern slavery did not necessarily translate into racial tolerance. White workers shared the racist attitudes that were so pervasive in American culture.

47. Cook, *Educational History of Illinois*, 32; Howard, *Illinois*, 129–38, 184–91; Harris, *The History of Negro Servitude in Illinois*, 27–98.

48. Cook, *Educational History of Illinois*, 544–45.

49. Foner, *Free Soil, Free Labor, Free Men*, 232–37.

50. Sandburg, *Abraham Lincoln*, 120.

51. *Illinois Teacher* 7, no. 5 (May 1861): 193. Public education reformers had always been vocal critics of southern slavery. Abolitionists had long been viewed as dangerous radicals who threatened the nation's unity, but tension over the spread of slavery in the federal territories increased antislavery sentiment in the North. As is widely quoted, Horace Mann wrote: "I consider no evil so great as the extension of slavery." In 1848, the Free Soil Party was organized to stop the spread of slavery in the territories. In 1854, the Free Soil Party merged with the Republican Party on an antislavery platform. Public empathy for enslaved people increased dramatically in the lead-up to the Civil War. In 1852, Harriet Beecher Stowe's best-selling novel *Uncle Tom's Cabin* turned public opinion in the free states against slavery. The book depicted slavery as an evil that violated basic Christian values. The conflict known as "Bleeding Kansas" (1854–59) and the *Dred Scott v. Sandford* decision (1857) convinced many in the North that southern planters were determined to spread slavery throughout the nation. John Brown's 1859 raid on the Harpers Ferry arsenal polarized public opinion over slavery. Leaders in the South were convinced that the free states were determined to outlaw slavery. The 1860 election of Abraham Lincoln confirmed their fears.

52. *Illinois Teacher* 8, no. 1 (January 1862): 8.

53. *Illinois Teacher* 9, no. 2 (February 1863): 42.

54. *Illinois Teacher* 8, no. 1 (January 1862): 11.

55. *Illinois Teacher* 11, no. 6 (June 1865): 189–93.

56. *Illinois Teacher* 12, no. 4 (April 1866): 106–8; 12, no. 8 (August 1866): 241; 12, no. 10 (October 1866): 308.

57. Butler, *Through Thunder and Lightning*, 3.

58. *Illinois Teacher* 15, no. 2 (February 1869): 48. Bateman was a former ISTA president. The 1870 ratification of the Fifteenth Amendment undermined racist exclusion of Black children from public schools. An educated electorate was widely viewed as a necessity in a democratic republic. If Black people had voting rights, they should be included in the public school system.

59. *Illinois Teacher* 17, no. 6 (June 1871): 243.

60. *Illinois Teacher* 17, no. 6 (June 1871): 243, and see 240–45.

61. Marshall, *Grandest of Enterprises*, 131.

62. Marshall, 131–32. Racial slurs spelled out in original.

63. Marshall, 110.

64. Marshall, 132.

65. *Illinois Schoolmaster* 6, no. 66 (November 1873): 388, 391.

66. *Illinois Schoolmaster* 7, no. 72 (May 1874): 160; Douglas, *Jim Crow Moves North*, 66–67, 80–81.

67. Cook, *Educational History of Illinois*, 544–45; Herrick, *The Chicago Schools*, 399–401; Dunphy, "How Alton Got Segregated Schools"; Douglas, *Jim Crow Moves North*, 115–17, 251–55; Freed, *Educating Illinois*, 119.

68. Eaton, *The American Federation of Teachers*, 1, 4.

69. *Report of the First Annual Session of the Federation of Organized Trades and Labor Unions of the United States and Canada*, 3.

70. *Proceedings of the Fourth Annual Session of the Illinois State Labor Association*, 2–3, and see 1.

71. *Illinois Teacher* 25, no. 3 (November 1936): 78.

72. Propeck and Pearson, *The History of the Illinois Education Association*, 31.

73. Murphy, *Blackboard Unions*, 12, and see 13–16.

74. *Illinois Teacher* 3, no. 2 (February 1857): 71–72.

75. Rousmaniere, *Citizen Teacher*, 32.

76. Spring, *The America School*, 266.

77. Herrick, *The Chicago Schools*, 404.

78. *Illinois Schoolmaster* 7, no. 2 (February 1874): 65.

79. *Journal of Proceedings of the Illinois State Teachers' Association*, 1899 meeting, 27.

80. *Journal of Proceedings*, 1906 meeting, 27.

81. *Biennial Report of the Superintendent of Public Instruction of the State of Illinois*, for years 1857–58, 7; for years 1898–1900, 2.

82. *Illinois Teacher* 2, no. 3 (April 1856): 65; 2, no. 5 (June 1856): 164; Cook, *Educational History of Illinois*, 505.

83. *Biennial Report of the Superintendent of Public Instruction of the State of Illinois*, for years 1867–68, 411–15.

84. *Journal of Proceedings of the Illinois State Teachers' Association*, 1905 meeting, 42.

85. *Biennial Report of the Superintendent of Public Instruction of the State of Illinois*, for years 1857–58, 9; for years 1878–80, 15.

86. *Journal of Proceedings of the Illinois State Teachers' Association*, 1905 meeting, 43.

87. *Journal of Proceedings*, 1868 meeting, 23; 1899 meeting, 31.

88. *Journal of Proceedings*, 1901 meeting, 27.

89. Cook, *Educational History of Illinois*, 519–20.

90. Propeck and Pearson, *The History of the Illinois Education Association*, 86–90.

91. In her study of US teacher unionism in the twentieth century, Marjorie Murphy points out that "tax-conscious organizations blocked any attempt to move school funding away from narrow, local taxation. Within these confines, teachers managed to win concessions but remained tied to a fiscally conservative system." Murphy, *Blackboard Unions*, 3.

92. Propeck and Pearson, *The History of the Illinois Education Association*, 89.

Chapter 2. Chicago Teachers Federation

The epigraph is quoted from Haley, *Battleground*, 72.

1. *Illinois Teacher* 14, no. 6 (February 1926): 110.

2. Herrick, *The Chicago Schools*, 96; Murphy, *Blackboard Unions*, 27.

3. There are a number of books that cover in detail the history of CTF, including Haley, *Battleground*; Herrick, *The Chicago Schools*; and Rousmaniere, *Citizen Teacher*. Here, I briefly summarize the most important events of CTF's history that affected the development of ISTA and the National Education Association (NEA).

4. Herrick, *The Chicago Schools*, 95–97. Haley, *Battleground*, 34–36.

5. Rousmaniere, *Citizen Teacher*, 37–39, 44–45.

6. *Journal of Proceedings of the Illinois State Teachers' Association*, 1901 meeting, 85.

7. Rousmaniere, *Citizen Teacher*, 59–61.

8. Herrick, *The Chicago Schools*, 105–6.

9. Herrick, 98–99. CTF publicly attacked Rothmann, accusing him of personally pocketing $20,000 annually in earned interest over a seven-year period when he served as chair of the police retirement fund.

10. Herrick, 96–98.

11. Herrick, 106–7. Haley, *Battleground*, xxiii.

12. Rousmaniere, *Citizen Teacher*, 159.

13. Haley, *Battleground*, xxvi–xxvii.

14. Haley, 129.

15. Haley, 133.

16. Haley, 134; see also Rousmaniere, *Citizen Teacher*, 106–11.

17. Haley, *Battleground*, 135–36.

18. Haley, 280–81.

19. Haley, 112; Rousmaniere, *Citizen Teacher*, 95; Herrick, *The Chicago Schools*, 96–97.

20. Haley, *Battleground*, xxvii, 129, 146.

21. *Illinois Union Teacher*, October 1955, 3–4.

22. Cook, *Educational History of Illinois*, 561.

23. Smith, *Ella Flagg Young*, 63–64.

24. Rousmaniere, *Citizen Teacher*, 156; see also Herrick, *The Chicago Schools*, 116–18.

25. Smith, *Ella Flagg Young*, 106–10.

26. Haley, *Battleground*, 87–89.

27. *Journal of Proceedings of the Illinois State Teachers' Association*, 1910 meeting, 7, 11–48.

28. *Journal of Proceedings*, 1909 meeting, 47.

29. *Journal of Proceedings*, 1909 meeting, 48.

30. *Journal of Proceedings*, 1910 meeting, 95.

31. *Journal of Proceedings*, 1910 meeting, 18.

32. *Journal of Proceedings*, 1913 meeting, 20. See also *Illinois Teacher* 4, no. 1 (September 1915): 2; 4, no. 2 (October 1915): 18–19.

33. *Journal of Proceedings of the Illinois State Teachers' Association*, 1909 meeting, 43–44.

34. *Journal of Proceedings*, 1911 meeting, 11–13, 27–28.

35. *Journal of Proceedings*, 1912 meeting, 29–33, 142–45.

36. *Illinois Teacher* 1, no. 3 (June 1913): 1–4.

37. *Journal of Proceedings of the Illinois State Teachers' Association*, 1912 meeting, 142–45.

38. *Illinois Teacher* 1, no. 3 (June 1913): 6.

39. Propeck and Pearson, *The History of the Illinois Education Association*, 195–96.

40. *Journal of Proceedings of the Illinois State Teachers' Association*, 1913 meeting, 23.

41. *Journal of Proceedings*, 1913 meeting, 31.

42. Propeck and Pearson, *The History of the Illinois Education Association*, 93–94.

43. *Illinois Teacher* 6, no. 1 (September 1917): 5.

44. Herrick, *The Chicago Schools*, 136; *Illinois Teacher* 11, no. 6 (February 1923): 74–75.

45. *Illinois Teacher* 25, no. 8 (April 1937): 243.

46. *Journal of Proceedings of the Illinois State Teachers' Association*, 1915 meeting, 17–21.

47. Propeck and Pearson, *The History of the Illinois Education Association*, 135–36, 152–55.

48. Propeck and Pearson, 94–95.

49. *Journal of Proceedings of the Illinois State Teachers' Association*, 1909 meeting, 35.

50. *Journal of Proceedings*, 1909 meeting, 15–16, 23–29.

51. *Journal of Proceedings*, 1911 meeting, 16–19.

52. *Journal of Proceedings*, 1911 meeting, 18.

53. *Journal of Proceedings*, 1911 meeting, 22–23.

54. *Journal of Proceedings*, 1911 meeting, 26.

55. *Journal of Proceedings*, 1911 meeting, 26; 1913 meeting, 47–48.

56. *Journal of Proceedings*, 1919 meeting, 36.

57. *Illinois Education* 41, no. 8 (April 1954): 318–21.

58. *Illinois Teacher* 7, no. 5 (January 1919): 64.

59. Herrick, *The Chicago Schools*, 136.

60. *Illinois Teacher* 7, no. 7 (March 1919): 92.

61. *Illinois Teacher* 9, no. 5 (January 1921): 52.

62. *Illinois Teacher* 16, no. 9 (May 1928): 14.

63. *Illinois Teacher* 17, no. 6 (February 1929): 172.

Chapter 3. ISTA and Labor Union Allies

The epigraph is from *Illinois Teacher* 15, no. 9 (May 1927): 185.

1. *Journal of Proceedings of the Illinois State Teachers' Association*, 1915 meeting, 10.

2. *Illinois Teacher* 4, no. 1 (September 1915): 14.

3. *Illinois Teacher* 3, no. 10 (June 1915): 3.

4. *Journal of Proceedings of the Illinois State Teachers' Association*, 1913 meeting, 27.

5. Cook, *Educational History of Illinois*, 472.

6. Herrick, *The Chicago Schools*, 117–19; *Illinois Teacher* 4, no. 5 (January 1915): 14.

7. *Illinois Teacher* 1, no. 2 (May 1913): 5, 8.

8. *Journal of Proceedings of the Illinois State Teachers' Association*, 1913 meeting, 31.

9. *Illinois Teacher* 3, no. 5 (January 1915): 14.

10. Goldstein, *The Teacher Wars*, 88.

11. *Illinois Teacher* 5, no. 6 (February 1917): 104.

12. *Illinois Teacher* 6, no. 7 (March 1918): 77–78.

13. *Illinois Teacher* 6, no. 5 (January 1918): 56; 6, no. 7 (March 1918): 77.

14. *Illinois Teacher* 8, no. 6 (February 1920): 76.

15. *Illinois Teacher* 4, no. 9 (May 1916): 138.

16. Herrick, *The Chicago Schools*, 123.

17. Haley, *Battleground*, 169–74.

18. Haley, 171.

19. *Illinois Teacher* 4, no. 2 (October 1915): 20.

20. Herrick, *The Chicago Schools*, 122–23.

21. *Illinois Teacher* 4, no. 2 (October 1915): 20.

22. Herrick, *The Chicago Schools*, 125.

23. Rousmaniere, *Citizen Teacher*, 162, 169.

24. Haley, *Battleground*, 175.

25. *Illinois Teacher* 4, no. 6 (February 1916): 90; Herrick, *The Chicago Schools*, 126–27.

26. Rousmaniere, *Citizen Teacher*, 171–73.

27. "Mary J. Herrick Collection, 1924–1969," biographical sketch, Explore Chicago Collections, accessed May 15, 2024, https://explore.chicagocollections.org/ead/uic/25/sc84/.

28. Haley, *Battleground*, 178–79; Herrick, *The Chicago Schools*, 128–29.

29. *Illinois Teacher* 5, no. 10 (June 1917): 179.

30. Haley, *Battleground*, 179.

31. Herrick, *The Chicago Schools*, 135.

32. Herrick, 131–35.

33. *Illinois Teacher* 6, no. 1 (September 1917): 10.

34. *Journal of Proceedings of the Illinois State Teachers' Association*, 1900 meeting, 213.

35. *Journal of Proceedings of the Illinois State Teachers' Association*, 1914 meeting, 19.

36. *Illinois Teacher* 5, no. 9 (May 1917): 164.

37. *Illinois Teacher* 7, no. 1 (September 1918): 6; 7, no. 2 (October 1918): 16.

38. *Illinois Education* 39, no. 2 (October 1950): 44; Herrick, *The Chicago Schools*, 245; *Chicago Union Teacher*, November 1950, 2.

39. *Illinois Teacher* 7, no. 1 (September 1918): 5–6.

40. *Illinois Teacher* 10, no. 6 (February 1922): 64.

41. *Illinois Teacher* 17, no. 1 (September 1928): 14–15.

42. *Illinois Teacher* 18, no. 7 (March 1930): 216–19.

43. *Illinois Teacher* 18, no. 7 (March 1930): 219.

44. *Illinois Teacher* 1, no. 3 (June 1913): 7.

45. *Illinois Teacher* 7, no. 7 (March 1919): 93; 8, no. 10 (June 1920): 127.

46. *Illinois Teacher* 9, no. 10 (June 1921): 115–16.

47. Illinois State Teachers' Association, "The Crisis in Public Education in Illinois," 3.

48. *Illinois Teacher* 16, no. 8 (April 1928): 20; 17, no. 2 (October 1928): 34–39.

49. *Illinois Teacher* 17, no. 2 (October 1928): 60.

50. *Illinois Teacher* 16, no. 5 (January 1928): 7.

51. *Illinois Teacher* 16, no. 5 (January 1928): 2–4; 17, no. 1 (September 1928): 4–7; 21, no. 4 (December 1932): 125.

52. *Illinois Teacher* 17, no. 1 (September 1928): 4.

53. *Illinois Teacher* 15, no. 3 (November 1926): 46.

54. *Illinois Teacher* 4, no. 6 (February 1916): 75.

55. *Illinois Teacher* 15, no. 5 (January 1927): 91.

56. *Illinois Teacher* 15, no. 9 (May 1927): 185.

57. *Illinois Teacher* 15, no. 9 (May 1927): 184–91.

58. *Illinois Teacher* 18, no. 9 (May 1930): 316.

59. *Illinois Teacher* 17, no. 9 (May 1929): 264.

60. *Illinois Teacher* 18, no. 8 (April 1930): 267.

61. Herrick, *The Chicago Schools*, 145–48; Haley, *Battleground*, 211; Rousmaniere, *Citizen Teacher*, 194.

62. *Illinois Teacher* 14, no. 6 (February 1926): 110.

63. Herrick, *The Chicago Schools*, 147.

64. *Illinois Schoolmaster* 9, no. 97 (June 1876): 213–14; *Illinois Teacher* 13, no. 1 (January 1867): 36–43.

65. *Journal of Proceedings of the Illinois State Teachers' Association*, 1899 meeting, 70.

66. *Illinois Teacher* 8, no. 10 (June 1920): 129.

67. *Illinois Teacher* 11, no. 8 (April 1923): 103–4.

68. Hosman, *State Teacher Organizations*, 57; *Illinois Teacher* 13, no. 4 (December 1924): 80.

69. *Illinois Teacher* 11, no. 8 (April 1923): 104.

70. Herrick, *The Chicago Schools*, 261.

71. *Illinois Teacher* 17, no. 1 (September 1928): 12.

72. *Illinois Teacher* 15, no. 9 (May 1927): 185.

73. *Illinois Teacher* 14, no. 5 (January 1926): 88–92.

74. Cannella, *171 Years of Teaching in Chicago*, 10–12; Herrick, *The Chicago Schools*, 147.

75. Rousmaniere, *Citizen Teacher*, 205–209.

76. Rousmaniere, 209–10.

77. Haley, *Battleground*, 270.

Chapter 4. The Great Depression

The epigraph is from *Illinois Teacher* 20, no. 8 (April 1932): 268.

1. Rousmaniere, *Citizen Teacher*, 210.

2. *Illinois Teacher* 24, no. 6 (February 1936): 171; 25, no. 6 (February 1937): 168.

3. *Illinois Teacher* 18, no. 4 (December 1929): 10.

4. *Illinois Teacher* 19, no. 2 (October 1930): 53.

5. Herrick, *The Chicago Schools*, 184–87.

6. *Illinois Teacher* 19, no. 7 (March 1931): 271; Rousmaniere, *Citizen Teacher*, 200–203.

7. *Illinois Teacher* 23, no. 8 (April 1935): 251; 24, no. 6 (February 1936): 167.

8. *Illinois Teacher* 23, no. 7 (March 1935): 205.

9. *Illinois Teacher* 19, no. 5 (January 1931): 170.

10. *Illinois Teacher* 20, no. 1 (September 1931): 23.

11. *Illinois Teacher* 19, no. 10 (June 1931): 442.

12. *Illinois Teacher* 23, no. 3 (November 1934): 67.

13. *Illinois Teacher* 25, no. 2 (October 1936): 41.

14. Herrick, *The Chicago Schools*, 189.

15. Herrick, 198.

16. *Illinois Teacher* 24, no. 2 (October 1935): 60–61.

17. Herrick, *The Chicago Schools*, 202.

18. *Illinois Teacher* 21, no. 5 (January 1933): 156.

19. *Illinois Teacher* 24, no. 2 (October 1935): 61.

20. Herrick, *The Chicago Schools*, 190.

21. *Illinois Teacher* 19, no. 8 (April 1931): 322. See also Herrick, *The Chicago Schools*, 195, 200.

22. *Illinois Teacher* 22, no. 2 (October 1933): 58–59.

23. Herrick, *The Chicago Schools*, 203, 238–41.

24. Steve Tisza, "RIP Mollie Lieber West Member/Retiree Chicago Typographical Union No. 16," Communication Workers of America Local 4250, posted August 10, 2015, https://cwalocal4250.org//article?id=a_1439248327–3014. As a member of the Illinois Labor History Society board of directors, I had numerous conversations with Mollie about her experiences, including her arrest and the Memorial Day Massacre.

25. Eaton, *The American Federation of Teachers*, 51–55; Herrick, *The Chicago Schools*, 239–40; *Illinois Teacher* 21, no. 10 (June 1933): 328–29.

26. Herrick, *The Chicago Schools*, 200, 207.

27. Herrick, 209–10.

28. Herrick, 210–12.

29. Herrick, 241–43.

30. *Illinois Teacher* 20, no. 4 (December 1931): 119.

31. *Illinois Teacher* 18, no. 7 (March 1930): 219.

32. *Illinois Teacher* 23, no. 10 (June 1935): 324.

33. *Biennial Report of the Superintendent of Public Instruction of the State of Illinois*, for the years 1932–34, 83–84.

34. *Illinois Teacher* 24, no. 9 (May 1936): 298.

35. *Illinois Teacher* 23, no. 3 (November 1934): 76; 24, no. 3 (November 1935): 74.

36. *Illinois Teacher* 24, no. 4 (December 1933): 112, 117.

37. Herrick, *The Chicago Schools*, 193–97.

38. Herrick, 197–98.

39. Herrick, 198.

40. *Illinois Teacher* 21, no. 9 (May 1933): 290–91.

41. *Illinois Teacher* 22, no. 1 (September 1933): 11, 19; 22, no. 6 (February 1934): 167–69.

42. *Illinois Teacher* 22, no. 8 (April 1934): 246, 248.

43. *Illinois Teacher* 21, no. 9 (May 1933): 290–91.

44. *Illinois Teacher* 25, no. 1 (September 1936): 14; 25, no. 2 (October 1936): 40.

45. *Illinois Teacher* 18, no. 10 (June 1930): 365; 19, no. 2 (October 1930): 62.

46. *Illinois Teacher* 22, no. 10 (June 1934): 300; 24, no. 6 (February 1936): 180.

47. *Illinois Teacher* 23, no. 8 (April 1935): 265.

48. Lyons, *Teachers and Reform*, 42.

49. Lyons, 42.

50. *Illinois Teacher* 23, no. 1 (September 1934): 14, 22.

51. *Illinois Teacher* 23, no. 1 (September 1934): 22.

52. *Illinois Teacher* 23, no. 1 (September 1934): 23–24.

53. Propeck and Pearson, *The History of the Illinois Education Association*, 95.

54. *Illinois Teacher* 23, no. 10 (June 1935): 324.

55. Propeck and Pearson, *The History of the Illinois Education Association*, 99–100.

56. *Illinois Teacher* 26, no. 7 (March 1938): 218.

57. *Illinois Teacher* 27, no. 2 (October 1937): 36; 27, no. 6 (February 1938): 171–73.

58. *Illinois Teacher* 25, no. 8 (April 1937): 238.

59. Herrick, *The Chicago Schools*, 223, 228–31.

60. Herrick, 214–15.

61. *Illinois Teacher* 24, no. 6 (February 1936): 183.

62. *Illinois Teacher* 25, no. 4 (December 1936): 114; 25, no. 5 (January 1937): 138, 154.

63. *Illinois Teacher* 28, no. 1 (September 1939): 7, 30; 28, no. 2 (October 1939): 37–38.

64. *Illinois Teacher* 26, no. 2 (October 1937): 45.

65. *Illinois Teacher* 28, no. 1 (September 1939): 6.

66. *Illinois Teacher* 27, no. 1 (September 1938): 4–11, 29–30.

67. *Illinois Teacher* 27, no. 8 (April 1939): 266.

68. *Illinois Teacher* 27, no. 1 (September 1938): 10–11.

69. Herrick, *The Chicago Schools*, 244–45.

70. *Illinois Teacher* 26, no. 9 (June 1938): 304.

71. *Illinois Teacher* 26, no. 9 (June 1938): 304.

72. Herrick, *The Chicago Schools*, 245.

Chapter 5. Democratic Reform and Increasing Teacher Militancy

The epigraph is from *Illinois Education* 31, no. 2 (October 1942): 39.

1. *Illinois Teacher* 26, no. 6 (February 1938): 167.

2. *Illinois Teacher* 27, no. 8 (April 1939): 243.

3. *Illinois Teacher* 28, no. 5 (January 1940): 134.

4. *Illinois Teacher* 26, no. 9 (June 1938): 281.

5. *Illinois Teacher* 24, no. 6 (February 1935): 116.

6. *Illinois Teacher* 27, no. 8 (April 1939): 271.

7. *Illinois Teacher* 27, no. 8 (April 1939): 256.

8. *NEA Handbook: 1973–74*, 237–44.

9. *Illinois Teacher* 26, no. 9 (June 1938): 304.

10. *Illinois Education* 29, no. 5 (January 1941): 154.

11. *Illinois Teacher* 28, no. 9 (May 1940): 300–301.

12. *Illinois Teacher* 28, no. 6 (February 1940): 176.

13. *Illinois Education* 30, no. 5 (January 1942): 150.

14. *Illinois Teacher* 28, no. 8 (April 1940): 261.

15. *Illinois Teacher* 27, no. 5 (January 1939): 135, see also 136, 159; and see Herrick, *The Chicago Schools*, 252, 255.

16. *Chicago Principals Club Reporter* 48 (December 1957–January 1958): 26.

17. Herrick, *The Chicago Schools*, 239–241.

18. *Illinois Education* 30, no. 5 (January 1942): 148; *Weekly News Bulletin*, December 9, 1939, 2.

19. *Illinois Teacher* 28, no. 7 (March 1940): 222–23.

20. *Illinois Education* 30, no. 5 (January 1942): 148.

21. Lyons, *Teachers and Reform*, 54.

22. Herrick, *The Chicago Schools*, 251.

23. *Illinois Union Teacher*, December 1939, 3.

24. Lyons, *Teachers and Reform*, 94; Herrick, *The Chicago Schools*, 255.

25. Herrick, *The Chicago Schools*, 250–51.

26. Herrick, 257; see also *Illinois Education* 35, no. 1 (September 1947): 7, 24.

27. Herrick, *The Chicago Schools*, 271–73, 277, 281.

28. Donley, *Power to the Teacher*, 149.

29. *American Teacher*, November 1944, 6–11; Weil, *Teachers beyond the Law*, 13–14; "A Contract or Memoranda of Agreement by and between the Grade School Board of the Benld Public Schools and the Progressive Trades and Labor Unions of America Representing the Progressive Teachers Union 1," 1934, author's collection. This and subsequently cited items in the author's personal collection will be donated to the IEA archives in Springfield upon publication of this book.

30. NEA, "AFT Membership by States and Locals: 1971–73," 8–10, author's collection.

31. Weil, *Teachers beyond the Law*, 20.

32. Weil, 10.

33. *Illinois Teacher* 27, no. 5 (January 1939): 158.

34. *Illinois Teacher* 27, no. 7 (March 1939): 202.

35. *Illinois Teacher* 28, no. 4 (December 1939): 104, 126.

36. *Illinois Teacher* 28, no. 1 (September 1939): 29.

37. *Illinois Union Teacher*, February 1940, 1.

38. *Illinois Teacher* 28, no. 9 (May 1940): 294.

39. *Illinois Education* 42, no. 1 (September 1953): 12, 18.

40. *Illinois Education* 30, no. 7 (March 1942): 211.

41. *Illinois Education* 31, no. 1 (September 1942): 22.

42. *Illinois Education* 31, no. 1 (September 1942): 22.

43. *Illinois Education* 44, no. 6 (February 1956): 212.

44. *Illinois Education* 55, no. 7 (March 1967): 303.

45. *Illinois Education* 59, no. 4 (December 1970): 52.

46. *Advocate* 6, no. 7 (February 1972): 2.

47. *Illinois Education* 31, no. 1 (September 1942): 7.

48. *Illinois Education* 31, no. 2 (October 1942): 39.

49. *Illinois Education* 31, no. 1 (September 1942): 42.

50. *Illinois Education* 31, no. 2 (October 1942): 39.

51. *Illinois Education* 31, no. 1 (September 1942): 8.

52. Propeck and Pearson, *The History of the Illinois Education Association*, 102.

53. *Illinois Education* 34, no. 8 (May 1946): 244.

54. *Illinois Teacher* 27, no. 3 (November 1938): 71.

55. *Illinois Teacher* 26, no. 4 (December 1937): 110–11.

56. *Illinois Education* 34, no. 1 (September 1945): 10, 27.

57. Propeck and Pearson, *The History of the Illinois Education Association*, 102; *Illinois Education* 36, no. 3 (November 1947): 73.

58. *Illinois Education* 40, no. 1 (September 1951): 14.

59. *Illinois Education* 36, no. 2 (October 1947): 45.

60. *Illinois Education* 36, no. 1 (September 1947): 16–17; 36, no. 5 (February 1948): 148; *History Highlights of the Illinois Education Association*.

61. *Illinois Education* 34, no. 1 (September 1945): 10, 27–29.

62. Wikipedia, s.v. "McAuley School District No. 27," last modified March 30, 2021, https://en.wikipedia.org/wiki/McAuley_School_District_No. 27.

63. *Illinois Education* 34, no. 4 (December 1945–January 1946): 115.

64. *Illinois Education* 34, no. 4 (December 1945–January 1946): 115.

65. *Illinois Education* 34, no. 4 (December 1945–January 1946): 115–16.

66. *Illinois Education* 34, no. 4 (December 1945–January 1946): 116.

67. *Illinois Education* 34, no. 4 (December 1945–January 1946): 115.

68. *Illinois Education* 36, no. 5 (February 1948): 153.

69. Ming, "The Elimination of Segregation in the Public Schools"; Fishbein, "School Segregation Still Issue in S. Illinois," 3, 5; Douglas, *Jim Crow Moves North*, 138–48, 251–55; Williams, "Illinois School Desegregation."

70. *Illinois Education* 38, no. 7 (March 1950): 249–51.

71. *Illinois Education* 38, no. 6 (February 1950): 202; see also 41, no. 6 (February 1953): 208–10.

72. *Illinois Teacher* 25, no. 7 (March 1937): 211.

73. *Illinois Education* 35, no. 3 (November 1946): 76.

74. *Illinois Education* 40, no. 2 (October 1951): 50; 40, no. 3 (December 1951): 150; Education International, home page, accessed August 1, 2024, http://www.ei-ie.org.

75. *Illinois Teacher* 18, no. 10 (June 1930): 365; *Illinois Education* 29, no. 5 (January 1941): 148.

76. Spring, *The America School*, 330.

77. *Illinois Education* 42, no. 7 (March 1954): 275–77.

78. Lyons, *Teachers and Reform*, 118–21.

79. Lyons, 127.

80. *Illinois Education* 39, no. 6 (February 1951): 222.

81. Herrick, *The Chicago Schools*, 294–98; Lyons, *Teachers and Reform*, 117–32.

82. *Illinois Education* 45, no. 3 (November 1956): 92.

83. *Illinois Education* 44, no. 4 (December 1955): 130.

84. *Illinois Education* 41, no. 8 (April 1953): 292.

85. *Illinois Education* 44, no. 1 (September 1955): 19.

86. *Illinois Education* 44, no. 1 (September 1955): 19.

87. Lyons, *Teachers and Reform*, 130–31. See also *Illinois Union Teacher*, December 1956, 1–2.

88. *Illinois Education* 54, no. 3 (November 1965): 148–49.

89. *Illinois Education* 28, no. 6 (February 1940): 176.

90. *Illinois Education* 45, no. 1 (September 1956): 2.

91. *Illinois Education* 35, no. 3 (November 1946): 83. The department was later renamed the Association of Classroom Teachers. Like ATA, it became a powerful voice for collective bargaining within NEA.

92. *Illinois Education* 35, no. 3 (November 1946): 83.

93. *Illinois Education* 39, no. 1 (September 1950): 8.

94. *Illinois Education* 50, no. 7 (March 1962): 283.

95. *Illinois Education* 49, no. 1 (September 1960): second cover.

Chapter 6. Professional Solidarity or Professional Unionism

The epigraph is from *Illinois Education* 38, no. 4 (December 1949): 155.

1. Weil, *Teachers beyond the Law*, 119.

2. *Illinois Education* 43, no. 8 (April 1955): 306; 43, no. 9 (May 1955): 350–51.

3. West, *The National Education Association*, 235.

4. *Illinois Education* 39, no. 7 (March 1951): 259.

5. Propeck and Pearson, *The History of the Illinois Education Association*, 145–47.

6. *Illinois Education* 54, no. 3 (November 1965): 131.

7. *Illinois Education* 34, no. 4 (December 1945–January 1946): 116; 35, no. 1 (September 1946): 8, 39, 60–61; 35, no. 9 (May 1947): 272, 291.

8. *Illinois Education* 39, no. 2 (October 1951): 53.

9. *Illinois Education* 42, no. 4 (December 1953): 149.

10. *Illinois Education* 48, no. 4 (December 1959): 165.

11. Barnard, "The Changing Role of the Illinois Education Association," 21.

12. Superintendent of Public Instruction, "Illinois Teacher Salary Study, 1973–74," 7.

13. *Illinois Education* 45, no. 7 (March 1957): 264–65; 58, no. 2 (October 1969): 75.

14. *Illinois Education* 53, no. 3 (November 1964): 127–28.

15. *Insight* 3, no. 6 (April 1969): 2.

16. *Insight* 5, no. 10 (May 1971): 1.

17. *Insight* 4, no. 8 (March 1970): 2.

18. *Illinois Education* 60, no. 1 (September 1971): 7.

19. *Illinois Education* 36, no. 6 (March 1948): 171.

20. Barnard, "The Changing Role of the Illinois Education Association," 25–26; Donley, *Power to the Teacher*, 39–41.

21. *Illinois Education* 54, no. 8 (April 1966): 352–53.

22. Information compiled from issues of *Illinois Education*, 1945–66.

23. *American Teacher*, November 1944, 6–11.

24. Weil, *Teachers beyond the Law*, 2.

25. *Illinois Union Teacher*, September 1950, 4.

26. Weil, *Teachers beyond the Law*, 1–3, 23.

27. *Illinois Union Teacher*, March 1947, 1.

28. Herrick, *The Chicago Schools*, 290.

29. Weil, *Teachers beyond the Law*, 18.

30. *Illinois Education* 39, no. 9 (May 1951): 342–43.

31. *Illinois Education* 39, no. 9 (May 1951): 343.

32. *Illinois Education* 39, no. 9 (May 1951): 343–44.

33. *Illinois Union Teacher*, November 1957, 1, 4.

34. Weil, *Teachers beyond the Law*, 23–25, 35–37.

35. *Illinois Education* 46, no. 6 (February 1958): 206.

36. *Illinois Education* 46, no. 6 (February 1958): 206.

37. *Illinois Education* 46, no. 8 (April 1958): 298.

38. *Illinois Union Teacher*, January 1958, 4.

39. *Illinois Education* 46, no. 1 (September 1957): 8; 46, no. 6 (February 1958): 207, 220; *Illinois Union Teacher*, January 1958, 1, 4.

40. *Illinois Union Teacher*, November 1963, 1.

41. *Illinois Union Teacher*, November 1956, 1.

42. *Illinois Union Teacher*, April 1958, 298.

43. Lyons, *Teachers and Reform*, 166.

44. Lyons, 165, 167, 259n159; James Chiakulas, pers. comm., c. 1990.

45. Donley, *Power to the Teacher*, 160.

46. Weil, *Teachers beyond the Law*, 37.

47. Weil, 25–27, 40–41.

48. *Illinois Education* 51, no. 1 (September 1962): 14; *Illinois Union Teacher*, November 1962, 4.

49. *Illinois Education* 51, no. 1 (September 1962): 15.

50. *Illinois Education* 51, no. 1 (September 1962): 15–16.

51. *Illinois Education* 51, no. 1 (September 1962): 14. Another major event that propelled public employee unionism was President John F. Kennedy's executive order 10988 (July 1962), which gave federal government workers the right to organize and bargain collectively.

52. *Insight* 5, no. 7 (February 1971): 2.

53. Barnard, "The Changing Role of the Illinois Education Association," 29.

54. Barnard, 75.

55. Stinnett, Kleinmann, and Ware, *Professional Negotiation in Public Education*, 1–3.

56. Robert Jensen, pers. comm., 2019–20.

57. Barnard, "The Changing Role of the Illinois Education Association," 81–82.

58. Barnard, 11–12; Stinnett, Kleinmann, and Ware, *Professional Negotiation in Public Education*, 17–18.

59. *Illinois Education* 54, no. 3 (November 1965): 131.

60. Barnard, "The Changing Role of the Illinois Education Association," 93.

61. Stinnett, Kleinmann and Ware, *Professional Negotiation in Public Education*, 103, 114–20.

62. Stinnett, Kleinmann and Ware, 58, 66–67; *Insight* 5, no. 2 (September 1970): 1.

63. *Illinois Union Teacher*, March 1967, 7.

64. Laird Lawlyes, pers. comm., 2020.

65. *Illinois Education* 51, no. 1 (September 1962): 15.

66. Barnard, "The Changing Role of the Illinois Education Association," 98.

67. *Illinois Education* 51, no. 1 (September 1962): 15.

68. *Illinois Education* 54, no. 4 (December 1965): 160–62.

69. *Illinois Education* 51, no. 1 (September 1962): 36.

70. *Illinois Education* 56, no. 3 (November 1967): 139.

71. West, *The National Education Association*, 47; Urban, *Gender, Race, and the National Education Association*, 176.

72. *Illinois Education* 49, no. 7 (March 1961): 278–79; 55, no. 5 (January 1967): 210.

73. *Insight* 4, no. 5 (December 1969): 2.

74. NEA, "Should Public School Teachers Ever Strike?," research information for UniServ units, special memo F-4, October 1974, author's collection. Many NEA documents are also available in the NEA collection, Gelman Library, George Washington University.

75. Barnard, "The Changing Role of the Illinois Education Association," 46–47.

76. Goldstein, *The Teacher Wars*, 135.

77. *Illinois Union Teacher*, May–June 1970, 3.

78. *Insight* 1, no. 3 (November 1966): 1; "IEA Strikes—1970 through 1975," author's collection.

Chapter 7. A Radical Transformation

The epigraph is from *Illinois Union Teacher*, September 1967, 4.

1. *Advocate* 8, no. 8 (May 1974): 17.

2. *Illinois Union Teacher*, February 1964, 1, 4.

3. Herrick, *The Chicago Schools*, 331–32.

4. Barnard, "The Changing Role of the Illinois Education Association," 90; *Insight* 1, no. 3 (November 1966): 1; *Illinois Education* 56, no. 1 (September 1967): 10–11.

5. Herrick, *The Chicago Schools*, 332.

6. Rousmaniere, *Citizen Teacher*, 210.

7. Earl Rudolph, pers. comm., 2020.

8. Rudolph.

9. Barnard, "The Changing Role of the Illinois Education Association," 92, 100.

10. For an early history of proposed bargaining legislation, see Fletcher, "The Judicial and Legislative History of Public School Employee Collective Bargaining Legislation in Illinois," 3, 150.

11. *Illinois Education* 58, no. 8 (April 1970): 249–51. As his Republican political career developed and as the IEA became more aggressive in its efforts to secure teacher rights, Representative Hoffman eventually came to oppose much of IEA's legislative agenda. Laird Lawlyes, pers. comm., 2019.

12. Lawlyes, "Legislative History of Collective Bargaining in the Illinois General Assembly," 6–7.

13. Weil, *Teachers beyond the Law*, 469.

14. *Illinois Education* 58, no. 1 (September 1969): 5, 8, 33.

15. Robert Jensen, pers. comm., 2019.

16. *Advocate* 6, no. 1 (August 1971): 2.

17. *Illinois Education* 57, no. 1 (September 1968): 2.

18. *Illinois Education* 54, no. 1 (September 1965): 8–9.

19. *Illinois Education* 57, no. 6 (February 1969): 243.

20. *Illinois Union Teacher*, April 1966, 1.

21. *Affiliated Local Associations—Illinois: 1973–74*, 237–44.

22. Joseph Pasteris, pers. comm., 2018.

23. *Illinois Education* 58, no. 5 (January 1970): 201.

24. *Insight* 5, no. 2 (September 1970): 1.

25. *Insight* 5, no. 1 (August 1970): 4.

26. *Advocate* 7, no. 5 (January–February 1973): 13.

27. *Illinois Education* 58, no. 8 (April 1970): 333–34.

28. *Illinois Education* 59, no. 1 (September 1970): 12, 32.

29. *Insight* 5, no. 2 (September 1970): 1.

30. IEA, "IEA Affiliates: 1970–71," internal document, August 24, 1971, author's collection.

31. *Advocate* 7, no. 5 (January–February 1973): 12.

32. *Illinois Education* 59, no. 1 (September 1970): 8–9.

33. *Advocate* 7, no. 6 (March 1973): 9.

34. *Illinois Education* 59, no. 1 (September 1970): 5.

35. *Illinois Education* 59, no. 4 (April 1971): 156.

36. *Illinois Education* 59, no. 4 (April 1971): 157; *Insight* 5, no. 10 (May 1971): 1.

37. *Insight* 5, no. 8 (March 1971): 3.

38. *Insight* 5, no. 8 (March 1971): 4.

39. *Insight* 5, no. 8 (March 1971): 4.

40. *Insight* 5, no. 2 (September 1970): 1.

41. *Illinois Education* 59, no. 4 (April 1971): 158.

42. John McCluskey, pers. comm., 2021.

43. *Advocate* 6, no. 3 (November 1971): 1. On a personal note, I served one term as IEASO secretary, was an IEASO delegate at numerous annual meetings, and participated in various NSO organizing efforts throughout my IEA career.

44. John McCluskey, pers. comm., 2021.

45. *Advocate* 7, no. 1 (September 1972): 4–5.

46. "Who Strikes More: Collective Bargaining, Question and Answers," undated IFT campaign flyer, author's collection.

47. *Insight* 5, no. 7 (February 1971): 1; *Illinois Education* 59, no. 4 (April 1971): 144–45.

48. John McCluskey, "Those Daring Young Folk on the Flying Trapezoids," unpublished IEA history distributed among IEA staff, February 9, 1988, 3, author's collection.

49. Curtis Plott, "Reorganization and Realignment of the IEA Staff," memorandum to IEA board of directors, April 16, 1971, author's collection.

50. Curtis Plott, "Staff Reorganization," memorandum to IEA board of directors, February 8, 1974, 1–2, author's collection.

51. *Advocate* 7, no. 2 (October 1972): 24; McCluskey, "Those Daring Young Folk on the Flying Trapezoids," 1.

52. *Illinois Education* 60, no. 1 (September 1971): 26–27.

53. *Illinois Education* 59, no. 4 (April 1971): 158.

54. *Illinois Education* 60, no. 1 (September 1971): 25; "Map of Illinois: Number of School Districts by County Staff," author's collection.

55. "IEA UniServ Committee Report to the Association Leaders," December 23, 1971, author's collection.

56. *Advocate* 7, no. 1 (September 1972): 4–5; 7, no. 4 (December 1972): 10; 9, no. 2 (October 1973): 3.

57. *Illinois Education* 58, no. 7 (March 1970): 276.

58. *Illinois Education* 60, no. 3 (February 1972): 113.

59. *Illinois Education* 60, no. 3 (February 1972): 112.

60. Herrick, *The Chicago Schools*, 312–13; *Martin Luther King Jr. Encyclopedia*, s.v. "Raby, Albert," Stanford University, Martin Luther King Jr. Research and Education Institute, accessed March 14, 2022, https://kinginstitute.stanford.edu/encyclopedia/raby-albert.

61. *Advocate* 8, no. 8 (March 1974): 10–11.

62. *Advocate* 8, no. 8 (March 1974): 10.

63. *Advocate* 6, no. 9 (April 1972): 7; 8, no. 1 (September 1973): 21.

64. Patricia Brown-Barnes, pers. comm., 2020.

65. *Advocate* 7, no. 6 (March 1973): 9.

66. Reginald Weaver, pers. comm., 2020.

67. IEA, *Pride and Progress*, 4–10.

68. Patricia Brown-Barnes, pers. comm., 2020.

69. IEA, *Pride and Progress*, 3–17.

70. IEA Office of the President, pers. comm., 2020.

71. *Illinois Education* 61, no. 1 (September 1972): 8–10, 24.

72. *Advocate* 8, no. 5 (January 1974): 11; 8, no. 7 (March 1974): 14.

73. *Advocate* 6, no. 7 (February 1972): 3.

74. *Illinois Education* 59, no. 4 (April 1971): 160.

75. *Advocate* 6, no. 8 (March 1972), 3; Laird Lawlyes, pers. comm., 2019.

76. *Advocate* 6, no. 7 (February 1972): 3; Laird Lawlyes, pers. comm., 2019. Over the years, the IPACE contribution has increased; members pay thirty dollars annually as of 2024. The local rebates now range from three to fifteen dollars.

77. *Advocate* 6, no. 1 (August 1971): 5.

78. Laird Lawlyes, pers. comm., 2019.

79. In 2014, the State Board of Education reported that IFT, conversely, lacked K–12 locals in fifty-six counties. See Illinois State Board of Education, *Teacher Salary Study*, for years 2013–14.

80. *Advocate* 8, no. 8 (May 1974): 17.

81. Laird Lawlyes, pers. comm., 2019. In 1973, Terry Bruce received an IPACE Legislator of the Year Award. *Advocate* 7, no. 6 (March 1973): 6.

82. Larry Phillips, "A Proposal for IEA Executive Staff Reorganization," January 4, 1974, 2, author's collection.

83. "Meet the Top Members of Assembly's '3d House,'" *Chicago Tribune*, April 30, 1978.

84. *Advocate* 6, no. 2 (September 1971): 1–2; 6, no. 3 (October 1971): 1, 6.

85. Weil, *Teachers beyond the Law*, 267–68, 547.

86. James Penca (IFT staff), transcribed interview by Robert Breving (IFT staff), March 25, 2009, author's collection.

87. United Teachers of Chicago, "Join United Teachers of Chicago: A Manifesto for Quality Education," September 1972, 11, author's collection.

88. *Advocate* 6, no. 2 (October 1971): 1.

89. *Advocate* 6, no. 3 (November 1971): 2.

90. Weil, *Teachers beyond the Law*, 649.

91. *Advocate* 6, no. 2 (October 1971): 1.

92. Lawlyes, "Legislative History of Collective Bargaining in the Illinois General Assembly," 9. Ryor, "History of Collective Bargaining Legislation in In Illinois," 86.

93. Lawlyes, "Legislative History of Collective Bargaining in the Illinois General Assembly," 9.

94. *Advocate* 6, no. 10 (May 1972): 1; 7, no. 1 (September 1972): 8.

95. *Advocate* 7, no. 1 (September 1972): 8.

96. Weil, *Teachers beyond the Law*, 548, 554.

97. Weil, 539.

98. Weil, 641.

99. *Advocate* 10, no. 10 (June 1976): 5.

Chapter 8. Bargaining without a Law

The epigraph is from *Advocate* 8, no. 1 (September 1973): 2.

1. *Advocate* 6, no. 1 (August 1971): 1, 6–7.

2. I worked with these three high school districts during my career as an IEA organizer. Oak Park and River Forest High School rejoined IEA in 1998. In 2017, District 214 affiliated with the Illinois Federation of Teachers (IFT). District 113 affiliated with IEA in 2022.

3. *Advocate* 6, no. 1 (August 1971): 6.

4. I learned about this practice at a Region 25 meeting in spring 1983.

5. Vern Thistlewaite, pers. comm., 2020.

6. *Illinois Education* 60, no. 3 (February 1972): 101–2; Alan Stang, "The NEA, Dictatorship of the Educariat," *American Opinion* (John Birch Society), March 1972.

7. Vern Thistlewaite, pers. comm., 2020; *Illinois Education* 60, no. 3 (February 1972): 103.

8. *Illinois Education* 60, no. 3 (February 1972): 102.

9. *Illinois Education* 60, no. 3 (February 1972): 102.

10. *Illinois Education* 60, no. 3 (February 1972): 102–3.

11. *Illinois Education* 60, no. 3 (February 1972): 103–4.

12. *Illinois Education* 60, no. 3 (February 1972): 104.

13. Vern Thistlewaite, pers. comm., 2020.

14. *Illinois Education* 60, no. 3 (February 1972): 104.

15. *Illinois Education* 60, no. 3 (February 1972): 105.

16. *Illinois Education* 60, no. 3 (February 1972): 105.

17. *Illinois Education* 60, no. 3 (February 1972): 106.

18. Vern Thistlewaite, pers. comm., 2020.

19. Thistlewaite.

20. *Advocate* 6, no. 4 (November 1971): 2; 6, no. 7 (February 1972): 8.

21. *Advocate* 8, no. 3 (January 1974): 24.

22. *Advocate* 6, no. 3 (November 1971): 2.

23. Memorial Dr. Roy J O'Neil, Ill. S.R. 0293, 91st G.A. (1999–2000). In 1982, East Aurora teachers affiliated with IFT.

24. *Advocate* 12, no. 4 (December 1977): 10.

25. "Injunction Request by Board Not Granted," *Tri-County Today* (Yorkville, IL), September 14, 1977, 1, 4; SCTA, "Sandwich Classroom Teachers Association Countersteps," September 13, 1977, author's collection.

26. *Advocate* 12, no. 4 (December 1977): 10; 12, no. 10 (Summer 1978): 5.

27. Mary Ann Beil, pers. comm., 2020.

28. *Advocate* 8, no. 1 (September 1973): 17.

29. Superintendent of Public Instruction, "Illinois Teacher Salary Study, 1973–74," 26–72. When I was hired in 1985 as an organizer, all teachers in large school districts in northern Illinois, except for District 200 (Oak Park and River Forest High School) and District 113 (Highland Park–Deerfield High School), had bargaining agreements. District 214 (Palatine) teachers had an independent agreement. From 1985 to 1999, I organized teachers in nine elementary districts and three special education cooperatives having fewer than eighty teachers.

30. *Advocate* 7, no. 2 (October 1972): 18–20.

31. *Advocate* 8, no. 1 (September 1973): 15.

32. *Advocate* 7, no. 2 (October 1972): 20, 23.

33. Steven Fischer, "Tales Told Out of School, A Didactic Narrative for Educators" (unpublished manuscript, 2015, in author's possession, ch. 11, 1.

34. Fischer, ch. 11, 2.

35. *Advocate* 16, no. 6 (February 1982): 11–12.

36. *Lake Park Education Association vs Board of Education of Lake Park District No. 108, DuPage County, Illinois,* 526 F. Supp. 710 (N.D. Ill. 1981).

37. *Advocate* 16, no. 6 (February 1982): 11–12.

38. Steven Fischer, pers. comm., 2020.

39. *Advocate* 8, no. 8 (May 1974): 18.

40. UniServ directors David Sneddon and Michael Cook, pers. comm., 2020.

41. *Advocate* 8, no. 8 (May 1974): 18.

42. David Sneddon and Michael Cook, pers. comm., 2020.

43. *Advocate* 13, no. 2 (October 1978): 7; 14, no. 1 (September 1979): 28.

44. David Sneddon and Michael Cook, pers. comm., 2020.

45. Sneddon and Cook.

46. Sneddon and Cook.

47. DuPage Bargaining Council, "D.B.C.," undated flyer, received from UniServ director Bruce Lund, 2020.

48. Jo Anderson, pers. comm., 2020.

49. Anderson.

50. Anderson.

51. *Advocate* 10, no. 3 (November 1975): 4.

52. Bruce Lund, pers. comm., 2020.

53. MBC, "M.B.C. Proposed Platform," February 1976 flyer, received from UniServ director Bruce Lund, 2020.

54. *Affiliated Local Associations—Illinois: 1973–74*, 243.

55. John McCluskey, pers. comm., 2020.

56. Edward Meridian [pseud.], *SIU, the First 50 Years: Transforming a Region* (Edwardsville: Southern Illinois University, 2007), 158–59. Ellen Nore (professor emerita, Southern Illinois University Edwardsville) was the author of this booklet and confirmed for me the accuracy of its content; Nore, pers. comm., 2022.

57. John McCluskey, pers. comm., 2020.

58. Mike Cook, pers. comm., 2021.

59. Cook.

60. IEA organizer David Vitoff, pers comm., 2021.

61. *Advocate* 8, no. 1 (September 1973): 2. La Vonne Whipple, *District U-46 Transportation Union History* (Elgin, IL: District U-46 Transportation Union, 1986), 1–15.

62. Whipple, *District U-46 Transportation Union History*, 8.

63. *Advocate* 10, no. 6 (February 1976): 12; Robert Jensen, pers. comm., 2019.

64. *Advocate* 13, no. 1 (September 1978): 4.

65. *Advocate* 16, no. 2 (October 1981): 12–13; Robert Jensen, pers. comm., 2019.

66. *Advocate* 11, no. 2 (October 1976): 18.

67. *Advocate* 13, no. 2 (October 1978): 7.

68. *Advocate* 12, no. 6 (March 1978): 15; 13, no. 1 (September 1978): 4.

69. *Advocate* 13, no. 6 (February 1979): 5.

70. "Bus Drivers Gain Wage Hikes," *Danville (IL) Commercial-News*, August 20, 1975, 1.

71. IEA executive director Clayton Marquardt, pers. comm., 2020.

72. "Supreme Court Rules Labor Board Lacks Jurisdiction in Parochial Schools Cases," *Wall Street Journal*, March 22, 1979.

73. "Transportation Pact Approved," *Decatur (IL) Herald*, March 23, 1977, 3.

74. "Bus Drivers for School Ask Vote on Union," *Decatur (IL) Herald*, August 3, 1979, 24.

75. Superintendent of Public Instruction, "Illinois Teacher Salary Schedule and Contract Provision Study: 1980–1981," 1.

Chapter 9. Internecine Warfare and the IFT Challenge

The epigraph is from Curtis Plott, "Reorganization and Realignment of the IEA Staff," memorandum to IEA board of directors, April 16, 1971, 1, author's collection.

1. Selden, *The Teacher Rebellion*, 141–43, 204, 191–92, 210–11.

2. *Illinois Union Teacher*, January–February 1969, 1, 6.

3. *Illinois Union Teacher*, March–April 1970, 7.

4. *Advocate* 6, no. 4 (February 1972): 4.

5. *Illinois Union Teacher*, April 1972, 9.

6. *Advocate* 6, no. 1 (September 1972): 11–13; 7, no. 5 (January–February 1973): 3, 7; "Toward a Confederation of American Public Employees," *Today's Education*, December 1972, 47; "Public Employee Coalition Formed," *Public Employee*, March 1973, 1, 7. From 1977 to 1982, civil rights icon James Farmer served as executive director of the national CAPE. Joining NEA, AFSCME, and the International Association of Fire Fighters in the national CAPE by 1978 were the American Nurses Association, National Association of Social Workers, National Treasury Employees Union, and Physicians National House Staff Association.

7. *Advocate* 8, no. 3 (January 1974): 3. After the death of AFSCME president Jerry Wurf in 1981, AFSCME rejoined the AFL-CIO's public employee department, ending its ties to CAPE.

8. Laird Lawlyes, pers. comm., 2020.

9. *Illinois Union Teacher*, October–November 1970, 3.

10. Oscar Weil, "Memorandum on the Proposed Dues Increase," addressed to local union leaders, March 16, 1971, 1, author's collection; *Illinois Union Teacher*, January–February 1970, 4–5; January 1971, 9; September 1971, 5.

11. *Illinois Union Teacher*, May–June 1970, 3.

12. *Illinois Union Teacher*, October–November 1970, 5; January 1971, 6; Superintendent of Public Instruction, "Illinois Teacher Salary Study, 1973–74," 26–72; Thomas A. Muer (Region 17 UniServ director), "Summary of Minority Units," January 5, 1972, 1–4, author's collection.

13. *Illinois Union Teacher*, September 1972, 2; October 1972, 3, 7.

14. NEA, "AFT Membership by States and Locals: 1969–1971," author's collection; NEA, "Teacher Representation Elections, as reported to the National Education Association," August 1972–June 1975, author's collection.

15. *Illinois Union Teacher*, April 1968, 1; May 1969, 2; November 1969, 10; April 1972, 6.

16. *Illinois Union Teacher*, January–February 1976, 3.

17. CCCTU (Cook County College Teachers Union) Local 1600, home page, accessed March 24, 2022, https://www.ccctu.org.

18. Leonard Aronson, "Mr. Raby and the Teachers Unions," *PTA Magazine*, January 1973, 21–23. See also "Join United Teachers of Chicago: A Manifesto for Quality Education," *United Teachers of Chicago* (UTC newspaper) 1, no. 1 (September 1972): 1–2, author's collection; Edith Herman, "IEA Seeks Control over Chicago Teachers," *Chicago Tribune*, August 16, 1972, 2.

19. *United Teachers of Chicago* 1, no. 1 (September 1972): 4, author's collection.

20. *United Teachers of Chicago* 1, no. 2 (October 1972): 2, author's collection.

21. Joseph Pasteris, pers. comm., 2020.

22. Curtis Plott, "Staff Reorganization," memorandum to UniServ staff, February 8, 1974, 3, author's collection.

23. Plott, 6–7.

24. Curtis Plott, "Reorganization and Realignment of the IEA Staff," memorandum to IEA board of directors, May 6, 1971, 7, author's collection.

25. *Oh Shit!*, February 27, 1976, 2.

26. Joseph Pasteris, pers. comm., 2020.

27. Gary Randolph, written statement to IEA board of directors, April 3, 1976, author's collection.

28. *Illinois Union Teacher*, November 1976, 7.

29. "Then . . . the Nebulous Network," *Common Sense*, undated flyer published by IFT, author's collection.

30. "Summary of IEA Board of Directors Minutes and Actions," September 10–11, 1976, author's collection. After his presidency, Woody Lee applied for an IEA staff position without success. In 1979, IFT hired Lee as an organizer.

31. Curtis Plott, "Zaremba Petition," IEA memorandum to all staff, September 17, 1976, author's collection.

32. "The Record," six-page memo by Region 26 UniServ director, attached to Plott, "Zaremba Petition," September 17, 1976, author's collection.

33. Linda Bailey, written statement to District 211 membership, September 1977, author's collection; "District 211 Now AFT," *It's Happening* (Illinois Federation of Teachers), Winter 1977–78; author's collection.

34. *Illinois Union Teacher*, February 1975, 10.

35. "IEASO Grievance Committee," *Oh Shit!*, March 4, 1976, 2.

36. "IEASO Accused of Unfair Labor Practice," *Oh Shit!*, April 1, 1977, 1; "IEASO Sued," *Oh Shit!*, April 25, 1977.

37. Charles DesEnfants, pers. comm., 2020.

38. "Psychology 101," *Oh Shit!*, December 1977, 1–3.

39. "Contingency Plan Should Agreement Not to Be Reached and Corporation Would Be Faced with Strike or Lockout," confidential memorandum to the IEA board of directors, June 10–11, 1977, author's collection.

40. Melvin Smith to Barbara Spooner, July 28, 1977, author's collection.

41. UniServ director George Dodd, "IFT Organizing Efforts," undated letter to all IEA local leaders, author's collection.

42. "Special Federation Project: Central Illinois," undated confidential document, files of UniServ director Karl Nagle.

43. *Illinois Union Teacher*, February 1978, 1; see also IFT Peoria staffer Michael Thompson, "Central Illinois Project: Organizing Grant," n.d., author's collection.

44. James Penca (IFT staff), transcribed interview by Robert Breving (IFT staff), March 25, 2009, author's collection.

45. UniServ director David Sneddon, "Response to the Latest AFT Mailing," memorandum to Michael Butera, May 5, 1981, author's collection.

46. Penca, interview by Breving; Michael McNalley (IFT staff), transcribed interview by Robert Breving (IFT staff), June 22, 2009, 1–11, author's collection.

47. "Psychology 101," *Oh Shit!*, December 1977, 2.

48. Laird Lawlyes, pers. comm., 2020.

49. UniServ director James Clark, pers. comm., 2020.

50. ISBE, "Illinois Teacher Salary Schedule and Contract Provision Study: 1982–1983," 15.

51. IEA, "IEA Announces Personnel Changes," news release, April 17, 1978.

52. *Advocate* 13, no. 4 (December 1978): 5; 13, no. 9 (May 1979): 13.

53. James Nagle, pers. comm., 2020.

54. *IEASOlidarity* 1, no. 2 (June 13, 1980): 4.

55. *IEASOlidarity* 1, no. 1 (May 30, 1980): 2.

56. UniServ directors David Sneddon and Michael Cook, pers. comm., 2020.

57. *IEASOlidarity* 1, no. 2 (June 13, 1980): 2–3.

58. *IEASOlidarity* 1, no. 2 (June 13, 1980): 3.

59. David Sneddon and Michael Cook, pers. comm., 2020.

60. "Blue Zoo Caper . . . a Success," *IEASOlidarity* 1, no. 3 (September 2, 1980): 2; "The Blue Zoo Revisited," *IEASOlidarity* 1, no. 4 (September 12, 1980): 1.

61. "Dialogue on the Picket Line," *IEASOlidarity* 1, no. 4 (September 12, 1980): 1.

62. E. Jay Hammer, letter to IEA teacher and leaders, September 5, 1980, 3, author's collection; see also Stephen G. Katz (IEA general counsel) to E. Jay Hammer, September 12, 1980, author's collection.

63. James Nagle, pers. comm., 2020.

64. Nagle.

65. David Sneddon and Michael Cook, pers. comm., 2020.

66. "No End in Sight: Chaos in IEA Continues," *Illinois Union Teacher*, January 1981, 5.

67. James Nagle, pers. comm., 2020.

68. "Teacher Representation Elections," as reported to the NEA, 1977–78 through 1981–82, author's collection.

69. Penca, interview by Breving, 2–3; McNally, interview by Breving, 1.

70. Gerald Gordon, pers. comm., 2020.

71. "IFT Score Card: Teachers Reject IEA," *In Focus* (IFT), Fall 1983, 4.

72. *Illinois Union Teacher*, June 1983, 12.

Chapter 10. President Weaver and Bargaining Legislation

The epigraph is from *Illinois Union Teacher* 44, no. 1 (January 1981): 5.

1. IEA executive director Clayton Marquardt, pers. comm., 2020. In 1985, IEA changed the job title of executive secretary to executive director. The duties of these management positions remained unchanged.

2. ISBE, Data Analysis and Progress Reporting, "Illinois Public School Enrollment Projections: 2004–05 through 2012–13," February 2004, table 1, https://www.isbe.net/Documents/public_school_enrollment.pdf.

3. *Advocate* 17, no. 6 (April 1983): 12–14.

4. *Advocate* 17, no. 6 (April 1983): 14.

5. Reginald Weaver, pers. comm., 2021.

6. Weaver.

7. "The Illinois Education Association–NEA during the 1980s: A Decade of Progress," IEA-NEA, 1990, 1, 45, author's collection.

8. *Advocate* 7, no. 5 (January–February 1973): 10, 16; 15, no. 7 (May–June 1981): 12–13; Clayton Marquardt, pers. comm., 2020.

9. Laird Lawlyes, pers. comm., 2019.

10. *Advocate* 17, no. 2 (October 1982): 8–9.

11. *Advocate* 17, no. 2 (October 1982): 8–9.

12. ISBE, *Teacher Salary Study*, for years 2013–14, 13–53.

13. *Illinois Union Teacher*, October 1982, 4–5.

14. *Advocate* 17, no. 2 (October 1982): 9–11.

15. Laird Lawlyes, pers. comm., 2019.

16. Lawlyes.

17. Wikipedia, s.v. "Shakman Decrees," last modified December 14, 2020, https://en.wikipedia.org/wiki/Shakman_Decrees.

18. Kenneth Bruce, pers. comm., 2020.

19. Bruce.

20. Superintendent of Public Instruction, "Illinois Teacher Salary Schedule and Contract Provision Study: 1980–1981," 11, 14.

21. *Advocate* 16, no. 1 (September 1981): 3; 16, no. 2 (October 1981): 3.

22. *Advocate* 16, no. 1 (September 1981): 16.

23. James Penca (IFT staff), transcribed interview by Robert Breving (IFT staff), March 25, 2009, author's collection.

24. NEA, "Profiles of State Associations: 1982–83," 3.

25. "The Illinois Education Association–NEA during the 1980s," IEA-NEA, 1.

26. Laird Lawlyes, pers. comm., 2019.

27. *Advocate* 17, no. 7 (May 1983): 16.

28. Laird Lawlyes, pers. comm., 2019.

29. Kenneth Bruce, pers. comm., 2020.

30. Martin H. Malin, "Implementing the Illinois Educational Labor Relations," *Chicago-Kent Law Review* 61, no. 1 (January 1985): 102.

31. "Illinois Educational Labor Relations Act," IEA-NEA, inside cover. Senate Bill 536, the Illinois Public Employees Labor Relations Act (Public Act 83-1012), also became law on the same day.

32. *Advocate* 18, no. 3 (January 1984): 32.

33. "Illinois Educational Labor Relations Act," IEA-NEA, 1–2. The labor board created by the IELRA originally had three members and has had either three or five members since 1984.

34. "Illinois Educational Labor Relations Act," 3, 6; Mitchell Roth (IEA general counsel), pers. comm., 2021.

35. Mitchell Roth (IEA general counsel), pers. comm., 2021.

36. Roth.

37. "Illinois Educational Labor Relations Act," IEA-NEA, 8.

38. Mitchell Roth (IEA general counsel), pers. comm., 2021.

39. Roth.

40. Wikipedia, s.v. "Janus v. AFSCME," last modified January 28, 2022, https://en .wikipedia.org/wiki/Janus_v. AFSCME.

41. IEA Membership Processing, membership data as of January 5, 2021.

42. "Illinois Educational Labor Relations Act," IEA-NEA, 9, author's collection; Laird Lawlyes, pers. comm., 2019.

43. Clayton Marquardt, pers. comm., 2020.

44. Marquardt.

45. "Yesterday . . . and . . . Today, Illinois Educational Labor Relations Act: 25th Anniversary, 1983–2008," IEA, 2009, 7, author's collection.

46. "The Illinois Educational Labor Relations Act and the Illinois Education Association–NEA: A Five Year Perspective," IEA, 7, author's collection; "IEA-NEA Field Services Activity: August 31, 2002–August 31, 2003," IEA, 2003, 1, author's collection.

47. Mitch Roth (IEA general counsel), synopsis of the 2003 Illinois majority interest law, based on a study by University of Illinois professor Bob Bruno, December 30, 2020, author's collection.

48. Illinois School Code, Sec. 10–22.34c (2020).

49. IEA Membership Processing, membership data as of January 5, 2021.

Chapter 11. Organizing K–12 under the Act

The epigraph is from Clay Marquardt, pers. comm., April 15, 2020.

1. "Activity and Membership Data: September 1, 2012–August 31, 2013," IEA Field Services Series, 2013, 2. This report includes data as far back as 1983.

2. I was hired as a part-time organizer under the NEA organizing project. In June 1985, I became a full-time organizer. Ted Tunison and Jo Anderson were my supervisors. This information is based on my personal knowledge.

3. "The Illinois Education Association–NEA during the 1980s: A Decade of Progress," IEA-NEA, 1990, 1, author's collection; ISBE, "Illinois Teacher Salary and Contract Provision Study: 1983–84," February 1983, 15–16.

4. "The Illinois Education Association–NEA during the 1980s," 46–47; "Analysis of IEA-NEA Growth, 1981–2010," IEA Membership Processing, 2010.

5. Clay Marquardt, pers. comm., April 15, 2020.

6. After Marquardt retired in 2005, his successor, Patricia Hodges, continued to produce these reports until 2013.

7. "IEA-NEA Field Services Activity: August 31, 2001–August 31, 2002," IEA-NEA, 2002, author's collection.

8. Jo Anderson, "Recommendations for New Flexible Staffing Position," memorandum to Clay Marquardt, June 1, 1987, author's collection; ISBE, *Teacher Salary Study*, for years 1985–86, 17; Bob Ray, pers. comm., 2024.

9. Clay Marquardt, pers. comm., April 15, 2020; Marquardt résumé, provided to author, 2020.

10. Laird Lawlyes, pers. comm., 2019.

11. "The Illinois Education Association–NEA during the 1980s," IEA-NEA, 3, 45; "Activity and Membership Data: September 1, 2012–August 31, 2013," IEA Field Services, 5.

12. ISBE, "Illinois Teacher Salary Schedule and Contract Provision Study: 1982–1983," 36–84.

13. IEA, "Election and Voluntary Recognition Activity," 1996–97.

14. "Activity and Membership Data: September 1, 2012–August 31, 2013," IEA Field Services Series, 2013, 36–39.

15. Mitch Roth (IEA general counsel), synopsis of the 2003 Illinois majority interest law, based on a study by University of Illinois professor Bob Bruno, December 30, 2020, author's collection.

16. Much of this narrative about District 16 is based on my wife's and my own personal experiences.

17. Mazur, Barbara, and I sat together in the front row at the board meeting. Mazur had been picket captain in the 1972 strike.

18. *Barbara Suhrbur v. Board of Education of Queen Bee School, District 16, DuPage County, Illinois, and Dr. Joseph Kariotis, Superintendent of Queen Bee School, District 16*, No. 84 C 7606 (N.D. Ill. 1985). We settled the case out of court for $10,000 and used some of the money to take our children on a European vacation, while Kariotis, for his part, was brought up on charges. Our first day in Europe, July 1, 1986, was the first day of Kariotis's sentence.

19. "District 16 Board President Resigns," *Glendale Heights (IL) Examiner*, June 5, 1985, 1.

20. "Indicted Dist. 16 School Chief Fired," *Glendale Heights (IL) Press*, July 3, 1985, 1–2; "School Official to Be Arraigned," *Chicago Tribune*, May 10, 1985, section 2, 1, 9.

21. "Ex Schools Chief Pleads Guilty," *Chicago Tribune*, June 11, 1986, section 2, 1, Barbara Suhrbur's newspaper clippings file.

22. Lake Park High School teacher Steven Fischer, pers. comm., 2020.

23. *Advocate* 21, no. 5 (January–February 1987): 4.

24. *Advocate* 21, no. 5 (January–February 1987): 4.

25. Tim Mitchell, "Two Decades Later, Homer Teachers' Strike Still Sore Subject," *News-Gazette* (Champaign, IL), November 12, 2006.

26. *Advocate* 21, no. 6 (March 1987): 4.

27. Mitchell, "Two Decades Later."

28. *Advocate* 21, no. 6 (March 1987): 4.

29. Mitchell, "Two Decades Later."

30. *Advocate* 21, no. 5 (January–February 1987): 4.

31. Mitchell, "Two Decades Later."

32. *Advocate* 21, no. 9 (July–August 1987): 3.

33. *Advocate* 21, no. 7 (April 1987): 5.

34. UniServ director Gerald Gordon, pers. comm., 2020.

35. Gordon.

36. Gordon. Gordon and I together helped the Elgin custodial/maintenance union bargain its contract after the election.

37. "The Illinois Education Association–NEA during the 1980s," IEA-NEA, 1, 46.

38. "The Illinois Education Association–NEA during the 1980s," 47.

39. IEA, "Election and Voluntary Recognition Activity," 1991–92, 30.

40. "Rival Union Backs DEA in Bargaining," *Herald and Review* (Decatur, IL), September 12, 1986, A3; Donald Jordan of IEA Membership Processing, membership data provided on March 19, 2021.

41. Michael Gibler provided this information when I was assigned to assist in the 1989 IFT election challenge of DEA. DEA was chartered in 1927; it is among the oldest IEA locals.

42. "Salary Not the Only Issue," *Herald and Review*, September 19, 1986, A3.

43. "Strike Begins," *Herald and Review*, September 12, 1986, 1.

44. "Salary Not the Only Issue," *Herald and Review*, A3.

45. "DEA Asks Ruling on Settling Key Issues," *Herald and Review*, September 19, 1986, A3.

46. "Strike Begins," *Herald and Review*, 1.

47. "Rival Union Backs DEA in Bargaining," *Herald and Review*, A3.

48. "Bargainers Given New Directions," *Herald and Review*, October 8, 1986, 1.

49. "There's Guilt to Share," *Herald and Review*, October 18, 1986.

50. "Why Won't Jane Talk?," *Herald and Review*, September 19, 1986, A3.

51. "School Board, DEA Chastise Each Other," *Herald and Review*, October 4, 1986, 4.

52. "School Board, DEA Chastise Each Other," 4.

53. "New Calendar Still Uncertain," *Herald and Review*, October 1, 1986, 5.

54. "New Calendar Still Uncertain," 5; "Bargainers Given New Directions," *Herald and Review*, 1.

55. "Board, DEA Resolve Pact Snafu," *Herald and Review*, November 15, 1986, 1.

56. "Board, DEA Resolve Pact Snafu."

57. Laird Lawlyes, pers. comm., 2021.

58. "Decision Led to Contract," *Herald and Review*, October 9, 1986, 1.

59. "Strike Ends—at Last!," *Observer* (Stephen Decatur High School), October 10, 1986, 1; "Teachers, Board Seem Happy with New Contract," *Decatur (IL) Tribune*, October 15, 1986, 4–5.

60. Laird Lawlyes, pers. comm., 2021.

61. Lawlyes; "Board, DEA Resolve Pact Snafu," *Herald and Review*, 1.

62. *Decatur Federation of Teachers v. Illinois Educational Labor Relations Board*, 556 N.E.2d 780 (Ill. App. Ct. 1990).

63. Donald Jordan of IEA Membership Processing, membership data provided on May 19, 2021.

64. "Twin Wins for Decatur," *Advocate* 25, no. 1 (August–September 1990): 14.

65. "Decatur Teachers to Vote on Bargaining Agent Today," *Herald and Review*, April 13, 1989, 72.

66. *Decatur Federation of Teachers v. Illinois Educational Labor Relations Board*, 556 N.E.2d 780 (Ill. App. Ct. 1990).

67. *Decatur Federation of Teachers v. Illinois Educational Labor Relations Board*.

68. "Board: Teachers' Election Invalid," *Herald and Review*, July 11, 1989, 5.

69. The organizers were Marcus Albrecht, Jerry Harrison, Robert Furnace, Mona Wiggington, and myself.

70. "DEA Ready to Bargain, While DFT May Appeal," *Herald and Review*, October 6, 1989, 4.

71. "Local Teachers Retain DEA," *Herald and Review*, April 25, 1991, 1.

72. UniServ director Patrick Bihn, pers. comm., 2021.

73. "Teacher Representation Elections," as reported to the NEA, 1972–73, author's collection.

74. "Teacher Representation Elections," as reported to the NEA, 1980–81, 2, author's collection.

75. Patrick Bihn, pers. comm., 2021.

76. Bihn.

77. IEA, "Election and Voluntary Recognition Activity," 1990–91, 13, 23, 64; 1992–93.

78. Patrick Bihn, pers. comm., 2021.

79. Bihn.

80. Bihn.

Chapter 12. Organizing Higher Education

The epigraph is from Donald J. Keck and Marcus Albrecht, "New Threats to Academic Freedom Emerge in 1980s: The Traditional Concept Must Be Expanded and Re-Defined for 1990s," unpublished essay widely circulated at SIUE and SIUC, c. 1985, author's collection.

1. "Higher Education Locals," provided by Donald Jordan, IEA Membership Processing, June 1, 2022.

2. John McCluskey, pers. comm., 2020.

3. David Rathke, pers. comm., 2021.

4. Marcus Albrecht, "SIU-E Election Overview," April 1, 1997, author's collection.

5. Albrecht. Marcus Albrecht also spoke on this history at the thirty-year SIUE celebration, March 9, 2019.

6. IEA, "Election and Voluntary Recognition Activity," 1990–91, 20. The number of eligible voters who signed each petition were as follows: 1,159 SIUC faculty, 282 SIUC professional staff, 472 SIUE faculty, 247 SIUE professional staff, and 45 School of Dental Medicine faculty.

7. IEA, 20.

8. *Advocate* 23, no. 7 (April 1989): 3.

9. "Faculty Bargaining to Get Board Decision in June," *Daily Egyptian* (Southern Illinois University), April 24, 1987.

10. Albrecht, "SIU-E Election Overview."

11. "Opinion and Order," IELRB, 1987, case nos. 85-RC-0022-S, 85-RC-0027-S, 85-RC-0030-S, 85-RC-0031-S, 85-RC-0032-S, 85-RC-0033-S, 85-RC-0035-S, and 86-RC-0011-S.

12. "Labor Board Decision Rendered—IEA Wins Total Victory on SIU Labor Board Unit Determination Ruling," flyer circulated by the SIU-E Professional Staff Organizing Committee, September 30, 1988, author's collection.

13. "SIU Showdown," *Advocate* 23, no. 3 (November 1988): 4. In 1987, Jim Nagle was hired as the IEA higher education director after his term of office as secretary-treasurer ended.

14. Keck and Albrecht, "New Threats to Academic Freedom Emerge in 1980s."

15. Edward Meridian [Ellen Nore], *SIU, the First 50 Years: Transforming a Region* (Edwardsville: Southern Illinois University, 2007), 160–62.

16. Meridian, 163.

17. Meridian, 160–64.

18. "IEA Sparks SIUE Affirmative Action Probe," *Advocate* 22, no. 6 (March 1988): 7.

19. "IEA Sparks SIUE Affirmative Action Probe."

20. "IEA Sparks SIUE Affirmative Action Probe."

21. "IEA Sparks SIUE Affirmative Action Probe."

22. "Report Rejects Discrimination Allegations," *News-Democrat* (Belleville, IL), February 25, 1988.

23. "King Day Celebration," *Advocate* 22, no. 5 (January–February 1988): 6.

24. Marcus Albrecht, "Remember Fannie: SIU Gave Her Lemons and She Made Lemonade," *East St. Louis (IL) Monitor*, July 6, 1988.

25. "SIU Board Upholds Dismissal of Former Teacher's Aide," *News-Democrat*, April 15, 1988, 13.

26. Albrecht, "Remember Fannie."

27. "Outcome of SIUE *Alestle* Fracas Hard to Foreknow," *Telegraph* (Alton, IL), May 16, 1987, A3.

28. "*Alestle* Editor Tells of Battle with SIUE Administration," *Telegraph*, May 30, 1987, A3.

29. Marcus Albrecht, pers. comm., 2022.

30. Leonard Van Camp, "Why I Favor Collective Bargaining," *Alestle* (SIUE), April 2, 1987, 3; Sheila Ruth, "Collective Bargaining: A Mechanism for Making Things Better," *Alestle*, April 30, 1987, 3.

31. Meridian, *SIU, the First 50 Years*, 163.

32. Meridian, 164–65; "Last SIUE Vote to Be Feb. 22," *Edwardsville (IL) Intelligencer*, January 18, 1989, 1.

33. "SIU Victory," *Advocate* 23, no. 7 (April 1989): 3.

34. Michael Cook, pers. comm., 2022.

35. Cook.

36. IEA, "Election and Voluntary Recognition Activity," 1990–91, 4.

37. David Vitoff, pers. comm., 2022; IEA, "Election and Voluntary Recognition Activity," 1996–97.

38. James Clark, pers. comm., 2021.

39. James Clark, pers. comm., 2022.

40. "SIUE Term Faculty Vote to Unionize," *Daily Egyptian*, September 28, 2004.

41. James Clark, pers. comm., 2022; IEA, "Election and Voluntary Recognition Activity," 2004–5, 2005–6.

42. "Update from the SIUC Faculty Association, IEA-NEA," March 11, 2011, and "Outcome of Mediation, Last Offer from Board," March 29, 2012, both items posted to SIUC Faculty Association website, https://siucfa.org/author/siucfa.

43. "Opinion and Order," IELRB, December 2014, case nos. 2011-CA-0037-S, 2011-CA-0038-S, and 2011-CA-0039-S.

44. Dave Johnson, "Strike Ends," SIUC Faculty Association, November 9, 2011, https://siucfa.org/2011/11/09/strike-ends/.

45. "Understanding the SIUC FA Furlough Victory," SIUC Faculty Association, IEA-NEA flyer, 2014, author's collection; James Clark, pers. comm., 2022.

46. "Opinion and Order," IELRB, December 2014, case nos. 2011-CA-0037-S, 2011-CA-0038-S, and 2011-CA-0039-S.

47. "Union Wins Furlough Fight, Judge Says SIU Acted Illegally in 2011," SIUC Faculty Association, NTTFA, and Association of Civil Service Employees, joint news release, August 4, 2014, author's collection.

48. David Vitoff, pers. comm., 2022.

49. Tom Suhrbur, "Coalition Building at the University of Illinois," *Sunrise*, Fall 2008, 4. This article was based on an interview with Gene Vanderport in 2008. Vanderport and Belden Fields founded the Champaign-Urbana Socialist Forum in the mid-1990s (thanks to Peter Miller for mentioning this). The Socialist Forum provided opportunities to discuss socialist readings and to organize around social justice issues. Vanderport died in 2016.

50. Suhrbur, 4, 6.

51. Suhrbur, 6.

52. New Hampshire NEA organizer Peter Miller, pers. comm., 2022; Maryland State Educational Association organizer Daniel Chambers, pers. comm., 2022.

53. Peter Miller, pers. comm., 2022.

54. Tom Suhrbur, "Coalition Building at the University of Illinois."

55. Suhrbur, 6.

56. Suhrbur, 6.

57. Joe Berry, pers. comm., 2022.

58. Berry, *Reclaiming the Ivory Tower*, 1–25. Much of this discussion is also based on my own experience in organizing adjunct faculty units in the Chicago metropolitan area.

59. "Opinion and Order: Harper Community College v. Harper College Adjunct Faculty Association Sunrise, IEA-NEA," IELRB, October 26, 1993, case no. 92-RC-0008-C, p. 4.

60. Tom Suhrbur, "Organizing P-T Faculty in the Chicago Area: A Metro-Wide Strategy," *Sunrise*, July 2007, 10–11.

61. "Degrees of Difficulty," *Chicago Tribune Magazine*, July 12, 1998, sec. 10, 16.

62. "New Deal or No Deal: Roosevelt's Part-Time Teachers Organize for More," *Chicago Reader*, November 19, 1999, 5, 8.

63. IEA organizer Robert Ray, pers. comm., 2022; IEA, "Election and Voluntary Recognition Activity," 1990–91, 34.

64. "Opinion and Order: Harper Community College," 6–7; IEA, "Election and Voluntary Recognition Activity," 1993–94. IFT Local 3791 organized Elgin Community College in 1994.

65. "Amends the Illinois Educational Labor Relations Act," Ill. H.R. 2581, 91st Gen. Assembly (1999–2000).

66. "Columbia College Part-Timers Mark Milestone with Contract," *Chicago Tribune*, March 18, 1999, sec. 2, 3. After sixteen years with IEA, P-Fac under new leadership ended its affiliation with IEA; several years later, P-Fac affiliated with SEIU.

67. IEA, "Election and Voluntary Recognition Activity," 1999–2000.

68. Steve Vaughan and I, along with a number of city college adjunct activists, attended the vote count.

69. "Higher Education Organizing Briefing Paper," IEA Field Services report, circulated among IEA staff, January 25, 2011. I kept a record of the outcomes of all my organizing activities between 1983 and 2011, and between 2014 and 2015. I participated in 155 election campaigns in that time, winning 80 percent of them.

70. "Part Timers to Form City-Wide Teachers Union," *Streetwise: Chicago*, November 10, 1998, 2, 6; Suhrbur, "Organizing P-T Faculty in the Chicago Area," 10–11.

71. Suhrbur, "Organizing P-T Faculty in the Chicago Area," 10–11.

72. Tom Suhrbur, "Not in My Backyard: St. Xavier University Fights Union Organizing," *Sunrise*, Fall 2011, 6.

73. St. Xavier Adjunct Faculty Organization (SAFO), "A Quick History of St. Xavier Adjunct Faculty Organization," SAFO blog, c. 2017, author's collection.

74. Suhrbur, "Not in My Backyard," 6.

75. Suhrbur, 7; SAFO, "A Quick History of St. Xavier Adjunct Faculty Organization."

76. Suhrbur, "Not in My Backyard," 6.

77. Suhrbur, 6.

78. Suhrbur, 7.

79. Suhrbur, 7.

80. Peter N. Kirstein, "Saint Xavier University Adjuncts Vote for Union," *Academe Blog*, September 27, 2016, https://academeblog.org/2016/09/27/saint-xavier.

81. Deanna Issacs, "After 40 Years, Saint Xavier University Wipes Out Its Faculty Union," *Chicago Reader*, June 10, 2020.

82. "NLRB Withdraws Protection from Catholic College Faculty; Saint Xavier University Busts Faculty Union," Catholic Labor Network, news release, June 15, 2020.

83. "Activity and Membership Data: September 1, 2012–August 31, 2013," IEA Field Services, 2013, author's collection.

84. Deanna Isaacs, "Columbia College's Feisty Part-Time Faculty Union Goes Its Own Way," *Chicago Reader*, November 18, 2015; Constitution of the Columbia College Faculty Union, approved May 2, 1998, amended January 21, 2015, and August 27, 2019.

Chapter 13. School Reform

The epigraph is from "Henry Giroux on Striking Teachers Beating Back the War on Public Schools," *Tikkun*, May 27, 2018, https://www.tikkun.org/henry-giroux-on-striking.

1. James M. McGeever, "The Decline of Standardized Test Scores in the United States from 1965 to the Present," Appalachia Educational Laboratory, October 1983, 20–24; Veera Korhonen, "Educational Attainment Distribution in the United States from 1960 to 2022," Statistica, October 6, 2023, https://www.statista.com/statistics/184260/.

2. William Lowe Boyd, "President Reagan's School-Reform," *Education Week*, March 18, 1987.

3. Gary K. Clabaugh, "The Education Legacy of Ronald Reagan," *Educational Horizons* 82, no. 4 (2004): 256–59.

4. Gracie Chen, "The Ongoing Debate over School Choice," *Public School Review* (blog), February 10, 2020, https://www.publicschoolreview.com/blog/the-ongoing-debate-over-school-choice.

5. Clabaugh, "The Education Legacy of Ronald Reagan," 258; Sean Cavanagh, "Reagan's Legacy: A Nation at Risk, Boost for Choice," *Education Week*, June 16, 2004.

6. Jo Anderson, pers. comm., July 18, 2022; Tom Suhrbur, "Education Reform in Illinois," *Sunrise*, Fall 2016, 3.

7. Jo Anderson, pers. comm., 2022.

8. Anderson.

9. Anderson.

10. "District 200 Impasse," *Daily Journal* (Wheaton, IL), August 27, 1985, 1.

11. WWEA president Kathy Wessel, pers. comm., 2022.

12. Jo Anderson, pers. comm., 2022.

13. Anderson; Suhrbur, "Education Reform in Illinois, 4.

14. "Consortium for Education Change: History, Status and Summer Institute," National Louis University, 1991, 2, author's collection.

15. Jo Anderson, pers. comm., 2022.

16. "Consortium for Education Change," National Louis University, 4.

17. Robert Haisman, pers. comm., 2022.

18. Lynn Adler, pers. comm., 2022; Jo Anderson, pers. comm., 2024.

19. IEA Hickory Ridge Commitment, August 7, 2003, author's collection.

20. Lynn Adler, pers. comm, 2022; Jo Anderson, pers. comm., 2022.

21. "Consortium for Education Change," National Louis University, 3; Jo Anderson, pers. comm., 2022; *Collaborating for Student Success: A Comprehensive, Practical Guidebook for Increasing Shared Decision Making through Lasting Partnerships* (Washington, DC: National Labor-Management Partnership, 2022), 1.

22. Lynn Adler, pers. comm., 2022; Jo Anderson, pers. comm. 2022; Mary Jane Morris, pers. comm., 2023.

23. Catalyst for Educational Change, homepage, accessed May 15, 2024, https://www.cecweb.org; Jo Anderson, pers. comm., 2023; Audrey Soglin, pers. comm., 2023; Mary Jane Morris, pers. comm., 2023; Shelley Taylor, pers. comm., 2023.

24. Jordan Sekulow, "What Is School Choice?," American Center for Law and Justice, June 23, 2020, https://aclj.org/school-choice/what-is-school-choice.

25. Wikipedia, "Category: Magnet Schools in Illinois," last modified October 11, 2023, https://en.wikipedia.org/wiki/Category:Magnet_schools_in_Illinois.

26. Talia Milgrom-Elcott, "Unionized Charter Schools: An Unlikely Course Our Democracy Depends On," *Forbes*, May 21, 2019.

27. Milgrom-Elcott.

28. Jonathan Kozol, "The Big Enchilada," *Harper's Magazine*, August 2007, 8.

29. "Fast Facts: Charter Schools," National Center for Education Statistics, accessed May 15, 2024, https://nces.ed.gov/fastfacts/display.asp?id=30; "Characteristics of Traditional Public, Public Charter, and Private School Teachers," National Center for Education Statistics, last updated May 20, 2020, https://nces.ed.gov/programs/coe/indicator/sld/

public-private-school-teachers; Mike Pompeo, "Randi Weingarten and the Teachers Unions Should Focus on Education, Not Attacking Parents," American Center for Law and Justice, March 31, 2023, https://aclj.org/school-choice/randi-weingarten-and-the -teachers-unions-should-focus-on-education-not-attacking-parents.

30. Jim Edgar, oral history interviews, sessions 19 (August 30, 2010) and 20 (September 2, 2010), interviewed by Mark R. DuPue, Abraham Lincoln Presidential Library and Museum, https://presidentlincoln.illinois.gov/oral-history/collections/edgar-jim-1/ interview-detail/.

31. Theodore Williams III, "Education Reform in Chicago Public Schools," *Capital Commentary* (Center for Public Justice), November 25, 2013.

32. Jeff Archer and Ann Bradley, "Despite National Defeat, NEA and AFT Work toward Mergers in States," *Education Week*, August 5, 1998.

33. Illinois State Board of Education, *Illinois Charter School Biennial Report*, for years 2019–21, 2.

34. Illinois Public Act 89-450, codified at 105 ILCS 5/27A-1 (1996).

35. ISBE, *Illinois Charter School Biennial Report*, for years 2019–21, 6–9.

36. "Our History," Ball Charter School, accessed May 15, 2024, https://ballcharter schools.org/our-history; Springfield Educational Association president Cinda Klickna, pers. comm., 2022.

37. I filed the IELRA representation petition on behalf of the Cambridge Lakes teachers, based on legal advice that I received.

38. Madeline Will, "The Nation's First Charter School Strike Has Ended with a Union Victory," *Education Week*, December 10, 2019; Alia Wong and Natalie Escobar, "The Charter-School Teachers' Strike in Chicago Was 'Inevitable,'" *Atlantic*, December 6, 2018.

39. ISBE director of charter schools David Turovetz, pers. comm., 2022.

40. Evie Blad, "Timeline: Party Platforms & Charter Schools," *Education Week*, June 18, 2019.

41. Celeste F. Busser, "NEA Adopts Charter School Statement," NEA press release, July 4, 2017.

42. Mitchell Roth, "SB7: A Union Perspective," *Illinois Public Employees Relations Report* 29, no. 2 (Spring 2012): 5–6.

43. Roth, 6–7.

44. Roth, 6–7.

45. Roth, 7–8.

46. Roth, 7–8.

47. "Illinois Pension Reform: Legislation Approves Massive Overhaul," *HuffPost*, May 25, 2010; "EZ Guide to Tier 1 and Tier 2 Retirement under Public Act 96-0889," Teachers' Retirement System of the State of Illinois, July 2020, https://www.trsil.org.

48. Rich Miller, "How Stand for Children Snuck into the Statehouse," *Illinois Times* (Springfield), July 21, 2011; Adam Sanchez and Ken Libby, "For or Against Children: The Problematic History of Stand for Children," *Rethinking Schools* 26, no. 1 (Fall 2011): https:// rethinkingschools.org/articles/for-or-against-children/; Rich Miller, "Who's behind Stand for Children," *Illinois Times*, October 21, 2010.

49. Roth, "SB7," 9–10.

50. Roth, 10.

51. Roth, 10–12.

52. George N. Schmidt, "Performance Counts Is Dead (for Now): Largest Unified Mobilization in Illinois Teacher Union History Defeats Billionaires' Teacher Bashing Plans for Illinois," *Substance News*, January 13, 2011.

53. Roth, 10–28. Audrey Soglin, pers. comm., 2022.

54. George N. Schmidt, "The Union-Busting Billionaires behind Phony 'Grass Roots' Groups Like Stand for Children and Advance Illinois Have Emerged from the Shadows: Complete Transcript of the Remarks of Ross Wiener, James Crown and Jonah Edelman at the Aspen Institute," *Substance News*, July 12, 2011.

55. Schmidt; Larry Duncan, "CTU Strike: 2012," *Labor Beat*, September 25, 2012; Audrey Soglin, pers. comm., 2022.

56. Teresea Moran, "Behind the Chicago Teachers Strike," *Labor Notes*, September 10, 2012; Audrey Soglin, pers. comm., 2022.

57. Moran, "Behind the Chicago Teachers Strike."

58. Robert Bruno, pers. comm., 2024. For a detailed account of the 2012 strike and its aftermath, see Ashby and Bruno, *A Fight for the Soul of Public Education*.

59. Wikipedia, s.v. "2019 Chicago Public Schools Strike," last modified May 4, 2024, https://en.wikipedia.org/wiki/2019_Chicago_Public_Schools_strike.

60. Robert Bruno, pers. comm., 2024.

61. Keith Geiger, Monica Garcia, and Rick Pearson, "U.S. Supreme Court Gives Rauner a Major Victory over Labor, in a Ruling That Could Undercut Public Sector Unions Nationwide," *Chicago Tribune*, July 27, 2018.

62. IEA Membership Processing, "Membership Trends Data by Membership Type:1998–2021," data provided January 5, 2021.

63. Rick Pearson, "State Employee in Major Union-Undermining Supreme Court Case Will Join Conservative Think Tank, Tour the Country," *Chicago Tribune*, July 22, 2018.

64. Mitchell Roth, pers. comm., 2022.

65. "Invest in Kids," Illinois Department of Revenue, accessed May 16, 2024, https://tax.illinois.gov/programs/investinkids.html.

66. Laura Welch, "Voucher Program Allows Inequality," *Daily Herald* (Arlington Heights, IL), October 27, 2023.

67. "Invest in Kids Program," EdChoice, last updated January 17, 2023, https://www.edchoice.org/school-choice/programs/illinois-invest-kids-program/; Kathi Griffin, pers. comm., 2023; Will Lovett, pers. comm., 2023.

Epilogue

1. Wikipedia, s.v. "List of School Districts in Illinois," last modified February 14, 2024, https://en.wikipedia.org/wiki/List_of_school_districts_in_Illinois; Wikipedia, s.v. "List of Colleges and Universities in Illinois," last modified March 1, 2024, https://en.wikipedia.org/wiki/List_of_colleges_and_universities_in_Illinois; "Membership Numbers: 1998 through 2021," provided by Donald Jordan, IEA Membership Processing, March 19, 2021.

2. This information is based on numerous conversations with IEA leaders and staff as well as my personal experiences of more than thirty years of involvement in the association.

3. IEA president (2017–23) Kathi Griffin, pers. comm., 2023; IEA vice president Al Llorens, pers. comm., 2022.

4. "Graduated Dues Structure," IEA, accessed May 17, 2024, https://ieanea.org/graduated-dues-structure/.

5. Ginger Ostro, "Assessing Equity in Higher Education" (presentation, Illinois Board of Higher Education, August 4, 2020), 15–24; Eric Lichtenberger, pers comm., 2022.

6. "FTC Targets False Claims by For-Profit Colleges," Federal Trade Commission, news release, October 6, 2021; Michael Nietzel, "The FTC Takes New Aim at Deceptive For-Profit Colleges," *Forbes*, October 8, 2021.

7. Milton Friedman, "The Role of Government in Education" (1955), EdChoice, accessed May 15, 2024, https://www.edchoice.org/who-we-are/our-legacy/articles/the-role-of-government-in-education/.

8. Friedman.

9. Douglas, *Jim Crow Moves North*, 195.

10. "Update: Covid-19 Causes Surge in TRS Retirements During July and August," *Topics and Report Newsletter* (Teachers' Retirement System of the State of Illinois), Fall 2020, 5 6. In 2020, there were an abnormally high number of retirements in July and August, largely caused by the stress of remote learning.

Selected Bibliography

Books and Dissertations

Ashby, Steven K., and Robert Bruno. *A Fight for the Soul of Public Education: The Story of the Chicago Teachers Strike*. Ithaca, NY: Cornell University Press, 2016.

Barnard, Robert C. "The Changing Role of the Illinois Education Association in Teacher Negotiations during the 1960s." EdD diss., Illinois State University, 1971.

Berry, Joe. *Reclaiming the Ivory Tower: Organizing Adjuncts to Change Higher Education*. New York: Monthly Review Press, 2005.

Charney, Michael, Jesse Hagopian, and Bob Peterson, eds. *Teacher Unions and Social Justice: Organizing for the Schools and the Communities That Our Students Deserve*. Milwaukee, WI: Rethinking Schools, 2021.

Cook, John Williston. *Educational History of Illinois: Growth and Progress in Educational Affairs of the State from the Earliest Day to the Present*. Chicago: Henry O. Shepard, 1912.

Crocker, Brandt G. "A Comparison of Members in Illinois Teacher Organizations for Differences in Selected Characteristics." EdD diss., University of Missouri–Columbia, 1969.

Donley, Marshall O., Jr. *Power to the Teacher: How America's Teachers Became Militant*. Bloomington: Indiana University Press, 1976.

Douglas, Davison M. *Jim Crow Moves North: The Battle over Northern School Segregation, 1865–1954*. New York: Cambridge University Press, 2005.

Eaton, William Edward. *The American Federation of Teachers, 1916–1961: A History of the Movement*. Urbana: Southern Illinois University Press, 1975.

Fletcher, James Logsdon. "The Judicial and Legislative History of Public School Employee Collective Bargaining Legislation in Illinois: 1921–1971." PhD diss., Northwestern University, 1971.

Foner, Eric. *Free Soil, Free Labor, Free Men: The Ideology of the Republican Party before the Civil War*. Oxford: Oxford University Press, 1970.

Freed, John B. *Educating Illinois: Illinois State University, 1857–2007*. Virginia Beach, VA: Donning, 2009.

Goldstein, Dana. *The Teacher Wars: A History of America's Most Embattled Profession*. New York: Anchor Books, 2015.

Haley, Margaret. *Battleground: The Autobiography of Margaret A. Haley*. Edited by Robert L. Reid. Chicago: University of Illinois Press, 1982.

Harris, N. Dwight. *The History of Negro Servitude in Illinois and of the Slavery Agitation in That State, 1719–1864*. New York: Negro University Press, 1904.

Herrick, Mary J. *The Chicago Schools: A Social and Political History*. Beverley Hills, CA: Sage, 1971.

Howard, Ronald P. *Illinois: A History of the Prairie State*. Grand Rapids, MI: William B. Eerdmans, 1972.

Lyons, John F. *Teachers and Reform: Chicago Public Education, 1929–1970*. Chicago: University of Illinois Press, 2008.

Marshall, Helen E. *Grandest of Enterprises: Illinois State Normal University, 1857–1957*. Normal: Illinois State Normal University, 1956.

McCaul, Robert L. *The Black Struggle for Public Schooling in Nineteenth-Century Illinois*. Carbondale: Southern Illinois University Press, 1987.

Mondale, Sheila, and Sarah B. Patton. *School: The Story of American Public Education*. Boston: Beacon Press, 2001.

Murphy, Marjorie. *Blackboard Unions: The AFT and the NEA: 1900–1980*. Ithaca, NY: Cornell University Press, 1990.

Murray, Robert K. *Red Scare: A Study in National Hysteria, 1919–1920*. New York: McGraw-Hill, 1964.

Pearson, Irving F. *Three Score Ten and More: An Autobiography*. Chicago: Adams Press, 1971.

Pegram, Thomas R. *Partisans and Progressives: Private Interest and Public Policy in Illinois, 1870–1922*. Urbana: University of Illinois Press, 1992.

Propeck, George. "The History of the Illinois Education Association and Its Influence upon the Development of Public Education within the State." EdD diss., Northwestern University, 1959.

Propeck, George, and Irving F. Pearson. *The History of the Illinois Education Association*. Springfield: Illinois Education Association, 1961.

Roediger, David. *The Wages of Whiteness: Race and the Making of the American Working Class*. New York: Verso Books, 1999.

Rousmaniere, Kate. *Citizen Teacher: The Life and Leadership of Margaret Haley*. Albany: State University of New York Press, 2005.

Sandburg, Carl. *Abraham Lincoln: The Prairie Years and the War Years*. New York: Galahad Books, 1993.

Selden, David. *The Teacher Rebellion*. Washington, DC: Howard University Press, 1985.

Shelton, Jon. *Teacher Strike! Public Education and the Making of a New American Political Order*. Urbana: University of Illinois Press, 2017.

Smith, Joan K. *Ella Flagg Young: Portrait of a Leader*. Ames, IA: Educational Studies Press, 1979.

Spring, Joel. *The America School, 1642–1990*. 2nd ed. New York: Longman, 1990.

Stampp, Kenneth M. *The Peculiar Institution: Slavery in the Ante-Bellum South*. New York: Vintage Books, 1956.

Sternsher, Bernard, ed. *The Negro in Depression and War: Prelude to Revolution, 1930–1945*. Chicago: Quadrangle Books, 1969.

Stinnett, T. M., Jack H. Kleinmann, and Martha L. Ware. *Professional Negotiation in Public Education*. New York: Macmillan, 1966.

Tyack, David, and Elisabeth Hansot. *Managers of Virtue: Public School Leadership in America, 1820–1980*. New York: Basic Books, 1982.

Tyler, Alice Felt. *Freedom's Ferment: Phases of American Social History from the Colonial Period to the Outbreak of the Civil War*. New York: Harper and Row, 1944.

Urban, Wayne J. *Gender, Race, and the National Education Association: Professionalism and Its Limitations*. New York: RoutledgeFalmer, 2000.

Urban, Wayne J. *Why Teachers Organized*. Detroit, MI: Wayne State University Press, 1982.

Weil, Oscar. *Teachers beyond the Law: How Teachers Changed Their World*. Bloomington, IN: iUniverse, 2012.

Wesley, Edgar B. *NEA: The First Hundred Years, the Building of the Teaching Profession*. New York: Harper and Brothers, 1957.

West, Allan. *The National Education Association: The Power Base for Education*. New York: Free Press, 1980.

Wrigley, Julia. *Class Politics and Public Schools: Chicago, 1900–1950*. New Brunswick, NJ: Rutgers University Press, 1982.

Booklets, Pamphlets, and Documents

Affiliated Local Associations—Illinois: 1973–74. Washington, DC: National Education Association, 1974.

Butler, Susan Lowell. *The National Education Association: A Special Mission*. Washington, DC: National Education Association, 1987.

Butler, Susan Lowell. *Through Thunder and Lightning: NEA's Journey for Justice*. Washington, DC: National Education Association, 1989.

Cannella, Nicholas R. *171 Years of Teaching in Chicago, 1816–1987*. Chicago: Chicago Teachers Union, 1987.

From the Beginning. Westmont: Illinois Federation of Teachers, 1992.

History Highlights of the Illinois Education Association. Bloomington: Illinois Education Association, 2010.

History in the Making: A Collection of IEA-NEA Local Association Histories as of December 2003. Bloomington: Illinois Education Association, 2003.

Hosman, Everett M., ed. *State Teacher Organizations*. N.p.: National Association of Secretaries of State Teachers Associations, 1926.

Lawlyes, Laird. "Legislative History of Collective Bargaining in the Illinois General Assembly." Unpublished essay, 1983, author's collection.

NEA Handbook: 1973–74. Washington, DC: National Education Association, 1974.

Ryor, John. "History of Collective Bargaining Legislation in Illinois." Memorandum to the Illinois Education Association board of directors, September 9, 1983.

Journals and Periodical Articles

Advocate (Illinois Education Association). 1971–88.

American Teacher (American Federation of Teachers). 1944.

Bone, Robert Gehlmann. "Education in Illinois before 1857." *Journal of the Illinois State Historical Society* 50, no. 2 (Summer 1957): 119–40.

Chicago Union Teacher (Chicago Teachers Union). 1950.

Dunphy, John J. "How Alton Got Segregated Schools." *Alton (IL) Telegraph*, January 22, 2012.

Fishbein, Justin. "School Segregation Still Issue in S. Illinois." *Chicago Sun-Times*, June 20, 1954.

Hagopian, Jesse. "A People's History of the Chicago Teachers Union." *International Socialist Review*, no. 86 (November 2012). https://isreview.org/issue/86/peoples-history -chicago-teachers-union/.

IEASOlidarity (Illinois Education Association Staff Organization). 1980.

Illinois Education (Illinois Education Association). 1940–73.

Illinois Schoolmaster: A Journal of Educational Literature and News. 1872–76.

Illinois Teacher (Illinois State Teachers' Association). 1855–71, 1913–40.

Illinois Union Teacher (Illinois Federation of Teachers). 1939–95.

Insight (Illinois Education Association). 1966–71.

Marshall, Helen. "Charles E. Hovey: Educator and Soldier." *Journal of the Illinois State Historical Society* 50, no. 3 (Autumn 1957): 243–76.

Ming, William R., Jr. "The Elimination of Segregation in the Public Schools of the North and the West." *Journal of Negro Education* 21, no. 3 (Summer 1952): 265–75.

Muir, Douglas. "The Strike as a Professional Sanction: The Changing Attitude of the National Education Association." *Labor Law Journal* 19 (October 1968): 615–27.

Oh Shit! (Illinois Education Association Staff Organization). 1976–77.

Prairie Farmer: Devoted to Western Agriculture, Mechanics and Education. 1843–44.

Public Employee (American Federation of Labor and Congress of Industrial Organizations). 1973.

Pulliam, John. "Changing Attitudes toward Free Public Schools in Illinois: 1825–1857." *History of Education Quarterly* 7 (Summer 1967): 191–208.

Sunrise (National Education Association, unofficial/independent journal). 1987–2018.

Today's Education (National Education Association). 1972.

Weekly News Bulletin (Chicago Teachers Union). 1939.

Williams, John L. "Illinois School Desegregation: What Next?" *Illinois Issues*, January 1984.

Winslow, Barbara. "Education Reform in Antebellum America." *History Now* (Gilder Lehrman Institute), no. 30 (Winter 2012). https://www.gilderlehrman.org/history-now.

Reports

Biennial Report of the Superintendent of Common Schools. 1851. HathiTrust.

Biennial Report of the Superintendent of Public Instruction of the State of Illinois. 1857–1912. HathiTrust.

Illinois Education Association (IEA). "Election and Voluntary Recognition Activity: Comparison of Illinois Education Association–NEA and Illinois Federation of Teachers–AFT." 1990–97.

Illinois Education Association. "Platform, Resolutions, and Legislative Program." Adopted at the Ninety-Sixth Annual Meeting, Chicago, December 1949.

Illinois Education Association. *Pride and Progress: IEA-NEA The Educational Professionals*. Annual report, 1990.

Illinois State Board of Education (ISBE). *Illinois Charter School Biennial Report*. 2019–21.

Illinois Education Association. "Illinois Teacher Salary and Contract Provision Study: 1983–84." February 1983.

Illinois Education Association. "Illinois Teacher Salary Schedule and Contract Provision Study: 1982–1983." February 1983.

Illinois Education Association. "Illinois Teacher Salary Schedule and Policy Study: 1984–1985." February 1985.

Illinois Education Association. *Teacher Salary Study*. 1985–2014.

Illinois State Teachers' Association (ISTA). "The Crisis in Public Education in Illinois." March 1921. HathiTrust.

Journal of Proceedings of the Illinois State Teachers' Association. 1869–1919. HathiTrust.

National Education Association (NEA). "Profiles of State Associations." For years 1978–99.

Proceedings of the Fourth Annual Session of the Illinois State Labor Association, Held in Springfield, January 25–27, 1887. 1887. HathiTrust.

Report of the Educational Commission of the City of Chicago, Appointed by the Mayor, Hon. Carter H. Harrison, January 19th, 1898. Chicago: University of Chicago Press, 1899.

Report of the First Annual Session of the Federation Organized Trades and Labor Unions of the United States and Canada, September 15–18, 1881, Pittsburgh, Pennsylvania. Cincinnati, OH: Robert Clarke, 1882.

Superintendent of Public Instruction. "Illinois Teacher Salary Study, 1973–74." 1974. Illinois State Board of Education archival collection.

Superintendent of Public Instruction. "Illinois Teacher Salary Schedule and Contract Provision Study: 1980–1981." February 1981. Illinois State Board of Education archival collection.

Index

THOMAS J. SUHRBUR is an affiliate of the Illinois Labor History Society and a retired IEA organizer.

The University of Illinois Press
is a founding member of the
Association of University Presses.

———————————————

Composed in 10.25/13 Marat Pro
with Trade Gothic LT Std display
by Lisa Connery
at the University of Illinois Press

University of Illinois Press
1325 South Oak Street
Champaign, IL 61820-6903
www.press.uillinois.edu

Printed and bound by CPI Group (UK) Ltd, Croydon, CR0 4YY

07/05/2025

14666870-0001